An Introduction to

Social Media Research

Editors:
Charmaine du Plessis
and
Ashiya Abdool Satar

JUTA

An Introduction to Social Media Research

First published 2020

Juta and Company (Pty) Ltd
PO Box 14373, Lansdowne 7779, Cape Town, South Africa

© 2020 Juta and Company (Pty) Ltd

www.juta.co.za

ISBN 978 1 48513 084 0

eISBN 978 1 48513 085 7 (WebPDF)

Publisher: Corina Pelser
Project specialist: Valencia Wyngaard-Arenz
Copy Editor: Chantelle Hough-Louw
Proofreader: Jenny De Wet
Cover designer: Drag and Drop (Jacques Nel)
Typesetter: Henry Daniels at Elinye Ithuba

Typeset in 11.5 pt on 14 pt Adobe Caslon Pro Regular

Acknowledgements

It is true that a single seed sown can yield a bountiful harvest. As the editors, we can attest to this as we see the fruits of our labour in the form of this publication. It all began with a single idea that gradually evolved and progressed, ultimately culminating in this handy resource on social media research that we hope will benefit you, the reader. Social media has permeated our lives in the contemporary world to a level where it shapes our understanding of the world. Therefore, as researchers, it bodes us well to gain an understanding of, *inter alia*, social media trends and communication patterns, as well as their implications and influence through research. It goes without saying that knowledge of the social media research process is thus vital to ensure sound and ethical insight into these phenomena. We see this book as a fundamental handbook, a sort of 'blueprint' to guide the social media researcher on this complex journey. This book is a culmination of many months of hard work and dedication, which would not be possible without the invaluable contributions of various people, without whom this publication would not have been realised.

First, the combined work, interaction, research and sharing of ideas between us, the editors, have been monumental and extremely rewarding. It is good to note that our collegial interactions helped us to complement our strengths and collective perseverance. We mention this here as we feel that the pooling of ideas, resources, strengths, and academic and professional insight add to research integrity. Without each other, our work would not have been as fulfilling or insightful.

However, our vision could not have been realised without the indelible efforts of the many people involved in this publication and we would like to express our appreciation to everyone who made the publication of this book possible. These include our authors, publisher, the project specialist, copy editor, proofreader and cover designer, the reviewers as well as the Loving Thy Neighbour non-profit organisation who made available the case study for chapter 1. In particular, we would like to thank Corina Pelser for believing in this publication and for assisting us through the entire publication process.

About the Authors

Ashiya Abdool Satar

Ms. Ashiya Abdool Satar is an academic in the Department of Communication Science at the University of South Africa (UNISA). She has diverse research interests that mirror her educational pursuits in the areas of organisational communication, media studies, inclusive education, and Open Distance and e-Learning (ODeL) in the Higher Education sector. Ashiya is currently involved in projects focusing on active youth citizenship, social justice, media identity and representation, public sector communication, and inclusive education, with a particular focus on the universal design for learning (UDL) approach. Ashiya's interest in inclusive and accessible education transcends national borders. Not only is she representing the College of Human Sciences at Unisa in a project linked with Curriculum Transformation with particular focus on students with disabilities, she is also part of the transnational Steering Group that heads the International Collaboratory for Leadership in Universally Designed Education (INCLUDE) that has a growing social media presence.

Wasim Ahmed

Dr Ahmed is a Lecturer in Digital Business at Newcastle University, United Kingdom, with a specialism in social media research in the Department of Marketing, Operations and Systems. His PhD, completed at the University of Sheffield, examined the role of social media during infectious disease outbreaks. Dr Ahmed also holds an MSc in Information Systems and a BA (Hons) degree in Philosophy from the University of Sheffield. Dr Ahmed has authored over 20 peer-reviewed outputs and has delivered over 70 external talks around the world. Dr Ahmed holds strong links in South Africa and, as an invited speaker, has talked about his research to the South African Broadcasting Corporation (SABC) offices, spoken on Lotus FM, and delivered a live SABC news interview based on the topic of social media.

Esther Emmanuel Awuah

Ms Esther Emmanuel Awuah is a communications professional based in Ghana, a researcher, and a PhD student with the University of South Africa. She holds a BSc (Hons) degree in Media and Society Studies from the Midlands State University in Zimbabwe, and a MA degree in Media and Communication Science from the University of Ilmenau in Germany. She has worked for several years as a communication professional in the pharmaceutical and industrial engineering industries in Germany, managing communication projects across European countries such as Germany, the United Kingdom, Spain, Italy, and France. She is currently an active communications consultant serving major Ghanaian corporations, consulates, and international organisations.

Tanja Bosch

Prof Tanja Bosch is an Associate Professor of Media Studies and Production in the Centre for Film and Media Studies at the University of Cape Town, where she also holds the position of Deputy Dean of Research and Postgraduate Affairs. She teaches journalism and multimedia production, social media, radio studies and research methods at undergraduate and postgraduate level. Her first book, *Broadcasting Democracy: Radio and Identity in South Africa*, was published by the HSRC Press in 2017. She is currently working on a second monograph titled *Social Media and Everyday Life in South Africa* (Routledge, forthcoming 2020). Prof Bosch has published widely in the field of radio studies in South Africa and is currently emerging as one of the few academics locally publishing in the area of social media activism, with her work on #RhodesMustFall and #FeesMustFall.

Yolandi Botha

Prof Yolandi Botha (previously Slabbert) is an Associate Professor in the Department of Communication Science at the University of South Africa. She has five years' experience in the communication and public relations industry, specialising in the financial and banking sectors and has worked in higher education since 2011. She is a Y2 NRF-rated researcher and her areas of specialisation include strategic communication, stakeholder relationship building, stakeholder engagement, stakeholder inclusivity, and change-orientated communication. Her current research aims to highlight the pragmatic relevance of postmodern, contemporary developments in strategic communication, especially related to the process of stakeholder engagement.

Prof Botha has published and presented various articles and papers, both locally and internationally, and currently supervises masters students and doctoral candidates in organisational communication related to her areas of expertise. She serves on the Editorial Board of the *Athens Journal of Mass Media and Communications* and is a member of the editorial advisory team of the *Journal of Management and World Business Research*.

Jacobus Marthinus (Koos) de Villiers

Mr Jacobus Marthinus De Villiers, or Koos, is a lecturer at the North-West University's (NWU) Vaal Triangle Campus, where he teaches various communication subjects (such as social media, communication theory, corporate communication and development communication). He completed his MA degree in Communication at North-West University which focused on the facilitation of participatory communication on social media platforms.

Ronesh Dhawraj

Dr Ronesh Dhawraj is a *Specialist Researcher: Politics* with South Africa's national public broadcaster, the South African Broadcasting Corporation (SABC). Having worked across print, radio, television and digital media platforms throughout his media career, the SABC also regularly uses Dr Dhawraj as their in-house political commentator to give his assessment of the burning political issues of the day, notably around elections. Dr Dhawraj holds a National Diploma in Journalism from the ML Sultan Technikon (now Durban University of Technology), undergraduate degrees in Communication Science from the University of South Africa (UNISA), an MA degree in political communication (*cum laude*), and a PhD in political communication from the same institution. In terms of published works, Dr Dhawraj previously published a book chapter on South African by-elections for a book conceptualised on the 2011 local government elections.

Charmaine du Plessis

Prof Charmaine du Plessis is a Full Professor in the Department of Communication Science at Unisa and a National Research Foundation (NRF) rated researcher. Apart from a PhD in Communication (UNISA), she also holds a Postgraduate Diploma in Marketing Management (UNISA) and a certificate in Brand Management (University of Cape Town). She has published and presented both locally and internationally. Some of her publications include papers in accredited journals and conference proceedings while she also contributed chapters to several books. She further supervises numerous masters students and doctoral candidates. Prof du Plessis specialises in brand communication with a focus on content marketing on social media. She was a communication practitioner at the Department of Trade and Industry and a marketing and public relations practitioner at UNISA's College of Economic and Management Sciences respectively before becoming an academic.

Christelle Swart

Dr Christelle Swart is a Senior Lecturer in the Communication Science Department of the University of South Africa (UNISA). She holds a PhD in Communication from UNISA and her fields of specialisation are social media communication, corporate communication, and corporate brand communication. She is particularly interested in contemporary corporate communication issues, and specifically in social media communication in corporate settings. In 2018, she proposed *A conceptual framework for social media brand communication in non-profit organisations in South Africa: An integrated communication perspective* by adopting an interdisciplinary perspective.

Fortune Tella

Fortune Tella was a Lecturer at the Department of Communication Studies, Christian Service University College (CSUC), Kumasi – Ghana for 10 years. His academic interests are in public relations, advertising, integrated marketing communications and electronic media. He is the immediate-past Dean of Students of CSUC and also served as a member of the Management Board of CSUC. He currently has a lectureship position with the Kwame Nkrumah University of Science and Technology (KNUST), Kumasi. Fortune has a Master of Arts in Communication Studies, a Graduate Diploma in Communication Studies, and a Bachelor of Arts in English and Theatre Arts. He is a proud alumnus of the University of Ghana, Legon. He is currently pursuing a doctorate degree programme in Communication Science at the University of South Africa, South Africa.

His professional background includes over 15 years experience in public relations, advertising, marketing, business development and logistics support. He has helped provide advisory and consultancy services to multinationals and government agencies such as Newmont Ghana, Shell Ghana, Metrica and the Department of Commerce of the United States of America.

His research and consultancy interests include crisis communication management, social media communication strategy, corporate social responsibility initiatives and internal communication.

He is married with three children.

Braam van der Vyver

Dr Braam van der Vyver has obtained degrees in law, marketing, communications and information systems. This includes an LLB from the University of Pretoria, as well as BSc (Hons), MComm (Marketing) and D. Litt et Phil in Communication Studies from UNISA. He has occupied management positions in all three spheres of government, two parastatals and the private sector. His lecturing experience spans over 24 years. This includes 15 years in the Faculty of Information Technology at Monash, South Africa. His research interests are social media, development informatics, intellectual property, and Massive Open Online Courses (MOOCs). He has 38 publications to his credit in which he covered a wide array of topics spanning from e-democracy and e-education to the use of the social media for management purposes. In his Twitter research, he dealt with #FeesMustFall, #PayBacktheMoney, #Listeriosis, and #SASSA. He is at present conducting research on MOOCs.

Contents

Introduction

Introduction to Social Media Research: Theory and Application is an extensive, fundamental reference work for social media scholars, students, and practitioners across various disciplines to conduct social media research scientifically and systematically. Written by an experienced local and international multidisciplinary team, the authors bring depth and individuality to their respective chapters. The authors do not align with individual academic or professional disciplines but allow readers from any branch of learning to gain theoretical and practical knowledge about the social media research process when following the scientific method. As such, the book serves as a portal for social media research and a starting point for any investigation or study about social media. The book has been written to appeal to novices as well as those who are more experienced in social media research.

The Fourth Industrial Revolution (4IR) has ushered in a new era with emerging technologies which means more data for research is being generated than ever before. As a result, researchers also have more opportunities to make a positive impact with their research, especially since social media research has become more established. Nevertheless, conducting a social media study remains complex and requires wide-ranging knowledge of all its aspects such as adopting a focused theoretical point of departure, selecting suitable paradigmatic approaches and methods, working with social media data as well as understanding the implications of social media research and the networked society. Social media research also still experiences many methodological challenges and issues affecting the reliability and validity of results.

This book, consisting of 11 chapters, deals with all essential aspects of the social media research process and also guides the reader to overcome or avoid the numerous obstacles associated with the social media research process. The information is presented in an easy to follow manner and explained with case studies and some illustrations. Each chapter ends with a relevant case study, learning activities, and suggestions for further reading, which allows the reader to reflect on the content presented in the chapter and its practical application in actual and/or hypothetical social media research studies.

The content is divided into four sections and structured in such a way to allow readers to study a specific area of interest, to consult topics in the book as needed, or to examine it straight through. The chapters are inter-reliant and should be read in conjunction with other chapters in this book.

Section A: Introduction to the Social Media Process

In Section A, the reader is introduced to social media for research, the social media research process, and how to select a suitable theoretical underpinning for a social media study.

Chapter 1, *Introduction to social media for research*, introduces the reader to social media platforms that can be used for research, the types of research that have been conducted as well as the aspects of communication that have been researched in these studies. Next, the different forms of textual, audio, visual (infographics, memes, gifs, and emojis), audio-visual (micro-videos, videos, live-streams, and VR-videos) and interactive content (#tags and hyperlinks) that are used on social media are highlighted. Lastly, the theoretical foundations of social media are presented.

Chapter 2, *Introduction to the social media research process*, acts as a point of reference and provides an overview of the entire research process and research design (with practical examples) that are discussed in more detail in other chapters in this book. The chapter also addresses not only the advantages but also disadvantages, limitations, and methodological challenges and issues that researchers may face when conducting social media research.

Chapter 3, *Prominent theoretical frameworks in social media research*, elaborates on prominent theoretical frameworks that could be applied in social media research following the themes of personal behaviour, social behaviour and media influence and also advises on future theoretical developments in social media.

Section B: Paradigmatic approaches and methods for Social Media Research

In Section B, the reader is introduced to paradigmatic approaches and methods for qualitative, quantitative, and mixed-method social media studies respectively.

Chapter 4, *Using a qualitative research approach in social media research*, explores a qualitative research design in social media research and considers the different research methods available to analyse visual and textual data within the social media context. Justification of the use of qualitative research of social media is provided, and precise challenges that the researcher might encounter are highlighted in context. Furthermore, the focus of this chapter is on possible research paradigms to direct the research actions, knowledge and perceptions of a qualitative researcher, and the various methods and techniques to qualitatively examine content on social media. Finally, a holistic qualitative approach that could be fitting to explore social media data is proposed and concisely outlined. In chapter 5, *Using a quantitative research approach in social media research*, the focus shifts to worldviews or paradigms, quantitative research approaches and quantitative research methods in social media research. The importance and development of a codebook using social media datasets are particularly impressed upon in the chapter. The chapter also describes the context for quantitative social media research, provides some computational methods used in the field and introduces the reader to various tools and applications that can be used in data mining and analysis, as well as in detecting deceptive content on social media sites. Chapter 6, *Using a mixed-methods approach in social media research*, concentrates on the typologies and designs of mixed-methods research (MMR) and proposes the use of paradigmatic perspectives as a guide for the MMR social media process. This chapter is especially important since MMR is a growing field with little guidance on how to conduct effective research. Consequently, there lies great potential in paradigms to add a greater depth and breadth of information to guide and inform MMR.

Section C: Working with Social Media Data

In Section C, the reader is introduced to sampling, collecting and analysing social media data by adopting different research approaches.

Chapter 7, *Sampling social media data*, explains how to sample social media data from both qualitative and quantitative approaches. Different sampling methods, such as probability and non-probability type of samples, are proposed within each of these approaches while the chapter also highlights some challenges that may be encountered such as external validity (generalisation). Chapter 8, *Collecting social media data*, presents an overview of the type of data that can be collected for social media research, the data collection process (both manual and automated), as well as which pitfalls to avoid. Chapter 9, *Analysing social media data*, gives an overview of social media data analysis from a quantitative, qualitative, and mixed-methods approach respectively and explains the importance of data cleaning and storage. Different social media data analysis tools are highlighted while a case study is used to illustrate one of these tools.

Section D: Implications of Social Media Research

In Section D, the reader is introduced to the implications of social media research such as ethical considerations and the consequences of new media data. Chapter 10, *Ethical issues in social media research*, introduces the reader to a broad range of ethical implications inherent in social media studies as well as potential contraventions. Chapter 11, *Implications of new media data* is the final chapter of this book and outlines the strengths and weaknesses associated with different forms of Big Data and Big Social Data. It further highlights the implications, for individuals and communities, of new media data in the hyper-connected networked society. Finally, a discussion of access to data, digital exclusion and the effects on targeted populations, samples, and the general aspects of the online research process related to new media data is presented in order to understand the implications that these elements have on research findings. The chapter concludes with how research based on Big Data (and particularly Big Social Data) affects the underlying epistemologies and ontologies of research. The diagram below is a schematic outline of the book.

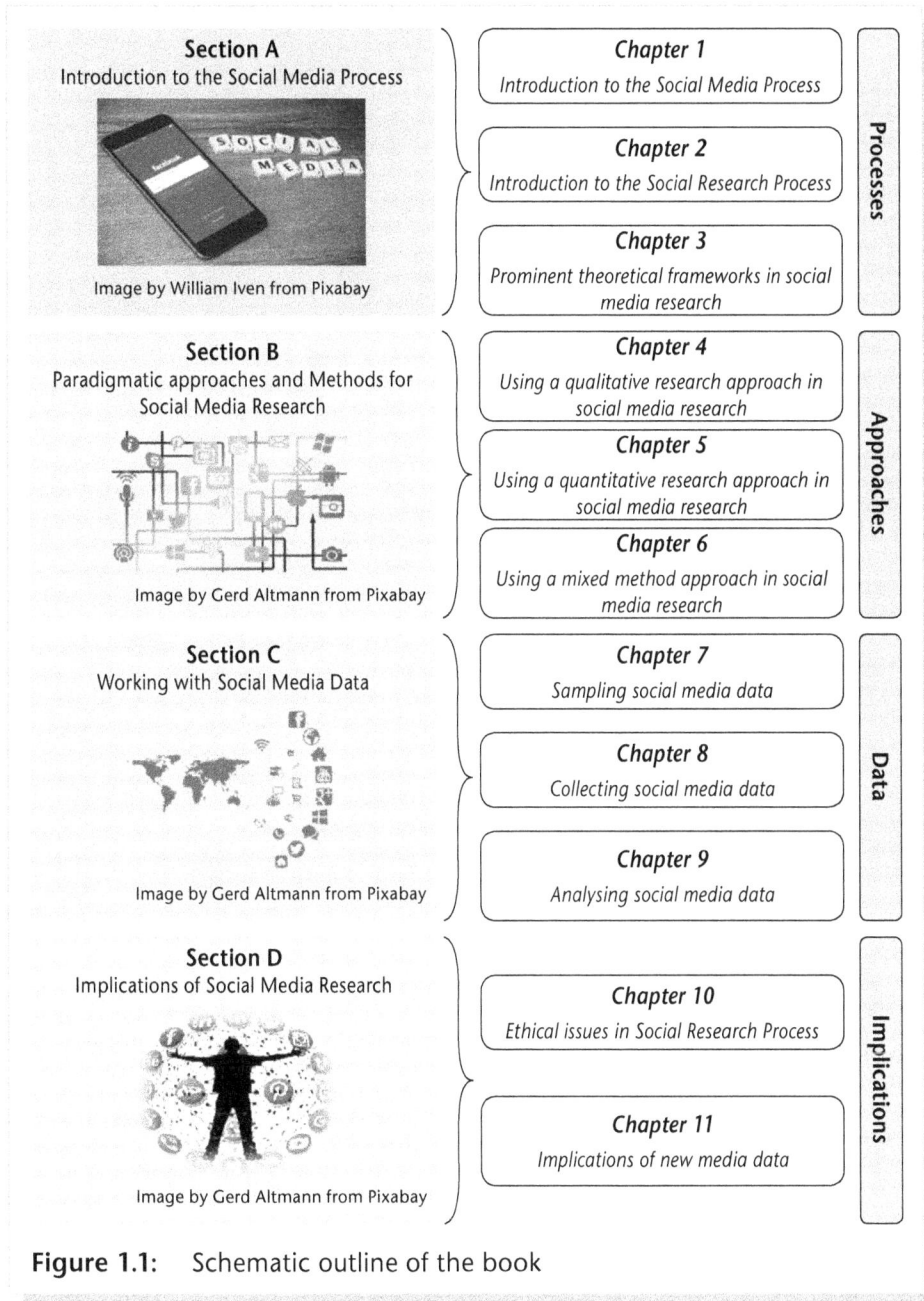

Section A	Chapter 1
Introduction to the Social Media Process	Introduction to the Social Media Process
	Chapter 2
	Introduction to the Social Research Process
	Chapter 3
	Prominent theoretical frameworks in social media research

Processes

Section B	Chapter 4
Paradigmatic approaches and Methods for Social Media Research	Using a qualitative research approach in social media research
	Chapter 5
	Using a quantitative research approach in social media research
	Chapter 6
	Using a mixed method approach in social media research

Approaches

Section C	Chapter 7
Working with Social Media Data	Sampling social media data
	Chapter 8
	Collecting social media data
	Chapter 9
	Analysing social media data

Data

Section D	Chapter 10
Implications of Social Media Research	Ethical issues in Social Research Process
	Chapter 11
	Implications of new media data

Implications

Figure 1.1: Schematic outline of the book

We hope that you will find the book and its many resources helpful in your journey as a social media researcher.

No research is ever quite complete. It is the glory of a good bit of work that it opens the way for something still better, and this repeatedly leads to its own eclipse – Mervin Gordon.

Section A

INTRODUCTION
TO THE SOCIAL MEDIA PROCESS

Processes

CHAPTER 1

Introduction to Social Media for Research

Jacobus Marthinus de Villiers

Social media isn't a fad, it's a fundamental shift in the way we communicate
– Erik Qualman

Learning Outcomes

After completing this chapter, the researcher should be able to:

- reframe the concept of social media based on the different definitions thereof;
- differentiate between and critique the different communication models available for social media research;
- analyse the various types of multimedia content available for social media research;
- categorise the differences between content creators on social media;
- compare the various social media platforms and their impact on social media research within different communication contexts; and
- develop a potential social media research topic using Power's four-tier approach to communication research.

1.1   INTRODUCTION

Social media technologies and applications are constantly changing within a world characterised by virtual interconnectivity and social interaction through text, audio, images, and video. Therefore, before social media research can be explained, social media, its current state and what it entails first need to be investigated. As a result of the changing nature of social media, the question arises: Are social media technologies and applications changing to suit the needs of the people, or are people changing social media technologies and applications through their use of social media?

No matter how you see it, social media has had an impact on the way we communicate as individuals, groups, communities, businesses, and professionals. To research social media, it is necessary to first be able to define social media. However, this task is in itself problematic as there is no consensus on the definition of social media. Since the development of social media, several definitions have been conceptualised, yet no single definition of social media has been established. The task of defining social media is inherently problematic due to the dynamic and changing nature of social media and social media platforms. This chapter will set out to identify a workable definition of social media. Once this is done, it will briefly discuss the models of communication applicable to social media. This chapter will then provide an alternative model for social media research. The different tiers applicable in this model will then be unpacked according to the different aspects of social media, such as content, content creators and social media platforms, before presenting a case study contextualising the importance of social media research.

1.2   WHAT IS SOCIAL MEDIA?

There are various definitions of the concept of social *media*. Earlier researchers defined social media as web-based services (social network sites) or internet-based applications (Web 2.0) that allow individuals to:

- create a public or semi-public profile within a bounded system (online);
- communicate a list of other users with whom they share a connection; and
- view and navigate their list of users within the system.

However, the way these users interact differs from site to site ranging from brand-generated content to user-generated content (Boyd & Ellison, 2008:211; Kaplan & Haenlein, 2010:61). More recent researchers expanded on the description of the concept of social media. Mahoney and Tang (2017:26), for example, perceive social media as the overarching term that includes all forms of exchange, interaction, and engagement in a digital space. According to Cornelissen (2020:39), social media can be described as 'involving all kinds of online or digital technologies through which people create, share and exchange information and ideas'. For (Bosch, 2017a:40) the term social media refers to internet-based websites or web-based applications which connect audiences virtually so that they can create content and share information. Others refer to social media as new forms of media that involve interactive participation (Manning, 2014:1158). Lipschultz (2018:8) added a further dimension to what social media encapsulates – it is interactive, allows for identity development and formation, and grants different communities the opportunity to exchange content with others.

Although different definitions for social media have existed since 2008, Carr and Hayes (2015) criticise most of these definitions based on the following criteria:

- It involves an oversimplified view and definition of social media that do not consider the unique characteristics that differentiate social media from other communication technologies such as email.

- It attributes capabilities and functionalities of specific social media platforms (like Facebook or YouTube) without considering the unique traits and characteristics of social media.

- It presents a narrow view of social media as many of the definitions constructed focus only on the technological affordances synonymous with Web 2.0 and exclude the communicative possibilities of Web 3.0 and Web 4.0.

Carr and Hayes's (2015:47–49) critique is quite important, taking into account the dynamic nature of social media to continuously change and adapt as new social media platforms emerge (such as Snapchat, WhatsApp, TikTok, etcetera) and existing social media platforms adapt by incorporating more digital enhancements (such as Facebook and Instagram) (Freberg, 2019:34). Considering how rapidly social media has changed over the past years it is important to keep in mind Carr and Hayes's definition to allow space for future developments within social media that will change the way we communicate.

Carr and Hayes (2015) define social media as:

Internet-based channels that allow users to opportunistically interact and selectively self-present, either in real-time or asynchronously, with both broad and narrow audiences who derive value from user-generated content and the perception of interaction with others.

Even though Carr and Hayes's definition provides a solid foundation for understanding social media from a user perspective, it does not address the individual and cultural identity development and formation as articulated by Lipschultz, (2018:8) and excludes brand-generated content. The author, therefore, constructed a proposed definition that does not only incorporate Carr and Hayes's definition, but all elements discussed thus far in this section. In terms of this proposed definition, social media can be defined as:

Internet-based channels and platforms that allow various users and brands to opportunistically interact and selectively self-present according to their individual and cultural identity, either synchronously or asynchronously with a variety of other participants from different backgrounds with their unique individual and cultural identities, who derive value from content (user-generated or brand-generated) and their interaction with various communicators.

In the following sections, the different models of communication that could be used in social media research are discussed.

1.3   MODELS OF COMMUNICATION USED IN SOCIAL MEDIA RESEARCH

Now that a broad understanding of what social media entails has been established, the following section will briefly discuss the communication process on social media to frame the different models of communication that apply to social media. Social media research and what it entails is explained in section 2.2 of chapter 2. However, before discussing the models of communication, it is important to note that social media researchers will most likely frame their research within the various traditions of communication (rhetorical, socio-psychological, socio-cultural, critical, etcetera) depending on the research being conducted (Griffin et al., 2015:47). The same can be said for communication models. Although some of the models that apply to social media will be discussed, social media research should not be limited to a specific model of communication. Different types of research and communication contexts may require a researcher to approach the research being conducted from a specific perspective. For this reason, it is important to note that all models of communication may apply when communicating on social media. Only when researching interactions on social media can it be determined what model was used and the effectiveness thereof.

Before discussing the different models, it is important to note that Holmes (2005:10), in his analysis of interactive media versus broadcast media, specifically indicates that interactive media:

* is decentralised as many speak to many;
* uses two-way communication;
* are not controlled by the state;
* participants being communicated to are seen as individuals; and
* influences the individual experience.

The issue with this comparison is that although it provides some guidance in terms of what models will most likely apply to social media; it does not take into account the dynamic nature of social media and the various social media platforms. Aspects such as power, ownership, context, platform design, content, time, and access can all play a role when communicating on social media (Van Dijck, 2013:28; Fuchs, 2017:7). These aspects can all influence the communication action which, in turn, can ultimately influence our conceptualisation of the models of communication that apply to social media. Furthermore, current models of communication may also fail to consider the future forms of interaction and interactivity that may arise as social media changes (Carr & Hayes, 2015).

Nonetheless, it is important to briefly discuss the different models and the variations of models of communication research that apply to social media research as well as a proposed alternative model for, amongst others, communication research but which could be extended to other disciplines as well.

1.3.1 Linear model of communication

One of the first communication models of mass media was the linear model of communication that provided a basic structure for classic mass media through which a passive audience could receive messages for information and entertainment purposes (Mahoney & Tang, 2017:10). This model entails a communicator sending a message to a receiver, who then makes sense of the message using their senses (channels) (West & Turner, 2018:9).

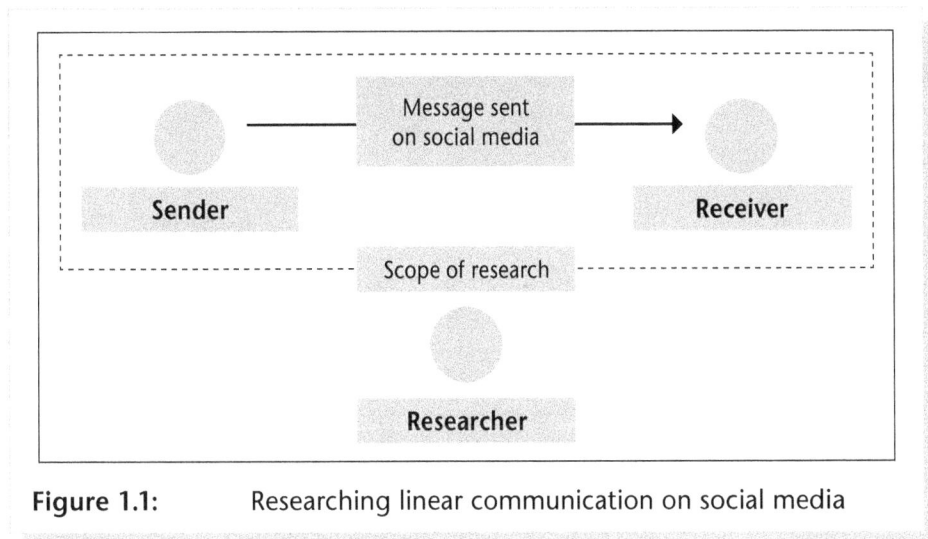

Figure 1.1:   Researching linear communication on social media

When first conceptualised, the sender within the linear model of communi-cation consisted of broadcasting organisations that had access to technological equipment enabling them to produce and send messages to audiences (receivers) (Mahoney & Tang, 2017:10). David Berlo expanded on the linear model of communication by unpacking the factors that affect the elements (that is, sender, message, channel, and receiver) (Businesstopia, 2018). Although this model does have some aspects that may be relevant to social media research, the one-way nature of the model poses a problem for social media researchers due to the dynamic nature of social media to facilitate two-way communication. The linear model of communication provides a basic model for communication within the mass media context, the applicability of this model within social media is questionable. Communication on social media is never really linear, as a message can be consumed by a person who was not the intended receiver of the message. Furthermore, synchronous and asynchronous capabilities of social media also make the view of a linear model impossible.

Although someone might not be engaging with your messages today, it might not mean that they will not engage with your message in the future.

1.3.2   Interactional model of communication

The interactional model of communication is considered a two-way model of communication where a sender encodes a message, sends it through a medium to a receiver who then decodes the message and provides feedback to the sender (West & Turner, 2018:11). The feedback loop differentiates the interactional model of communication from the linear model of communication.

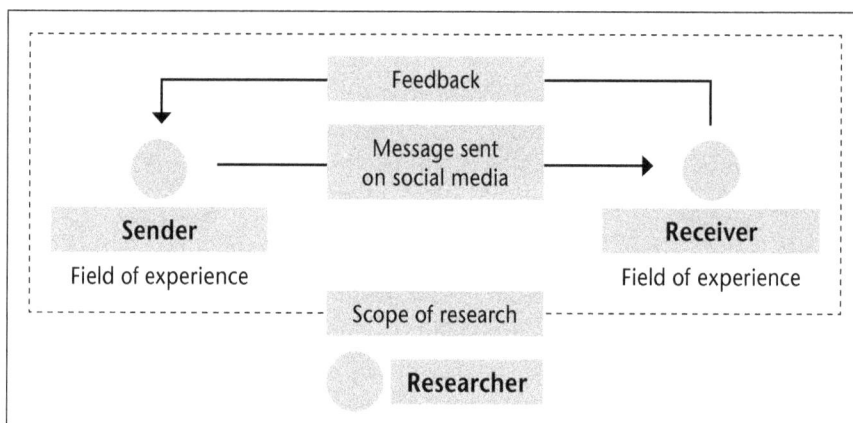

Figure 1.2:   Researching interactional communication on social media

A further element of the interactional model of communication is that both sender and receiver come with their personal field of experience (West & Turner, 2018:11). This model can be applied to the social media context where, for example, an organisation shares content with their audience and in turn their audience reacts to the message by loving or liking it. Organisations can then use this information to create another message based on the users' reaction. However, the interactional model of communication has been criticised for its narrow view of communication. For one, this model can easily explain communication within an interpersonal communication setting but may be problematic when applied to a broader context like group or public communication (Businesstopia, 2018). Social media messages are sent to a specific receiver or receivers, but unintended receivers may consume the message. The feedback loop within this model is accordingly problematic as both unintentional and intentional receivers may provide feedback, but it may not necessarily be to the sender.

1.3.3   Transactional model of communication

In the transactional model of communication, participants are simultaneously seen as senders and receivers of messages (West & Turner, 2018:13). Like the interactional model, communicators in the transactional model also come with their personal field of experience (based on their history, identity, etcetera), and create a shared field of experience through communication. Viewing social media from a transactional perspective provides a dynamic interpretation of the communication process by equalising power and creating an opportunity for mutual understanding where participants share meaning (Mahoney & Tang, 2017:12).

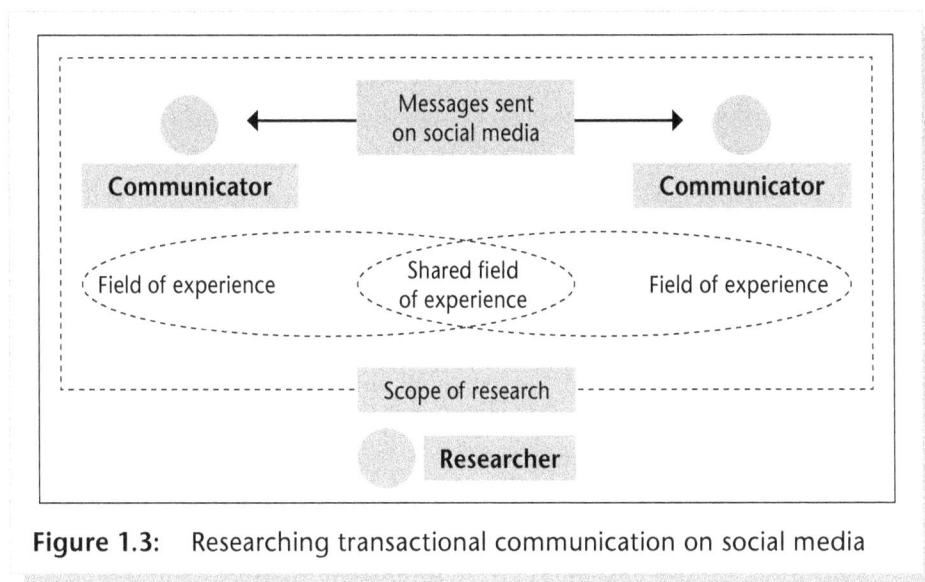

Figure 1.3:   Researching transactional communication on social media

Due to the many-to-many capabilities of some social media platforms, users can communicate with one another as they please, causing communication to be more transactional within social media as every user has the opportunity to initiate communication.

1.3.4   Alternative model of communication research

Although this chapter discusses the different models of communication that can be relevant to social media scholars for research purposes, it is difficult to frame social media research within a simplified or even existing model of communication due to the dynamic and ever-changing nature of social media content and platforms (West & Turner, 2018:13). Consequently, it might be better to approach social media research from the angle of the different intellectual tiers of communication. Power's seminal work (1995) identifies four tiers of communication that provide a foundational model for communication research, which defines the core concepts of the communication discipline and explains how these concepts build on each other (Littlejohn et al., 2017:36–40). The four tiers are discussed next.

- **Tier 1 – Message:** Within the first tier of Power's model the nature of the message (verbal, non-verbal, signs, symbols, intentional or unintentional) is emphasised. This tier focuses on aspects such as message structure and content that can be seen as the core to understanding social media research.

- **Tier 2 – Communicator:** The second tier of Power's model focuses on the communicator who, through communication, tries to accomplish certain goals. The communicator can be researched from an individual, relational, or cultural perspective concerning certain aspects of the message. For example, on social media, the effect of memes as non-verbal messages and the impact thereof on relationships can be researched.

- **Tier 3 – Level:** Within the third tier of Power's model the nature of the domain of communication is vital to approach communication research. Communication usually takes place at an interpersonal, small-group, public, mediated, and societal level. As a result, the number of people, the power of individuals in a communication interaction, the degree of formality, and the personal information exchanged among communicators all have an impact on the message design and the behaviour of the communicator.

- **Tier 4 – Situation:** The fourth tier of Power's model emphasises the situation in which communication takes place (corporate, government, education, health, etcetera). It is important to note that researchers in social media do not study health as a context, but they study the message, communicator, and nature of communication within a specific social media situation.

Although Power's model was conceptualised for communication research, it is also relevant to other disciplines. In essence, all social media research, no matter the discipline, is concerned with what is being said, by and to whom, on what platform and level and lastly to what effect. For example, a researcher in public administration may want to investigate the impact of government initiatives on social media to reduce road accidents during the festive season (See Table 1.1 below). The context of the research falls into the disciplines of both education and health since social media messages about road safety need to take into account pedagogy for it to be effective, while the nature of the messages is to educate drivers to reduce fatalities and hospitalisation.

Table 1.1: How Power's model relates to interdisciplinary social media research

	Tier 1: Message	Tier 2: Communicator	Tier 3: Level	Tier 4: Situation
Government	Reducing accidents during the festive season	The Department of Transport	Public	Education, health
Health	Coping with stress in higher education	University of South Africa	Internal	Medical, corporate, and education
Marketing	Parents' responses to sexist advertisements on social media	Social media users	Individual	Media, family, and religious

Power's model of communication thus creates an excellent framework for scholars who wish to study social media. The rest of this chapter will unfold according to the four tiers:

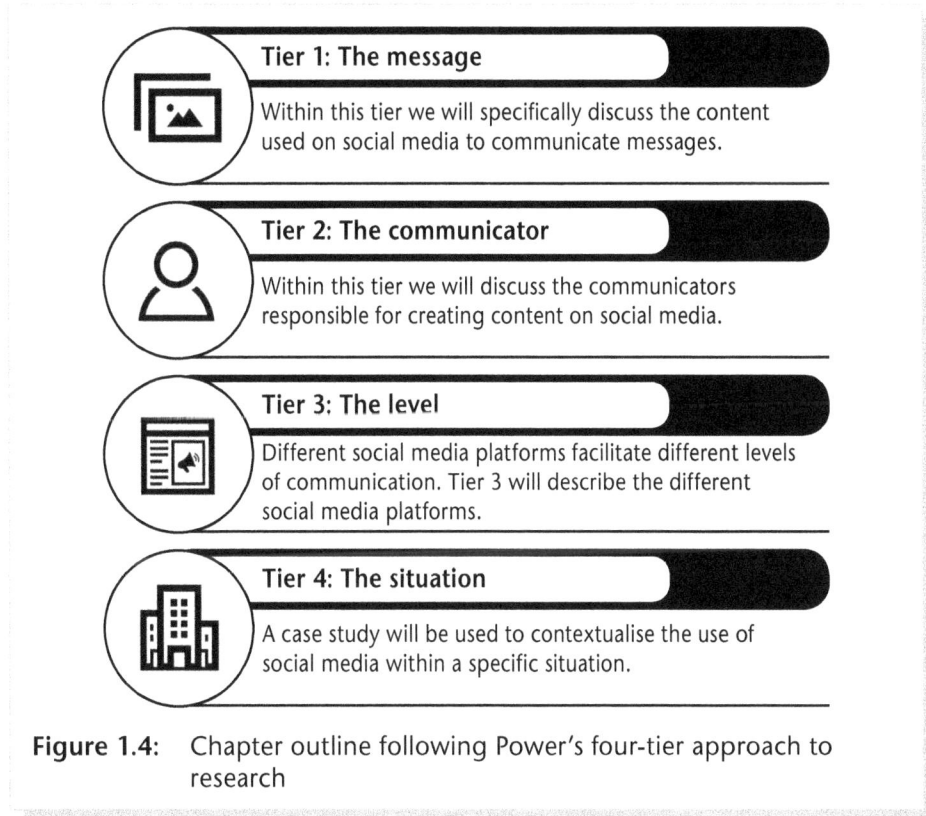

Tier 1: The message

Within this tier we will specifically discuss the content used on social media to communicate messages.

Tier 2: The communicator

Within this tier we will discuss the communicators responsible for creating content on social media.

Tier 3: The level

Different social media platforms facilitate different levels of communication. Tier 3 will describe the different social media platforms.

Tier 4: The situation

A case study will be used to contextualise the use of social media within a specific situation.

Figure 1.4: Chapter outline following Power's four-tier approach to research

1.4   TIER 1: THE SOCIAL MEDIA MESSAGE (TYPES OF MULTIMEDIA CONTENT)

Just like any other form of media, social media provides us with various multimedia tools to construct verbal and non-verbal messages that allow us to interact with one another to not only understand ourselves but the world around us (Siapera, 2012:9). These messages or multimedia content act as a catalyst to set in motion the interaction and engagement that facilitate this understanding (Schaefer, 2018:49). During the age of mass media, people relied on formal structures of power (broadcasters) for multimedia content creation to set in motion the processes of understanding (Holmes, 2005:10). However, in the information age, everyone is a content creator and two-way communication can occur between various communicators. For this reason, users become responsible for creating their content to set in motion these processes of understanding. The downside to this is that users can experience communication and information overload and turn to content that creates a skewed view of such users and the world around them. The role of social media researchers should thus be to critically analyse social media messages and content to determine which content helps users understand the world and which content contributes to a misinterpretation of the world around us.

Before the various multimedia content that can be used to research social media messages can be discussed, it first needs to be established what is meant by the term multimedia. Multimedia can be seen as the

production, transmission, and interpretation of a composite text, where at least two of the component-texts use different representational systems in different modalities (Purchase, 1998:13).

In other words, multimedia can be seen as a combination of various media elements like pictures and text. For researchers to investigate and understand verbal and non-verbal messages packaged into multimedia content, an overview of the different types of multimedia content is needed. Furthermore, various social media platforms distribute multimedia content differently which will influence the way in which multimedia content is researched due to the different rules (formal and informal), designs, aims, opportunities, and limitations of these platforms (Lindgren, 2017:22). Multimedia content can be divided into different categories based on their structural elements.

The different types of multimedia content will be discussed in the following categories: typography, audio, visual, audio-visual and interactive elements. Different multimedia elements are combined to engage users for different purposes, and it is important to note that no multimedia content is better than another. Rather different types of multimedia content will be used to engage different users (Mahoney & Tang, 2017:185).

1.4.1 Typography

Although typography is not a multimedia element, it is a design element that forms the basis of most social media messages. Typography is the visual application of text and can be seen as the basic structural element of any social media content (Lee & Boling, 1999). In social media, typography is the most used element due to the minimal production effort it takes to produce messages like instant messages, status updates, posts, blogs, and so forth (Clark & Mayer, 2016). Although text is one of the most basic structural elements used on social media, it is important to note that social media platforms are becoming more visual. This can in part be ascribed to the amount of effort it takes to read text-heavy multimedia content. Therefore, text should always be kept to the minimum to keep users engaged (Mahoney & Tang, 2017:329). An example of content on social media that consists of typography are blogs and microblogs. Social media research can be conducted by analysing typography like blogs and microblogs to determine perceptions, feelings, and meaning through content and textual analysis. When users comment on posts, a discourse analysis of textual comments can also be conducted.

(i) Blogs and microblogging

Blogs or online logs are online diaries, created on platforms such as WordPress, where users share episodes of written ideas, thoughts, or experiences over a period of time (as users deem fit) (Du Plessis, 2018:181). Bloggers usually cover a variety of topics (like politics, travel, experiences, etcetera) with the goal of connecting individuals who share the same interests (Page, 2014:43). Microblogging, on the other hand, follows the same structure as blogs but differs in size as the content is usually restricted to a certain number of characters (Engelbrecht & Ngcongo, 2018b:217). Twitter is an example of a microblogging social media platform as it restricts the information that users can post to a limited number of characters.

The difference between blogging and microblogging is also evident when considering the ownership of the platform. Blogs are owned by the user who can decide on the features and design of the platform itself. Microblogs are social media platforms that allow users to create profiles, but the platform is owned and designed by an organisation (Freberg, 2019:46).

Blogs and microblogs are forms of textual communication, that enable users to share who they are by providing a space for them to share their internal monologues (intrapersonal communication) while providing an opportunity for engagement by directing their communication to peers (interpersonal communication). Blogs and microblogs can provide insight to social media researchers into how users and organisations participate within the participatory culture, through a process of self-creation that is meaningful to them (Burger, 2017:384–385).

1.4.2 Audio

Audio is an important form of multimedia content as it is easy to process and allows users to process information by creating mental images (Safko, 2010:511). Within the context of social media research, audio is crucial as many social media platforms such as WhatsApp and Facebook Messenger allow users to communicate through voice clips. After text, audio is the second easiest content to create since many platforms, technologies, and applications allow users to create audio with minimal production effort (Clark & Mayer, 2016:115). Two examples of audio content relevant to social media researchers are podcasts and voice notes. These two forms of content will be discussed below.

(i)   Podcasts

Podcasts are a series of digital episodes or programmes that deliver specific information (news, comedy shows, industry-specific content, stories, and so forth) to a target audience. This form of content has become exceedingly popular in recent years as it provides targeted users with relevant information (Quesenberry, 2019:197). Podcasts can be considered audio blogs and are very effective as the content is automatically delivered when shared. When distributed on social media, podcasts also bypass the gatekeepers involved in traditional media and allow users to tell their stories (Quesenberry, 2019:197).

The strength of a podcast lies in the simplicity of the content. First, podcasts are easy to create, consume and share. Secondly, podcasts allow the user to target a narrow audience and lastly, podcasts can be streamed from platforms and can circumvent the barriers of literacy and access (podcasts consume less data than video) (Breslin et al., 2009:127; Handley & Chapman, 2011:206).

For social media researchers, the use of podcasts can still be relevant as podcasts can provide insight into storytelling and the dissemination of professional content. As a result, social media researchers can analyse the content communicated in podcasts. Because many podcasts take the form of talk shows (for example the Gareth Cliff show podcast), discourses between various communicators on shows can also be researched.

(ii)   Voice notes

One of the most important forms of audio content that has not received much attention in the literature is voice notes. Voice notes provide an alternative to text-based messages and allow synchronous (real-time) and asynchronous (any-time) communication, while at the same time providing a cheaper alternative to phone calls (Talhouk et al., 2016:338).

Although voice notes have been around for some time, research conducted on this multimedia content has mainly been in the field of health and education (especially language studies or open-distance learning). As WhatsApp mainly focuses on interpersonal communication and small-group communication, it does create challenges to researchers interested in researching voice notes as multimedia content. Issues and challenges relating to privacy and access to voice notes may prevent social media researchers from accessing voice notes. However, voice notes are very important within the South African context as WhatsApp is fairly accessible and provides an alternative form of communication for people who are not proficient in reading and writing.

1.4.3 Visual content

Visual content, in the form of either still or moving images and graphics, has become one of the most important multimedia content on social media, not only due to the quick and succinct way this content facilitates communication but also because most social media users prefer visual content (Cassinger & Thelander, 2017). Visual content on social media can take various formats and can be anything from emojis, Graphic Interchangeable Formats (GIFs), photographs, comics, memes, and so on. Visual content has also impacted how we communicate. Instead of commenting on a post, we react to the message using emojis. Graphical images have become so popular that social media platforms have even changed their text-based status update feature to include a variety of visual multimedia content (Mahoney & Tang, 2017:329). This is because graphical images are more than just a representation of users' emotions, experiences, and memories; they are a tool to engage others through capturing and maintaining attention (Carah, 2014:138).

Graphical images are important to social media research as they provide not only a cultural perspective but also insights into the impact of images on people's identities and how they assign meaning (Cassinger & Thelander, 2017). Therefore, this section will focus on some of the graphical images used on social media to communicate.

(i)   Emojis

Emojis is not a new concept and has been around since the first person combined a colon with a bracket to simulate being happy or sad. The first mention of the use of emoticons dates back to 1881 when a magazine spoke about how symbols and characters can be arranged to represent emotional feelings (Kannan & Shreya, 2017:50). Since the first conceptualisation of the emoticon, it has changed according to the various devices, social media platforms, and even from static to moving. Emojis have also evolved to the extent that they now provide various choices to represent several races, products, causes, cultures, countries and even brands. Each time an application, social media platform, or website is updated new emoticons are added to create a large databank of emoticons for users to choose from (Kannan & Shreya, 2017:50).

Emojis provide a form of non-verbal communication to illustrate and communicate various feelings on social media to various audiences (individual or group) and provide a form of participation that allows users to react to the content being shared (Engelbrecht & Ngcongo, 2018a:49–50). Different platforms (like Facebook, Instagram, Twitter, LinkedIn, etcetera) have even added quick-respond emojis (liking, clapping, being angry at, caring, and so forth) that users can choose from to respond to content and messages from other content creators. According to Engelbrecht and Ngcongo (2018a:50) high arousal caused by certain types of content or messages, leads to the use of emoticons, while low arousal leads to the conversation.

(ii)   Memes

It is not easy to explain the meme phenomenon to a person who does not have an understanding of memes, as they are usually constructed by individuals sharing a bizarre sense of humour (Lindgren, 2017:43). Memes can be defined as

> *the spread of various types of content to convey socially constructed ideas, jokes or even general mind-sets from one person to another via the internet* (Shifman, 2014:2).

Memes create narratives using a picture and a caption to convey meaning or connotations about a person, place, thing, event, or combination of the aforementioned (Woodworth, 2018:87). Social media offers platforms for the diffusion and dissemination of this socially constructed multimedia content and furthermore creates opportunities for shared content to be reproduced and remixed in various ways (Mahoney & Tang, 2017:43).

According to Shifman (2014:4) academics should research memes as they encapsulate some of the fundamental aspects of digital culture. Memes are at their core user-generated and are in essence linked to the idea of the participatory culture of social media. Furthermore, they may seem like 'trivial pieces of pop culture, but they provide an overview and a deeper understanding of the defining events of the twenty-first century' (Shifman, 2014:4–5). Memes serve an important communication function as vehicles to convey various forms of commentary and perspectives (Woodworth, 2018:88).

(iii)   Graphic Interchangeable Format

A GIF is an animated (moving), short, silent, looping, untitled image (Eppink, 2014:298). Although earlier GIFs consisted only of animations, recent GIFs are constructed by creating screenshots from media products (movies, series, events, etcetera) overlaid with writing (user-generated or embedded subtitles from the media product itself) (Adami & Jewitt, 2016:265). Although GIFs are derived from a familiar existing source (for instance a television programme), observers do not have to be familiar with the original media source of the graphic to understand the new construction (Highfield & Leaver, 2016:53). GIFs are usually used as a substitute for communication and like memes can be used to convey emotions, share opinions, provide a punch line or serve as a reaction to communication (Highfield & Leaver, 2016:53). GIFs can, therefore, be shared and reused beyond the intent and purpose of the original creators.

GIFs are successful on social media due to the simplicity of the content (Eppink, 2014:303). They are easy to share, view, and process and have even been incorporated into social media platforms such as Facebook and WhatsApp, simplifying access to this type of content. Despite the success of GIFs within digital culture, research of this form of content from a cultural or sociological perspective is still lacking (Ash, 2015:119). GIFs can provide researchers with a new understanding of how users communicate and even construct meaning within the participatory culture. Thus, research on GIFs could be conducted through visual semiotics.

(iv) Infographics

An infographic is a visual representation of data or ideas that communicates complex information to users in an easy-to-understand and digestible manner (Smiciklas, 2012:3). This is achieved by creating a visual and mental model of the complex information in the minds of the users to enable them to understand and comprehend the information (Dunlap & Lowenthal, 2016:44). Although infographics are new to social media, this form of content has been around for some time. Newspapers have been using infographics before social media to illustrate, for example, information on how an accident occurred.

Infographics are especially shared on social media because it packages information in a creative, interesting, and understandable manner that can be shared at the click of a button (a phenomenon coined 'word of mouse') (Smiciklas, 2012:15).

However, infographics are not without criticism. Researchers, like Featherstone (2014:148), have criticised infographics for oversimplifying complex information and research, causing many users to draw the wrong conclusion from the information. Caution should, therefore, be exercised when creating infographics with information that could potentially harm individuals. For example, infographics that convey harmful or unscientific facts on health and the healthcare industry can be shared on social media, which can cause social media users to unknowingly engage in harmful medical practices. Due to the availability of free online graphic design software, individuals can easily construct and share infographics. This can be potentially harmful since fake news and propaganda can be communicated in this way to manipulate people (to change their behaviour, buy products, etcetera).

Social media researchers can approach infographics from various perspectives. Researchers can investigate the content used in infographics, how people and brands use infographics, the effectiveness of infographics to engage audiences, and even the effectiveness of infographics on social media to create awareness.

1.4.4   Audio-visual multimedia content

In recent years, audio-visual multimedia has also become a powerful medium due to its visual nature and its ability to convey information consistently and entertainingly (Zhang et al., 2006). Audio-visual material is more likely to go viral than text-based content (Handley & Chapman, 2011:195). Audio-visual multimedia is also very engaging as it brings stories to life through video and allows content to be more authentic (Kerpen, 2011:135). Although audio-visual multimedia has been synonymous with video, it is important to discuss other audio-visual multimedia that may also be relevant to social media researchers like augmented reality (AR) and virtual reality (VR).

(i)   Video

The concept of video has become increasingly difficult to define, as the change of technology throughout the years has impacted the use of this type of content. Video can be seen as an umbrella concept for audio-visual objects that cannot be separated from the idea of a medium that combines, but are not necessarily dependent on, all channels of communication (speech, sight, hearing, touch) (Vonderau, 2014:498). It combines various practices that are still the foundation of this type of content, even on social media, like 'recording, collecting, copying, repeating, deleting or sharing'. These practices add an inherent advantage to video as they have sustained the test of time.

Video is not only vital content on social media as users are starting to look for visual content that grabs their attention (Azionya & Sitto, 2018:15) but it also provides versatile multimedia content when it comes to social media. YouTube, for example, has numerous user-generated and brand-generated videos ranging from corporate videos, advertisements, demonstrations, movies, series, documentaries, and many more. Furthermore, social media platforms also provide various features to consume video, from uploading, sharing and live streaming to even hosting 'watch parties'. However, one of the issues with video on social media is that there is an endless supply of videos, but not all videos are produced to reflect quality content (Azionya & Sitto, 2018:15). For videos to consequently be consumed, they have to be exceptionally engaging and of high quality.

On social media, we also find video blogs or vlogs as they are known. Vlogs follow the same structure as a blog but differ as they use video instead of text as a blogging medium (Du Plessis, 2018:187). They can also be seen as a form of web television (ranging from 5 minutes or less to 30 minutes or more) that covers a variety of topics from politics, pop culture, comedy to fictional dramas (Breslin et al., 2009:130; Quesenberry, 2019:147). As multimedia content, vlogs offer a more multimodal and engaging experience than blogs and podcasts, as non-verbal behaviour enriches what is being explained in the video (Biel & Gatica-Perez, 2013:41). Vlogs also focus on a specific target audience with whom blog creators (usually called influencers) tend to build trust and credibility (Du Plessis, 2018:187). Although vlogs are more engaging than blogs, the length of a vlog can determine the effectiveness thereof. If a vlog is too long, usually more than 30 minutes, it will not be consumed (Breslin et al., 2009:130).

(ii)   Augmented reality

AR is 'the term for a constellation of digital technologies that enable users to display and interact with digital information integrated into their immediate physical environment' (Bolter, 2014:30). In other words, AR refers to the integration of real-world environments with technological environments. An example of AR is Snapchat where users can take a picture of themselves and overlay digital images on their pictures. Recent technological advancements (mobile phones and social media) have created opportunities for different mediums to incorporate AR onto their platforms and have created opportunities for cultural expression. An excellent example of AR within social media is Snapchat, as users on this platform can augment their realities by manipulating videos and pictures by incorporating animation to real-world situations (Azionya & Sitto, 2018:21).

AR is also becoming increasingly important for both social media users and brands. Social media users are continuously looking for new experiences, while brands need to create compelling and consistent brand experiences to make sure their content stands out from all the other content available on social media (Azionya & Sitto, 2018:33). As AR evolves, organisations will also find opportunities for branded content to be inserted into conversations (Scholz & Smit, 2016:155). Although this is a future perspective, AR is becoming increasingly relevant and may impact the way social media platforms are structured and the tools that will be available on social media platforms (Kane, 2017:44). The inclusion of AR capabilities will not only have an impact on how brands communicate with users but also how individuals and organisations communicate, create, and share knowledge. The more AR is incorporated into social media the more AR content will be utilised in social media. It is also important to realise that AR may also have an impact on how other content is consumed. For example, Snapchat allows users to not only send videos and photos but also to create an opportunity to make this multimedia content more engaging and 'fun' using filters and lenses. The impact of AR on content, communication, knowledge sharing, and production and marketing will make the integration of AR into social media research increasingly important.

(iii)   Virtual reality

VR can be viewed as a device that produces technologically-simulated experiences by constructing virtual worlds (that is, resembling a new world or replicating the actual world) (Hillis, 2014:512). Oculus rift headsets are examples of expensive devices that can be acquired to access virtual realities, while products such as Google Cardboard and VR Box allow users to access VR by combining their mobile device with their glasses. Although many internet articles and blogs state that VR will change how we interact on social media by creating computer-simulated places to communicate, no platform currently exists that combines social media with VR. However, as VR technology evolves current social media platforms may embrace incorporating VR technology within their platforms. Currently, many social media sites are starting to embrace 360° and 180° photos and videos as a way of experimenting with VR capabilities on their social media platforms (Calero, 2015).

Little research currently exists regarding the use of VR on social media platforms. However, social media researchers can use 360° and 180° videos and pictures as a starting point for social media research in the domain of VR. Especially marketing research can use the opportunity to determine the impact and effect that VR on social media can have on user and consumer behaviour, while social scientists can investigate the impact VR has on communication by creating opportunities to share experiences through social media by transporting people away from their everyday lives.

1.4.5   Interactive elements

The following interactive elements are applicable:

(i)   Tagging features

Although tagging is not content per se, the functionality of tags plays a key role in content consumption. According to Mahoney & Tang (2017:133), social media provides various forms of tagging to link individuals (random or specific) to a communication event (such as a message, picture, video, and so forth). They add that tagging is an interactive element to link people who share the same interests or link designated topics and ideas together. Social media users can tag their friends, a person, and even a brand in photos, messages, and posts. They can further tag a location that they are visiting or even tag an interest they may have (by posting a message, graphic, or video) in order to share their thoughts with like-minded individuals. Tagging is thus 'the way social-bookmarking programs organize links to resources' (Quesenberry, 2019:184). Social media researchers can thus use social media tags to find information on a certain topic that they would like to analyse and report on their research. For example, social media researchers who are interested in feminism can look for the #menaretrash tag on social media platforms to find various posts on this topic.

Social media researchers should furthermore distinguish between the various types of tagging and how they relate to the different types of studies when they plan to conduct social media research. The types of tagging are:

- **Geotagging:** Content (text, images, or video) can be perceived as geotagged when such content is associated with a geographic location indicating where the content was constructed. Geotagging is closely linked to geosocial networking, which is a type of social networking in which users' GPS data coordinates are used to connect them to people, businesses and events (Flatow et al., 2015; Quesenberry, 2019:160)

- **Location tagging:** This form of tagging allows users to tag a specific location (place, business, destination, etcetera). Unlike geotagging which embeds a tag into content, location tagging allows the user to share their location via social media by 'checking-in' (Quesenberry, 2019:163)

- **Collaborative tagging:** Collaborative tagging describes the process by which many users add metadata in the form of keywords to shared content. This form of tagging can be used to follow and analyse trends as different sources converge and collaborate over time (Golder & Huberman, 2006:198; Quesenberry, 2019:184).

Tagging should consequently be seen as an important tool that does not only create awareness of new or relevant content but also allows users and brands to engage with each other and the content. Tagging provides an opportunity to group together different types of content that may be different in format but communicate and share the same ideas. Furthermore, many brands have constructed campaigns in which they gamified the use of tagging to increase brand engagement.

1.5 TIER 2: THE COMMUNICATOR (SOCIAL MEDIA CONTENT CREATORS)

From the previous section, it is evident that various types of multimedia content exist that can be communicated on social media. This different multimedia content can be used to engage and communicate with various users. Referring back to Power's (1995) model of communication research, the communicator as an individual, the relationship, and their culture needs to be researched with the message. However, the question then becomes who is the communicator and who the creator of the message/content on social media?

This is a particularly important question as communicators' approaches to social media differ significantly from person-to-person. For example, people tend to use social media informally as an extension of their social life by talking to friends, gossiping, sharing their photos, and so forth. (Van Dijck, 2013:6–7). While brands, on the other hand, strategically manage their social media to achieve certain objectives aligned with the organisation's strategy (Du Plessis, 2017:356). Thus, there is a clear differentiation between the communicative intent of the different communicators. The next two sections consider the different content creators to gain a basic understanding of the different communicators that should be kept in mind when researching social media.

1.5.1 User-generated content

User-generated content is the process where social media users collaborate to construct content that is then distributed among various platforms and consumed by different communities (Mahoney & Tang, 2017:26). At the core of user-generated content lies the idea of active participation, where users are actively involved either by creating content or co-creating content through their interaction with the content from other users (Fourie, 2017:20). The idea of active participation by users encompasses the whole idea of a 'participatory culture' conceptualised by (Jenkins et al., 2006:3). User-generated content on social media, in a participatory culture, plays a vital role in enhancing the connection between users, while creating a space for users to articulate their culture, opinions, views, interests, and so forth. (Van Dijck, 2013:35). This is an important aspect of social media as it to some extent questions power relations in society and shifts the control of media from organisations and government to the users who can then democratise the media landscape through their participation (Lindgren, 2017:41).

Despite the cultural and participatory value of user-generated content, it is not without criticism. User-generated content is usually considered as amateurish because of the low production value of some content that is seen as 'unfinished, recyclable input in contrast to the professionally polished and finished content of mainstream media' (Van Dijck, 2013:35). This can be ascribed to low barriers to the artistic expression of the participatory culture (Jenkins et al., 2006:3).

Therefore, in the new information economy content that violates expectations (good or bad) has a high probability of going viral on social media (electronic word of mouth (eWOM)). According to Freberg (2019:38), eWOM can be described as the rapid spread of content through various networks and communities in a limited amount of time. Researchers on social media need to take into account these perceptions and the impact thereof on information consumption and the spread of content on social media.

1.5.2 Brand-generated content

Brand-generated content (also referred to as firm-generated content, enterprise-generated content or marketer-generated content) is a multifaceted construct that refers to all the messages and content created by brands and shared on the various social media platforms owned by the brand to further business objectives (Kumar et al., 2016:9). Thus, brand-generated content is a strategy used by organisations to engage users and consumers via social media to build relationships, communicate with customers, market products, create awareness of the brand, etcetera. By doing this, communications on social media are more consumer-centric or driven to allow brands to co-create content with users and to minimise the risks caused by communication about brands on social media (Berthon et al., 2008:20; Du Plessis, 2017:356). According to Muir and Verwey (2018:5), social media users have more control over the messages communicated by the organisation, than the organisation itself. Co-creation is therefore pivotal to brands as user-generated content shapes their customers' brand perceptions (Smith et al., 2012:100). There is evidently a need for organisations to carefully construct their social media strategy and messages (both when initiating the communication and when responding to a message) on both traditional and social media, as users can keep organisations accountable for what they say. It is important to note that organisations and brands within this context should not just be seen as organisations functioning in the corporate sector. To illustrate, the government, as a brand, also uses social media strategically to build relationships with citizens.

For researchers, it is important to keep in mind the differences between these two communicators. Although social media researchers can research these communicators from an individual, relational, or cultural perspective, there is a clear difference between the communicative intent with which these two communicators approach messages and multimedia content. There can be an overlap between the two concepts (user-generated content and brand-generated content) in the case of influencers and even personal branding of individuals. When researching these individuals and the messages they communicate, the true nature of the content can be determined.

1.6 TIER 3: LEVELS OF COMMUNICATION (SOCIAL MEDIA PLATFORMS)

Social media serve as gateways through which various types of content and conversations can be shared between individuals, groups, brands, organisations, and nations (Freberg 2019:37). The nature and design of these platforms can to a certain extent determine the level of communication that takes place on a specific social media platform. For example, WhatsApp can facilitate communication both on an interpersonal and group level, while Twitter can facilitate communication on a public level. Furthermore, communicators share messages and content on various platforms based on the different levels of communication that platform can facilitate (Mahoney & Tang, 2017:92). It will be virtually impossible to discuss all the social media platforms and their features; however, this section will provide a brief overview of the different types of social media platforms and some of the most popular platforms used in South Africa and around the world (see Box 1 for credible sites where social media statistics can be obtained). According to Statista (2020) Facebook, YouTube, Instagram, and TikTok are some of the most used social media platforms around the world. However, within this section a discussion of the different platforms, Twitter, LinkedIn and Snapchat, will be included due to the popularity of these platforms in South Africa and due to their platform features (World Wide Worx, 2019). This section will also illustrate at what level communication can take place on that specific platform and the impact thereof on research:

Social media statistics

Numerous websites contextualise the most used social media platforms used around the world, but not all these sites provide credible statistics. The following sites offer credible information regarding social media usage patterns and consumption patterns:

- Datareportal: https://datareportal.com/
- Hootsuite's and We Are Social's digital reports: https://wearesocial.com/digital-2020
- Statista: https://www.statista.com/statistics/272014/global-social-networks-ranked-by-number-of-users/
- Statcounter: https://gs.statcounter.com/social-media-stats
- Our World in Data: https://ourworldindata.org/rise-of-social-media
- Smart Insights: https://www.smartinsights.com/social-media-marketing/social-media-strategy/new-global-social-media-research/

1.6.1   Social media platforms and research

Social media platforms and users can be researched using both traditional (surveys, questionnaires, interviews, etcetera) and digital (for example big social data, social network analysis, multi-platform analysis) quantitative and qualitative research methods (McCay-Peet & Quan-Haase, 2017:14). The type of research that will be conducted depends on the research objective of the researcher and what they want to investigate. For example, researchers in communication may be more interested in the content structure, whereas researchers in marketing may be more interested in the click-through rate of content to online stores. Jordan (2018:913) indicates that one of the issues social media researchers face is their decision to base social media research on the people who use social media platforms or the platforms themselves. As social media platforms form part of a broader social media ecosystem, with cross-platform capabilities, researchers can also take a multi-platform approach when researching social media (Jordan, 2018:913).

That being said, some social media platforms may be better suited for specific types of research due to access to data and factors such as ethics. Hence, various opportunities exist in conducting social media research regarding users and social media platforms. Table 1.2 below provides some examples of the types of research that can be conducted on different social media platforms.

Table 1.2:   Suggestions for research that can be conducted on different platforms

Social media platform	Type of research	Research methods examples
Facebook	Quantitative, qualitative and mixed-method research	Content analysis, discourse analysis, semiotic analysis, social network analysis, case study research, ethnography, etc.
Twitter	Quantitative, qualitative and mixed-method research	Content analysis, discourse analysis, social network analysis, case study research, ethnography, etc.
YouTube	Quantitative, qualitative and mixed-method research	Semiotic analysis, content analysis, discourse analysis, etc.
Instagram	Qualitative research	Content analysis, semiotic analysis, content analysis, Case study research, ethnography etc.
LinkedIn	Quantitative, qualitative and mixed-method research	Discourse analysis, social network analysis, content analysis, case study research, ethnography, etc.
Tik Tok	Quantitative, qualitative and mixed-method research	Semiotic analysis, content analysis, case study research, ethnography, etc.
Snapchat	Qualitative research	Traditional research methods, discourse analysis

It is important to note that the table above serves only as a starting point for the social media researcher. Before conducting social media research, the researcher needs to investigate different and new social media research opportunities due to the dynamic and changing nature of social media users and platforms.

1.6.2   Facebook

One of the biggest social media networks is Facebook with its 2 498 million active users (Statista, 2020). There exist various research opportunities for social media researchers when looking at Facebook due to the versatility of the platform in terms of networking, marketing, branding, and so forth. Facebook is a social media platform that provides various messaging and chatting functions that not only allow users to choose between asynchronous and synchronous communication but also provides a combination of mass and interpersonal communication (Mahoney & Tang, 2017:106). According to Russell and Klassen (2019), Facebook can be observed as a social interest graph, meaning that users simultaneously have the opportunity to maintain relationships on an interpersonal level and share their reactions and feelings to a broad audience on a public level (depending on the privacy settings). They add that Facebook uses an asymmetrical friendship model as users need to accept each other's 'friend requests' first before being able to view each other's information. Facebook as a social media platform does not only create a space where people can connect and share experiences, it also gives users insight into one another's lives and psychology and demonstrates a unique social perspective (Vaynerchuk, 2013:30; Yang et al. 2017:78).

Facebook can be seen as a hybrid social media platform, facilitating communication at all levels, as it provides a space for different contexts of communication:

- intrapersonal by sharing your thoughts (status updates);
- interpersonal communication (through chatting in the private chat section);
- organisational communication (by using Facebook workplace or groups as an internal communication platform);
- business communication (facilitated through Facebook marketplace and pages); and
- public communication (by simply sharing your ideas or responding to the posts of other individuals).

The messages and content on Facebook, therefore, differ depending on the intent of the communicator and their specific needs. This creates various opportunities for researchers who wish to study Facebook by focusing on aspects like representation, the relationships between individuals and groups, or even how users communicate in different situations (Bosch, 2017b:67).

Facebook is still one of the biggest social media platforms that connects social media users. The various content formats used on Facebook along with developments that enable users to engage through messages and interactions provide rich research opportunities for social media researchers. Social media researchers can use various qualitative and quantitative research techniques to understand not only content but the behaviour, motivation, and attitude of users (Vitak, 2017:627). Various quantitative research methods can also be employed to gain an understanding of the data generated by Facebook.

1.6.3   Twitter

One of the platforms that are important for social media research is Twitter. Although Twitter only has 340 million active monthly users (We are Social, 2020), Twitter has become the go-to platform for politicians, academics, and journalists. Twitter can be seen as a synchronous microblogging service that allows users to share short thoughts and ideas in the form of Tweets to a timeline (Russell & Klassen, 2019). Communication on Twitter is asymmetrical, which means that users can read and access anyone's messages, even though they do not 'follow' that specific person. Twitter thus facilitates public communication, due to the unidirectional and bidirectional connections on this platform where anyone can create, access and share messages to anyone (Weller et al., 2014:xxx).

Although Twitter can facilitate both interpersonal and public communication it is mostly used as a source for real-time information (Weller et al., 2014:xxx). Therefore, Twitter is the ideal site for journalists, politicians, and organisations to communicate breaking news and updates (Lipschultz, 2018:79). This causes information on Twitter to have a short lifespan as up to date information is added every minute (Mahoney & Tang, 2017:91). Despite this, Twitter is still an important social media platform for politicians, academics, journalists, and brands due to its participatory capabilities. Various politicians use Twitter to communicate their stance on political issues or engage with voters regarding issues that are important to them. Twitter users (like politicians, journalists and brands) can easily track information on certain topics by following hashtags (Freberg, 2019:42) thereby not only providing the opportunity to stay up to date with breaking news but also becoming an excellent source of crowd-sourced information from users.

Twitter can be valuable for researchers as it provides insight into discipline-specific research, to find new and innovative research methodologies (although this can be said for all social media platforms), give insights into big data (see chapters 8 and 9), investigate issues of policy and privacy, etcetera (Weller et al., 2014).

Due to the various opinion leaders on social media research, the societal impacts remain a research interest for many social media researchers. Social and material practices on Twitter also provide research opportunities related to a variety of methods and methodology (Stewart, 2017:251). As machine learning and computer analysis applications develop, Twitter researchers will be able to use mixed-method research to understand different perspectives and interactions on social media (Murthy, 2017:569). Twitter provides social media researchers with various qualitative and quantitative research approaches to understand the complex data generated by Twitter. Furthermore, discourse and conversational analyses can also be researched to gain insight into how users engage with each other and user-generated content.

1.6.4 YouTube

One of the second largest social media platforms is YouTube with 2 billion active users (Statista, 2020). YouTube is a video-sharing site, where users and brands can upload a variety of video messages and content (For example movies, documentaries, advertisements, educational videos, and training videos) (Quesenberry, 2019:145). Users can then subscribe to channels that disseminate information about topics that they find relevant (Lange, 2009:71). Although we can explain YouTube, it cannot be defined from a computer science perspective as YouTube is a database. However, from a humanistic perspective, it can be viewed as a cultural institution that archives memories, surroundings, portrayals, and voices of various users (Snickars & Vonderau, 2009:2013; Pennington, 2017:233). YouTube can, therefore, provide insights into not only the present but also the past.

Just like all other social media platforms, YouTube provides capabilities for users to react and respond to the content of other users (Uricchio, 2009:34; Salmons, 2017:179). However, YouTube also creates a space where various voices can meet and communicate, from governments, organisations, non-profit organisations (NPOs), or religious groups who can come together to share and archive their memories and affective moments while at the same time providing meaning to individuals and communities (Uricchio, 2009:34; Grusin, 2009:66). The nature of these messages differs from organisation to organisation, while adding value to not only the intended audience but also for those who could derive value from the content in the future.

YouTube creates a platform where users can share affinity videos that can establish personalised communicative connections between users on a social media platform (Lange, 2009:71). These videos are constructed to connect the creator of the video to the consumer of the video by connecting both the creator and the user through mutual beliefs or interests (Lange, 2009:83). Videos of affinity can be either user-generated or brand-generated and differ in personalisation, expectation, and interactivity depending on the communicator.

For social media researchers, YouTube thus has tremendous value as not only the platform, but the communities that form around various topics can be researched to gain an understanding of the platform.

The videos on YouTube have created a whole repository and archive of popular culture and knowledge artefacts for social media research (Arthurs et al., 2018:3). As YouTube develops synchronically, new research opportunities regarding content and engagement with the content on social media platforms emerge every day. YouTube provides social media researchers, especially social scientists, with artefacts to understand digital society. The naturalistic content and professional content, stretching over various contexts, provide social media users with many data formats to analyse for research purposes (Pennington, 2017:232). YouTube functionalities like comments, sharing, and liking also provide insight into communities that form around content channels. Video content also creates opportunities for social media researchers to investigate the psychological and sociological effects of visual artefacts (Pennington, 2017:233).

1.6.5   Instagram

Instagram is a social media site that provides users with the functionality to apply filters to visual content (video and photos) and users then have the opportunity to like and share content (Quesenberry, 2019:148). Instagram provides users with the option of shareability where content shared on Instagram can be shared with other social media platforms like Facebook and Twitter to increase content awareness and engagement (Vaynerchuk, 2013:136). Because of this, Instagram has high engagement rates and is very rich in user-generated content (Quesenberry, 2019:148). In an analysis of social media statistics, Chaffey (2020) reported that Instagram is one of the most popular social network sites for millennial and Generation Z users. For researchers, this is particularly important as Instagram has approximately 1 billion active social media users (Statista, 2020).

Although Instagram is a great social media platform to share visual content, the downside to the platform is that it does not allow users to organically connect (Mahoney & Tang, 2017:91). This means that you can follow a person, but they have the choice if they are going to follow you back. Instagram is important to social media researchers as the platform provides insight into the visual generation.

McDowell and De Sousa (2018:17) argue that Instagram holds the potential for 'data-driven cultural research beyond data visualisation or hashtag sentiment analysis'. Due to the visual nature of Instagram production and consumption patterns can be investigated along with quantitative data like followers, likes, network mapping, population research, etc. (McDowell and De Sousa, 2018:17). Furthermore, the number of influencers on Instagram can also provide opportunities for case study research related to brands and individuals. Media effect research and psychological research can also be conducted on platforms like Instagram due to the graphic nature of the content and the psychological impact of these messages on individuals.

Instagram research covers various topics and subject-fields that capture the daily lives and aspirations of social media participants. Instagram provides data that can help researchers understand younger generations and popular culture. Images/videos, text, emoji, and hashtags can be analysed together as unified artefacts. Although Instagram provides an opportunity to research content, there is a need to understand social media users and content creation (Laestadius, 2017:588). Instagram provides various qualitative research opportunities using semiotic analysis of symbols used in posts, images, and videos. However, uses and gratification research can provide more information to understand Instagram users. The psychological and sociological impact of Instagram content also needs to be investigated to understand the impact they have on users.

1.6.6 LinkedIn

Although LinkedIn is not one of the most used social media platforms globally, it does serve as an important platform to research. LinkedIn is a professional social media platform allowing users (future employees or customers) and organisations to build relationships (Russell & Klassen, 2019). Unlike Facebook and Twitter, the LinkedIn profile is structured in a way that reflects a resume by adding aspects like work experience, skills and education-related sections to the profile (Quesenberry, 2019:117). Due to the professional and specialised nature of LinkedIn focusing specifically on professionals and organisations, it makes sense to research LinkedIn despite the fact that this platform has 610 million users (Statista, 2020). LinkedIn also provides users with a group function although the nature of the group is mostly professional, and groups tend to be closed. Due to the professional nature of LinkedIn, messages and content posted on LinkedIn tend to be carefully formulated and constructed by users to convey a positive image (Mahoney & Tang, 2017:91). Thus, information and messages posted on LinkedIn differ from users' social media accounts due to the networking and lead generating capabilities of this professional platform. Therefore, Engelbrecht and Ngcongo (2018a:51) suggest that the following should be considered when managing your LinkedIn account as opposed to your profile on other social media platforms:

- **Language:** A more formal register of language is used on LinkedIn because you need to convey and maintain a professional image. This also means that language and grammar need to be checked to maintain the appearance of being a professional.
- **Content:** Your LinkedIn profile is used to share professional information and should not be used to share content intended for staying in touch with friends. Thus, always think if you would advertise what you are publishing on your social media on a billboard for everyone to see.
- **Reputation:** LinkedIn should not be used to write bad messages. What may be seen as freedom of speech to you may be seen as a potential reputational risk to organisations. Therefore, it is also important to moderate the comments and posts made by others on social media to ensure your reputation is not harmed and your credibility not influenced.

The types of messages shared on LinkedIn between users and organisations are usually focused on industry-related information (like opportunities, success, development, training, inspirational stories, etcetera) or information that can increase a person's personal brand as either a professional or expert.

LinkedIn as a social media platform provides many opportunities for human resource management professionals, industrial psychologists, branding specialists (organisational and personal), and leadership communication (among many other possibilities). For example, a study conducted by Koch et al. (2018:14) found that social media, especially LinkedIn had an impact on recruiting during the sourcing process. Considering this type of research, it becomes important for social media users to think about how they represent themselves and what they communicate on social media platforms like LinkedIn.

As a professional social media platform, LinkedIn allows researchers to understand the corporate communication context and how individuals present themselves through their communication. LinkedIn's functionality of connecting professionals can also provide interesting insights by using social network analysis tools. Using content analysis research methods LinkedIn can also provide interesting case studies of how organisations and individuals position themselves and their personal brands.

1.6.7   TikTok

TikTok is a short video-sharing application that enables users to create quirky and creative videos (Wang, 2020:5). The idea behind TikTok is to create a platform for users to be creative and to express their creativity (TikTok, 2019). TikTok allows users to create short videos between 15 seconds to 60 seconds and cover a wide variety of topics (singing, lip-syncing, dancing, cooking, beauty, real-life, etc.) (Wang, 2020:5). Short video is becoming increasingly more popular among social media users due to the rich content, personalisation of content and interactive format (Xu, Yan & Zhang, 2019:59). Due to its alternative format of video-sharing TikTok is becoming one of the fastest-growing social media platforms with 800 million active users worldwide (Oberlo, 2020).

Just like most social media platforms, TikTok enables users to follow other users, see trending TikTok posts, follow hashtags, allow tagging, and allows users to comment and share content.

Research conducted by Bresnick (2019) indicated that the fundamental features of TikTok are playful and may lead to increased video creation. He adds that 'TikTok liberates young people to play without adhering to the visual styles, narratives, and online cultures of the past'. The playful and creative nature of TikTok can provide researchers with interesting insights into changes in content creation and adapting messages for younger audiences. However, Anderson (2020) indicates that TikTok does have regular videos that reflect the real-life context. She adds that there is an element of uncertainty created by the contrast between the different types of content which can be researched from a cultural perspective to gain insight into the digital lives of younger generations. Social media researchers must take cognisance of TikTok due to the potential research opportunities that will arise from this fast-growing social media platform.

1.6.8 Snapchat

Snapchat is a social media platform that provides users with the opportunity to circulate visual gags and jokes to satisfy the needs of those who cannot stand boredom (Vaynerchuk, 2013:175). Unlike many other social media platforms Snapchat *snaps* (vertical photos or ten-second videos), only live for a few seconds or disappear after reading and pose an interesting challenge for researchers as these messages are pure erasure (Lindgren, 2017:83; Quesenberry, 2019:150). What makes Snapchat different from other social media platforms is that messages and content are not shared with the masses, but rather focused on engaging a preselected group of friends (Mahoney & Tang, 2017:152). Snapchat provides various features (like lenses, filters, text, emoji, etcetera) that can be combined with the visual content uploaded on the platform (Quesenberry, 2019:150). According to Freberg (2019:42), Snapchat is becoming one of the dominant platforms and is being used a lot by the younger generation due to the visual and 'snackable' nature of the content being generated and shared on this platform. According to Statista (2020), Snapchat has 398 million active users with a majority of users below 25 years of age and a sizable portion of its users between the ages of 13 to 17 years. Marketers and brands can still target audiences on Snapchat by choosing from various paid and native advertising options (Quesenberry, 2019:151).

Although Snapchat is increasingly being used, there is a small issue of content ownership. According to Freberg (2019:90), Snapchat has updated its terms of use by stating that the platform has the power to use content created by users as the content is posted on their platform.

Lindgren (2017:111–112) states that Snapchat, like Instagram and YouTube, is changing the way people communicate and even our culture and politics by placing prominence on imagery. He adds that this new focus combined with our ability to alter images for various results (humour, deception, etcetera), demands that new perspectives be developed through research to understand the new modes of expression and communication.

According to Mahoney and Tang (2017:321), the interpersonal, one-to-one model of communication used by Snapchat requires researchers to research Snapchat from a more interpersonal perspective rather than from a mass media perspective. Researchers in social media should always be aware that although platforms are structured in a specific manner, social media research can be framed within different contexts of communication. Thus, different approaches can lead to different results and findings.

Snapchat is developing and evolving, just like many other social media platforms, thus providing various research opportunities as new technological affordances are incorporated into the platform. Snapchat research is still in its early stages and provides opportunities for social media researchers to understand content creation, user interaction and communication phenomena (Grieve, 2017:136).

1.7   TIER 4: SITUATION (SOCIAL MEDIA CASE STUDY)

Social media research is becoming increasingly important in various fields as more users are turning to social media for their information and communication needs. Various studies have been conducted about the use and impact of social media on health, organisations, politics, marketing, and education (to mention but a few). Due to its affordability and the diversity of audiences, social media provides various research opportunities to social media researchers.

The following case study contextualises how NPOs are turning more towards social media to communicate with donors. It is hoped that the case will provide not only insight into the importance of researching social media within an NPO context but also spark some interest in researching NPOs on social media.

1.7.1   A decline in support of charity and charitable projects

There are several reasons why so many charitable organisations and projects suffer financially. Many NPOs struggle to get financial support as South Africans tend to suffer from donor fatigue. Furthermore, people supporting NPOs feel that there is no return on investment for their donations. There is a need for NPOs to not only be visible to attract support, but to provide proof that their donations are being used to facilitate social change (Kanter & Fine, 2010). This is not always possible as NPOs only have a limited amount of resources and do not always have the time or skills to communicate how they are spending donors' contributions. Thus, traditional funding and communication are no longer effective and need to accommodate the needs of individuals who want instant gratification from doing good, while reducing the effort of electronic funds transfers (EFTs). NPOs are faced with the burden of implementing expensive systems to ensure donor convenience when providing support (Taljaard, 2019).

The only solution for NPOs to reduce this decline is to find alternative media for communication. However,

> [a]s mainstream media only focus on events that are considered newsworthy, most day-to-day challenges remain unknown to the greater public. Above-the-line awareness is completely out of reach for most charities, because they simply cannot afford it, leaving NPOs with social media as the only strategy to share their story (Loving Thy Neighbour, 2019).

This, however, poses a challenge as the dynamic nature of social media requires social media managers to constantly stay up to date with the latest trends and tools. As most NPOs are constrained by limited resources, skills, and time, they need continuous training to manage social media effectively. Even though various courses exist that provide NPOs with social media training, these courses are too expensive for most NPOs to attend (Loving Thy Neighbour, 2019). This impedes NPOs' abilities to provide the return on investment that individuals require for instant gratification with a minimum amount of effort from donating to charitable organisations.

1.7.2   Empowering non-profit organisations the Loving Thy Neighbour way

Inequity Holdings (Pty) Ltd started Loving Thy Neighbour (LTN) in an attempt to address their social responsibility. They aim to help other charities by establishing a visibility platform to share work done by NPOs and sponsor social media and financial training for organisations to manage their relationships and finances effectively via different mediums of communication. By providing this support to NPOs, LTN aims to focus on improving NPOs' ability to help themselves to create improved sustainability, as they continuously have access to knowledge, skills training, and the support of the digital communication environment. LTN, as a meta-charity supporting other charities, focuses all their energy on working with charities to achieve the following goals (Loving Thy Neighbour, 2019):

- Advise NPOs on how to fix the current business structures to provide sustainable support.
- Provide training and support on all necessary skill levels (social media, strategic planning, and more).
- Provide a visibility platform where they can load and distribute their activities and results.
- Integrate message flow with money flow by providing seamless donation buttons.

Although LTN focuses on the whole range of services to support NPOs, two of the important aspects of support for NPOs are social media planning and management.

1.7.3   The Loving Thy Neighbour model

As mentioned before, LTN empowers NPOs in two ways: by providing (i) social media training and (ii) a visibility platform where NPOs can load and distribute their activities. These two activities will be discussed next.

(i)   Social media training

On a bi-weekly basis, LTN provides social media and digital communication training, together with systems training that enables NPOs to communicate more effectively with their target audience. During this training, they focus on the brand identity being communicated through an organisation's social media platform, the levels of communication facilitated by different social media platforms, and how to strategically use the correct platform for the specific target audience. After organisations gained an understanding of how to utilise different social media platforms to communicate with their target audiences, LTN supports NPOs to construct a Digital Communication Strategy Plan and weekly social media calendars (Taljaard, 2019).

Figure 1.5:   An example of a banner created by LTN for their own social media page

During the social media training, LTN teaches other NPOs to create similar high-quality content for their social media platforms.

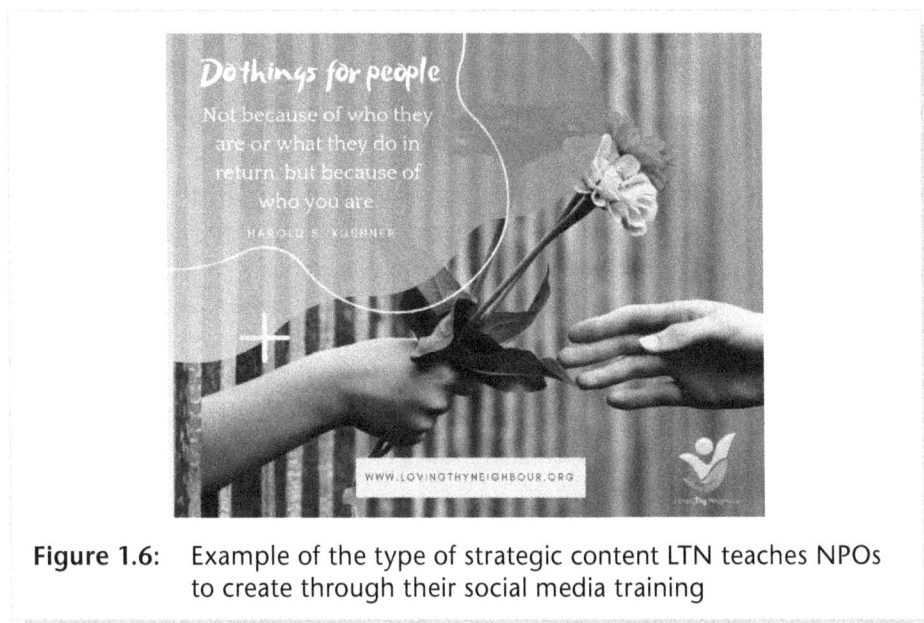

Do things for people

Not because of who they are or what they do in return, but because of who you are

HAROLD S. KUSHNER

WWW.LOVINGTHYNEIGHBOUR.ORG

Figure 1.6:   Example of the type of strategic content LTN teaches NPOs to create through their social media training

(ii)   Providing a visibility platform

LTN does not only provide NPOs with training to effectively manage social media platforms they also use their own social media presence to share the stories and projects of the NPOs they serve. Once an organisation is successfully registered on their platform and has undergone and passed a strict vetting process with their sponsoring bank, LTN can post about the good work they are doing, giving donors a peek into the projects, events, and operations they have helped fund. Their platform is therefore just like a news feed on your typical social media platforms. On every post, donors or interested parties can FOLLOW this organisation, SHARE the story to their own social media platforms, or DONATE to that particular organisation. LTN further supports NPOs by directing donors to their website where they also share stories, upcoming events, and all the different projects that LTN is supporting (Taljaard, 2019).

It is thus evident that social media plays an important role in many NPOs addressing issues in many different situations. The lack of skills and knowledge on how to communicate their messages, create and construct content, and use social media platforms strategically to engage with stakeholders on different levels causes NPOs to lose donor support. By empowering NPOs to manage their social media platforms effectively and providing a supportive platform that provides a catalogue for different NPOs, donors can have instant gratification while being provided with proof that their investments are being used to facilitate social change.

1.7.4   Experience from a previous participant

To assess the effectiveness of the support that LTN provided, a former communication practitioner working in the non-profit sector was asked to share her experience of the organisation:

> *Loving Thy Neighbour helped me realise that social media can serve as a less expensive tool to help my organisation grow and adapt to the new digital era. Their support also helped me realise that social media can serve as a vehicle to help us reach our strategic goal and to nurture our online communities. The practical examples for managing the various social media platforms proved to be invaluable. These practical examples included the different types of marketing, the use of emotions, the four posts building blocks, improving your writing skills and the importance of a call-to-action proved to be very insightful. Their support enables Non-Profit Organisations to build relationships and experience a boost in both donations and brand awareness. Paying attention to this has helped my organisation to improve our chances to secure support and donations from potential untapped supporters/donors.* (Degenaar, 2019).

1.7.5   Social media research and the importance of researching the non-profit sector

It is important to research the use of social media within the non-profit sector as there are lessons and insights to be gained by investigating how they creatively find ways to communicate with various stakeholders (Freberg, 2019:494). Unlike for-profit organisations, NPOs are continuously trying to improve on social media practices and without knowing it, they are creating new business and communication models due to their strategic management of social media. The limited resources and the nature of NPOs cause these organisations to think strategically and creatively when considering content creation and social media management.

Research on the NPO sector will not only contribute to the body of knowledge of social media but is also important due to the role NPOs play in society. The significant work NPOs do in terms of raising awareness of and addressing various issues or challenges (such as abuse, discrimination, poverty, health and illiteracy) and addressing the needs of vulnerable communities, increase the importance of social media research in this context (Freberg, 2019:495).

Social media research can not only help NPOs understand different case studies or improve strategic plans of organisations but it can also help to document the return of impact regarding issues faced by society (Freberg, 2019:495). In this case, we can see that LTN is not only providing social media training and social media fundraising opportunities for NPOs but is also equipping other

NPOs to address issues faced in society adequately by providing them with a platform to share their stories and to document their impact.

1.8 SUMMARY

From the previous section, it is evident that social media research should be approached taking into account the different tiers of communication research. The message and content lie at the core of any social media research and therefore researchers should be attentive of the nature of the message. Furthermore, the communicator and communicative intent of the communicator should be considered when conducting social media research as different communicators approach content creation differently. Social media researchers should also keep in mind the capabilities of the social media platform and the level of communication that these platforms can facilitate. Finally, the situations will determine how social media is used as a form of communication. Social media researchers should also keep in mind that the situation plays an important role not only in understanding the impact of social media on how we communicate but also by noting the important role that social media plays within the communication landscape.

When deciding how to approach your social media research, it is important that you carefully plan what you want to investigate. According to Lindgren (2017:269), the multiplicity of the internet should be taken into account when conducting social media research. It is, therefore, important to keep in mind that research can be conducted by looking at the content being shared on a specific platform, by looking at the platform itself, or by focusing on both aspects. Couldry and Van Dijck, (2015:2) add to this idea by stating that research on social media should be more than merely describing the functionalities and potential of current and new social media platforms. Social media should describe how platforms have redefined what it means to be social and how users not only enact the social but also indicate the ethical implications of mediated spaces on our social life.

Social media researchers need to be aware that social media is dynamic and evolving and they need to be constantly informed on how social media and social media platforms are continuously changing. These changes will create new challenges and opportunities for social media researchers.

Learning activities (Test yourself)

1. Discuss why it is difficult to define the concept of social media?

2. Why do you think it is problematic to research social media within existing models of communication?

3. Analyse the social media presence of any individual or organisation according to Power's four tiers of research:
   - What message is being communicated and what content are they using to communicate this message?
   - What type of communicator do we find on this social media platform?
   - Which social media platform do they use and what level of communication is facilitated on this social media platform?
   - What context and situation does the communication within this platform fall into?

Further reading

Lindgren, S. (2017). *Digital media and society*. London: SAGE Publications.

Mahoney, L.M. & Tang, T. (2017). *Strategic social media: From marketing to social change.* 1st edition. Chichester: Wiley-Blackwell.

Prichard, M. & Sitto, K. (eds.). (2018). *Connect: Writing for online audiences.* Cape Town: Juta.

Quesenberry, K.A. 2019. *Social media strategy: Marketing, advertising and public relations in the consumer revolution.* 2nd edition. Lanham: Rowman and Littlefield.

CHAPTER 2

Introduction to the Social Media Research Process

Charmaine du Plessis

Research is about what everybody else has seen and thinks what nobody has thought – Albert Szent-Györgi

Learning Outcomes

After completing this chapter, the researcher should be able to:

- identify how to extend traditional research to a social media study;
- describe how social media research supports traditional research;
- recognise the advantages and disadvantages of social media research;
- explain all the challenges of a social media study;
- summarise the differences between social media as a research methodology and using social media data for research;
- discover all the essential components of a social media study's research design; and
- relate to the different components of the social media research process.

2.1   INTRODUCTION

This chapter introduces the reader to the social media research process and makes cross-references to the different chapters in this book where these topics are explored in more detail. The chapter thus acts as both a starting point and a point of reference for all social media researchers and should be read together with other chapters.

The number of conversations on social media provides the social media researcher with unique and ample opportunities to uncover qualitative insights on a quantitative scale (Smith, 2016). Apart from knowing how to conduct social media research, it is imperative to be well-informed about all the trends in qualitative, quantitative, and mixed methods research for social media (Snelson, 2016) and have a sound theoretical point of departure (see chapter 3).

This chapter will explain why social media research must follow the same rigorous process as traditional research methods and why social media research has become mainstream. Social media research, however, is not without criticism and there are plenty of pitfalls that the researcher must avoid.

This chapter provides an overview of the social media research process starting with what traditional research is and how social media supports traditional research. The chapter explains the need for more scientific results when using social media, the advantages and disadvantages, as well as methodological challenges and issues related to social media research. Like traditional research, a social media study must have a conceptual structure within which to conduct the inquiry. It is therefore important to explain a study's purpose and the different considerations in the research design, for example, identifying the research problem, formulating a central research question or hypothesis, setting out the sampling methods, data collection, analysis, and reporting. Some of the topics introduced in this chapter concerning the research design are merely introductory to the different chapters in the book and will assist the reader to make appropriate choices. The social media research process is also illustrated in a case study.

2.2   TRADITIONAL RESEARCH

Research is an exploration of the world in all its various forms and is an opportunity to create and share knowledge about contested and multiple realities. As a result, research has become a multi-dimensional concept (Pather & Remyenyi, 2019).

Traditional research follows systematic steps to solve a research problem with traditional research methods such as interviews, focus groups, Grounded Theory, a survey, or experiments, amongst other methods. By doing so, researchers adopt a research approach which can be quantitative and/or qualitative or mixed-method – see section 2.7.4, Table 2.3 below (Cary, 2011).

Social media research is an extension of traditional research and follows the same systematic steps (see Figure 2.2 in section 2.7 below). Social media studies can be mainly qualitative and/or quantitative or mixed method. The main differences between traditional research and a social media study are that the researcher can collect and analyse data much faster and reach a wider audience while a social media study is often also more cost-effective than a traditional study. Moreover, novel research methods that are tailored only for social media studies have emerged, for example, sentiment analysis and social network analysis (see chapter 5). Also, innovative data collection and analysis tools have become available to collect and analyse large social media datasets – see chapters 5, 8 and 9 (Hynd, 2018).

The social media research process is explained in much detail in section 2.7 and illustrated in Figure 2.2. Keep in mind that the sequence of steps for a social media study is also applicable to the traditional research process and will not be repeated in this section.

2.2.1 How social media research supports traditional research

Although social media research has become mainstream and many researchers consider it a stand-alone research method, it is also important to consider arguments that social media could complement and support traditional research. Social media is indeed becoming more prominent, but it will not replace, for example, traditional research methods such as focus groups, surveys, interviews, and ethnography. Some traditional research methods are also used for social media studies as explained in chapters 4 and 5 (Hynd, 2018).

Before a researcher decides on whether to use social media or traditional research methods, it is important to consider the types of analysis that could be performed on social media as opposed to traditional research methods. For example, social media provides insight into online behaviour as well as information about that behaviour, whereas in a traditional survey a reply also includes offline behaviour (Petitt, 2011). On the other hand, social media provides a wealth of information about user behaviour without the limitations of a survey which could yield more natural results. In a survey, it is also not always possible to connect responses about behaviour with actual behaviour. While a survey often includes demographic information about respondents and assists with arguments about age, gender, and socio-economic information in findings, it is not possible to obtain accurate demographic information about users on social media platforms. Many social media users do not disclose their locations or do not use their real names (for example, on Twitter) (Buntain et al., 2016).

There are many arguments in favour of combining social media with surveys to obtain richer results, especially when it comes to context (Buntain et al., 2016). A case in point is Petitt (2011) who illustrates that a survey aiming to determine where respondents want to buy their coffee would need many response options that could cause responder fatigue. When analysing coffee conversations on social media, only the most relevant coffee shops could be identified and assist with narrowing down response options for the traditional survey. Social media data could, therefore, help identify item options and topics for a survey, interviews, and focus groups or in providing more contexts to complement the results of traditional research methods.

For example, using social media to analyse online conversations could be a useful first step in a larger research project and one way of triangulation in research. Social media data could, amongst other things, also identify new categories, products and questions for a survey. Besides, social media data could provide preliminary information before using traditional research methods. Since quick results can be obtained with social media as opposed to surveys, interviews and focus groups (that are time-consuming to plan, implement, and analyse), organisations often turn to social media to collect information that will aid faster decision-making (Nguyen, 2014).

However, there are still many arguments that social media research is not a method of doing systematic research but merely a method to monitor and notice content and information on different social media channels. This book will, however, illustrate that social media can be used as a scientific research methodology. There are already some studies that found similar results when doing a social media study followed up with a traditional research method. These studies' findings counteract arguments that social media research cannot be generalised to the larger population (Bruns & Stieglitz, 2013; Olteanu, Vieweg & Castillo, 2015).

2.3   WHAT SOCIAL MEDIA RESEARCH IS AND IS NOT

Social media research has seen tremendous growth over the last decade. As is evident from chapter 1, social media has become a universal tool that is used for both business and leisure purposes. Social media research is an extension of traditional research and typically uses tailor-made tools and techniques to collect and analyse real-time or historical data from different social media platforms to address a research problem (Vis & Thelwall, 2013).

It is, however, important to distinguish between social media as a methodology and using social media data for research. Hynd (2018) defines social media research as a methodology when it

utilizes public-facing content from a variety of online & social sites in order to aggregate, monitor, and analyse content surrounding a topic, issue, product or service as a research methodology.

In 2011, Poynter, who is the Managing Director of The Future Place and a renowned social media researcher, explained that social media research could simply be traditional research with social media as a sample source that must adhere to the same rigour as other research (Poynter, 2011). For example, social media studies that use categorisation and semantic tagging follow the same techniques as Grounded Theory, qualitative content analysis, or thematic analysis (Wills, 2016) – see chapters 4 and 9.

More generalised methods of using social media data include tools such as listening and monitoring social media conversations. Social media as a methodology is used to answer specific research questions, to identify consumer insights, study consumer behaviour, sentiment, or perceptions, amongst other things. Also, analytical social media data could assist to test hypotheses (Hynd, 2018).

Academics and professionals across different disciplines apply social media as a methodology to study topics of interest and concern to obtain greater insight on problems that could also be useful for organisations. As a result, many social media studies use case studies to explain a problem and to contribute to the literature with practical applications. Studies about social media may typically adopt a qualitative, quantitative, or mixed-method research approach (see chapters 4, 5 and 6) using different research methodologies (Carrigan, 2016; Mollett et al., 2017).

In addition, academics and practitioners also adopt more generalised methods of using social media data across different fields on a variety of topics ranging from studying real-time interactions, gaining consumer insight, or improving social media strategies, amongst other things. Organisations also use social media as a methodology in obtaining consumer sentiment, opinions (feedback) and reactions to events as well as to identify new trends (Hynd, 2018; Mollett et al., 2017). As a result, organisations invest millions in strategies and technologies to assist with their social media presence and to build relationships with consumers by connecting with them (McCorkindale & DiStaso, 2014). A 2019 benchmark study on 150 organisations from 12 industries globally indicates that these organisations are invested in social media platforms Facebook, Instagram and Twitter (Feehan, 2019). Another study by Buffer (2019), an online traffic metrics organisation, indicates that although social media has become a key component of organisations' marketing strategies, marketers are still unsure how to measure social media success. This study shows that there are still numerous social media research opportunities available in terms of developing more advanced tools and methods to measure social media success.

Hence, as social media is evolving, social media researchers continue to develop new research methods and ways of using social media data, for example, advanced social listening and audience intelligence tools and platforms. Social media data can nowadays be extracted from social media, the World Wide Web (WWW), blogs, forums, and news sites (McCorkindale & DiStaso, 2014). Also important is the application of social media research in the fourth industrial revolution (4IR) to more smart devices, for example, mobile phones, cars, home appliances, and wearable technology such as Fitbit, an activity tracker for improved health. Because of the Internet of Things (IoT), data has become more interconnected but also poses more ethical concerns. The IoT extends connectivity to devices that can be controlled and monitored remotely – refer to chapter 11 to read about the implications of the networked society (Social Media Research Group, 2016).

It is also important to mention that scientific social media research is not about launching opinion polls on, for example, Twitter, Facebook, or Instagram as the results are deemed too idealistic. However, many organisations use opinion polls on social media to obtain some quick ideas about the perceptions of consumers on an event or topic. Nevertheless, the organisation will not know how real these results are since many social media users might participate, but not necessarily care about the topic of the poll. Opinion polls on social media will merely complement traditional research but not replace traditional opinion surveys (Sajuria & Fábrega, 2016). Table 2.1 below depicts some of the main differences between social media as a research methodology and using social media data for research.

Table 2.1:   The main differences between social media as a research methodology and using social media data for research

Social media as a methodology	Using social media data for research
Uses a scientific inquiry to combine, monitor, and analyse content surrounding a topic, issue, product or service to solve a research problem and research question(s)	Using social media data tools such as listening and monitoring, for example, to understand real-time conversations or to improve organisational strategies
Follows a systematic and scientific procedure to obtain and interpret results (systematic steps similar to traditional research)	Not always concerned with following a systematic and scientific procedure although in some studies it might (depending on the purpose of the social media study)
Can be time-consuming to complete	Concerned with fast results
Concerned with ethical issues and permission	Ethical issues are a concern, but not to the extent as social media as a methodology where ethical clearance should be sought before the study may continue

Sources: Dharmapalan (2012), Hynd 2018, McCorkindale & DiStaso (2014)

Scientific social media studies share the following characteristics (Dharmapalan, 2012):

- The study follows a proper research design and is carefully planned, accurately implemented, and solves a research problem (see section 2.7 below).
- The study is guided by a research problem, central research question or hypotheses (see section 2.7.5).
- The study has a purpose and clear objectives (see sections 2.7.1 and 2.7.2).

- Reasoned arguments are necessary to support conclusions about findings (see section 2.7.12).
- When a research problem is resolved, further problems often arise which need resolving.
- Ethical considerations are important.

2.4   ADVANTAGES AND DISADVANTAGES OF SOCIAL MEDIA RESEARCH

Conducting social media research has many advantages but also some disadvantages. The advantages of using social media data for research are numerous as indicated below. By using social media data for research purposes, the social media researcher (FoodRisc Resource Centre, 2019; Hynd, 2018; Buntain et al., 2016; Social Media Research Group, 2016):

- collects and analyses data in real-time which means that the researcher has access to the latest conversations and opinions about a specific topic;
- has access to data of influencers on a topic. Since influencers start many conversations on social media, the researcher has access to dominant and present-day perspectives;
- may collect data from a diverse group of people which include both spontaneous to more reflective responses to a topic;
- has access to data of a large sample of people irrespective of geographical areas or boundaries;
- may collect data either longitudinally (over several periods) or cross-sectionally (over a specific period) depending on the research question;
- does not need to do any data transcriptions as the conversations on social media can be used verbatim for analysis;
- will have access to conversations that are honest and transparent. Since social media encourages people to share their opinions, conversations often reflect the real feelings of social media users. However, the researcher must take care not to consider fake information and always be aware of the presence of social media trolls (social media users who disrupt conversations with inflammatory or off-topic messages);
- may be able to analyse the reach of posts (Facebook, Instagram) or tweets (Twitter) or the spreading of the information from those posts or tweets across social media networks (see chapter 1);
- has access to data which can be collected quicker and more cost-effectively than data collected through traditional research methods;

- might remove what is referred to as the Hawthorne (observer) effects that could lead to skewed results. This means that participants or respondents' behaviour changes because they are aware that they are being observed, for example, responding to questions in a survey or focus group differently and not revealing their true opinions on a topic; and
- will have access to social media analytics that provide much insight into information needed to base decisions on, for example, branding, campaigns or brand positioning.

There are also a number of disadvantages of using social media for research. The social media researcher (see Phillips, 2011; Buntain et al., 2016; Hynd, 2018; FoodRisc Resource Centre, 2019):

- may deal with the same messages several times, for example, social media users who post messages twice or the same messages that were shared by several people. This could lead to a biased interpretation of the data as well as the over-representation of the sample;
- may need to invest in expensive social media subscriptions for social media data analysis software to effectively deal with a large sample of data;
- may need to explain the reliability and validity of the findings with much more rigour than for traditional research;
- must spend much time on the data analysis to obtain deep and rich results because of the size and unstructured nature of the data. A study using social media data may, therefore, be very time-consuming to complete, especially because the results need to be proven as reliable and valid;
- may find it difficult to collect historical data on social media unless using complicated methods, for example, using the Twitter public API (application programming interfaces). However, access to historical tweets may still be limited;
- may face privacy and confidentiality issues since behaviour on, for example, Facebook and Twitter could be argued as being private and not public behaviour and consent will be required to use these posts in research (depending on whether the research problem involves studying behaviour on social media);
- may face additional ethics and privacy concerns because of the recent concerns and revelations around privacy issues in several countries, especially when it comes to Facebook. These ethical and privacy concerns may also extend to other social media networks in future as social media users and organisations are becoming more aware of the implications of how their data are being used;

- needs to accept that what is relevant on a specific social media platform today, may no longer be relevant in a year or beyond because of the evolving nature of social media. Social media research could thus become unrelated soon;

- needs to realise that when dealing with vast quantities of data it is often necessary for more than one researcher to do the coding which could result in concerns about interrater reliability;

- deals with fears of results not being statistically significant because the sample may not be representative of the target population. There are, for example, many arguments questioning the results of studies using sentiment analysis as it is believed that sentiment cannot be recorded and analysed scientifically (see chapter 5);

- faces reliability issues because many social media studies cannot be replicated due to privacy restrictions on social media networks; and

- should rigorously ensure the quality of the social media data to be used for the study because many posts may not be relevant to the research question(s). In social media spam posts, fake news, and rumours abound (see section 2.6.4).

Furthermore,

- it is not always possible to generalise findings to the larger population unless the study was complemented with additional data analysis procedures and research methods such as a survey or face-to-face interviews;

- quantitative analysis of social media data is often criticised as being superficial because this type of analysis does not consider the richness and context of social media users' conversations and responses;

- not all people have access or prefer using social media and samples could, therefore, exclude an important part of the target population;

- the researcher will not have access to the non-verbal communication of the sample which could affect the interpretation of the data. Emoticons (symbolic illustration of a facial expression used in online conversations) may be helpful but might not reflect the overall perspectives of the topic under investigation.

- the researcher relies only upon publicly shared information and will need consent and access to study private data which is not available in the public domain;

- samples could be subject to criticism because of researcher bias – that is, only testing those individuals' opinions who are more interested in the topic;

- social media may give researchers access to diverse perspectives, but social media users are not necessarily representative of the target population. It is therefore always important to highlight this weakness in any social media study and argue that the sample is more diverse than usual; and
- observational data, specifically, might pose numerous limitations which is explained in more detail in section 2.5 below.

2.5   METHODOLOGICAL ISSUES AND CHALLENGES: THE BATTLE FOR SCIENTIFIC RESULTS

As mentioned elsewhere in this chapter, there are still many researchers who avoid conducting social media research especially because of the many methodological issues and challenges. These issues and challenges are depicted in Figure 2.1 and explained below.

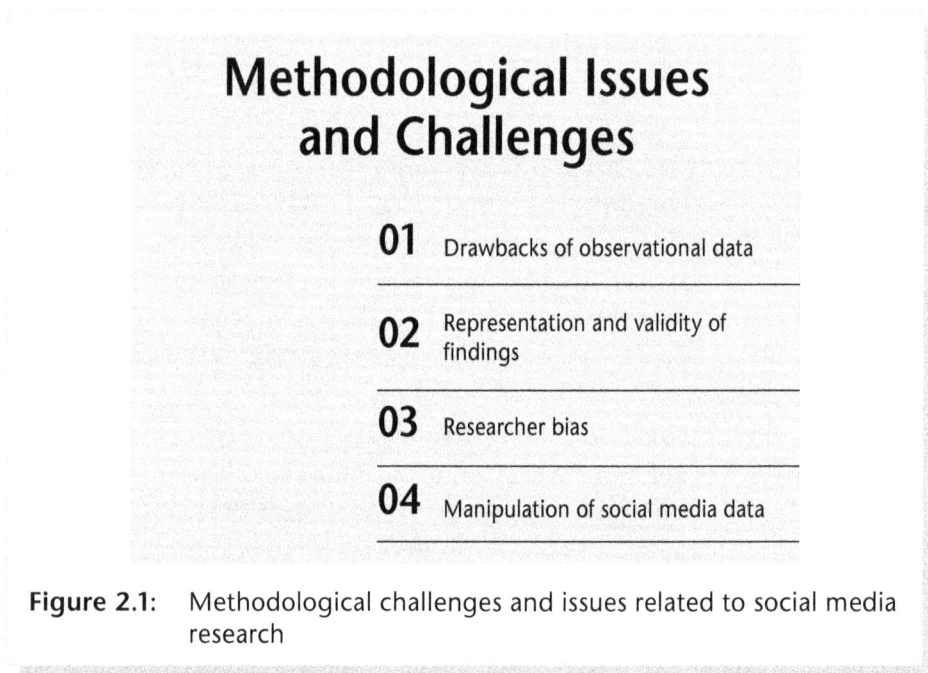

Methodological Issues and Challenges

01 Drawbacks of observational data

02 Representation and validity of findings

03 Researcher bias

04 Manipulation of social media data

Figure 2.1: Methodological challenges and issues related to social media research

2.5.1   Drawbacks of observational data

Although social media seems to be a very attractive way of obtaining observational data, there are many pitfalls when it comes to methodological issues as explained by Poynter (2018) below.

Similar to traditional research, a researcher gathers observational data for a social media study when individuals do not have to be involved when collecting the data, for example, not being interviewed, not recording a research diary or responding to a questionnaire. Observational data can also be collected as a census (studying everyone in a population) or with a sample using different social media listening and monitoring tools. Observational data has become popular because researchers realise that survey questions can be limiting, and response rates are declining while observational data is widely available.

However, observational data poses challenges for a social media study because it often does not account for all the variables in a population which might lead to the wrong conclusions. It is also very difficult to determine cause and effect although there may exist a relationship between variables in the data. The relationship may also be too complex to measure when models made up of linear components are not applicable. Also, an analysis may reveal the specific patterns in the data but not the reason for the patterns to reach valid conclusions. Traditional market research often comprises pre-testing of advertisements. However, observational data will not be able to predict the success of any advertisement. In some instances, researchers will need to complement observational data with a survey (Poynter, 2018).

2.5.2   Representation and validity of findings

Social media data differs from platform to platform and does not necessarily reflect the larger online and offline population. Therefore, social media researchers are often facing challenges of whether the data will be helpful to understand an entire target population. This means that social media researchers must consider and address this concern which could be overcome by how the sample is drawn and reported on (Carson, 2016).

Tufekci (2014) explains that especially the validity and representativeness of big social data analyses pose some methodological challenges. Social media researchers also often overemphasise a single social media platform or select a sample frame that is unrepresentative. The interpretation of big social data could also be compromised by 'invisible data' which the social media algorithms could not identify, for example, subtweeting, mock-retweeting and using screen captures to analyse text. One of the biggest methodological challenges of analysing big social data is an insufficient understanding of the denominator (a numerical number representative of the total population in terms of which statistical values are expressed). For example, it will not be of any value to the social media researcher to only know how many social media users liked a post without being aware of how many saw the post. Inferences and interpretation of big social data can also be compromised by not understanding the issues of why social media users clicked through on a link, retweeted a post, or the context in which this occurred (Tufekci, 2014). Big social data is further explained in chapter 5.

2.5.3   Researcher bias

As is the case with traditional research methods, also when dealing with a social media study, the researcher might face several types of researcher bias. Researcher bias refers to the process where the researcher who conducts the study influences the results to generate a certain outcome that could be intentional or unintentional (Leedy & Ormrod, 2013).

However, unlike with traditional research methods, how to reduce researcher bias in social media research is still an ongoing debate and is not yet fully known (Carson, 2016).

There are several instances where a social media researcher must be careful not to be biased. A researcher may resort to selection bias by drawing a sample on social media without considering the exclusion of potential social media users resulting in inaccurate results. Most researchers do not consider full Twitter datasets for a study that involves this microblogging social media platform but instead draw a sample with various sampling strategies. However, it must be an important consideration of whether the chosen sample will provide objective data (Zhang, Hill & Rothschild, 2018) – see also section 2.5.4 below.

In addition to selection bias, a social media researcher may also face issues of non-participation bias which might impact the reliability of the results in unknown ways. For example, those conversations or individuals that were not included in the sample may have entirely changed the results if they were included (Devault, 2018).

Read more about sampling in chapter 7.

2.5.4   Manipulation of social media data

Manipulation that often happens on social media challenges the reliability and validity of social media studies. For example, activists or haters might make a hashtag trend through coordinated efforts, while social media is also full of spam and other types of bots who intercept conversations to direct them in a different direction (Tufekci, 2014). A spam bot can create fake accounts on social media platforms and will even attempt to disguise their activities as coming from a real social media user. Often creating a social media account is relatively easy and only involves completing a form (which spambots can also do with the assistance of a programmer), for example, Instagram and especially Twitter. Other social media platforms, such as

Facebook, are more stringent when it comes to preventing fake accounts. It, therefore, remains a methodological challenge for the social media researcher to include only authentic data in the sample for analysis (Morstatter, Sampson & Liu, 2016). Many researchers use machine learning models based on machine learning algorithms to detect spam, for example, the Support Vector Machines based spammer detection model. However, these types of models require some knowledge of computing and are not always feasible for the social media researcher (Zheng et al., 2015). How to effectively deal with data on social media which could have been manipulated remains one of the biggest methodological challenges for the social media researcher.

2.6   OPPORTUNITIES: FINDING REAL AUDIENCE INSIGHTS

Doing social media research has many opportunities as explained in section 2.4 when it comes to all the advantages. One of the advantages that need further explanation is the opportunity to find real consumer insights. Consumer insights are original and interesting information about an organisation's customers which could include but are not limited to, demographics like age, gender, and location, but also sentiment towards certain topics and which topics they find interesting (Chan, nd). While it is also possible to obtain audience insight with traditional research methods, social media could provide more authentic data since conversations are happening in real-time about real issues.

Also, since there are millions of conversations happening on social media every day, the social media researcher could have the opportunity to obtain qualitative insight on a quantitative scale. The quantitative understanding is thus complemented with rich data. However, this can be a daunting exercise as the researcher must cut through all the noise on social media to find the right data to address the research question(s) adequately (Smith, 2016). For example, it is not enough to only rely on social media metrics (likes, shares and comments) for audience insight but to know where to search, how to detect a trend, what is important and to be able to discuss the findings in context. It is therefore important for the researcher to ask the right research question(s) to find the right answer(s). This means that the social media researcher should not first consider the methodology for the study but rather be focused on identifying the right research problem and question(s). Only once the research question(s) are clear, concerns about how to conduct the study should become a consideration (Smith 2016). Consumer insight is also only worthwhile when the information that is found on social media is new, unexpected, relevant, and worthy of further investigation (Chan, nd).

2.7   THE RESEARCH DESIGN

The rise of social media research presents new possibilities for discovery but also encourages differences over how the scientific method should be conducted and applied. Social media research is not about collecting social media data to interpret knowledge but should be a rigorous inquiry to solve a specific problem. All scientific research needs to follow a logical plan or process to come to valid and reliable conclusions (see Leedy & Ormrod, 2013). As Sutton & Austin (2015) explain, research begins in the mind of the researcher because of a curious and observant attitude that recognises a problem that exists and needs further investigation. Also, Pather & Remyenyi (2019) confirm that a scientific inquiry always starts with a research question, respects what has previously been learned while being sceptical, uses a structured methodology, seeks alternative explanations, looks for application of the findings, while being aware of the limitations.

Thus, scientific research always starts with observations of a phenomenon. The researcher thus notes what is happening to explain a phenomenon. For example, when it comes to social media, the researcher might access different social media platforms to observe how they function or are being used to obtain different types of results. The researcher might also observe conversations about a topic which is trending on social media (Poynter, 2018).

Like traditional research, social media as a research methodology must also have an overall strategy (or blueprint) to guide the different components of the study. A well-thought-out research design enables the researcher to address the research problem adequately and to answer the research question(s) or hypotheses. The study's overall strategy thus assists in obtaining the right evidence to assess the phenomenon that is being studied in a logical and clear-cut manner. This entails collecting the data, measurement as well as data analysis. It is always the research problem that determines the type of research design to be used and explained. If a study's research design is not well-developed, the findings could be at risk to be insubstantial and unconvincing (Leedy & Ormrod, 2013). For findings to be convincing and to be taken seriously social media research also must follow the scientific method. Figure 2.2 below depicts the generic steps of a social media study and the chapters in which these steps are discussed in more detail.

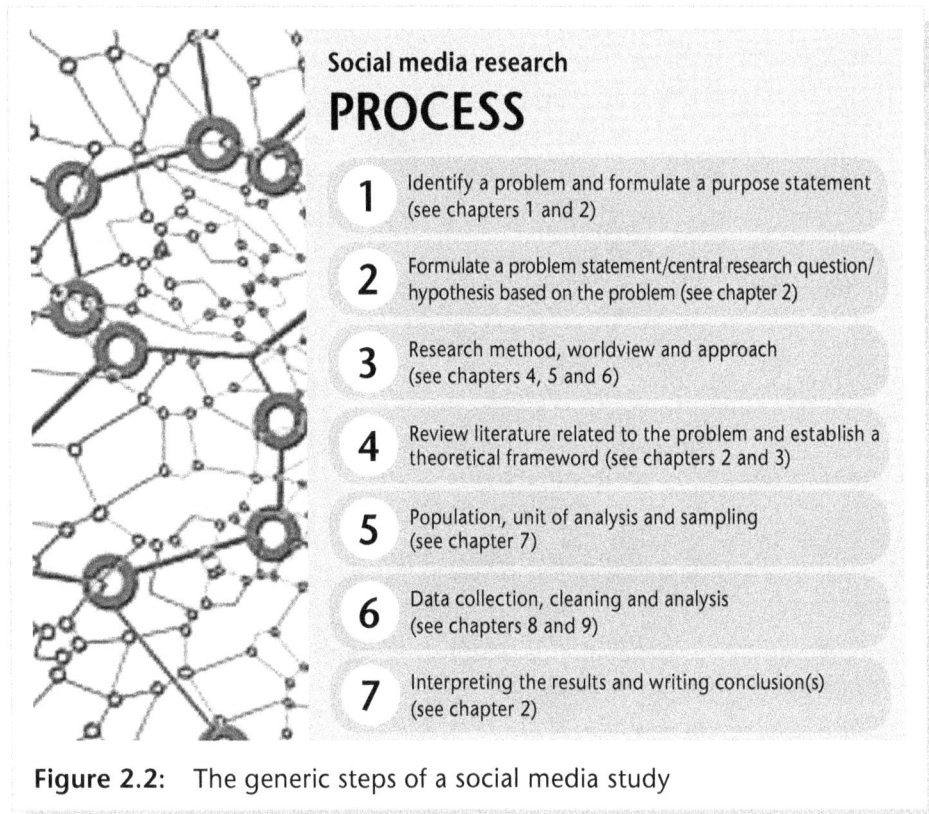

Figure 2.2:   The generic steps of a social media study

By following the above steps as depicted in Figure 2.2, a research design for a social media study typically considers the following aspects which are explained in the sections below (but which will differ per the epistemologies and ontologies of researchers).

2.7.1   Purpose of the study

The purpose of a study comprises a statement about the reason for or the intent of the social media study and should be understandable, precise, and informative (Cresswell, 2014).

More specifically the purpose statement is a statement (unambiguous or implied) that indicates the overall focus for the study in one or more brief sentences. In a social media study for a journal article the researcher typically states the purpose of the study at the end of the introduction while in a thesis and dissertation the statement is provided in a separate section. However, the purpose statement is often neglected during the research proposal writing stage, while authors on research methodology often incorporate it into other topics such as the research questions or the research problem. The purpose statement outlines the plan for the study and should not be confused or treated like the research problem or research questions (Cresswell, 2014).

Therefore, for this book, we propose that social media researchers should consider giving more importance and prominence to the purpose statement of their studies and not to incorporate it into other sections.

A purpose statement can be formulated for both quantitative and qualitative studies. For example, a purpose statement for a qualitative social media study can be formulated as follows (Cresswell, 2014:124):

'The purpose of this _____(strategy of inquiry, such as Grounded Theory, qualitative content analysis or other type) study is to _____ (understand/describe/develop/discover) the _____ (central phenomenon being studied) for _____ (the participants, such as the individual, groups, organisation) at _____(research site). At this stage in the research, the _____(central phenomenon being studied) will be generally defined as _____ (provide a general definition)'.

For a quantitative social media study, the purpose statement can be formulated as follows (Cresswell, 2014:128):

'The purpose of this _____ (network analysis) study is (was/will be) to test the theory of _____ that _____ (compares/relates) the _____ (independent variable) to _____ (dependent variable), controlling for _____ (control variable) for _____ (participants/respondents) at _____ (the research site). The independent variable (s) _____ will be generally defined as _____ (provide a general definition), and the control and intervening variable (s), _____, (identify the control and intervening variables) will be statistically controlled in the study'.

The purpose statement thus explains the 'why' of the study and paves the way for the 'how' of the study.

While the purpose statement provides the focus of the study, research objectives identify specific aims to be accomplished (Cresswell, 2014).

2.7.2   Research objectives of the study

An objective guides a study in the right direction and should be clearly and concisely defined. There are various types of objectives which can range from the general to the specific. General objectives are broad goals to be achieved by the study and are stated in general terms. Specific objectives, on the other hand, are more focused and narrower (Sreejesh, Mohapatra & Anusree, 2014).

Specific objectives of a study clarify ways to measure the variables and might be to **explore** or **describe** a concept or to **explain** or **predict** a situation or solution to a situation that indicates the type of study to be conducted (Cresswell, 2014).

When formulating an objective, it is recommended that the social media researcher use the SMAART formula. We have adapted the well-known SMART formula (see Lawlor & Hornyak 2012:267), namely for the objectives to be:

- S – specific (what exactly should be achieved by the study?)
- M – measurable (how will the researcher know whether the objective was achieved or not?)
- A – attainable (how realistic is the objective?)
- A – accessible (will the social media data be accessible and available?)
- R – relevant (why should this study be conducted and will the study at any value to the body of knowledge?)
- T – timely (will the study be achievable within a reasonable time?)

An example of a specific objective for a qualitative study is:

- To explore how the content in tweets on Twitter reflect social media users' acceptance of the microblogging site's new camera features to ascertain how brands can use these features to better connect with consumers on social media.

An example of a specific objective for a quantitative study is:

- To explain the effect of social media users' complaints about service delivery on the responses of an organisation on Facebook to propose some guidelines for best practices for customer service in a Web 2.0 environment.

The above author-formulated objectives comply with the SMAART formula in that they are relevant, feasible, logical, observable, unambiguous and can be measured within a reasonable time. In addition, social media data must be obtained ethically (see chapter 10) and be accessible by the researcher. Historical social media data are more difficult to retrieve and require the use of sophisticated software while the social media researcher will also need some technical skills (unless an organisation specialising in gathering historical data on social media is sourced) – see chapters 8 and 9 in this regard.

2.7.3   The research paradigm (worldview)

A research paradigm is a conceptual lens through which the researcher sees the world objectively and affects every decision made during the research process.

Interestingly, when two researchers adopt different research paradigms to study the same phenomenon they will arrive at different results. A paradigm helps the researcher to decide which research question(s) to address or hypotheses to test and consists of overall ideas or underlying beliefs that a group of people may have to understand a theory. Kuhn's (1962:45) seminal definition of a paradigm as 'the set of common beliefs and agreements shared between scientists about how problems should be understood and addressed' reflects a philosophical way of thinking. Guba and Lincoln (1994:105) define a paradigm as 'a basic set of beliefs or worldview that guides research action or an investigation.' More recent schools of thought see a paradigm as fundamental in how researchers construct meaning from the data, based on individual experiences as guided by their worldview (see Kivunja & Kuyini, 2017).

Once a social media researcher has a research problem in mind to investigate, it is important to reflect on how the study will be conducted. As mentioned, all researchers have their views of the world that will guide their beliefs and assumptions about a study. It is therefore important to clearly state the paradigm in which the social media study is located (see Kivunja & Kuyini, 2017).

A research paradigm has four elements, namely epistemology (how a researcher arrives at reality), ontology (an understanding of the things that constitute the world, as it is known), methodology (research design, methods, approaches and procedures used in a study) and axiology (ethical issues that need to be considered in a study) (Kivunja & Kuyini, 2017).

Currently, the dominant research paradigms in social media research are positivist, interpretivist, constructionist, critical and pragmatic and are addressed in detail in chapters 4, 5 and 6.

2.7.4   The research approach

Each research paradigm has a corresponding research approach and research method(s). A research approach is the selection of research and data gathering methods to solve the research problem. However, the social media researcher can adopt research methods across different paradigms, depending on the research question(s) that need(s) answering (Wagner, Kawulich & Garner, 2012).

To illustrate, a researcher that uses a positivist research paradigm will adopt a quantitative research approach and research methods such as a social media network analysis or other quantitative methodologies for social media studies that have numerical measurements or counts (see chapter 5). For an interpretivist research paradigm, the research will adopt a qualitative research approach and use research methods such as semiotics, Grounded Theory and ethnography, amongst other things (see Cresswell, 2013 and chapter 4).

Table 2.2 below summarises the differences between a qualitative and quantitative research approach.

Table 2.2: The differences between a qualitative and quantitative research approach

Qualitative research	Quantitative research
No single reality exists but is subjective and exists only concerning the observer. The researcher is not separated from the data.	The study has objectivity without bias while the researcher is separated from the data.
The study's design often evolves during the research and can be adjusted or even changed as the study advances.	The study's research design is considered before the study and guides the implementation of the study.
Exploratory objectives (although in some instances a qualitative study might also have descriptive objectives).	Descriptive, predictive, or explanatory objectives.
Smaller sample size.	Larger sample size.
Data cannot be counted.	Data is numerical.
Uses methodologies to develop a deep (information-rich) understanding of the phenomenon under investigation.	Uses methodologies to measure the phenomenon quantitatively.
Creative and interpretive data analysis.	Uses statistics to summarise data, describing patterns and relationships and can be descriptive and inferential.
Conventional standards of reliability and validity cannot be applied.	Others can replicate studies
Findings cannot be generalised to the larger population.	Findings can be generalised to the larger population.

Source: McCleod (2019)

Table 2.3 below summarises some research paradigms that could apply to social media research with corresponding research approaches and examples of research methods.

Table 2.3:   Research paradigms that could apply to social media research with corresponding approaches and examples of research methods

Research paradigm	Underlying philosophy	Research approach	Examples of research methods
Positivist	Emphasising empirical studies using appropriate methodologies and measurement	Quantitative	Survey, experimental, opinion poll, data mining
Post-positivist	All studies are fallible and have errors. All theory can be revised in an endless search for the truth	Quantitative	Survey, experimental, opinion poll, data mining
Interpretivist	Integrates human interest into a study	Qualitative	Qualitative content analysis, focus groups, interviews, ethnography, discourse analysis, Grounded Theory, participant observation, conversation analysis
Social constructivism	Human development is socially situated. Humans construct knowledge	Qualitative	Grounded Theory, conversation analysis, participant observation
Critical theory	Oriented toward critiquing and changing society	Critical and action-oriented	Ideology critique Action research
Pragmatic	Focuses on what works as the truth regarding the research questions under investigation	Mixed methods	For example, sentiment analysis and a thematic analysis, amongst other methods
Postcolonial/ indigenous	Promotes transformation and social change among the historically oppressed	Mixed methods	Methodologies that draw from indigenous knowledge
Transformative/ emancipatory	Destroys myths and empowers people to change society radically	Mixed methods	Action research, participatory research

Adapted from Cresswell (2013); Given (2008); Wagner et al. (2012)

Corresponding research approaches and research method(s) are explained in more detail in chapters 4, 5 and 6.

2.7.5   The research problem and key issues

Any social media study starts with a research problem, namely what problem needs solving which could include a gap in existing knowledge or an area of concern that needs investigation. The researcher needs to identify why the research problem is important and requires some resources. This problem then follows an investigation to reach a feasible solution with a suitable research design. A good research problem creates some focus for the study and often leads to further studies while a problem statement is typically formulated (see Creswell, 2013; 2014).

A social media study may either have a research problem statement (with sub-problems), a central question (with sub-questions) or a hypothesis as explained in the sections below (see Shi & Tao, 2008; Creswell, 2013; 2014 & Doody & Bailey, 2016).

(i)   *Research problem statement*

Depending on the research design, a research problem may culminate into a problem statement that clearly outlines the issue by explaining the ideal, the reality and the outcomes of the study and assists the researcher to obtain better results.

There are different ways to write a research problem statement. Also, not all qualitative studies necessarily include a statement. However, the statement typically includes what the problem is, how the problem will be solved and what the purpose of the study is.

An example of a problem statement for a qualitative study is: To explore through a visual semiotic analysis how Instagram users respond to brand messages that encourage them to share selfies while using the brand to provide brands with guidelines on how to resonate more with visuals.

The research statement should then be divided into sub-problems. A sub-problem divides the main problem statement into manageable parts and must be stated in logical order as they set the direction of the study. A sub-problem states what the researcher wants to find out with the study and not how the researcher wants to find the information. For example, the following three sub-problems can be formulated for the above problem statement.

Sub-problem 1: To identify the reasons why brands use brand messages on Instagram to encourage consumers to share selfies while using the brand.

Sub-problem 2: To trace brand messages on Instagram that encourage consumers to share selfies while using the brand.

Sub-problem 3: To visually explain consumers' shared selfies while using the brand.

In many theses and dissertations, each sub-problem eventually becomes a separate chapter in the final document.

(ii)   The central research question (qualitative or quantitative)

Rather than formulating a problem statement, the researcher may also formulate a central research question to guide the study depending on the research design. Research questions are essential for a study as they guide the researcher's selection of methodology, sample methods, data collection and analysis techniques.

A **qualitative research question** is a broad, non-directional question to explore the central phenomenon or concept(s) in a study. The researcher poses this question as a general issue to not restrict the investigation. It is always a good idea to start a qualitative research question with the words 'what' or 'how' or 'in what way' to encourage an open design and not to ask a question that could merely invite a yes or no response.

For a qualitative research design exploratory verb such as to 'discover,' 'seek to understand,' 'experience' or 'explore,' will speak to the design of the study. A qualitative research question is suitable for (but not limited to) a historical/narrative, case study, netnography, phenomenology, textual analysis, qualitative content analysis and Grounded Theory – see chapter 4.

Here is an example of a qualitative central question: How do conference attendees at the Third Digital Public Relations Conference in Dubai experience the use of Twitter to broadcast their paper presentations during the conference?

A **quantitative research question**, on the other hand, is concerned about the relationships among variables that the researcher wants to discover and includes words such as 'relate', 'relationship', 'association' and 'trend'. In addition, a quantitative research question could also compare two or more groups using the word 'compare' or can be causal to determine the effect of X on Y. The question is also often descriptive to quantify variables or responses and starts with 'What is' or 'What are?'

Here is an example of a descriptive quantitative central question: What are the main reasons for the youth to abandon Facebook to join Instagram?

It is also recommended to separate quantitative and qualitative research questions for **a mixed-method** study but only if the main focus is to emphasise the quantitative and qualitative approaches followed to highlight the different phases of a study (see chapter 6). Mostly, a research question for a mixed-method study reflects the integrated content of the topic.

Here is an example of a mixed-method central question: How often do social media users retweet posts on Twitter when following a trending topic with a hashtag as opposed to a non-trending topic without a hashtag?

The above research question has both a quantitative and qualitative component but reflects the integrated content and not separate issues with separate questions.

The central research question thus represents the **umbrella question** to which the researcher does not know the answer yet but will need to do an investigation to find the answer. The research question must also be well-grounded and not too narrow, broad, or challenging. A narrow research question merely invites a yes or a no answer, while a broad research question cannot be answered with one study only. A challenging research question is either opinionated or based on subjective feelings and not objective research.

The researcher may also formulate sub-questions that are narrow questions to help answer specific aspects of the central research question. Examples of sub-questions for a qualitative study are:

Sub-question 1: How often do conference attendees use Twitter while attending the Conference?

Sub-question 2: Do conference attendees retweet mentions of conference papers being presented? (yes or no answer)

(iii)   The hypothesis

When a researcher formulates a quantitative hypothesis, a prediction is made about the expected relationships among variables. In other words, the researcher uses some statistical procedures to predict inferences about the population from a sample by observing the effect of an independent variable on the dependent variable. An independent variable is a cause and the dependent variable is the effect on the issue. Also, the independent variable can be changed whereas the dependent variable is expected to change or not to change.

Hypotheses are mostly used in experimental research to compare groups. The six most common types of hypotheses are a simple hypothesis, complex hypothesis, empirical hypothesis, the null hypothesis (HO), the alternative hypothesis (H1), empirical hypothesis, logical hypothesis, and statistical hypothesis. Table 2.4 summarises the differences between these hypotheses.

Table 2.4:   The differences between the six types of hypotheses

Type of hypothesis	The purpose of a social media study
Simple hypothesis	The researcher predicts the relationship between variables.
Complex hypothesis	The researcher investigates the relationship between two or more independent variables and two or more dependent variables.
Empirical hypothesis	The researcher uses observation and an experiment to test a theory. For example, the researcher might use lab experiments that are conducted repeatedly.
Logical hypothesis	The researcher applies this hypothesis to a field of study as an assumption first and becomes an empirical hypothesis afterwards.
Statistical hypothesis	The researcher examines a portion of a population on social media.
Alternative hypothesis	The researcher attempts to contest a null hypothesis.
Null hypothesis (HO)	The researcher believes that there is no relationship between two variables (independent and dependent) or there is a lack of evidence to formulate a scientific hypothesis.

Source: Adapted from Allen (2017)

Examples of the six types of hypotheses

Examples of types of the six types of hypotheses can be found at: https://examples.yourdictionary.com/examples-of-hypothesis.html

An example of a quantitative null hypothesis for a social media study might be as follows: There is no statistically significant relationship between the type of images posted on Instagram (independent variable) and follower growth (dependent variable).

This hypothesis can be experimented with and possibly be proven wrong or right. The researcher will also be able to support the hypothesis with a high level of confidence. Testing the null hypothesis can tell the researcher whether the results are because of manipulating the dependent variable or due to chance.

2.7.6   The literature review

The research problem statement, central research question or hypothesis guide a study's literature review. A review of the literature provides not only the background but also explains previous research on the topic (what was said about the topic) grounded in a solid theoretical point of departure (see chapter 3). A literature review uses secondary sources, namely books, articles, published research, and newspaper articles, amongst other things, and does not report on original findings. For a social media study, most literature consulted and reported on should be recent to indicate the latest trends but also include some seminal views of major studies that stood the test of time. The literature review should thus reflect current knowledge and substantive findings, as well as theoretical and methodological contributions to a topic (Efron & Ravid, 2019).

It is also important to consider the study's research problem statement, central research question or hypothesis when deciding on the scope of the review which often is challenging to the researcher. To communicate an ordered sequence of ideas, a clear logical argument is required which should be evident throughout the discussion (Efron & Ravid, 2019). A logical flow of arguments is enhanced by using transitional verbs and phrases to connect arguments, ideas, and paragraphs (Randell et al., 2014).

Managing references and sources can be a daunting task. A number of reference management software systems are available to manage references and sources, for example, Mendeley, Zotero, RefWorks, EndNote and CiteULike. Some of this software is free while others are paid for (Efron & Ravid, 2019).

The researcher must adhere to the writing style as prescribed by the publication which will also influence how a source is listed in the text and the bibliography. Examples are the American Psychological Association (APA), Chicago Press (Chicago Manual of Style), the Modern Language Association (MLA) and Harvard (Efron & Ravid, 2019).

See chapter 3 for a comprehensive discussion of a theoretical framework that could be a theoretical point of departure for a social media study.

2.7.7   Research methods

This section must be read together with section 2.2 in this chapter as well as chapters 4, 5 and 6 in this book. There are several research methods available to a researcher to conduct a social media study. In addition, a researcher may adopt a qualitative, quantitative, or mixed-method research approach when conducting a social media study (see section 2.7.4).

Interestingly, Snelson (2016) indicates that from a systematic review of 229 qualitative or mixed-methods research articles published from 2007 to 2013 focusing on social media research, a total of 55 of these studies deal with mixed-method research (see section 2.7.4 and chapter 6). Also, the analysis indicates that social media researchers tend to use a qualitative content analysis with

Facebook, Twitter, YouTube and other social media posts as data sources (see chapter 4). As mentioned earlier in the chapter (section 2.3), there is a difference between social media as a research method and using social media data for research as also put forward by Sloan and Quan-Haase (2017). Both procedures can yield interesting results with a novel and interesting research problem.

2.7.8   Research population and sample methods

A social media study's research problem, the context of the research and research questions or assumptions all shape how the researcher will consider the target and accessible population. In a scientific social media study, a research population focuses on many individuals or things. Examples of a target population are the population of a city, country, or in the case of social media all posts related to a specific topic (see Asiamah et al., 2017).

The **target population** (also referred to as the theoretical population), is the group to which the study's findings are generalised. When findings and conclusions are generalised, it means that they can be extended to the population. The generalisation of findings and conclusions depend on the type of sample (probability versus non-probability) and the sampling method which can be qualitative or quantitative (see Asiamah et al., 2017). Sampling is discussed in detail in chapter 7.

The **accessible population** (also known as the study population), is the actual sample frame from which a sample is drawn. Many social media studies can base their conclusions only on the accessible population, for example, followers of a social media influencer who criticise a topic. Depending on the research design, findings can be generalised to the target population as explained above and in chapter 7 (see Asiamah et al., 2017).

Also, an important consideration for a social media study is the **unit of analysis**, namely the major entity which will be analysed (namely the focus of the data collection). Examples of units of analysis are (see Cresswell, 2013):

- individuals;
- groups;
- social artefacts (books, documents, images, newspapers, social media posts, videos, online media reports);
- geographical units (city, town, census region, state, province); and
- social interactions.

For example, for a survey, interviews and focus groups about social media, the unit of analysis will be individuals or groups, whereas, for qualitative content analysis, narrative analysis or document analysis using social media data, the unit of analysis will be social artefacts. Also, for a social media study using social media data for research, the unit of analysis could be social artefacts or social interactions.

Population parameters are more applicable to quantitative studies that are interested in describing the population and which are represented by numerical numbers. Population parameters are also referred to as population characteristics and are applied to studies interested in using numerical expressions to summarise the various aspects of the research population (Lee, 2008).

2.7.9   Data collection

Data collection is explained in more detail in chapter 8.

Social media data comprises all the information (raw data) collected from individual users on different social media networking sites, for example, on Facebook, Twitter or Instagram. This data can be in the form of images, videos, shares, comments, posts, and mentions (Segal, nd). However, Poynter (2012) points out that social media data comprises 'what is said in social media in locations that can legitimately be queried.' Especially collecting data on Facebook poses some ethical challenges (see chapter 10) while many social media users do not upload content or comment on topics discussed on social media networking sites.

Due to the vast amount of social media data that is constantly generated, various computer software programs are available to facilitate this daunting task, for example, NVivo, which is also discussed in more detail in chapter 8. Depending on the study, it is still possible to collect data manually on social media (by copying and pasting the data into a word processor). However, to manually collect a vast amount of social media data could result in inadequate data and is not recommended.

There are various advantages to collecting social media data (Snaptrends, 2019):

- Social media data is not only about demographics data but includes information which the social media researcher could analyse in terms of social media users' preferences, sentiment, activities and intent, amongst other things.
- Social media data is current (unless historical data is collected). This allows researchers to obtain a holistic view of the sample (see chapter 7) which can be used to analyse past and to predict future behaviour.
- Social media data represents a social media user's beliefs, actions and attitudes allowing insight on an individual level.

A social media researcher also faces the following challenges when collecting social media data (Snaptrends, 2019):

- Social media data is always changing and available which makes it challenging to collect useful data.
- Big data (such as big social data – see chapter 5) must be broken down into smaller segments that make sense. To analyse big social data, the researcher must have access and an understanding of complex analytical software.

Social media data can be used for academic research, audience segmentation, personalised brand messages and creating content, amongst other things (also refer to chapter 11). Depending on the research problem and research questions social media data can be collected across different social media networks and not focus on one social media network only (Segal, nd).

2.7.10 Data analysis

Data analysis and tools are discussed in detail in chapter 9 from a qualitative, quantitative, and mixed-method research approach respectively. Social media researchers may analyse social media data to support a research problem, to improve upon social media strategies to ensure a better social media presence or to gain valuable consumer insights for an organisation's brand. Consumer insight, for example, can be obtained by analysing conversations around a brand that could assist with more effective campaign planning (Smith, 2019).

When it comes to effective campaign planning at the time of publication some of the most popular paid social media analytics tools were Sprout Social, Curalate, BuzzSumo and Keyhole. Free social media analytical tools include (but are not limited to) Facebook Insights, Twitter Analytics, Instagram Insights, YouTube Analytics and Google Analytics. Google Analytics is often used to establish which social media sites direct visitors to a website. It is also possible to do a cross-platform analysis (analysing more than one social media networking site at the same time) by, for example, using the BrandWatch analytics tool or Social Mention (Smith 2019). However, in chapter 9, more advanced tools for quantitative analysis adopting the scientific method permitting different types of analysis, are highlighted.

It must be noted that analysing a large amount of social media data (big social data) for a scientific social media study must be more rigorous to ensure the validity and reliability of the findings than using social media analytics tools to make business decisions based on users' social media behaviour. However, validity and reliability are not only applicable to analysis but also when selecting the sample, doing data collection as well as the methods used (see Ruths & Pfeffer, 2014). Data analysis for social media studies that require more rigorous analysis can be done by adopting either a qualitative or quantitative approach as explained in chapter 9. Like collecting social media data, various software programmes are available to facilitate the analysis of a large amount of data. Most often the same software can be used for both the collection and analysis of social media data (see chapters 8 and 9).

2.7.11 Validity and reliability

Like other scientific studies, a social media study's findings must also be valid and reliable to be taken seriously. However, social media studies still face many methodological challenges and issues as explained in section 2.5. Nine years ago, before this publication, Poynter (2011) pointed out that the population, sample frame and 'complicit' participants in social media studies could be questioned which is still true today (see chapter 7).

Social media researchers must, therefore, put in much effort to report thoroughly on issues related to the validity and reliability of quantitative studies (Cresswell, 2014) and trustworthiness of qualitative studies (Mills & Birks, 2014). Validity refers to whether the study measures what it is supposed to measure to make solid claims in the findings. Reliability, on the other hand, refers to the extent to which a study produces consistent results when replicated. The research design, method(s) and data collection process of a social media study must be rigorous and transparent (see Cresswell, 2013; 2014).

(i)   Validity and reliability of a quantitative social media study

There are several ways to assess a quantitative social media study's validity similar to traditional quantitative research (see Cresswell, 2013:2014):

- **Construct validity**: Construct validity refers to how well the social media study measures what it is supposed to measure when it comes to variables that the researcher operationalised for empirical testing. The researcher could, for example, ensure that the theoretical framework of the study is solid and reflects in the measurement instruments and use several sources of evidence.

- **Face (logical) validity**: Face validity is the most basic type of validity to subjectively assess whether a social media study covers the concepts it is supposed to measure. As the initial step in the research process, a researcher may ask another expert to consider whether a social media study's measurement will be valid.

- **Content (sampling) validity**: The area (content) that is researched in social media is selected using a sample method that is well-explained, appropriate and justified. See chapter 7.

- **Criterion-related validity**: Criterion-related validity has two components. The results of a social media study can have concurrent or predictive validity. Concurrent validity refers to comparing the measure and outcome of the study with another measure that is known to be valid. Predictive validity is obtained when test scores are compared to future measures and when a study's findings can make accurate predictions about a future outcome.

- **Internal validity**: The extent to which evidence supports the researcher's claims in the study's findings. The researcher must be very transparent and rigorous when it comes to implementing a social media study. In addition, the research process followed must be the best way in which to address the study's research questions or hypotheses.

- **External validity**: Whether another study will have the same outcome when replicated in another setting. A social media study has external validity when the findings can be generalised to the population and not only to the specific situation of the study. The external validity of a social media study depends on the research design, sample method and sample size.

- A quantitative social media study could consider two types of reliability, namely across time and different samples (see Cresswell, 2013; 2014).

- **Reliability across time (test-retest)**: Whether the same researcher obtains similar results when the study is conducted at a different time.

- **Reliability across samples**: When the researcher uses a different sample, the results are similar.

(ii)   Validity and reliability of a qualitative social media study

There are several ways to assess a qualitative social media study's validity like traditional qualitative studies (see Mills & Birks, 2014). These include:

- **Trustworthiness**: Trustworthiness refers to the credibility of the research process and results as well as the overall quality of the social media study. The social media researcher must ensure that there is confidence in the truthfulness of the research process followed and the results. Also important is to ensure that the data collected represent the real world and not fake accounts or bots (Mills & Birks, 2014). Social media researchers could, for example, use a strategy known as dialogic engagement by sharing the research with experts to assess the process and interpretations (Ravitch & Carl, 2016).

- **Credibility (internal validity)**: Whether the research results are believable based on the richness of the data to allow for useful knowledge. This relates to the quality of the data gathered to reflect true and real viewpoints. Credibility is often a challenge because many social media researchers gather observational data (see section 2.5). Social media researchers could overcome this challenge with data triangulation. Data triangulation refers to when results can be verified with different data sources (typically more than two data sources).

- **Transferability (external validity)**: The degree to which the results are also applicable in other contexts and 'can be transferred'. Transferability, however, depends on the study's research design.

- **Confirmability**: How well the research findings are supported by actual data collected when examined by other researchers/experts. Social media researchers could have their results assessed and scrutinised by peers and experts.

- A qualitative social media study's reliability could, amongst other things, be ensured through the following measures (Mills & Birks, 2014; Neuendorf, 2017):

- **Interrater reliability**: Reflects the extent to which different coders agree on independent coding processes, for example, when coding social media data for qualitative content analysis or Grounded Theory study. Cohen's kappa coefficient is a robust measure to calculate interrater reliability and is a metric that compares the random chance of an observed accuracy with an expected accuracy.

- **Intracoder reliability**: The consistency with which the same researcher codes the data at different times with the same outcome.

- **Dependability**: The consistency with which the findings could be repeated in another context with similar results. The social media researcher could ensure the dependability of results by carefully documenting the entire research process and data collected.

2.7.12 Interpreting and reporting results

After data analysis, the researcher must interpret and explain the study's results. The study's literature review plays an important role when it comes to the interpretation of the results (see section 2.7.6). It is not enough to merely summarise the results because a summary is not interpretation. Interpretation of the results is rather to confirm the study's sub-problems or research questions, or hypotheses substantiated with what was said in the literature review. Arguments need to be clear and conclusive to the reader (StatisticSolutions, nd).

For a qualitative study, the interpretation of the findings could be argued around themes or categories and related to previous studies (depending on the research design). It is also important to explain how and why the findings confirm or contradict previous studies and to expand on novel information. It is often valuable to also indicate both the practical and theoretical contributions of the study (StatisticSolutions, nd).

For a quantitative study, the findings could focus on the hypotheses or research questions substantiated with literature from the literature review (depending on the research design). It is also important to explain non-significant findings which a researcher might find challenging. Like a qualitative study, the practical and theoretical contributions of the findings could be highlighted while novel information is explained (StatisticSolutions, nd).

The explanation of the study's results must have some theoretical depth and any new understanding or insights must be meticulously clarified. A discussion of the results must increase understanding of the topic by interpreting facts or ideas and reaching some conclusions. Reasoned arguments based on results are necessary to support conclusions.

Social media researchers will interpret and discuss results for a thesis, dissertation, report, or academic journal article. The length and depth of the discussion of the results will, therefore, depend on the type of publication.

The case study below illustrates the research process of a social media study.

2.8   CASE STUDY

A researcher is interested in investigating customer service on social media and starts observing organisations' responses to customer queries on social media and reading widely about the phenomenon.

Research problem

The researcher identifies a problem related to good customer service on social media and wishes to propose a social media customer service framework that could serve as a heuristic for service organisations with a social media presence. Consequently, a responsive mobile service provider with a long-standing social media presence is identified which could be studied.

Purpose statement

The following purpose statement is formulated to guide the research design:

The purpose of this Grounded Theory study is to understand excellent customer service on social media. At this stage in the research, the concept of excellent customer service on social media will be generally defined as 'being responsive to customer inquiries, providing solutions and helpful information.'

➥

Central research question

The study's central research question is as follows:

What constitutes excellent customer service on social media?

The study also has three sub-questions to narrow down the scope of the central research question.

Sub-question 1: How responsive is the mobile service provider to customer questions on social media?

Sub-question 2: How often does the mobile service provider offer solutions in the form of information to customer queries?

Sub-question 3: How do customers react to the mobile service provider's replies to their queries?

Objectives

The study only has exploratory objectives (the SMAART formula was followed).

Objective 1: To explore how responsive the mobile service provider is on social media.

Objective 2: To explore what kind of solutions and information the mobile service provider offers to customer queries.

Objective 3: To explore how customers react to the mobile service provider's replies to their queries.

Literature review

A comprehensive literature review is conducted to conceptualise the main concepts related to the study, to ascertain what previous work was done and to clarify the study's theoretical position and framework. Seminal authors are used to illustrating ideas that stood the test of time while recent work (not older than 10 years) demonstrates current thinking and ideas.

Research paradigm

The worldview adopted for this study is the social constructivist paradigm. The researcher explains why this worldview suits the study also in terms of ontological, epistemological, and methodological underpinnings.

Research approach

The researcher adopts a qualitative research approach and explains the rationale for this approach.

Research method

The research method is Grounded Theory and is explained, also why this is the best research method to address the study's sub-questions (see also chapter 4 for an explanation of Grounded Theory).

Population and sampling

The target population is all service organisations with a presence on Twitter and Facebook. The accessible population is the mobile phone service provider's profiles on Twitter and Facebook. The sampling method is purposive since only posts and replies related to customer service are sampled. The researcher also explains the sample size. The initial sample consisted of 2 000 tweets with 600 replies and 800 Facebook posts with 300 replies. After data cleaning and purposive sampling, the final sample consisted of 500 tweets with 320 replies and 550 Facebook posts with 115 replies. The unit of analysis is identified as social artefacts.

Data collection

A corpus of tweets and posts that includes customers' replies on Twitter and Facebook was collected with the NVivo Plus software programme's NCapture function.

Data analysis

After data cleaning, data analysis is done inductively as the researcher is guided by social media data to propose a framework for social media customer service. The researcher does the coding in different phases, namely line-by-line (open) coding for initial codes and then focused coding while also writing memos that document the coding process for transparency. The researcher meticulously follows the coding processes of Grounded Theory.

The researcher uses dialogic engagement by sharing the research with experts to assess the process and data interpretation to enhance the study's trustworthiness. Data from Twitter and Facebook are triangulated to add credibility to the results. The findings cannot be transferred to other contexts or settings and are only applicable to the mobile service provider.

Interpretations and findings

The researcher is guided by the study's research questions when interpreting the data. The theoretical framework of the literature review is expanded because of gaining more insight evident in the data. Based on the results, the researcher proposes a social media customer service framework as a heuristic for other service organisations.

2.9   SUMMARY

This chapter acted as a point of reference and provided an overview of the research process and research design that are discussed in more detail in other chapters in this book. Researchers need to avoid pitfalls when conducting a social media study. Consequently, the chapter addressed not only the advantages but also disadvantages, limitations, and methodological challenges and issues when conducting social media research. The differences between social media as a research methodology and using social media data for research were also highlighted.

Learning activities (Test yourself)

1. Explain the differences between social media as a methodology and using social media data for research. Illustrate your answer in table format.

2. What are the main methodological challenges and issues when using observational social media data for research?

3. Can you think of a research problem for which a pragmatic research paradigm will be suitable as a worldview for a social media study?

4. How would a quantitative social media study achieve construct validity?

5. How can a researcher enhance the trustworthiness of a qualitative social media study's findings?

Further reading

Cary, S.S. 2011. *A beginner's guide to scientific method*. 4th edition. Boston: Wadsworth Cengage Learning.

Centre for Social Media Research. n.d. *Papers*. Available from: https://www.westminster.ac.uk/camri/publications [26 August 2019].

Du Plessis, C. 2019. Augmenting social media research with Q methodology: Some guiding principles. *The Electronic Journal of Business Research Methods*, 17(3): 155–164.

Khang, H., Ki, E.-J., & Ye, L. 2012. Social media research in advertising, communication, marketing, and public relations, 1997–2010. *Journalism & Mass Communication Quarterly*, 89(2): 279–298.

Lee, F.L.F., Leung, L., Qiu, J.L. & Chu, Donna. S.C. (Eds). 2013. *Frontiers in new media research*. New York: Routledge.

Mollet, A., Brumley, C., Gilson, C. & Williams, S. 2017. *Communicating your research with social media: A practical guide to using blogs, podcasts, data visualisation and video*. London: SAGE Publications.

Rusmussen, N.D. (Ed.). 2012. *Social media for academics: A practical guide.* Oxford: Ghandos Publishing.

Poynter, R. 2010. *The handbook of online and social media research: Tools and techniques for market researchers.* New Jersey: John Wiley & Sons.

CHAPTER 3

Prominent Theoretical Frameworks in Social Media Research

Yolandi Botha

Theory provides the backcloth and rationale for the research that is being conducted ... it provides a framework within which social phenomena can be understood and the research findings can be interpreted – Alan Bryman

Learning Outcomes

After completing this chapter, the researcher should be able to:

- recognise the difference between a theoretical construct, model, and theory that can serve as theoretical frameworks in a research project;
- infer the role of theoretical frameworks in a research project;
- define and describe the various theoretical frameworks that could be applied in a social media research context;
- discover various disciplinary, field or topic and social media platform applications of various social media theoretical frameworks; and
- judge various considerations towards the future developments of social media theoretical frameworks.

3.1   INTRODUCTION

The focus of this chapter is the importance and role of theoretical frameworks in a research project with a specific delineation of prominent theoretical constructs, theories, and models associated with social media research. Models are often regarded as theories in action and provide a map for viewing reality whereas a theoretical construct or concept serves as a set of ideas to define a specific phenomenon (Silverman, 2013). Theories consist of plausible relationships between concepts or a set of concepts in order to provide a foundation for understanding a specific phenomenon (Haugh, 2012). Although there are distinct differences, this chapter will explore various theoretical constructs, theories, and models as 'theoretical frameworks' to guide a social media research project.

Based on a solid understanding of the importance of theory and the role of theoretical frameworks in research, this chapter will categorise some of the most prominent theoretical frameworks that are often applied in social media research according to personal behaviour, social behaviour, and media influence (Ngai et al., 2015). The personal behaviour category encapsulates theoretical frameworks aiming to explain individuals' behaviour to specific internal and external stimuli, which can be used to provide an understanding of individual user behaviour in social media. The social behaviour category envelops theoretical frameworks where group dynamics seemingly have a direct impact on the individual's behaviour and their participation in social activities. In this capacity, these frameworks guide researchers to identify specific social factors that contribute to individuals participating in collective actions on various social media platforms (Ngai et al., 2015). Theoretical frameworks under the category of media influence will focus on the effects that the media (specifically mass media) could have on individuals in social communities.

A description of each theoretical framework will be provided with an emphasis on its origin and key thrusts and some examples of social media applications. The preceding sections will culminate into a tabulation that serves as a quick reference guide to outline each theoretical framework's key thrusts, seminal authors, disciplinary and field or topic applications, examples of social media applications, and allude to social media platforms. This chapter will conclude with considerations for the future development of social media theoretical frameworks and a case study to provide guidelines for the application of a theoretical framework.

3.2   IMPORTANCE OF THEORY IN RESEARCH

Contemporary web applications have radically increased individuals' capacity to interact with others online which has led to new social practices, sociability patterns, learning practices, leisure activities, social and political mobilisation as well as new business models (Urquhart & Vaast, 2012). These changes combined with a milieu where users act as both consumers and creators of media (Moreno & Koff, 2016), have placed the spotlight on social media theories and their development to assist researchers to make sense of the dynamics of the interactive communication environment.

3.2.1 Towards theoretical frameworks: Distinction between theories, theoretical constructs, and models

Theories considered the 'currency of our scholarly realm,' could be defined as a 'statement of concepts and their interrelationships that shows how and/or why a phenomenon occurs' (Corley & Gioia, 2012:12). A theory can further be described as a methodical explanation for the observations that relate to a specific facet of life (Babbie, 2007). Theories assist researchers to understand phenomena and serve as a conceptual framework from which knowledge could develop (Littlejohn, Foss & Oetzel, 2017). A theory consists of four dimensions (Littlejohn et al., 2017): philosophical dimensions or beliefs that underlie the theory; concepts that serve as its building blocks; explanations or dynamic connections; and principles to guide action. A good theory is comprehensive, cross-cultural, heuristic, falsifiable, rational, parsimonious, and practical (Thyer, Dulmus & Sowers, 2012:xxii). Furthermore, a good theory is also characterised by its theoretical scope (that is, its comprehensiveness and inclusiveness); its appropriateness (whether the epistemological, ontological, and axiological assumptions are suitable for the theoretical questions and research methods to be used) and from a pragmatic perspective, a good theory has sufficient openness to allow the integration of alternative possibilities (Littlejohn et al., 2017).

Theories, models, and theoretical constructs are terminologies that are used interchangeably to ground a research project. Although these terms are closely related, there are distinct differences. Both theories and models are abstractions of reality, but

> *a theory is not a model of practice. Theories explain whereas models provide direction to practitioners on what they are to do. A theory consists essentially of definitions and propositions; it defines, explains and it predicts, but it does not direct* (Reid, 1978:12).

Conversely, a model explicitly outlines steps for practical implementation. A model serves as a depiction of the relationships between various theoretical constructs. A theoretical construct is a concept that consists of specific attributes that serve as the foundation for a specific phenomenon to be explored. It can be regarded as a simple 'idea or notion' that is packaged into one or more words (Grix, 2010). More specifically, a theoretical construct or concept is the 'building blocks of theory, hypotheses, explanation, description and prediction' (Grix, 2010:112).

This chapter builds forth on the idea of theoretical frameworks as a collective term to refer to the blueprint that is applied by a researcher to build on their own research inquiry (Adom, Hussein & Agyem, 2018). In this capacity, this chapter explores prominent theories, models, and theoretical constructs as theoretical frameworks to serve as a foundation to guide social media research projects.

3.2.2   The role of theoretical frameworks in a social media research project

In the context of this chapter, theoretical frameworks fulfil various purposes, including, analysis, explanations, prediction as well as design and action (Urquhart & Vaast, 2012). It provides a means to evaluate new data, identify new research problems and offer direction towards formulating solutions to research problems (Littlejohn et al., 2017). Depending on the grade of abstraction, scope, and involvement with social reality, a theoretical framework could be applied as meta-theory, grand/formal theory, middle-range theory, or grounded theory (Grix, 2010): Meta-theory refers to the basic assumptions and philosophical underpinnings of all research. Grand/formal theories aim to put forward significant features of an entire society, for example, functionalism. Middle-range theories are the most popular and are often developed in accordance with a specific social issue, for example, the media ecology theory. Most of the theories that will be discussed in this chapter can be regarded as middle-range theories. Grounded theory is associated with inductive research strategies and aims to 'close the gap between theory and research (by grounding theory in empirical data)' (Grix, 2010:112).

The development of theoretical frameworks in social media specifically, is important for various reasons (Urquhart & Vaast, 2012): First, social media is a salient topic that has changed our working practices from the way we work together, transform, and manage to how we organise. Secondly, it is vital to maintain disciplinary plasticity; alignment with the interactive communication and business environment is essential for organisational survival and thirdly, a solid theoretical foundation in a research project is indispensable to render strong results.

3.3   CATEGORISATION OF SOCIAL MEDIA THEORETICAL FRAMEWORKS

Theoretical frameworks applied in a social media context should ideally consider both technological and social aspects (Urquhart & Vaast, 2012). The following categorisation, depicted in Figure 3.1 below, outlines, but is not limited to, the most prominent theoretical frameworks that could be applied in social media research according to personal behaviour, social behaviour and media influence themes (Ngai et al., 2015).

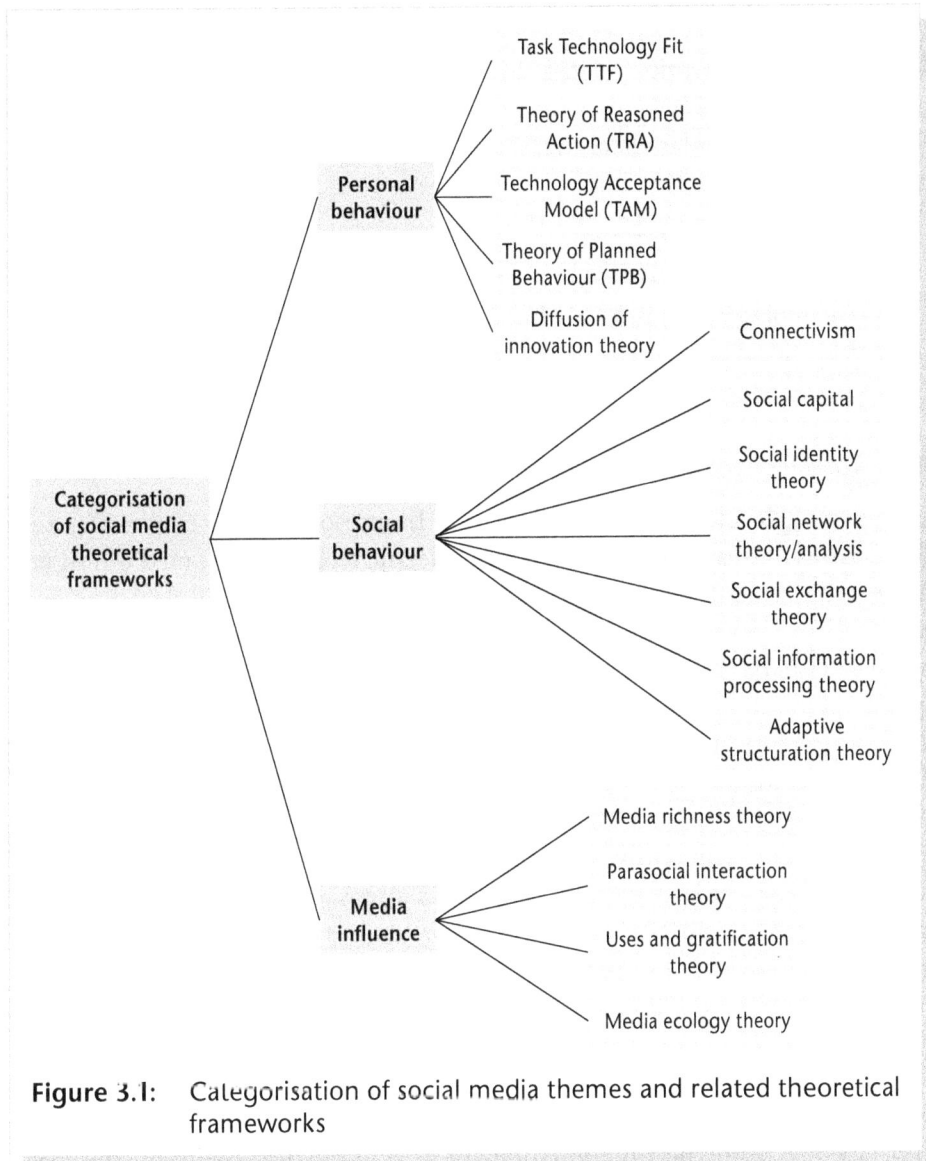

Figure 3.1:   Categorisation of social media themes and related theoretical frameworks

The sections to follow will specifically focus on defining, describing, and outlining the key thrusts of each theoretical framework and will serve as a foundation for section 3.4, which will elaborate on specific disciplinary and theme or topic applications related to these frameworks evident in social media research studies.

3.3.1 Personal behaviour

Theoretical frameworks related to the theme of personal behaviour are concerned with the behaviour of individuals in a social media context, on a personal level. Popular theoretical frameworks in this theme include, but are not limited to, the following:

- Task-Technology-Fit (TTF) model;
- Theory of Reasoned Action (TRA);
- Technology Acceptance Model (TAM); and
- Theory of Planned Behaviour (TPB) and the diffusion of innovation theory.

(i)   Task-Technology Fit model

This model, developed by Goodhue and Thompson (1995), emphasises that the features one can derive from using a specific technological medium should fit the requirements of a specific task. It provides a theoretical depiction as to how information technology could result in specific performance and usage impacts (Lu & Yang, 2014). The TTF model proposes that information systems will influence performance positively when there is a relation between its functionality and the task requirements of the user. More specifically, TTF refers to the 'correspondence between task requirements, individual abilities and the functionality of the technology' (Goodhue & Thompson, 1995:218). Put differently, information technology should fit the tasks it supports to be utilised and to influence a user's performance in a positive manner (El Said, 2015). 'Fit' in this context, is a predictor of performance benefits that could potentially be derived from utilising information systems (Dwyer, 2007). Goodhue and Thompson (1995) further argue that the precursors to TTF are the interactions between the task, technology, and the user. From this perspective, it is argued that certain tasks are dependent on specific technological functionalities. The further apart the requirements of a task are from the functionalities of a technological medium, the lower the TTF (Goodhue & Thompson, 1995). This model suggests that both the technology and task characteristics influence the user's perception of TTF which, sequentially, affects the degree to which the technological system is being used and the impact of the user's performance (El Said, 2015).

In a social media context, the TTF model could be used to explore the fit between a specific technology's features and the needs of the users of a specific social media platform. Ip and Wagner (2008), for example, used this model as a basis to evaluate the fit between technology features and the requirements of webloggers. Tasks in the conventional TTF model, as outlined above, normally refer to business-related tasks in an organisational setting. To consider a fit in the social domain, Ip and Wagner (2008) modified the TTF model and argued that tasks performed are stimulated by individuals' requirements in a blog-based virtual community. Organisations might, therefore, have to provide a vast array of publishing tools to encourage comment postings from its users. From this perspective, organisations need to be cognisant of their users' needs. In alignment with the propositions of the TTF model, their study discovered that the success of social technology (weblogging) is dependent on how well it resonates with technology features, in this case, the needs of its users (Ip & Wagner, 2015).

(ii)   Theory of Reasoned Action

TRA, originally developed by Fishbein and later refined by Fishbein and Ajzen (1975), is a psychological theory that proposes that an individual's volitional behaviour could be predicted based on their attitudes and subjective norms (Ngai et al., 2015). In essence, it is a theory that explores why an individual behaves in a specific manner. TRA purports that behavioural intention (an individual's intended actions) is the primary cause of behaviour (Trafimow, 2009). Behavioural intention is determined by attitude (an individual's assessment of the behaviour) and subjective norm (an individual's evaluation of what key influencers might perceive as the most desired action), which could guide a particular behaviour (Trafimow, 2009). Attitude is determined by behavioural beliefs (beliefs about the probability of different consequences) and evaluations of the positive and negative impacts of these consequences should they occur. Trafimow (2009) further states that beliefs as to how key influencers think one should act and the degree to which one is willing to comply with these beliefs, guide subjective norm.

TRA has widely been applied in social media contexts to assist organisations to develop strategies to advance customer engagement by drawing from the principles of volitional behaviour (Ngai et al., 2015). In alignment with the ideas of Lezin (2007), an example of TRA, in the context of this chapter, could be outlined as follows: When an individual aspires to use a specific social media platform to engage others on a topic of interest, TRA would first focus on exploring whether the individual has a positive or negative attitude towards the specific social media platform. Secondly, TRA would explore the perceived perceptions (subjective norm) that key influencers might have about the utilisation of the specific social media platform in relation to the topic of interest. These attitudes and subjective norms influence intention, which in turn motivates behaviour. The outcome of the behaviour (whether more information on the topic of interest could be obtained from utilising the particular social media platform) and the individual's evaluation of this outcome (whether more information on this topic and engaging with others on the particular social media platform rendered the desired benefits) would, therefore, determine an individual's attitude regarding the social media platform.

(iii)   Technology Acceptance Model

The TAM, proposed by Davis (1989), is an extension of TRA, customised to the information system context, and explores the effect of an individual's 'perceived ease of use (PEOU) and perceived usefulness (PU) on their attitude toward new technology adoption' (Ngai et al., 2015:786). The main purpose of this model is to offer a foundation to explore the influence of external variables on the internal beliefs, attitudes and intentions of an individual, where PEOU and PU are the most important factors in explaining the utilisation of a system (Legris, Ingham & Collerette, 2003). PEOU refers to the degree to which an individual anticipates no physical and mental issues in adopting the respective new technology and PU represents the individual's belief that the adoption of this new technology will ensure a more productive performance (Pinho & Soares, 2011). Collectively, these two components serve as relevant beliefs for determining attitude towards the utilisation of new technology (Pinho & Soares, 2011).

Various versions and extensions of TAM have been developed over the years (for example, TAM2 and TAM3), but the original model consisted of the following components: PEOU, PU, attitude towards using (AT), behavioural intention to use (BI) and actual use (U) (Legris et al., 2003). The PEOU and PU and one's attitude towards a new technology (in this case a specific social media platform) could arguably explain an individual's adoption of the respective social media platform (Pinho & Soares, 2011). PEOU has a direct impact on PU, provided that the PEOU contributes to a more productive performance. Thus, if two social media platforms offer the same functionalities, the individual will probably use the platform that is more user-friendly (Pinho & Soares, 2011).

In the social media context, an example is the exploration of the TAM model in social networking usage among university students. Pinho and Soares (2011) discovered that most students regard social networking easy to use, they easily become skilful users of social networking platforms (such as Facebook) and regard it as a flexible communication medium. They further discovered that PU has more influence on students' attitudes towards using social networking sites as opposed to PEOU. Moreover, a positive attitude towards use leads to a favourable BI to use a specific social networking site. This study highlights that an enthusiastic attitude towards social networking because of PEOU and PU leads to increased BI to use in the future and as a means for students to express their personality (Pinho & Soares, 2011). This study has, among others, reinforced PEOU and PU as determinants of a positive attitude towards the adoption of social networking sites.

(iv)   Theory of Planned Behaviour

The TPB, developed by Ajzen (1985), also serves as an extension of TRA but specifically includes 'perceived behaviour control' to explore the impact of attitudes and subjective norms on an individual's behaviour (Ngai et al., 2015). This model addresses a shortcoming of TRA by making provision for situations in which individuals do not have full control over a situation (Yousafzai, Foxall & Pallister, 2010). TPB proposes that one's intentions serve as the immediate determinant of one's behaviour and that attitude, subjective norm (as outlined in TRA) and perceived behaviour control are autonomous dimensions that predict intention (Kim, Lee, Sung & Choi, 2016). Perceived behaviour control refers to the extent to which an individual believes that he or she has control over performing the target behaviour (Kim et al., 2016). TPB is built on the premise of a three-fold belief system (Yousafzai et al., 2010): Human action is guided by *behavioural beliefs* about the probable results of the behaviour and the assessments of these results. Secondly, human action is directed by *normative beliefs* about the normative anticipations of others and motivations to adhere to such anticipations. Lastly, human action is steered by *control beliefs* about the available resources and opportunities to the individual and the possible hurdles that might impede on performing the target behaviour. It is argued that behavioural beliefs yield a positive or negative attitude towards the respective behaviour; normative beliefs result in social pressure or subjective norm; and control beliefs stimulate perceived behavioural control (Yousafzai, et al., 2010). Although Azjen (2011) later added motivations, background factors and past behaviour as additional dimensions; attitude, subjective norm and perceived behaviour control remain the standard dimensions of this model.

TPB has predominantly been applied to predict an individual's behavioural intentions. From a social media perspective, this model is often used to predict people's adoption of social networking sites (Baker & White, 2010; Pelling & White, 2009). Although no direct findings related to perceived behaviour control were recorded, Pelling and White (2009) discovered in their study that users' behaviour and intention to use social networking websites were influenced by attitude and subjective norm. Furthermore, Chang and Zhu (2011) conducted a study to identify the pre-adoption and post-adoption behaviour of social networking site users in China. This study revealed that the standard dimensions of TPB (attitude, subjective norm, and perceived behavioural control) all influenced individuals' intention to adopt specific social networking sites (Kim et al., 2016).

(v)   Diffusion of innovation theory

Diffusion of innovation (Rodgers, 1962) refers to 'the process by which an innovation is communicated through certain channels over time among the members of a social system' (Chang, 2010:23). Although this theory is focused on information that is being distributed about a specific innovation, this theory is conceptualised under the personal behaviour theme in this chapter as it could serve as a framework for understanding how an individual user views a unique idea, practice or object (in this case, a social media platform of functionality) as new. This theory is, therefore, both concerned with communication and the innovation-decision process on an individual level (Frank, Zhao & Borman, 2004).

In this theory, the diffusion process is conceptualised by the elements of innovation, the social system that is influenced by the respective innovation, the communication channels of the social system and time (Chang, 2010). More specifically, this theory proposes a process that consists of an independent individual's knowledge or awareness of a particular innovation, the development of perception towards the innovation, a choice to accept or discard an innovation, the implementation of the decision and the validation of the decision process (Frank et al., 2004).

To illustrate an example of the application of this theory in a social media context, Chang (2010) used elements of this theory to explore Twitter hashtag adoption. In this study, the diffusion of innovation theory served as a framework to outline individuals' motivations and adoption behaviour, which arguably provide reasoning for the spread of innovation and the driving forces behind expediting the adoption rate of the respective Twitter hashtag.

Further examples of theoretical frameworks that could serve as the foundation for social media research in accordance with the theme of personal behaviour are personality traits (Digman, 1990; Lu & Hsiao, 2010), social cognitive theory (Chiu, Hsu & Wang, 2006), and attribution theory (Porter & Donthu, 2008).

3.3.2 Social behaviour

Theoretical frameworks categorised under the theme of social behaviour, serve as blueprints for studying and interpreting social phenomena. These theoretical frameworks explore how the dynamics of a group could influence an individual's behaviour and their involvement in social activities (Ngai et al., 2015). Such frameworks are useful in an organisational context, as organisations could apply the principles of these frameworks to identify factors that stimulate individuals to par take in shared activities via their social media platforms (Ngai et al., 2015). Some of the prominent theoretical frameworks that could be aligned with this theme are as follows: Connectivism; social capital; social identity theory; social network theory; social interaction theory; social exchange theory; social information processing theory and adaptive structuration theory.

(i)   Connectivism

The perception of cyberspace being a 'globalised condition of connectedness' has resulted in the view that the 'digital age' is the 'connected age' (Caldwell, 2017). Connectivism, developed by Siemens (2004), aims to describe the process of learning in the digital age and proposes that the 'pipe is more important than the content within the pipe', which implies that the network itself serves as the foundation of the learning process (Pettenati & Cigognini, 2009:962). Connectivism is conceptualised as the successor to behaviourism, cognitivism, and constructivism (Bell, 2011). This theoretical construct is characterised by nine principles (Pettenati & Cigognini; Bell, 2011):

- learning and knowledge reside in a multiplicity of opinions;
- learning is a process of linking specialised nodes or information sources;
- knowledge rests in networks; learning could exist in non-human applications;
- the capacity to know is more significant than contemporary knowledge;
- connections have to be sustained to ensure continuous learning;
- the ability to view connections between phenomena is a critical skill;
- all connectivist learning activities intend to provide accurate and updated knowledge; and,
- decision-making is a learning process – what might be applicable today, might not be applicable tomorrow due to the decision being influenced by the volatile information context.

From a social networking perspective and in the milieu of user-generated content (UGC), Pettenati and Cigognini (2009) argue that connectivism is valued as a context where learning could easily occur due to technological advances. The idea here is that learning sprouts from the interactions among users of a social networking site. Furthermore, connectivism is enabled by an increasingly knowledgeable user (also defined as the 'prosumer') that participates in the creation, sharing and management of resources through social networking software and applications (Pettenati & Cigognini, 2009).

(ii)   Social capital

Bordieu's (1985) idea of social capital refers to

> *an aggregation of resources that is linked to the possession of a durable network of relationships of mutual acquaintance and recognition – or, in other words, to membership in a group* (Qi et al., 2018:97).

Social capital denotes the 'accumulated resources that have been derived from the relationships among people in a social context or network' (Bosch, 2017:54). Social capital arguably surfaces from trust and shared norms embedded within relationship networks and through brokering information and resources (Saffer, 2019). Each member that belongs to a specific social network has 'capital', a type of credential that entitles the member to 'credit' (Qi, et al., 2018). Thus, it can be deduced that the premise behind social capital is that individuals invest in social relations with anticipated returns (Lin, 1999). Individuals who are actively involved in social networks are considered to be building sustainable social network relationships (You & Hon, 2019).

Putnam (2000) differentiates between two social capital types: bridging social capital and bonding social capital. Bridging social capital can be attained by individuals using broader, weak-tie networks to, for example, broaden social horizons (You & Hon, 2019). Bonding social capital is created when emotional support could be derived from strong social networks, for example, family and friends (You & Hon, 2019).

From a social media perspective, social capital is accrued from network members by posting content on social media (Qi et al., 2018). It should be noted that online social capital is different from offline social capital due to the wide range of people that could be reached instantaneously (Qi et al., 2018). An empirical example of social capital applied to a social media context is You and Hon's (2019) exploration as to how individuals interact via social media to gain bridging and bonding social capital through strong and weak ties and how these interactions could impact on individuals' behavioural participation in online communities.

(iii)   Social identity theory

The social identity theory, originally developed by Taijfel (1974), explores how the surrounding social context (Hornsey, 2008) could influence intergroup relations. Social identity refers to how individuals see themselves in relation to their social group memberships, which serves as a key consideration in defining their self-concept (Coverdale & Wilbon, 2013). An individual's identity is then associated with the social groups to which he or she belongs and the social cognitive processes related to these groups guide the individual's behaviour (Coverdale & Wilbon, 2013). This theory further highlights that the notion of categorising oneself and others into 'in-groups' and 'out-groups' could influence one's perceptions, attitudes and behaviour (Ngai, et al., 2015). Self-enhancement drives these social categorisation processes and sets the direction for the group standard to favour members of the in-group (Coverdale & Wilbon, 2013). A key element of this theory is that equations between a pertinent in-group and out-group will tend to show favouritism towards the individual's in-group, and as a result, augment one's self-concept (Coverdale & Wilbon, 2013). Thus, it could be deduced that an individual's behaviour and attitude are driven by the perceptions of support from the attitudes of in-group members.

In the context of social media, Zhang, Jiang, and Carroll (2010) explored aspects of identity that are evident among the social interaction of Facebook communities. This study specifically revealed that identity in an online environment represents a process of constructing self-presentations rather than moderation and adjustment in social contexts.

(iv)   Social network theory/analysis

Various research traditions, such as sociometric analysis in mathematics, interpersonal relationships and community structures in anthropology (Barnes, 1954; Bott, 1957; Mitchell, 1969), have contributed towards crystallising contemporary social network theory (Liu, Sidhu, Beacom & Valente, 2017). Social network theory (also referred to as social network analysis) offers a guideline to 'understand media effects, enabling consideration of how micro- and macro-social structures mediate and moderate media effects' (Liu et al., 2017:5). More specifically, a social network is made up of 'nodes' (actors such as individuals or an organisation) and 'ties' (relationships between nodes) and underlines that social network nodes are rooted within ties, which could either enable or impede their actions (Wu, Wu & Ling, 2009). Networks are made up of weak ties (acquaintances) and strong ties (close friends and family), and it is argued that nodes with few weak ties will be curbed to the views of their strong ties (Bosch, 2017). Social network theory is further characterised by homophily (the notion that shared norms or values might bring nodes with shared traits together and vice versa), mutuality (the idea that relationships are reciprocal) and transitivity ('if A is tied to B, and A is tied to C, it is likely that B is tied to C') (Bosch, 2017:45).

In alignment with the abovementioned aspects, three important elements conceptualise network effects in the social network theory, namely, centrality, cohesion and structural equivalence (Liu et al., 2017): Structural centrality is measured, according to Freeman (1979), by means of degree, closeness, and betweenness. 'Degree centrality' is concerned with the links to and from an individual within a specific network. A person with high degree centrality could fulfil an activist or influencer role in an issue arena due to various social ties. 'Betweenness centrality' measures 'the frequency at which an individual node lies on the shortest path connecting other nodes in the network', and often serves as a bridge within the network (Liu et al., 2017:5). 'Closeness centrality' measures the approximate distance between a single node and the remaining nodes in the network. The higher an individual's closeness centrality, the less effort is required to reach other network nodes. Secondly, cohesion in a network refers to the extent of the interconnectedness among a group of nodes and is used as a guideline to identify subgroups or cliques in a social network. Lastly, structural equivalence refers to two or more network positions that share a comparable arrangement of connections with the remainder of the network. This includes nodes that share structural equivalence, share specific characteristics, such as celebrity status.

Wu et al. (2017) conceptualised the principles of social network theory as a mediator in the relationship between information technology usage and organisational performance. Such a study could further be extended to a social media context by focussing on a specific social media platform to establish whether the usage of a specific social media platform could contribute towards strengthening an organisation's inter- and intra-organisational networks as a means to enhance an organisation's performance.

(v)   Social exchange theory

The social exchange theory (Thibaut & Kelley, 1959; Emerson, 1962; Blau, 1964) purports that interaction between individuals is built on the exchange of rewards and costs (Dore, 2012). It proposes that individuals' relationships are driven by expectations of mutual advantage, presented as 'reward and punishment', 'pleasure and pain' and 'cost and benefit' (Dore, 2012). Although there are various perspectives on the theory (rooted in disciplines such as anthropology, social psychology and sociology), the idea that a set of interactions create obligations, is central to all these perspectives (Cropanzano & Mitchell, 2005). These interactions are usually mutually dependent and reliant on the actions of another individual (Cropanzano & Mitchell, 2005). Mutually dependent interactions are likely to result in sustainable relationships that eventually evolve into loyal and mutual commitments; provided that individuals adhere to specific rules of exchange (Cropanzano & Mitchell, 2005).

Lambe, Wittmann and Spekman (2008) underline four foundational premises of the social exchange theory: First, exchange interactions are driven by the expectations of economic and/or social outcomes. Secondly, individuals will only remain in a relationship if the desired outcomes are reaped from the relationship. In this regard, individuals will continuously compare the current economic or social outcomes to other exchange substitutes. Thirdly, positive outcomes eventually proliferate trust among relational parties. When one individual provides the other with a benefit, he or she should trust the other that such a benefit would be returned. Fourthly, relational parties' relational norms (explicit and/or tacit communal behavioural rules), that are established by a solid commitment to the relationship and positive exchanges, will direct the exchange relationship. As with trust, norms are a critical element of this theory as a social exchange is guided by norms.

The social exchange theory could specifically be applied in a social media context to explore the sense of community that is established within a specific social media platform. In a study to test the pragmatic value of a model of sense of virtual community, Blanchard (2008) utilised, among others, the principles of social exchange to measure the exchange of support as a possible rationale for the existence of a virtual community. In this capacity, this theory assisted Blanchard (2008) to better understand the behaviour between individuals within the respective virtual community.

(vi)   Social information processing theory

The roots of the social information processing theory could be traced back to Fulk et al. (1987) who developed a social information processing model to showcase how individuals' attitudes toward communication and media behaviour are affected by social influence processes. From a somewhat different perspective, Walther (1992) later developed the social information processing theory to

> describe the (individual) cognitive processing of socially revelatory information (and subsequent communication based on that information), rather than the social (conjoint) processing of information (about the medium) (Walhter, 1992:17).

This perspective of the theory relates to perception formation and social-cognitive processes evident in the psychology literature (Walhter, 1992).

The social information processing theory offers key propositions that provide a framework for understanding computer-mediated communication development (Walhter, 1992). Relational aspects of computer-mediated communication that are considered by this theory include (Olaniran, Rodriguez & Williams, 2012) the following: The rate of transmission of information, as opposed to the ability of the media to transmit information, distinguishes computer-mediated communication from face-to-face communication. Furthermore, in computer-mediated communication, the relational tone tends to change as a function of time. In this regard, the theory 'attempts to explain, as well as predict, an individual's interpersonal adjustment to computer-mediated communication and face-to-face communication' (Olaniran et al., 2012:47).

From an empirical perspective, social information processing theory could be used as a framework in a virtual team context (situated within a social media platform) for the development of trust, fostering group unity, and facilitating communication within international workgroups (Olaniran et al., 2012).

(vii)   Adaptive structuration theory

Adaptive structuration theory, which is a theory of social action developed by DeSantis and Poole (1994), aims to understand how individuals utilise information and communication technologies (Littlejohn et al., 2017). Different individuals, groups and organisations apply the same information communication technologies differently (Littlejon et al., 2017). Grounded in Anthony Giddens's structuration theory, adaptive structuration theory proposes that social structures coupled with innovative technology give way to 'technology-in-use' that is either comparable or different to the original intention behind the respective technology (Sinclaire & Vogus, 2011).

The theory outlines that the structures (rules and functionalities) of advanced information technologies (such as social media) may differ through contexts (subject to the task and the organisational environment) and due to interpersonal interaction with the technology, new structures could be developed (Sinclaire & Vogus, 2011). In essence, adaptive structuration theory proposes that advanced information technologies have the potential to prompt adaptive structurational processes that could eventually lead to amendments in the rules and resources that organisations utilise to guide social interaction (DeSantis & Poole, 1994).

In a social media context, this theory could be applied to explore the various social structures within specific social media platforms and the various interaction processes that are embedded in the usage of these platforms. In this regard, this theory could assist organisations to obtain a better understanding as to the implementation of a specific social media platform and provide guidelines to 'promote productive adaptations' (DeSantis & Poole, 1994:143).

Additional theoretical frameworks that could be applied in a social media context in relation to social behaviour are the social interaction theory (Fischer & Reuber, 2011), social influence theory (Cheung & Lee, 2010); social presence theory (Chung, Han & Koo, 2015) and social loafing (Shiue, Chiu & Chang, 2010).

3.3.3 Media influence

This theme aims to encapsulate theoretical frameworks that focus on the influence or role of the media (predominantly mass media) on the members of social communities (Ngai et al., 2015). Prominent theoretical frameworks in accordance with this theme that will be discussed in this section include media richness; parasocial interaction; uses and gratifications theory and media ecology theory.

(i)   Media richness

The theoretical construct media richness or information richness (Daft & Hengel, 1984) highlights that

> *communication channels differ in the extent to which they are able to bridge different frames of reference, make issues less ambiguous, or provide opportunities for learning in a given time interval* (Rice, 1992).

The richness of a medium is determined by the following elements: the presence of feedback; the utilisation of different prompts such as physical presence, body gestures and words; the usage of natural language to create an understanding of diverse concepts, and the subjective focus of the medium (Sheer, 2011). Different media are either more or less suited to convey rich communication content to execute a task (Rice, 1992). Face-to-face interaction is regarded as the richest medium because it has all the aforementioned elements (Sheer, 2011).

Media richness also proposes that specific media are more suited than others to transfer information in situations of uncertainty or equivocality (Dennis & Valacich, 1999). Uncertainty occurs when an interpretation framework is available, but a lack of information to process exists (Dennis & Valacich, 1999). Equivocality occurs when the information within a framework could be interpreted in multiple, and often contradictory, ways and requires negotiation among members towards a single interpretation (Dennis & Valacich, 1999).

Media richness could be used to serve as a guideline to understand social communication amid traditional and internet-based technologies (Koo, Wati & Jung, 2011). From a social media perspective, Koo et al., (2011) explored how social media could be applied by an employee to fit his or her task characteristics and how employees' social relationships guided media utilisation within the organisation as well as the impact thereof on task performance.

(ii)   Parasocial interaction

The theoretical construct, parasocial interaction, was developed by Horton and Wohl (1956) to describe the potential influence that media celebrities or media performers, portrayed in film and television media, might have on consumer behaviour (Ngai et al., 2015). Differently put, it is an asymmetrical relationship (also known as a parasocial relationship) between the viewer and media celebrity (Hartmann, 2008). Media performers specifically direct their social and communicative behaviour toward an audience who then, in turn, responds in ways as if these media performers were physically present and standing in front of them (Hartmann, 2008). Another perspective, especially relevant to marketing communication, is that parasocial interaction and narratives allow individuals to be captivated with the messages that are packaged as entertainment to conceal the persuasive part of the message (Littlejohn et al., 2017).

Despite the fact that the principles of parasocial interaction resonate with the social media context (Ngai et al., 2015), the application of parasocial interaction in social media could be challenging as social media differ from mass media in three ways (Hartmann, 2008): First, social media characters are less intuitive than mass media performers. Secondly, the interactive nature of social media allows for feedback, while mass media performers do not provide feedback. Thirdly, mass media performers are more authentic than social media characters. These reasons could be contributors to the limited application of parasocial interaction in social media research. Regardless of the current limited application, parasocial interaction has potential in organisations to serve as a basis for social media marketing strategies to establish parasocial relationships and to influence customer behaviour (Ngai et al., 2015).

(iii)   Uses and gratifications theory

Katz (1959) originally proposed the basic idea behind the uses and gratifications theory which was later refined by Katz, Blumler and Gurevitch (1974). This theory focuses on consumers or audience members as 'discriminating users of media' that actively use media content to satisfy their own goals (Littlejohn et al., 2017:174). Five assumptions underlie this theory (Littlejohn et al., 2017):

- Audience members actively select information from several media and decide what they want to hear, watch and see.
- Audience members are active and goal orientated. They are responsible for selecting specific media to fulfil their needs and these media selections are only one factor that contributes towards fulfilling audience members' needs.
- All media compete for the attention of audience members, which drives media institutions to create content in accordance with audience members' desires.
- Social and contextual elements guide the activity of audience members. Their context dictates which media they will consume.
- The effects of media and the usage of media are related; media will only influence audience members as they chose to consume the media.

The gratifications or rewards from the media usage could either be regarded as 'gratifications sought' or 'gratifications obtained' (Ruehl & Ingenhoff, 2015:2). Gratifications sought refer to the reasons behind the consumption of specific media and gratifications obtained refer to the realised gratifications from the media consumption. These realised gratifications could range, for example, from entertainment, information, personal identity as well as integration and social interaction (Littlejohn et al., 2017).

Commenting on the role of the uses and gratifications theory in contemporary society, Ruggiero (2000) argues that there is a need to expand the current body of knowledge on uses and gratifications 'to include concepts such as interactivity, demassification, hypertextuality, asynchronicity and interpersonal aspects of mediated communication' (p. 29). An example of research in this vein is Ruehl and Ingenhoff's (2015) study that focuses on the application of uses and gratifications and social cognitive theory to explore stakeholder intentions and usage types of specific corporate social networking sites. This study revealed that different stakeholders have varied intentions for using corporate social media. Another example of a study that explored uses and gratifications in the context of social media is Quan-Haase and Young's (2010) comparative analysis that examined users' gratifications obtained from Facebook in relation to instant messaging. It was discovered that the uses and gratifications of Facebook are related to increasing awareness of social activities within one's social network, while the uses and gratifications reaped from instant messaging were related to building and sustaining relationships.

(iv) Media ecology theory

To obtain a better understanding of the social impact of technology and communication, McLulan (1964) developed the media ecology theory, which proposes that the media directly shapes and organises culture (Moreno & Koff, 2016). Thus, the medium controls how individuals will use the content that is being disseminated (Cline, 2016). The theory aims to establish what roles the media forces individuals to play; how media orientates our perception of specific phenomena and why media provoke certain feelings and actions (Scolari, 2012).

According to Scolari (2012), media ecology has two dimensions: the environmental dimension and the intermedia dimension. The environmental dimension resonates with the term 'ecology', which refers to the exploration of the environment's structure, its content, and the influence on individuals (Plugh, 2018:182). The environment is a complex message system that surrounds and directs individuals to behave, feel and think in specific ways (Plugh, 2018). The intermedia dimension focuses on the interactions and relationships between media (Scolari, 2012).

Bosch (2017) contends that the media ecology theory is one of the most applicable theoretical frameworks for the social media context. Society has quickly become reliant on electronic media, especially social networking sites (Moreno & Koff, 2016). In this regard, media ecology theory could assist researchers to identify the reasons that motivate individuals to interact via certain social networking platforms such as Facebook and LinkedIn. A specific example of a study conducted in this context is Veltri and Atanasova's (2015) exploration of climate change on Twitter. In this vein, they, among others, explored the media ecology of tweets and the external web links that users shared. The media ecology analysis highlighted various sources of multidimensional discourse that contributed to fundamental links between climate change and its consequences.

Additional theoretical frameworks that could potentially be applied in the context of social media, in relation to the theme of media influence, are the cultivation theory (Stefanone, Lackaff & Rosen, 2010) and the agenda-setting theory (Meraz, 2009).

3.4   A BIRD'S EYE VIEW

To serve as a quick reference guide and building forth on the ideas of Ngai et al. (2015), Table 3.1 provides a summation of the theoretical frameworks discussed in this chapter in terms of its key thrusts; seminal authors; disciplinary and field applications; examples of social media applications and social media platforms.

Table 3.1: An overview of prominent theoretical frameworks in social media research

	Theoretical framework	Key thrusts	Seminal authors	Disciplinary application	Field/topic application	Sources: Social media application	Social media platform applications
Personal behaviour	TTF model	The features of a technological medium should fit the requirements of a task. The further apart the requirements of a task are from the functionalities of a technological medium, the lower the TTF.	Goodhue & Thompson (1995)	Knowledge management Organisational communication	Knowledge sharing	Ip & Wagner (2015)	Blogs Social networking sites (Facebook, LinkedIn)
	TRA	It explores why an individual behaves in a certain way. Behavioural intention is the primary cause of the behaviour.	Fishbein & Ajzen (1975)	Social psychology Marketing Health studies	Knowledge sharing Consumer behaviour	Hsu & Lin (2008)	Blogs
	TAM	As an extension of TRA, it provides a framework that serves as a foundation to explore the influence of external variables on the internal beliefs, attitudes and intentions of an individual.	Davis (1989)	Information science Marketing	Consumer behaviour Social capital	Pinho & Soares (2011)	Micro-blogging Social networking sites (Facebook)
	TPB	As an extension of TRA, it includes perceived behaviour control as an additional dimension to explore the impact of attitudes and subjective norms on an individual's behaviour.	Ajzen (1985)	Psychology	Behavioural studies (behavioural intentions) Knowledge sharing	Pelling & White (2009) Baker & White (2010) Chang & Zhu (2011)	Social networking sites
	Diffusion of innovation theory	This theory explores how information about innovation is being disseminated and how an individual perceives an idea as new.	Rodgers (1962)	Organisational communication Marketing Knowledge management	Innovation management and knowledge sharing	Chang (2010)	Twitter

➡

Theoretical framework	Key thrusts	Seminal authors	Disciplinary application	Field/topic application	Sources: Social media application	Social media platform applications
Connecti-vism	This theoretical construct describes the process of learning in the digital age. The network itself serves as the foundation for learning.	Siemens (2004)	Marketing Organisational communication Education	Consumer behaviour Learning organisation Open Distance Learning (ODL)	Pettenati & Cigognini (2009)	Social networking sites (UGC)
Social capital	This theoretical construct refers to the accumulated resources derived from the relationships among people in a social context.	Bordieu (1985)	Organisational communication Strategic communication Public relations Political science Economics	Stakeholder relationship management Stakeholder engagement Corporate social responsibility	You & Hon (2019)	Micro-blogging Online communities (created via various social media platforms) Social networking sites
Social identity theory	This theory explores the effect of social contexts on intergroup relationships.	Taijfel (1974)	Marketing Organisational communication Social psychology	Interpersonal communi-cation	Zhang et al. (2010)	Facebook Online communities (created via various social media platforms)
Social network theory/ analysis	Social network nodes are embedded within ties, which could either enable or impede actions.	Barnes (1954) Bott (1957) Mitchell (1969)	Mathematics Anthropology Social psychology Organisational communication	Interpersonal relationships Inter- and intra-organisa-tional communi-cation	Wu et al. (2017)	Facebook
Social exchange theory	Interactions between individuals are built on the exchange of rewards and costs.	Thibaut & Kelley (1959) Emerson (1962) Blau (1964)	Sociology Anthropology Social psychology Organisational communication	Relationship studies / relational exchange Change management	Blanchard (2008)	Virtual communities in various social media platforms

Social behaviour

➡

	Theoretical framework	Key thrusts	Seminal authors	Disciplinary application	Field/topic application	Sources: Social media application	Social media platform applications
Social behaviour	Social information processing theory	This theory is concerned with the cognitive processing of socially relevant information.	Fulk, Steinfeld, Schmitz and Power (1987) Walhter (1992)	Organisational communication Social psychology	Interpersonal communication Human behaviour studies	Olaniran et al. (2012)	Virtual teams/communities research related to various social media platforms
	Adaptive structuration theory	Since individuals apply the same information communication technologies differently, this theory is concerned with the manner in which individuals utilise information and communication technologies.	Poole & DeSantis (1994)	Organisational communication Change management	Organisational change Interpersonal communication sites	Sinclaire & Vogus (2011)	Social networking sites
	Media richness	Different media are more or less suited in conveying rich communication content towards executing tasks.	Daft & Hengel (1984)	Marketing	Marketing communication	Koo et al. (2011)	Corporate social media and -networking sites such as Facebook and LinkedIn)
Media influence	Parasocial interaction	This theoretical construct focuses on the asymmetric relationships that consumers create with media celebrities/ performers.	Horton & Wohl (1956)	Marketing Branding	Entertainment education Consumer behaviour Brand attitudes	Colliander & Dahlén (2011)	Social media in general
	Uses and gratifications theory	Consumers/audience members actively use media content to satisfy their own goals.	Katz (1959) Katz, Blumler & Gurevitch (1974)	Communication management Public relations Knowledge management	Stakeholder analysis Knowledge sharing	Ruehl & Igenhoff (2015)	Facebook Twitter YouTube
	Media ecology theory	The medium determines how individuals will utilise the information that is being disseminated.	McLulan (1964)	Mass communication	Media studies Marketing communication	Moreno & Koff (2016)	Facebook LinkedIn

It should be noted that the theoretical frameworks outlined in this chapter are by no means the only frameworks that could be applied in a social media context. To challenge existing media and behavioural theories (Moreno & Koff, 2016), other disciplines such as political science, economics, information science, and education also serve as excellent departures to explore theoretical frameworks to ground social media research.

3.5   THE WAY FORWARD: CONSIDERATIONS FOR FUTURE SOCIAL MEDIA THEORY DEVELOPMENT

The growing popularity and constant innovations of social media platforms and applications have transformed ways of interacting, working, creating value and innovating. There is a need to theorize these new environments, and the intriguing social and technical dynamics they make possible (Urguhart & Vaast, 2012:1).

In steering future theory development in social media research, the following considerations could be taken into account:

- The advent of social media has changed internet usage in general. The communication context is much more visual and collaborative in nature (Urguhart & Vaast, 2012).

- There is a need to account for the effects of social media users acting as both creators and distributors of content (Collins, Martino & Shaw, 2011).

- To highlight the all-encompassing influence of social media, the concept of 'mediatisation' must be carefully considered. Fourie (2017) argues that it is the most prevalent effect of social media and refers to the way the media infiltrate and influence society in a similar fashion than the state. From a social media perspective, mediatisation could be used to illustrate how social media 'have become 'life', metaphorically speaking – how they have become *the* culture (and not only part of the culture) and *the* world, and how *life is the media* and *the world is the media*' (Fourie, 2017:33).

- Since information systems are now being infiltrated as part of the larger societal context, social media research should consider the competitive setting of dynamic social systems (Kapoor et al., 2018).

- Existing media theories could be combined with new conceptual developments, such as the Facebook influence model (Moreno & Koff, 2016).

- Social media should not only be explored as platforms for socialisation, interaction and congregation, but also the ability of the medium to encourage aggregation (Kapoor et al., 2018).

- Social media research in an organisational context should aim to move past the dyadic view of the relationship between an online community and an organisation. Users of social media should be reconceptualised as an 'ecosystem of stakeholders' (Kapoor et al., 2018:554).

3.6 CASE STUDY: GUIDELINES FOR THE APPLICATION OF A SOCIAL MEDIA FRAMEWORK

Throughout this chapter, reference was made to pragmatic applications of the various theoretical frameworks in a social media context. The purpose of this section is to elucidate in greater detail how one could go about using a theoretical framework to ground a social media research project. In this regard, the following fictitious research topic, related to the theoretical framework of social capital, is used:

An exploration of corporate social networking sites as a means for employees to build social capital and to share knowledge.

Based on your research problem that will anchor your study (see chapter 2, section 2.7.5), the following steps pertaining to the application of the theoretical framework could be made.

1. The first point of departure is to conduct an extensive literature review on the theoretical framework, social capital, to identify the key thrusts (which could be structured as theoretical statements) of the framework (see chapter 2, section 2.7.6).

   Examples could include the following. Social capital is a relational resource; social capital consists of structural, relational and communication dimensions; social capital is built on trust and shared norms and it is an investment with expected returns. Furthermore, in this regard, the differences between online and offline social capital need to be operationalised and different types of social capital, such as bonding and bridging social capital have to be explored in the context of the study. Some of these thrusts would require the researcher to conduct additional research. For example, the concept of 'trust' and 'shared norms' should be studied to identify its intrinsic characteristics.

2. Once the researcher is satisfied with the key thrusts or theoretical statements, it is important that the researcher also explores the other key concepts of the study.

   In the context of this example, it would include, among others, organisational/corporate communication, corporate social networking sites, employee behaviour and relationships, and knowledge sharing.

3. Touchpoints between the theoretical thrusts or statements and related concepts need to be identified.

    For example, trust is both an element of social capital and knowledge sharing. Sometimes, it is advisable to group these 'touchpoints' into dependent and independent variables. In this context, trust could consist of the elements of ability, integrity and benevolence.

4. Once clear touchpoints are identified the researcher should structure the data collection instruments in accordance with these touchpoints (see chapter 8). This is a critical step as the researcher should determine whether the theoretical thrusts or statements are supported or rejected in a pragmatic context in answer to the research problem.

3.7   SUMMARY

This chapter aimed to elaborate on prominent theoretical frameworks that could be applied in social media research in accordance with the themes of personal behaviour, social behaviour, and media influence. A theoretical framework served as a blueprint for a research project and assisted the researcher to narrow the scope of the research. Future theoretical developments in social media should build forth on its collaborative and visual nature and make provision for theorising its continuous technical innovations and social dynamics.

Learning activities (Test yourself)

1. What is the difference between a theoretical construct, model, and theory?

2. What is the purpose of a theoretical framework in a research project?

3. Select a theoretical framework and apply it to a social media research project.

4. In alignment with the previous question, explain how the principles of the uses and gratifications theory could be used to explore graduates' usage patterns on Facebook as a corporate social networking site.

5. What additional elements should be considered in the future development of social media theory?

6. Can you think of any other theories that could apply to social media research not mentioned in this chapter?

Further reading

Coombs, W.T. & Holladay, S.J. 2000. Internet contagion theory 2.0: How internet communication channels empower stakeholders. In Duhe, S.C. (ed.) *New media and public relations*. New York: Peter Lang: 21–30.

Ngai, E.W.T., Tao, S.S.C. & Moon, K.K.L. 2015. Social media research: Theories, constructs, and conceptual frameworks. *International Journal of Information Management*, 35(1): 33–44.

Poore, M. 2014. *Studying and researching with social media*. London: SAGE Publications.

Rice, R. & Fuller, R. 2013. Theoretical perspectives in the study of communication and the internet. In Dutton, W.H. (ed.) *The Oxford handbook of internet studies*. Oxford: Oxford University Press.

Schroeder, R. 2017. Towards a theory of digital media, *Information, Communication & Society*, 21(3): 323–339.

Whiting, A. & Williams, D. 2013. Why people use social media: a uses and gratifications approach. *Qualitative Market Research*, 16(4): 362–369.

Section B

PARADIGMATIC APPROACHES AND METHODS FOR SOCIAL MEDIA RESEARCH

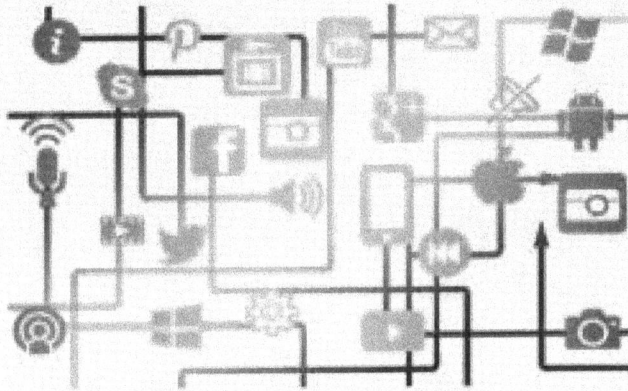

Approaches

CHAPTER 4

Using a Qualitative Research approach in Social Media Research

Christelle Swart

To qualitative researchers, social media offers a novel opportunity to harvest a massive and diverse range of content without the need for intrusive or intensive data collection procedures – Matthew Andreotta, Robertus Nugroho & Mark Hurlstone

Learning Outcomes

After completing this chapter, the researcher should be able to:

- argue the suitability of qualitative research for social media data;
- appraise the different research paradigms applicable to qualitative social media research;
- justify the research methods for researching textual and visual contents; and
- conceptualise a holistic qualitative research approach.

4.1 INTRODUCTION

The overall purpose of this chapter is to explore a qualitative research design in social media research, as well as the different research methods available to analyse visual and textual social media content. Related aspects such as the choices between for example, cross-sectional, experimental, and longitudinal designs; sampling methods; the different types of data analysis methods and the ways in which data is analysed, are addressed in subsequent chapters of this book.

This chapter is structured as follows: The rationale for the suitability of a qualitative research approach of social media content is first presented, followed by the scope of the investigation to outline the primary focus. Thereafter the challenges that are associated with qualitative research of user-generated content are considered. Secondly, insights are provided into applicable research paradigms within which qualitative research of social media content may be framed, including interpretivism, symbolic interactionism, narrative research, ethnographic research, and social constructionism (Burton & Bartlett, 2009; Bryman, 2012; Gergen & Gergen, 2012). A brief review is presented of distinct characteristics and goals of these research traditions, in context. These insights are based on a review of scholarly viewpoints in literature with an emphasis on the orientations concerning the creation of reality, knowledge, and meaning.

Thirdly, discussions concentrate on different methods and techniques to qualitatively examine user-generated content on social media. The understanding is that social media research involves an investigation of those social media platforms that permit users to create content in various forms such as posts, comments, tweets, photos (for example, selfies), and many other forms. The qualitative research methods explored in this chapter include ethnographic methods (for example, visual ethnography), qualitative content analysis, conversation analysis, semiotics, narrative inquiry, segmentation techniques, grounded theory, and multimodal research, (Altheide, 2008; Schreier, 2013; Belgrave, 2014; Stan, 2010; Hand 2017; Rasmussen Pennington, 2017; Salmons, 2018). In some instances, research methods such as qualitative content analysis, for example, thematic analysis and conversation analysis, are viewed as research methods and likewise as methods of analysis. The collection presented in this chapter is clarified according to the qualities of the *types* of approaches and methods, rather than the analysis, cleaning and storing of the qualitative data *per se*.

The chapter concludes with a brief outline of a holistic qualitative approach that comprises interconnected aspects of a research design that could be fitting for exploring social media data that is directly collected from these platforms. It is founded on the conception of Salmons (2017) and aligned to the current focus.

The focus of this chapter falls on the different qualitative research methods that could be applied to researching the data that is available on social media, but not on the application of social media as a research methodology (see chapter 2).

4.2   RATIONALE, THE PRIMARY FOCUS, AND CHALLENGES ASSOCIATED WITH A QUALITATIVE RESEARCH APPROACH OF SOCIAL MEDIA CONTENT

As already indicated, this section outlines the reasons for the suitability of a qualitative research approach of social media content that simultaneously underlines the primary focus of this chapter. This is followed by a concise discussion of the challenges that a researcher might expect when undertaking this research approach.

4.2.1 Rationale and the primary focus of a qualitative research approach of social media

The necessity to consider innovative approaches to using social media data for research is evident in scholarly literature. This can be ascribed to, among other facts, the unprecedented amount of information that is generated and stored as a consequence of the popularity of social media platforms; the embeddedness of social media in people's daily lives; and because the content generated by users on these platforms can provide access to real-time data that provide rich and thick information for research on diverse topics (Nevius, 2018; Salmons, 2017; Latzko-Toth, Bonneau & Millette, 2017).

The volume of data that are created and stored on social media is considered unequalled and believed to hold the benefit of being a rich source of information, as mentioned above (Quan-Haase & Sloan, 2017:4; McCay-Peet & Quan-Haase, 2017:14). The use of a qualitative research approach for social media research seems to be a perfect fit since it strives to investigate the quality of a certain event, experience or phenomenon, such as contained in social media data as a result of interactions or engagement on these platforms (Bryman et al., 2014:31; Quan-Haase & Sloan, 2017:4).

4.2.2 Challenges associated with qualitative research of social media content

According to Williams, Burnap and Sloan (2016:322–323), social media data and the qualitative investigation thereof present unique challenges that are worth mentioning as it is not confined to a specific discipline. These also include dealing with the well-known characteristics of Big Social Data (a concept first put forward by the Information Technology discipline) in terms of volume, variety, velocity, veracity, virtue, and value characteristics, but which are also applicable to qualitative research (see chapter 5, section 5.3 and Table 5.2).

4.3 RESEARCH PARADIGMS FOR QUALITATIVE SOCIAL MEDIA RESEARCH

It is widely accepted that the research paradigm (or worldview) and its philosophical assumptions, the research design, and the research method largely guide a distinct research approach, which, in context is qualitative in nature. It is the rationale or particular way in which a set of general beliefs about the world and reality directs the actions, knowledge, and perceptions of researchers of social media data (cf. Bryman 2012:5, 6). Ontology and epistemology are two philosophical rationales linked to a certain research paradigm. *Ontology* specifies the nature and form of reality, including the personal beliefs and views of the researcher, whereas epistemology refers to the way/s (methodology, data collection methods) in which a phenomenon can be understood (Byrne, 2017a). In qualitative research, ontological views primarily perceive the social world as being shaped by social actors and not external influences (Burton & Bartlett, 2009). *Epistemological* views state that knowledge about the social world can be obtained through the application of several qualitative methods to achieve an understanding of real-life situations (ibid). The focus falls on emerging and innovative research methods to attain research objectives. A summary of the paradigms is presented in this chapter, section 4.3.5, page. 114, Table 4.1. The researcher must realise that these philosophies relate to the reasoning, methods, and principles of a topic.

The scrutiny of research paradigms is intended to provide insights into the lenses that might be applied when researching social media data qualitatively, and that direct the way in which particulars of a study are viewed and approached (cf. Bryman, 2012:6).

A qualitative research paradigm generally aims to locate patterns of meaning through examining how people assign meaning to things, to obtain insights into what the meanings are, and to place what is said and done into context (Berg, 2008). Qualitative research data are mainly non-numerical and include textual and non-textual material that makes it suitable for social media data as it permits the researcher to, among others, analyse a wide array of data. Unique to qualitative research and an aspect that necessitates vital consideration in qualitative research, is the importance of being sensitive to the distinct contexts in which interactions and engagements on social media take place (Quan-Haase & Sloan, 2017:3).

4.3.1 Interpretivism

The interpretivist paradigm holds the view that the interactions between people create their social world. It is concerned with understanding the meaning behind the actions of people as they respond to certain events, and thus strives to bring about an understanding of the interpretations of actions and interactions between people (cf. Burton & Bartlett, 2009; Smith, 2008). To obtain such insights, studies within this paradigm may implement numerous research methods with a preference of natural types of data collection in natural settings, such as narratives and individual accounts gathered through observations and the like (cf. Burton & Bartlett, 2009). These are usually smale-scale studies aimed at acquiring detail and understanding of a particular situation.

Researchers in this paradigm believe that there is no single objective reality and that individuals each have their view of a situation or event, and will act based on their interpretation thereof (Burton & Bartlett, 2009). The view considers people as actors who create their social worlds, albeit in a subjective way (cf. O'Reilly, 2015). The basic task of researchers following this view is, therefore, to explore and understand people's 'actual common sense' with the purpose to obtain insight into their individual interpretation (Gephart Jr, 2018). This paradigm acknowledges that the involvement of the researcher is essentially to interpret elements of a study and is for this reason integrated into the study (Dudovskiy, 2018). As Dudovksiy (2018) affirms, researchers adopting this paradigm should recognise the effects of diverse personal, cultural, and social perspectives when they are the research instruments, and involved in interpreting elements of a study (cf. Harrison, 2018:155).

4.3.2 Symbolic interactionism

Symbolic interactionism can be explained as the 'way we learn to interpret the world' (Griffin, 2009:61) by considering humans as 'active agents who create shared meanings of symbols and events and then interact based on those meanings' (Ballantine 2014:51). This perspective reveals many similarities with the interpretivism paradigm. Jones et al. (2011:105) describe symbolic inter-actionism as the 'interaction of humans via the use of symbols' and underlines that reality is constructed through these symbols (cf. Dudovskiy, 2018).

Symbolic interactionism is deemed to underscore interaction as a two-way process that centres around the interpretations of all participants, and the view of action correspondingly as a *product* of the behaviour that was interpreted and as an *effect* on the person/s whose behaviour was interpreted (Jones et al., 2011:104, 105). Hence, meaning is created based on these interactions that eventually culminate in interpretation, and that shapes the way relationships with others are formed and social worlds are established (Pink, et al., 2016:81). The seminal thoughts of Mead (1934) which centres around the belief of *mind* – the emergence and development of one's thoughts, identity, and the self as a response to and part of one's interaction with others, the roles that other people take and the recognition of selves from others' perspectives – are of significance (Mead, 1934:133; Griffin, 2009: 62, 161; Gecas, 2009). Researchers following this paradigm focus predominantly on the subjective qualities of social life rather than the objective qualities of social systems (Berg, 2008).

At this point, the issue of *self-presentation* deserves attention as online activity does contain a certain level of anonymity. It is pivotal that researchers following this research paradigm with a focus on investigating matters such as self-presentation or online personalities, consider that a change in personality expressions could influence the way people present themselves online (Yang, Quan-Haase, Nevin & Chen, 2017:78). To explain, research has established that personalities expressed online are markedly different from those expressed offline and so are not always accurate reflections of the person. This poses special challenges. These personalities are said to influence among other things, the type of information posted on online platforms and that researchers use as research data (ibid). To further complicate matters, some scholars suggest the possibility of multiple personalities that, in the same vein increase the complexity when interpreting data. Also, according to Goffman's (1959) theory of action, the *selves* are instituted through other *actors'* performances and the responses of others, thereby emphasising the social nature of people and the way people present themselves online (Sandstrom, 2011). Due to anonymity, the effect of others' perceptions or actions may or may not affect the way people establish and present their *selves* that could, in turn, impact the outcomes of a study.

4.3.3   Narrative research

Kartch (2018) describes a narrative approach to research as 'the collection of narratives to make sense of the business of assigning meaning to lived experiences'. In Clandinin and Caine's (2012) opinion, these aims are achieved through an investigation into 'conversations, dialogue, and participation' in peoples' lives, which they classify as 'field texts' or simply 'data'. Certain research methods that are appropriate to this research approach are mentioned in section 4.4 below and include qualitative content analysis, conversational analysis, and a narrative inquiry – specifically storytelling.

The fact that social media form part of people's daily lives, and that their interactions and activities on these platforms provide rich and thick information for social media research, is ample motivation of the suitability of this type of research (Hiles, Erml, Chrz, 2017; see section 4.3.2). It is accordingly viewed as an essential way to gain access to the way people think and behave, to understand their experiences, and more extensively to identify social narratives.

4.3.4   Ethnographic research

According to Behar-Horenstein (2018) ethnography is grounded in the belief that meanings are formed through interaction with the world, and so are not newly created but rather brought into existence by combining different engagements. It seeks to present comprehensive accounts of experiences or situations within unique contexts (Berg, 2008). Furthermore, Venkatesh et al.'s (2017:4) assertion that ethnography literally is 'writing (graphy) about people (ethnos)' is of particular relevance to social media research as the actions of people or users in actual contexts are under scrutiny. A researcher following an ethnographic approach to qualitative research is considered to take part in the daily lives – or actions – of participants through concentrating either on verbal statements, sentences or phrases, or digital information, pictures, symbols, signs, visual or digital information (Ang, 2014; Hine, 2015:9; Venkatesh et al., 2017:16). It aims to generate knowledge about 'social worlds and social processes in a continued and disciplined manner' (Atkinson, 2015:191).

Ethnography is also, albeit infrequently, considered as either a type of qualitative research, or as a research method. The latter view is therefore dealt with in a subsequent section (see section 4.4.1, p. 115).

4.3.5   Social constructionism

Social constructionism typically denotes that knowledge and meaning, and the nature of reality, are outcomes of the actions produced within human relationships, hence as a result of the interconnections between people, as opposed to meaning-making that occurs in the individual's mind as with constructivism (Gergen & Gergen, 2012). Literature reveals different traditions or movements which, despite little agreement on the basic tenets of the term, are mostly linked to three *lines of argument* that are of particular relevance to the exploration of the topic in this chapter (ibid). First, there is an extant view that knowledge of the world originates in relationships and thus situated in such social processes; secondly, the idea that a concern with language is key to the social origins of knowledge; and thirdly, the adoption of a pragmatic conception of knowledge that mainly focuses on those concerns emanating from research as opposed to traditional truths and objectivity (Gergen & Gergen, 2012). The pragmatic focus to uncover knowledge for a specific situation, as a line of argument, is moreover in line with the conception that innovative approaches to social media data research are needed (cf. Biesenthal, 2014). The assumption that a pragmatic orientation allows for the selection of the most appropriate research methods, or even a combination of both qualitative and quantitative research methods (cf. Morgan, 2014), creates the expectation that the application of various qualitative research methods is possible in this paradigm.

The above sections highlight the different research paradigms that can be considered for qualitative research of social media data. As can be expected, a research method may be more fittingly linked to a particular paradigm. In other instances, a specific research method may not be tied to a single paradigm alone. For example, a content analysis may be valuable within interpretive and symbolic interactionism approaches. In this regard, Table 4.1 aims to indicate the research methods that could be associated with these paradigms, and that are explained in the following sections. This collection is, however, not anticipated to be exhaustive. It must be understood that these research methods are not mutually exclusively assigned to the paradigms, and the selection for a study should, therefore, be based on the philosophical assumptions of the researcher, the research purpose and context. See also chapters 5 and 6.

Table 4.1:   Qualitative research paradigms and principle philosophies

Research paradigm	Ontological philosophies on the creation of social worlds and realities	Epistemological philosophies
Interpretivism	Socially constructed	Ethnography, narrative inquiry, multimodal research
Symbolic interactionism	Constructed through shared symbols	Semiotics, grounded theory, content analysis
Narrative research	Interpreting and understanding experiences with a story form	Conversational analysis, content analysis, narrative inquiry
Ethnographic research	Through interaction with the world	Ethnography, conversational analysis, content analysis
Social constructionism	Outcomes of actions within relationships	Ethnography, conversational analysis, grounded theory

4.4   QUALITATIVE RESEARCH METHODS FOR TEXTUAL AND VISUAL SOCIAL MEDIA DATA

For qualitative researchers to take advantage of the social media data that are readily available on social media, they need to look attentively at research methods that generally allow for an in-depth understanding of how people interpret and assign meaning to the social world. The research methods outlined below focus uniquely on achieving this broad aim. Considering the information that follows will reveal overlaps between certain methods and techniques, for example, content analysis and semiotics that are both suitable for written and visual data. Thus, decisions about which method or technique to use should be based on the availability of resources, and the one/s that

- will answer the research questions;
- is/are generally accepted in the specific discipline;
- the researcher feels competent to use (cf. Byrne, 2017b).

Besides, thought should be given to the availability of resources (cf. ibid). It should be noted that this overview is not meant to be exhaustive and mainly highlights some of the popular research methods.

As argued in the previous section, the specific research paradigm should be an important consideration as the lens that is adopted for a study. Reflection on the points above should then allow the researcher to consider the most suitable method/s to address the research objective of the study. One should realise that in some cases these methods can be jointly used to research social media data and that it could be set apart in terms of the different research objectives, such as narrative analysis and its interest in *stories*. At this point, it is necessary to distinguish between *data* and *object*. Schwandt's (2007) view is that text can be regarded as an *object* for research that can be analysed through a narrative method. It thus suggests that, for present purposes, the term *object* can be used when referring to the social artefact or focal point of the research (Bryman 2012:557). Besides, a specific method might incorporate and allow different ways to research data, as with ethnography that combines observations and document analysis.

Many qualitative studies have used social media platforms as primary sources to examine pertinent aspects such as interactions, attitudes, sentiments in social media conversations, public opinion, consumer behaviour, and others. The point of departure here is a focus on *research methods*, as opposed to on different social media types as popularly found in the literature. This way, the application possibilities are explicit.

4.4.1   Ethnography

Caliandro (2018) identifies some of the *styles* of online ethnography that were developed to deal with social media environments and that simultaneously illustrate the many terms used when referring to these types of ethnography: *virtual ethnography* (Hine, 2000), *Internet ethnography* (Miller & Slater, 2001), *cyber-ethnography* (Escobar 1994), *digital ethnography* (Murthy 2008), and *ethnography of the virtual worlds* (Boellstorff, Nardi, Pearce & Taylor, 2012) and others.

When considering ethnography as a research method, it is driven by the desire to gain knowledge about and to make sense of social domains (areas of social life), relationships, community, events, experiences or practices (daily routines and habits) (Pink et al., 2016; Venkatesh et al., 2017). It is distinguished from a research methodology in that it encapsulates the varied tools and techniques to investigate social media research data. According to Harrison (2018:40), the focus falls on the 'meanings, categories, and practices that shape people's behaviors and perceptions'. In context, this methodology is applied *inter alia* to documents the 'forms of expression that arise online, [and] the social groups that emerge there ...' (Hine, 2017), to purposely recognise and search for ways to get to know other people's worlds that might be otherwise hidden. For this reason, people are studied in their natural settings to understand their activities and behaviour (Burton & Bartlett, 2009). O'Reilly (2015) maintains that present ethnographers increasingly strive to understand the creation of social life and distinctly aim to not only understand people's 'feelings and emotions, their experiences and their free choices, but also the wider constraints and opportunities that frame their agency'.

In response to the prominence of social media in the everyday lives of people, and equally of researchers, significant developments in and adaptations to ethnographic practices have taken place to consider these online spaces (cf. O'Reilly, 2015; Hine, 2017; Caliandro, 2018). The role of the qualitative researcher will thus incorporate new ways to engage, namely watching or observing people by tracking them, or becoming part of their social media practices; listening by reading and other ways of communication; using video blogging or video instead of ethnographic writing (Pink et al., 2016:3); conducting problem-centred interviews using different features on social media such as video, messaging, or text chat (Salmons, 2017:182). As technology advances, indications are that these applications will also continuously evolve (Postill & Pink, 2012:124).

Caliandro (2018) reveals two different modes in which ethnographers could deal with online environments, for example, virtual ethnography that is mainly concerned with both online and offline activities, and multi-sited ethnography that encourages researchers to follow users' movements across online platforms. In line with the virtual mode, Boellstorff et al., (2012:69) contend that ethnographers currently frequently use traditional offline methods, namely document analysis, interviews, and observations, and essentially adapt them to online settings such as social media, of which online surveys is an example (Hine, 2000; Nieuwenhuis & Smit, 2012:127; cf. Postill & Pink, 2012). Multi-sited ethnography considers the nature of the digital environment to track how social media platforms, including functions on these platforms, for example, Twitter hashtags and search engines, organise the flow of communication and interaction (Caliandro, 2018:558). This mode thus encourages researchers to follow users' movements across online platforms that shift the emphasis to the Internet as a 'source of methods' as opposed to an 'object of analysis' (cf. Rogers, 2010; Caliandro, 2018). Irrespective of the mode, the approach followed, or emerging trends, the significance of adhering to the fundamental principles of ethnography is emphasised, that refers to the immersion of the ethnographer over an extended time into certain contexts, to reveal practices and meanings as they develop (cf. Bosch, 2013; O'Reilly, 2015).

Specifically related to this research method and social media context, Pink et al's (2016:3) assertion that researchers are in mediated contact with others in online settings rather than being in their physical presence, is of relevance. It is thus fair to accept that social media generate new research sites or ethnographic places for ethnographic fieldwork that are distinctly unbounded and consequently require researchers to distinguish manageable sets of data

(Postill & Pink, 2012:124, 125, 128). Cook, Laidlaw and Mair (2009:60) mention that the ethnographer's field is a set of points that may be imagined as a space or a site. However, as Hine (2015:56) maintains, such sites are difficult to delimit in a social media environment, as is the case with Twitter. On social media, sites or groups are difficult to describe exactly but might be bound, for example, by tracking hashtags (on Twitter and Instagram) and keywords (on Facebook) (cf. Marwick, 2013).

4.4.2 Qualitative content analysis

According to Payne and Payne (2004), content analysis 'seeks to demonstrate the meaning of written or visual sources ... by systematically allocating the content to pre-determined, detailed categories ...'. Although the indicated areas of application – written and visual – are evident in this definition, texts can be justified as research objects (Schwandt, 2007), and therefore the focus now on written materials. Bryman (2012:557) states that this method, otherwise referred to as *thematic analysis*, is a dominant approach in qualitative research and essentially comprises the identification of codes and themes in documents or materials. This method is systematic and comprises different series of steps or phases, such as those conceptualised by Kowal and O'Connell (2014), Lapadat (2010), and Braun and Clarke (2006) – see a detailed explanation of Braun and Clarke's steps in chapter 9. Accordingly, the researcher may need to repeat some steps to adapt the coding frame that signifies the flexibility of this method (Schreier, 2013). Adaptations should be done without deviating from the sequence and ensuring that the categories contained in the coding frame match the data (ibid). In King and Brooks's (2018) view, a distinction should be drawn between codes and themes by considering codes as 'short comments or abbreviations' in a passage of text, that in the end will evolve into themes. King and Horrocks (2010:150) define themes as 'recurrent and distinctive features of participants' accounts, characterising particular perceptions and/ or experiences, which the researcher sees as relevant to the research question'.

Given the diverse types of content created by users online, this research method can be applied to various social media content ranging from tweets, posts, blogs, to photos, online videos, conversations and more. Caliandro (2018) refers to recent research into online content analysis and the view that native social media devices such as mentions (@), retweets (RT), or hashtags (#) should be acknowledged and used to filter and select texts. Many social media platforms present researchers with the tools required to measure interaction and sociality. The retweet function of Twitter is popularly used as an example of a social media platform that permits interaction between users, to measure the direction and intensity of these interactions (Caliandro, 2018).

In Hsieh and Shannon's (2018) view this qualitative method is popularly used to identify codes and common themes to interpret data, and to eventually form basic meanings and a detailed account of the content under investigation. The research purpose and existing knowledge in a specific area mainly determine the approach to content analysis, that can either be *inductive or conventional* where codes and themes emerge from the data, *deductive* to build initial codes that are guided by research questions, or *summative* where keywords and concepts are identified and counted (Hsieh & Shannon, 2018; Gabriel, 2013). Answers to research questions or objectives thus emerge from the data.

True to the nature of qualitative research this method aims to provide detailed descriptions of material with explicit consideration of the context. The advantages of content analysis are that the approach is unobtrusive, key techniques can be learned quickly, and it is more time-efficient when compared to other methods, such as ethnography (Hsieh & Shannon, 2018).

4.4.3   Conversation analysis

Conversation analysis is regarded as one of the approaches to discourse analysis. A brief overview of discourse analysis as a broad concept is thus warranted. Discourse analysis is described by Siegel (2018) as the 'broad term for the study of language usage', and looks at a wide range of data of which conversations, and spoken or written versions are examples (Byrne, 2017b). It focuses on any manner in which 'people make meaning' in a particular context (Siegel, 2018).

Byrne (2017b) states that the focal point of conversation analysis is solely on interpersonal communication between people, including verbal and non-verbal interaction, but excludes written material. Byrne's (2017b) concisely describes it as looking at 'patterns of interaction in communication'. It is hence well-suited to study the social interactions that are expressed as conversations on social media. It seeks to expose the sequential features of how conversations are constructed that involve aspects such as 'turn-taking, topic management, information receipt, and opening and closing talk' (Siegel, 2018). Markos-Kujbus and Gáti (2012) add that this approach centres around the *way/s* people communicate – the 'motivations, frequency and content'. The researcher of social media data should know that social media, in essence, is about conversations and that it permits users to exchange opinions and views unrestricted and in a multidirectional way (Romenti, Murtarelli & Valentini, 2014:10). Conversations can be followed as it unfolds and across multiple online platforms with the option to participate or not, as discussed in the next section, for example when creating a community. This analysis is based on the data available and patterns that occur repeated (Siegel, 2018).

Ethnography of communication is a certain approach to discourse analysis that likewise deserves mentioning. As seen by Siegel (2018) it pays attention to the *way of speaking* as a unique cultural interaction and is distinctly different from ethnography as discussed earlier. In this approach ethnographic fieldwork is undertaken to investigate the communicative patterns to understand how groups of people make sense of their contact and encounters (ibid). This approach seemingly requires attention to a particular setting, the participants and their characteristics, the end goal and purpose, activities and sequence, the tone of language, the linguistic code, 'norms of intention and interpretation'; and the type of event (Siegel, 2018).

4.4.4 Semiotics, and visual semiotics

Semiotics, or the theory of signs (Chandler, 2017:2), should be acknowledged as both a method of textual analysis and as a philosophical exploration of issues relating to reality. For present purposes, the focus falls on it being a particular research method to examine social media data. Chandler (2017:2) notes that semiotics embraces 'the whole field of signification', comprising many competing theories and models of the sign. This research method seeks to discover *latent content* existent in images with symbolic meaning or to reveal underlying meaning for example ethnicity in a protest (Hand, 2017).

Moreover, it is propounded that the construction of social reality is tied to sign systems, such as language and other media, and thereby points to a close link between social constructionism and semiotics (Chandler, 2017: xvi). A basic explanation of semiotics is that it is the 'study of signs', or in a broader sense as being concerned with 'everything that can be taken as a sign' (Eco, 1976:7). The concept is further clarified as including phenomena such as 'words and images' (Chandler, 2017:2). Central to these conceptions is the *mediating* role of signs and the roles of individuals in the construction of realities (Chandler, 2017:8). The notion is that people's prior knowledge contributes to an interpretive framework that guides expectations and behaviour (ibid). A sign is said to be the 'most basic level of language' (Rasmussen Pennington, 2017:240), and may include words, emotions, sounds, visuals, images, sounds, and many more (Matusitz, 2018; Chandler, 2017:11). Driven by the desire to make meanings, anything can become a sign when a specific meaning is assigned thereto (Chandler, 2017:11). Chandler (2017) identifies two distinct research directions that are both vital in semiotic research, namely the view by de Saussure (1890s) of it as a language (or semiology) and the view by Peirce (1860s) as logic (or semiotics). These directions focus respectively on signs as vehicles of communication through engagement in conversation, and the use of signs to reveal and understand the world (Shank, 2008).

Highfield and Leaver (2016:47) draw attention to the increased importance of visual media in social media (see the detailed discussion in chapter 1). Their list of some of the specific forms contains selfies (self-portrait images), profile pictures (cover photo)s, infographics (visual presentations of information)s, memes (humorous or mimicry concepts or activities), emojis (digital conversational elements), GIFs (animated images) and others that are popularly used on Instagram (visual), Facebook and Twitter (mix of text and visual) and other applications that allow visual presentation (ibid). Visual analysis is distinguished from other methods in that it primarily examines images. Researchers following this approach are interested in the content, arrangement of elements, the social context of the image, and the process of production (Byrne, 2017b). Whereas quantitative methods allow for the analysis of large sets of data, they are frequently not accessible to all and as such compel the use of alternative approaches to explore content and platforms, also from related disciplines, at a smaller scale and in a qualitative manner (Highfield & Leaver, 2016:49).

Shank (2008) highlights the scarcity of semiotic research tools and holds that in qualitative research it is inspired by presuppositions about the world that move between semiology and semiotics. The assumptions include: (1) an interest in the way the world is formed and in the roles of implicit and explicit therein; (2) as the world is permeated with signs, there is a reliance on the world to guide and affirm the meaning; (3) the notion that there are things in the world that are uniquely significant and not reliant on the meaning assigned by people; (4) an awareness that the world cannot be understood in human terms and that the presence or absence of things provides clues to the nature of what is real or existent. Hand (2017:245) emphasises the views, as expressed by Jewitt and Oyama (2001), on how meaning occurs through visual semiotics. Three types of meaning apparently occur concurrently and include (1) meaning that is inherent to the visual image as portrayed through the actions of individuals in the picture or the concepts in the picture referred to a representational meaning; (2) the relationship between the researcher and who or what is illustrated referred to as interactive meaning; and (3) compositional meaning that is presented in the images, such as physical arrangement in the image, and contrast between items.

It is apparent that visual analysis presents specific challenges that relate to the assessing of the images, videos and other files, and the studying thereof (Highfield & Leaver, 2016:48). Kariko's (2013) study of memes reveals a possible approach for semiotics as a research method with attention to (1) myths, together with (2) a qualitative-interpretive approach. It distinctly focuses on the notion that the *myth* comprises accounts of creation that formed the foundation of early social institutions. In support, Hawkes (2003:2) refers to the seminal view of Vico (1725), namely that the *myth* contains early sophisticated ways of 'knowing, of encoding, of presenting' the facts. A present-day example is about dreadlocks and the many connotations assigned thereto, such as associations with specific religious views, drugs, or fast living (n.a, 2016). The conception of the seminal scholar de Saussure (1980s) is evident in this example in that the image of dreadlocks contains a relation between a *signifier* (the material aspect), and the mental concept a *signified* (concept), and between itself and signs outside of it (cf. Cobley, 2014). Secondly, as illustrated in the study by Kariko (2013), a qualitative-interpretive approach is followed that focuses on signs and texts, and the interpretations and decoding thereof by using semiotics. In this study examples of memes that contain images and captions, are analysed.

The selection and classification of images pose unique challenges considering the countless images available on social media. Issues such as sampling, authenticity, representation, and comprehensiveness require meticulous attention (Hand, 2017:218) as also explained in chapter 7. To address issues of scale *per se* researchers need to use *geo-temporal* frames that sort tweets for example according to a specific timeframe and setting (ibid). As an illustration, one can think about selecting images during an event through hashtags (Twitter), that might need the use of the platforms' distinct codes, together with the organiser's classification, and also hashtags that emerge while following the event (ibid). Additionally, often the producers and regulators of images are unclear as some platforms allow users to reclassify images to prevent the researcher from following the narrative or story. Hand (2017:219) refers to photographs that require insight into the organising sequence.

4.4.5   Narrative inquiry

Diverse perspectives exist on the distinct key elements of this concept, such as the view that it encapsulates methods such as discourse or conversation analysis (Mazur, 2018). The outlook of this section is to intentionally view it as a separate research method or technique that seeks to 'explore and interpret, in a disciplined way, peoples' lived experience' (ibid) to contribute to an understanding of their social worlds. It is explicitly separated from content analysis and semiotics, and their foci on written text and images, as explained in the previous sections. The focus hence falls on narratives or stories that are generated by users or that are solicited by organisations on social media, and that represents their experiences and memories of their life stories, in part or in full. In literature differences between a narrative and a story are made, such as by Boje (2008) but for the sake of consistency, both the terms will be used interchangeably, as done by du Plessis (2015:85) when referring to users' original accounts of their experiences in story format.

Storytelling is not a novel technique and is central to many cultures. Behar-Horenstein (2018) conceptualises four frameworks in narrative research, namely (1) an interest in how stories are told when people form their identities and realities, (2) a focus on the link between the peoples' 'life stories and the quality of their life experiences', (3) concentrating on the way personal stories 'shape and are shaped by environment', and (4) when the researcher becomes part of the story by involving the participant in the research analysis and, in some instances, even the researcher's own stories.

Storytelling has become essential in an organisational context and Boje (2008) declares that 'every workplace' irrespective of their type of business, is a storytelling organisation. Storytelling is increasingly used by organisations to tell the organisation's story to attract customers to a brand, but also to permit customers to share their experiences employing stories (cf. du Plessis, 2015:86; Swart, 2018:282).

Atkinson (in Byrne, 2017b) alerts to the fact that narrative analysis is largely neglected as a qualitative research method and calls for a more systematic and disciplined analysis of narratives within their specific settings. The understanding is that narratives are usually merely reproduced rather than recognised as social forms and products that have specific form and purpose (ibid). It is maintained that they should be treated similar to any other data by collecting them in context and analysing them according to content, form or the way they are organised, indigenous inherent structures, functions and with attention to how these stories are constructed.

Behar-Horenstein (2018) points to the lack of a widely accepted method or approach to conduct a narrative inquiry but suggests that after gathering the stories, a combination of different methods could be applied. The main issue is to realise the different contexts and that peoples' stories will reflect multiple realities and truths.

4.4.6 Audience segmentation and persona research

To make provision for our professional readers it is also important to briefly examine audience segmentation and persona research, as their main purpose is to achieve a better understanding of customers, particularly in the digital age. There are diverse views on whether segmentation and persona research is completely different or the same thing (Williams, 2018; Shukairy, n.d.). This said the general idea is that both are valuable tools that should be used together (Williams, 2018; Collins, 2015). *Segmentation research* is a research technique through which valuable information about groups of social media users, or customers in business, is obtained. The purpose is to identify segments or groups in a specific market that entail the exploration and analysis of their characteristics. Depending on the specific context, the information provides insights into their demographics (gender, race, age, etc.), product use (brand affinity or use of a product), socioeconomic information (income, occupation, etc.), and the like (Devault, 2019). Thus, in marketing, for example, a business needs to know its target market to be able to direct its marketing efforts to well-defined groups in an attempt to reach certain goals (Devault, 2019). Additionally, information about psychographics – attitudes, opinions and so on; generation (people from a certain age group); geography (areas of living, religion, etc.); and the benefits consumers seek when they shop that provide information about the consumers' loyalty and attitude towards a brand could be obtained. Although it is proposed to be a complete process, it can be assumed that in context, the focus may fall on one or more of these categories (cf. Devault, 2019). To illustrate, in a social media setting a researcher may focus only on collecting information on psychographics. Besides, researchers should take into account that, depending on the social media type, certain information will not be readily available such as socioeconomic or demographic information.

Persona research is said to provide richer information of individual customers' psychological and emotional wants, needs, and behaviours that allow brands to exactly know how to target them (Williams, 2018; Collins, 2015). This differs from segmentation that aims to identify groups of homogenous customers (ibid). In the digital age, the vast volumes of information compel organisations to make sense of it at an individual customer level but in the same way provide opportunities to profile the individual customer (Williams, 2018).

Bock (2018) asserts that qualitative research is typical to market research and particularly ethnographic methods that are addressed in a previous section. Multi-sited ethnography allows a researcher to track and follow users across several online platforms to uncover certain categories and information needed for a study. In the spirit to identify innovative ways for qualitative research, some original ways to segment audiences on social media are proposed. Alton (2018) points out that the type of social media platform in itself segments the audience and illustrates it by referring to Pinterest that largely attracts women. This platform allows people to *pin* images and videos that are already grouped around common themes and, in this way, *self-segment* themselves by participating in such a community (Hines & Quinn, 2005). Alternative ways include Facebook post-filtering and Twitter lists to identify what the interests are or what conversations certain segments are involved in (ibid). Another original way, apposite here is the idea to build a community with shared interests – that can be open or closed and with or without the participation of the researcher – that may eventually lead to an understanding of the attitudes and opinions and other relevant information (Ollison, 2017).

4.4.7 Grounded theory

There are different approaches to conducting a grounded theory study with social media data. This chapter considers the seminal approach of Glazer and Strauss (1967) about grounded theory as the 'inductive construction of theory from systematically obtained and analysed data' (Gephardt Jr, 2018). In this way, this method is typically seen as inductive research that is anchored in the 'data itself' (Berg, 2008). The logic behind grounded theory is the identification of concepts in a wide array of data sources that mainly include written notes transcripts, other forms of documentation, reviews of records, observations, or even visual materials (Ang, 2014; Venkatesh et al., 2017:47), followed by establishing relationships between these concepts that form the basis for theory construction. Considering this, the suitability of this research method when dealing with a large collection of data sources generated by users on social media, which include conversations, posts, blogs, tweets, selfies, emojis and the like is underlined. The assumption in grounded theory is that concepts should emerge from the research data rather than being based on professional interests or predetermined hypotheses (cf. Holton, 2018). The coding of qualitative data in various stages and analytic procedures are central to grounded theory but are distinctly different from other types of qualitative coding (Ang, 2014; Charmaz & Bryant, 2008). The view is that grounded theory does not depend on the application of predetermined sets of codes to 'compare, sort, and synthesise' data, but instead elaborate on the codes or concepts through memo writing (Charmaz & Bryant, 2008). These memos provide intrinsic details about the codes' properties or characteristics, conditions under which the codes emerged, and comparisons with other codes and data (ibid) and thus add to the internal validity of the study – see also the discussion of credibility in chapter 2. A variety of data sources can be used for social media data, for example, interviews, observations, and review of records (Ang 2014). See also the case studies using grounded theory in chapters 2 and 8.

4.4.8 Multimodal research

Rasmussen Pennington (2017:245) argues that this research method was initially used to promote the incorporation of non-text documents in semiotic research. As a result, multimodel research is often used interchangeably with social semiotic research. The literature reveals two perspectives on multimodal research. The first perspective allows the researcher to holistically describe a depiction or application from multiple perspectives, through the application of *several techniques or methods* (Rasmussen Pennington, 2017:245; Salmons, 2018). For social media, this allows the researcher to obtain several perspectives by using more than one method, such as online observations and conversation analysis. The alternative view with the same objective is to combine different *modes of data* (multimodal), for example, the use of selfies (visual data), conversations (posts, tweets), and memes (visual and text) to understand peoples' lived experiences (Salmons, 2018). These views underline the importance of multimodal research when studying social media data, mainly for two reasons: on social media, many documents at a time can be accessed; and the combined use of pictures and words create meaning (Rasmussen Pennington, 2017:245).

In Rose's (2007:142) view a combination of both images and texts is needed to obtain knowledge and insights into how individuals understand the world that highlights the importance to consider this type of research (Rose, 2007:142). Van Leeuwen (2012) corroborates this view and says that communication inherently is multimodal, and so to grasp the meaning of modern written forms, such as those on social media, also demands the consideration of images. Hand (2017:245) maintains that in context, a text is thought to include many aspects such as videos, written language, images, sound, and others, while visual elements such as facial expressions, colours, movement, music, texture and the likes become interlinked data. Van Leeuwen (2012) offers a view of how both image and text stand in specific relation to one another: (1) where image and text predominantly rely on the same content though in different ways; (2) where text is primary and the image clarifies it in a specific context and for a certain group of people; or (3) where images are interpreted as the only data and without references to the text. In the research process, these elements could be detailed in a transcript that can include textual and non-textual accounts, such as by combining words, sounds, actions, and non-verbal communication (Van Leeuwen, 2012). This interrelatedness is evident in the use of captions to clarify images, or to add additional detail to clarify it (ibid). In multimodal research, the focal point should not only be on images but also visual design elements for example layout and other relevant aspects (ibid).

To conclude, Table 4.2 presents the insights included in this section together with the research objects on which they focus. According to the explanations given in section 4.3, objects refer uniquely to the social artefacts or items under investigation.

Table 4.2: Research methods and their research objects

Research method	Research objects
Ethnography	Observations of users by tracking them, document analysis, following online conversations, joining social media communities as an observer
Qualitative content analysis	Various texts
Conversational analysis	Conversations in posts, tweets, comment threads, communicative patterns
Semiotics and visual semiotics	Visual matter in posts, tweets, blogs, videos
Narrative inquiry	Stories in posts, tweets, blogs
Segmentation research	Tracks users across multiple social media sites, pins on Pinterest, filtering Facebook posts, building communities
Grounded theory	Visual matter, observations, text, selfies, emoji's, GIFs, written texts, using social media data to build a theory
Multimodal research	Texts that combine visual, written and audio (for example, video or photos with captions)

4.5   INTERCONNECTED ASPECTS OF A HOLISTIC QUALITATIVE RESEARCH APPROACH

The scarcity of distinct guidelines together with the intricacies associated with qualitative research consequently compel consideration of the pertinent elements of a comprehensive qualitative research approach of social media data. Salmons (2017:177–192) propounds an organising framework to approach qualitative research and to deal with the complexities linked to users' interactions online. The presented approach aims to accomplish an inclusive research outlook by considering the inter-related aspects associated with the design (cf. Salmon, 2017). It uses Salmon's (2017) conception, which is sequential and iterative in nature.

This framework combines all issues that require deliberation when a study is originally conceptualised, with special attention to the evaluation of proper research methods. As the centre of interest of the chapter is on the research methods to investigate data available on social media, and not on social media as a research instrument, the framework is adapted accordingly. Figure 4.1 below illustrates the elements of the proposed holistic framework.

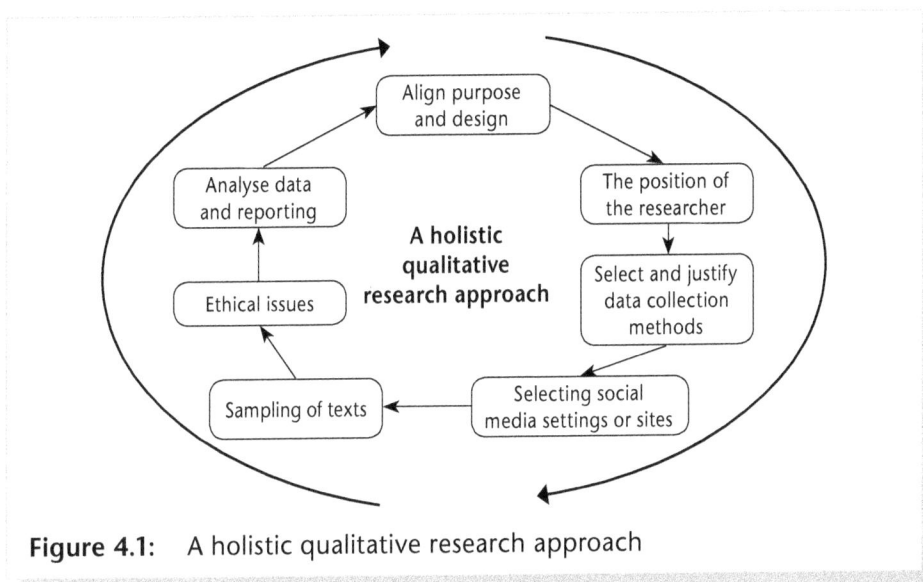

Figure 4.1:   A holistic qualitative research approach

- **Aligning purpose and design:** The researcher should consider all aspects of the research design, and so determine whether the research paradigm, theories, research purpose, and research methods are aligned. It should be clear why specific methods will be used, and how they will contribute to reaching the research purpose and answering the research questions (cf. Salmons, 2017:180).

- **The position as a researcher:** Certain research paradigms, for example, interpretivism openly appreciate the human interest in a study. In this regard, Salmons (2017:181) says the researcher should explain the aspects that motivate the study – either personal or scholarly interest or to address scarcity in the literature. Another aspect is the researcher's relationship to the phenomenon or participants that indicate possible prejudice when participants are known or familiar to the researcher (cf. Kaplan-Weinger & Ullman, 2014). As the researcher is the data collection instrument, he/she should be up-front about possible conflicts of interest. Once the research purpose and the position taken is known, it will be possible to consider the data collection methods (ibid). Another aspect that deserves thought is the extent of the interaction that is envisaged. In context and considering the main premise of qualitative research to investigate users in natural settings, this role should possibly mostly be *unobtrusive* to learn more about a phenomenon or population.

- **Selecting and justifying data collection methods:** A key question the researcher needs to answer is whether there is a convincing motivation for the selected methods and how it will contribute to answering the research purpose. As proposed in the section on multimodal research and as is evident in the presentations of other research methods, the selection of more than one method is often of value. Nonetheless, the fit between the method/s and the purpose of the study should be obvious.

Salmons (2017:181) proposes three categories typical to data collection methods: interviews, observations, and document or archival analysis. These are common to the traditional methods which are adapted to online settings, as indicated in the section on ethnography. To these original ways to collect data the following are added: extant, elicited, and enacted methods. These distinctions are made based on the 'degree of direct interaction the researcher has with the data and with participants', as summarised in Table 4.2 (adapted from Salmons, 2017:182). At this juncture, the researcher should reflect on the position he/she will take as touched on in the previous section.

Given the emphasis on different research methods to study social media data, as opposed to on social media as a research methodology, the categories in Table 4.3 below suggests useful ways to arrange these research methods (see also the discussion in chapter 2). In consequence, insights obtained throughout the chapter are incorporated. The role of the researcher is not envisaged to be the initiator of the content (such as asking questions), but mainly to observe, with limited involvement in already existing activities on social media platforms. Table 4.3 below illustrates how social media data collection methods could be organised.

Table 4.3:   Categorising data collection methods

Category	Social media data collection methods
Extant (no influence by the researcher)	Review of countless content created and shared on social media and available unrestricted (blogs, posts, discussions, conversations, images, videos, events and many more user-generated data)
	External observations of social media sites without researcher involvement (online behaviour and activities, for example, communities, events, etcetera)
Elicit (prompting involvement through limited participation by the researcher)	Becoming part of users' social media practices (specifically create communities with the purpose to allow the researcher to take part in discussions)
	Participant observations of social media sites with researcher involvement (online communities, etcetera)
Enacted (allowing participants to express opinions, etcetera)	Problem-centred interviews (eliciting information using text chat, video, messaging features)

Sources: adapted from Salmon (2017); Salmon (2012)

- **Selecting social media settings or sites:**

The researcher should consider the way/s communication with participants will take place, timing aspects of questions and responses, and the degree of access to the site and communication features (Salmons, 2017:182). Timing is seemingly a key consideration as the author distinguishes between asynchronous and synchronous communication, in which there is a time-lapse between messages and responses, and where message and response take place in real-time, respectively (ibid:183, Salmons 2012). As motivated in the previous section of this approach, the focus will primarily be on extant and elicit collection methods.

The social media contexts referred to throughout this chapter provides unique spaces in which users interact. Examples of these are; videos; communication in writing (text); posts, sharing and exchanges of an image; signalling – likes, dislikes, approval, disapproval of posts and tweets (for example, retweets); sharing of content (for example, retweets) (cf. Salmons 2017). It can thus be expected that the researcher needs to be able to distinguish and identify those sites that are appropriate to the research purpose and research methods. Adequate knowledge of the types of data available on these sites, including possibilities and challenges, is therefore a prerequisite.

- **The sampling of texts:**

This section speaks to the location and selection of suitable text on social media. In the section on content analysis, the uses of social media devices to filter and sample texts are proposed. In the section on semiotics, Hand (2107) highlights some of the specific issues that need to be deliberated when data is identified and selected, and that could be germane to the other methods included in this chapter – see also chapters 7, 8 and 9.

- **Ethical issues:**

As all studies require consideration of ethical issues, qualitative social media research is no exception. Salmons (2017:185) identifies aspects relating to informed consent and confidentiality. All research studies in which participants can be identified require informed consent, but some data does not contain personally identifiable information. Chapter 10 deals with pertinent ethical issues in social media research that should be considered at this point.

- **Collecting the data:**

The crucial question, in context, relates to the researcher's knowledge of the features of the technology and specific sites, the experience and skills needed to access the social media sites, conversations, archives, and to download images and so on (Salmons, 2017:186). The researcher has the freedom to decide whether the technique used should be structured (greater consistency), unstructured (more flexibility), or semi-structured (a mix of these) (Salmons, 2017:187). See chapter 8 for a more detailed discussion of data collection.

• **Analysing data and reporting:**

Following the collection of data, it needs to be analysed, interpreted, and reported. The method/s used for analysis will be determined on the method/s used to gather the data. Thus, the researcher needs to be familiar with these methods to allow for analysis. At this point, the researcher will be expected to separate data into parts and thereafter to combine it again. It is illustrated in the earlier section on *qualitative content analysis,* in which the coding (inductive or deductive) and the emerging themes are key. Atlas.ti is one of several qualitative data analysis software programmes that can be used to analyse qualitative data and that can assist with the analysis of large sets of social media data – video, audio, or textual (Friese 2014). Chapter 9 provides a more detailed overview of analysing social media data whereas in chapter 2 reporting is discussed.

4.6   CASE STUDY: A QUALITATIVE CONTENT ANALYSIS OF CORPORATE VIDEOS ON YOUTUBE

The case of A&B – A&B (pseudonym) is a building administrator organisation.

At a board meeting of A&B, a decision was taken to investigate the viability of producing corporate videos. Since this is a new initiative of the organisation and considering the limited knowledge of the possibilities and challenges that YouTube videos present, particularly on corporate videos, it was decided that the ideal way is to undertake a research project. In this way, an understanding of how competitors take advantage of corporate videos will be gained. The project has as its primary aim to uncover best practices by organisations that use corporate videos on YouTube.

Specific research aims include the identification of the purpose/s of these videos; the types of content; and the topics included.

4.6.1   Methodology

A semiotics paradigm was regarded as providing the most appropriate lens for the study as it generally focuses on the use of symbols to interact with people. The most suitable research method was deemed to be content analysis, as it allowed for the examination of the written and visual components of the corporate videos.

The unit of analysis is social artefacts. Based on the views of Payne and Payne (2004), a YouTube video is classified as a visual source. Videos of five organisations who operate in the same sector as A&B were purposively selected to ensure relevance. The two most viewed videos for each organisation were identified for the study, with a total of ten videos.

The study followed a two-pronged approach as associated with qualitative content analysis, namely, to undertake both deductive and inductive reasoning. A set of predetermined codes were compiled based on insights from scholarly literature to permit deductive coding, and in doing so to investigate the themes, namely the *purpose* of the videos, the *types* of content, and the *topics*. These codes were included in a coding framework. The second round of coding involved inductive coding that was applied to identify topics addressed in the videos. The limited information that exists about *what content* similar organisations use in their videos, necessitated this special focus.

Atlas.ti was used to code and analyse the data. The videos were uploaded as primary documents and appropriately titled. This programme allowed the researcher to open, view and code every video separately.

4.6.2   A Research strategy for the deductive coding

The research strategy assumed here required the researcher to become familiar with the data, and each video was viewed repeatedly. Next, preliminary coding was done on the first video to verify the correctness of the themes. Similarly, where the text offers another aspect of relevance, notes were made. Following, the videos were accessed one by one and sections or content relating to the themes were highlighted and assigned to the existing codes. The results are reported in Table 4.4 and Table 4.5.

The videos were studied and compared to the set of codes to identify those who meet the requirements. Based on the summary in Table 4.4, it is evident that most of the organisations clearly stated the main aim of their videos (n=7). Only four videos were professionally produced (n=4), and three acknowledged contributors by giving closing remarks (n=3). The last two categories can be linked to the professional production category, and only two had a title screen (n=2), and two used captions (n=2).

Table 4.4:   Results in respect of the purpose theme

Categories on the *purpose* theme	n = 10
Professionally produced	4
Presence of a title screen	2
Use of captions	2
Closing credits	3
The main aim of the videos	7

The second research aim pertains to the types of content used in the videos. As with the previous aim, the videos were compared to the set of codes. Out of the ten videos, six used content that was created by the organisations themselves (n=6). This included contributions by the managers of the different organisations and presentations from other staff members. Four videos used content that was created together with clients, for example, stories in which their experiences are discussed (n=4). Only two videos included some content from other sources and that were repurposed (n=2).

Table 4.5:   Results in respect of the types of content used in the videos

Categories in terms of the *types* of content themes in the videos	n = 10
Created content (by the organisation itself)	6
Co-created content (joint involvement of user and organisation)	4
Curated or repurposed content (aggregate information from other sources)	2

- **The research strategy for the inductive coding:**

For this activity, the researcher generated codes from the videos and then clustered them under potential and meaningful themes (broader units). Each video was loaded as a primary document. They were viewed more than once to identify and group similar issues (or codes) into the broad theme around 'content' provided in the videos.

Table 4.6 provides a summary, per organisation on the topic's theme. All videos provided contact information (n=10), and nine included a logo (n=9). Eight and six videos referred to their web addresses (n=8) and their services and products (n=6) respectively. Only two videos referred viewers to other social media sites used by the organisation.

Table 4.6:   The issues relating to the topic's theme, per organisation

Organisation	Emerging codes around the topics addressed in the videos					
	Web address	Logo	Contact info	References to service and topics	Call to action	Integration on other social media sites
A	2	2	2	2	0	2
B	2	0	2	2	0	0
C	2	2	2	0	2	0
D	0	2	2	0	0	0
E	2	2	2	0	0	0
Totals	8	9	10	6	2	2

In the final research report, the findings were summarised as in Table 4.7. All organisations provided contact information in their videos. Nine videos displayed an organisational logo, while eight provided their web address. Six organisations used the videos to identify their niche areas, with only two requesting participation or feedback and two combining the video on other social media sites.

Table 4.7:   A summary of the topics provided in the videos

Categories in terms of topics	n = 10
Web address	8
Logo	9
Contact information	10
References to services and topics unique to the sector	6
Calls to action (solicit stories, comment feature)	2
Integration on other social media sites	2

In the final research report of the study by A&B, the findings were elaborated on by linking them to theoretical aspects, the limitations pertaining to social media research were mentioned, and opportunities for further research were stipulated.

4.7   SUMMARY

This chapter explored a qualitative research design in social media research and also considered the different research methods available to analyse visual and textual data within the social media context. Justification for the use of qualitative research of social media was provided and precise challenges that the researcher might encounter were highlighted in context. Furthermore, the focus was on possible research paradigms to direct the research actions, knowledge, and perceptions of a qualitative researcher, and various methods and techniques to qualitatively examine content on social media. Finally, a holistic qualitative approach that could be fitting for exploring social media data was proposed and concisely outlined. The chapter concluded with a case study that aimed to illustrate the application of a semiotic research paradigm, using qualitative content analysis as well as deductive and inductive reasoning.

Learning activities (Test yourself)

1. In a paragraph or two, motivate the reasons why qualitative research is regarded as a fitting approach to investigate social media data.

2. Find a meme on social media that combines visual and textual content. Identify the research methods that could be used to study it.

3. Identify the research objects of ethnography, conversation analysis, and multimodal methods.

4. You are tasked with analysing the Facebook page of a known organisation. Identify the organisation and the most appropriate research paradigm. List all the suitable methods that could be applied to analyse the different aspects of the page by keeping in mind that this page should, for example, contain different aspects and not only text.

Further reading

Bauer, M.W. & Gaskell, G. (eds) 2011. Qualitative researching with text, image and sound. Available from: http://dx.doi.org/10.4135/9781849209731 [19 July 2019].

Flick, U. 2018. *The SAGE handbook of qualitative data*. London: SAGE Publications.

Flick, U. 2018. *Designing qualitative research*. 2nd ed. LA: SAGE Publications.

Denzin, N.K. & Giardina (eds.). 2011. *Qualitative inquiry and global crises.* Walnut Creek, CA: Left Coast Press.

Géring, Z. 2015. Content analysis versus discourse analysis: Examination of corporate social responsibility in companies' homepage texts. Available from: http://dx.doi.org/10.4135/978144627305014556732

CHAPTER 5

Using a Quantitative Research approach in Social Media Research

Tanja Bosch

The amount, scale and scope of social media data have created a need for methodological innovations that are uniquely suited to examine social media data. This is not only restricted to big data analysis of a quantitative vein, which has perhaps received the most media and scholarly attention, but also to new approaches in qualitative methodology – Luke Sloan & Anabel Quan-Haase

Learning Outcomes

After completing this chapter, the researcher should be able to:

- define the positivist research paradigm and a quantitative approach;
- identify the characteristics of Big Social Data and small data;
- recognise key issues related to quantitative sampling on social media;
- describe some quantitative methodologies for social media research;
- draw a sample of Big Social Data for analysis;
- critically reflect on the quantitative research approaches related to Big Data, particularly as they are often developed for commercial purposes;
- develop and implement a codebook for a quantitative content analysis of Big Social Data datasets; and
- formulate a Big Social Data research project, developing research questions, collecting and analysing the data, and writing up the findings.

5.1 INTRODUCTION

This chapter focuses on the positivist worldviews/paradigm, the quantitative research approach as well as some quantitative research methods used to conduct social media research. By the end of this chapter researchers will, therefore, be able to explain how quantitative research methods are used to study social media; including (but not limited to) a quantitative content analysis, data mining, sentiment analysis, geospatial and social media network analysis.

Social media platforms have become a central object of study for researchers across a range of disciplines from sociology and politics to media studies. While there are some critiques of these platforms, specifically around who has access, they are public platforms that enable citizens to express their views and engage in public debate. In recent times, platforms such as Facebook and Twitter have been used to choreograph social protest and activism. Political protest in North Africa, and the events that became known as the Arab Spring, were mediated by social media platforms which were used by protesters to disseminate information and organised protests. Similarly, in the South African context, social media platforms were used by student protesters in the national Fees Must Fall protests, to mobilise and raise awareness (Bosch, 2016).

This chapter provides an overview of a range of quantitative methods used by media researchers working in the field of social media research, describing the context for such research as well as some of the computational methods used in the field. The internet has been used extensively to conduct qualitative and quantitative research of content and users; and methods such as web-based surveys, online interviews and focus groups, as well as large scale quantitative approaches, are widespread. There is some debate about whether the analytic measures built into digital infrastructures qualify as social research methods or whether social media researchers simply use the tools of traditional social science whether quantitative or qualitative. Marres (2016) argues that social research methods have long had a computational dimension and that digital methods are not just another toolkit, but a way for researchers to use the digital to make sense of and gain knowledge about social life. There are many freely available and open-source third-party software applications which can be easily used by researchers with minimal computing skills to access data from sources like Twitter and to engage in analytic work using this software (see the list of tools and applications in chapters 8 and 9).

This chapter also provides an overview of the methodology of Social Network Analysis (SNA), which allows researchers to explore the relationships between individuals and groups online and draw insights from the patterns and implications of these relationships. SNA has its roots in classical sociology and explores relational ties and links between actors. Moreover, this approach focuses on investigating social structures through networks and graph theory, frequently providing visualisations of these community patterns. SNA approaches are often rooted in Big Data, a term used to refer to the existence of larger than usual datasets which are analysed using computer programmes to reveal patterns and trends, with specific reference to human online behaviour (see the detailed discussion in chapter 8).

Moreover, the chapter also explores the concepts of Big Data and Big Social Data, and reflects on the advantages and disadvantages of having access to these volumes of accessible data; with particular reference to data mining with Big Social Data. The chapter will explore how Big Social Data is changing how we do research, and what we lose or gain by having access to large datasets; as well as explore the idea of using 'small data' instead, or alongside Big Data approaches. In addition, one of the key tools used in SNA is data visualisation, and this chapter will provide an overview of the methods and tools used for visualising complex networks. Data visualisation is the technique of presenting complex data in graphical form.

Linked to Big Social Data approaches are the challenges of sampling in social media research, and we turn the attention here next (see also chapter 7). The chapter explores questions related to sampling on social media sites, for example, what is the population on social media platforms? How do platforms differ in population characteristics? How do we select cases or draw a sample from Big Social Data? Linked to this discussion on sampling, the chapter also briefly outlines how researchers might approach conducting a quantitative content analysis on social media datasets, to make broad generalisations about a corpus of social media posts.

In addition, this chapter also explores approaches and tools related to data mining and sentiment analysis. Sentiment analysis refers to the computational treatment of opinion, sentiment, and subjectivity in text. Methods for exploring the sentiment of large volumes of text could include quantitative content analysis and methods related to the analysis of content, such as text mining which identifies patterns and relationships within large volumes of text. Text mining software can analyse content and tone, and this technique of sentiment analysis computationally identifies and categorises opinions.

The chapter also provides a brief summary of the field of geospatial analysis, explaining the major issues associated with retrieving, sampling and geocoding. Social media applications track GPS locations of users, who in turn share their locations in various apps, and this section explores how this data can be used to gain insights about communities, communication patterns, the impact of events and so forth. Geospatial analysis can be used for forecasting political opinions on the internet, identifying and mapping virtual communities or studying the structure and dynamics of cities.

In the context of the growth of fake news, particularly on social media sites, the chapter then turns to an overview of online tools that tackle the problem of deception detection. In recent years, various conceptual tools dealing with language accuracy, objectivity, factuality, and fact-verification have become available across a number of disciplines in response to larger volumes of digital information. This section of the chapter explores the quantitative automated tools and approaches with which to identify potentially deceptive content on social media sites.

Even the exploratory phases of social media research tend to be quantitative, as searching, filtering and ranking are the only way to make sense of Big Social Data and thus form a logical first step in any analysis even in qualitative studies (Gaffney & Puschmann, 2014). While there are several methods for researching social media that might be considered to be 'quantitative', much of the research in this area comprises a mixed-methods approach, with a combination of quantitative and qualitative methods (see the discussion in chapter 6), and sometimes qualitative data is represented quantitatively. However, much of the data that is gathered from social media platforms is very large in scope, requiring quantitative analysis, and this phenomenon is referred to as Big Social Data, described in further detail below. It should also be noted that one can make a distinction between quantitative approaches to social media data and new computational methods which are slightly different, as data are not organised in a matrix of variables, but instead in a structure that more closely resembles a relational database rather than a spreadsheet. 'This is the reason why computational approaches do not necessarily need the use of statistics, even if univariate or bivariate data representations are useful to visualise some results' (Giglietto et al., 2012, 145). To some extent this chapter thus conflates traditional quantitative methods with computational methods.

Because it tends to be data-driven, quantitative research methods for social media focus primarily on 'measuring and comparing specific structural parameters in very large data samples, sometimes with little regard for the theoretical salience of these parameters' (Gaffney & Puschmann, 2014:64). There is a risk that these types of approaches are used simply because it is possible to easily collect this type of data; while it is specific research questions that should drive research. Much Big Social Data analysis is generated

> with no specific questions in mind, or the focus is driven by the application of a method or the content of the data set rather than a particular question, or the data set is being used to seek an answer to a question that it was never designed to answer in the first place (Kitchin, 2014:9).

5.2   RESEARCH PARADIGM FOR A QUANTITATIVE RESEARCH APPROACH IN SOCIAL MEDIA RESEARCH

Quantitative research methods in the humanities and social sciences are rooted in the positivist paradigm, which developed in the 19th century as social scientists attempted to show that their work was on par with researchers working in the natural sciences. 'Positivists see the overall aim of scientific inquiry as developing generalisations about the relations between social 'facts' that establish basic connections of cause and effect' (Deacon, et al., 1999:4).

The basic assumptions of positivism are thus that 'truth' can be observed and measured objectively, using a systematic and scientific approach to research. The positivist approach thus lends itself to a quantitative research approach and quantitative methods which aim to measure or quantify a phenomenon, as opposed to qualitative approaches which focus more on emphasising meaning through describing experiences as explained in chapter 4. The positivist research tradition is often referred to as empirical or quantitative research and uses the scientific method to conduct research. Research rooted in this paradigm thus assumes an objective truth and a measurable reality positions itself as objective, and relies on data and statistical, quantitative methods and approach (Cresswell, 2014).

Table 5.1 below summarises some of the characteristics of a social media study that adopts a positivist research paradigm and quantitative approach:

Table 5.1:   Characteristics of a social media study that adopts a positivist research paradigm and quantitative research approach

Statistical treatment of data collection	Drawing a representative sample of social media data in order to make broader inferences about a larger dataset
Large sample size	Sample size can depend on the overall size of the dataset, but typically, for a Twitter project, for example, a dataset might comprise thousands of tweets. Researchers should keep in mind that larger sample sizes do not necessarily produce better results if the large sample is not representative of the population to which the results will be generalised
Structured data in the form of numbers and statistics	Data is collected in a way which allows for statistical analysis
Objective interpretation based on statistics	Generalisable knowledge about a social phenomenon is generated through deductive reasoning
May determine relationships within a population	
Research design is descriptive (establishing associations between variables)	Correlation analysis can show the strength of relationships between two variables
Makes generalisations about a social media dataset	The analysis of a representative sample of the larger dataset allows the research to draw inferences and to test hypotheses

Source: Adapted from Cresswell (2014)

5.3   BIG SOCIAL DATA AND SMALL DATA

In this section pertinent issues not only related to Big Social Data, but also small data are highlighted.

5.3.1   The concepts of Big Data and Big Social Data

The concept 'Big Data' was first used by NASA in 1997 'to describe quantities of data so large that they taxed memory and hard disc capacity' (Hollander, et al., 2016:2). While there is no agreed universal definition for Big Data across multi-disciplinary academic scholarship, Big Data nearly always entails elements such as size, volume and how this data is eventually packaged to be better understood. The bulk of Big Data encountered today is 95 per cent unstructured and 5 per cent structured. With the broader goal being to seek understanding, Big Data analysis is about overcoming the 'noise' of the information to sift real, tangible 'knowledge' (Putting Big Data to Good Use 2017). Social media datasets constitute a part of what is referred to as 'Big Data' as they tend to make it possible for researchers to generate very large datasets. On Twitter, for example, half a billion messages are sent every day, and researchers have focused on developing new analytical tools and methods to efficiently process and analyse these massive volumes of real-time information to better understand virtual social networks (Hollander et al., 2016). On the other hand, while data collected through public posts on social media platforms is easy to collect, it has raised controversial ethical issues (refer to chapter 10 for a more detailed discussion on ethical considerations in social media research).

For the scholarly fraternity, this means the jobs of researchers have just become even more taxing on the ultimate quest to seek relevant meaning. In the social sciences, the term refers to data sets that are so large that they can only be processed by computers; but as Boyd and Crawford (2012:663) point out, Big Data is 'less about data that is big than it is about a capacity to search, aggregate, and cross-reference large data sets.' Moreover, Big Data is characterised 'by being generated continuously, seeking to be exhaustive and fine-grained in scope, and flexible and scalable in its production' (Kitchin, 2014:2). Analysing Big Datasets can thus reveal patterns or relationships that researchers may not even have known to look for.

Big Data is often analysed using a computational approach (see chapter 9), which is based on a web services-based approach, an Application Programming Interface (API) manipulation approach, the attempt to model the results (for example, by analysis of the graph structure) etcetera (Giglietto et al., 2012). APIs allow an exchange of information between clients and servers, and provide structured queries, allowing researchers to 'search' a platform and return data in a readable format. Social scientists usually use a web services approach – that is, tools and software available to researchers on the internet, which make data collection and analysis easy, versus computer scientists who tend to conduct social media research using the API manipulation approach which requires programming skills, for example, Python and Shah et al. (2015) describe computational social science as a subcategory of work on

Big Data and define it as an approach to social inquiry defined by the use of large and complex datasets, the use of computational or algorithmic solutions to generate patterns and inferences from these datasets.

The massive amount of social media data has resulted in an emerging topic known as Big Social Data that refers to technology-mediated interactions on social media. Social media researchers and professionals use Big Social Data to obtain insights from social media data and online social interactions for descriptive or predictive purposes (Olshannikova et al., 2017).

Because the majority of Big Data datasets often come from social media platforms like Facebook and Twitter, much of the discussion of quantitative research methods for social media in this chapter centres around these two platforms. Also, since much of the data that comes from social media sites is considered to be 'Big Social Data,' it is often analysed quantitatively, though qualitative approaches on smaller samples is also quite common.

Complicating matters during this sense-making exercise is the additional worry of researchers and students being compelled to contend with Big Social Data in multimedia formats such as audio, images, video and text (Gandomi & Haider, 2015:138). Scholars are, therefore, well within their right to claim disillusionment with the deluge of information coming to them at one go as such large volumes of information have that rare ability to confound, scare off and ultimately intimidate. However, to grasp how Big Social Data is structured, there is a need to peel away at its various layers, namely volume, variety, velocity, veracity, variability, and value. To fully comprehend the enormity and multi-layered texture of Big Social Data, reference is made to what scholars have classified as the six 'Vs' of Big Data scholarship, namely volume, variety, velocity, veracity (vague), variability and value as depicted in Table 5.2 below and which can be extended to social media data collection (Gandomi & Haider, 2015:138–139; Olshannikova et al., 2017).

Volume simply refers to the vast amount of data generated globally that presents challenges in terms of collecting, storing and sorting the data. Variety is associated with the diverse nature of the content on social media, such as images, text, audio and video (Williams, Burnap & Sloan, 2016:322; cf. Quan-Haase & Sloan, 2017:5). Velocity refers to the rate at which data are produced and propagated, specifically pertaining to the speed at which users respond, and that demands speedy reactions from researchers (Quan-Haase & Sloan, 2017:6). Veracity (vague) relates to accuracy, quality and originality of the data that result in the unavailability of information normally gathered, for example, demographics that could impact decisions around populations and sampling. Williams et al. (2016) explain that virtue refers to the ethical considerations in social media research (see chapter 10). While it is maintained that many users are aware that their information may be accessed by a third party after they have accepted the Terms of Service, it is crucial that researchers should follow the basic principles of social science ethics such as participant anonymity.

Table 5.2 provides a simple illustration of the six 'Vs' and their concomitant effect on one's understanding of the Big Social Data concept and how it relates to social media data collection.

Table 5.2:   The six Vs of Big Social Data and its relation to social media data collection

Dimension	Detail	How this affects data collection for the social media researcher
Volume	Refers to the size or magnitude of Big Data	Social media data collection is indeed about the 'volume' or 'quantity' of data one is confronted with. Social media data sets are by nature large, complex, noisy and at most times unstructured.
Variety	Refers to the 'structural heterogeneity' or different types of information contained within a data set	Large data sets also mean there is no homogeneity. Researchers will need to apply several processes to 'make sense' of what is seen.
Velocity	Refers to the speed at which data is generated and how quickly this is analysed	Technology over the last decade has 'sped up' the way information spreads. User-generated content is continually being created over social media platforms. Researcher agility is, therefore, needed to know how to manage large information-laden persistently coming through at any given 24-hour cycle.
Veracity (Vague)	Refers to the trustworthiness of Big Data: how credible is the data?	The open-source nature of social media data lends itself to questions of credibility. What is real, what is fake, what is usable and what is superfluous? These are some of the key 'gate-keeping' functions researchers need to perform to ensure final data sets enjoy both credibility and trustworthiness.
Variability	Commonly refers to the 'periodic' flow rates of Big Data. There will be times where data flow will be accentuated while at other times data flow will dip	Social media data operates mostly in real-time. Global users, however, log in according to where they are in the world from many different time zones. There will, therefore, be 'peaks' and 'dips' in terms of social media data flows.
Value	Relates to sense-making from Big Data and can only be attained after data cleaning and data analysis reduces the information to a workable 'structured' data set	For researchers, 'filtering' large amounts of social media data is non-negotiable. 'Data cleaning' is executed to make better sense of the data; it is also done to ensure only the most relevant aspects are extracted and subsequently analysed in the pursuit of knowledge creation.

Sources: Gandomi & Haider (2015:138–139); Olshannikova et al. (2017)

Although Big Data and especially Big Social Data scholarship is continual and evolving, several scholars within the discipline have since confirmed the multi-dimensionality and existence of these six 'Vs' of Big Data; they include Oweis et al. (2015), Günther et al. (2017), Oussous et al. (2018), Stieglitz et al. (2018) and Olshannikova et al. (2017), to name but a few.

Big Social Data has also commonly been approached with small scale content analysis, either analysing small numbers of users or small samples of tweets (Tinati et al., 2014). Issues related to sampling on social media, particularly on Twitter, are discussed further in the next section 5.4.

5.3.2 Small data

During the current computational turn, and while there are so many methods for quantitatively analysing social media data, we should not overlook the value of 'small data', as research insights can be found at even modest scales – 'the size of the data should fit the research question being asked' (Boyd & Crawford, 2014). The concept of 'small data' refers to smaller datasets which are more manageable and easier for researchers to analyse without the assistance of software and other automated data analysis tools. Latzko-Toth et al. (2017) argue that the value in these smaller datasets is in what they refer to as 'data thickness' (199), with such data containing fewer data points but more detail. The process of 'thickening' social media data could refer to, for example, interviewing users about their motivations to supplement data 'with richly textured information or, in other words, adding layers of thickness to them' (Latzko-Toth et al., 2017, 202).

While small data is too small to be representative, it can be useful for gaining insight into the phenomena under investigation and provides layers of additional data which contextualises the interpretive paradigm of qualitative inquiry. The difficulty (and sometimes the expense) of gaining access to big social media datasets creates a restricted culture of research and what Boyd and Crawford (2014) refer to as a new kind of digital divide in the current ecosystem around Big Data. Those who have the computational expertise to analyse Big Data produce biases in the data and the types of research questions that are answered through these datasets.

While Big Data and the resultant quantitative research approaches pose some challenges, they also present a number of 'opportunities for social scientists and humanities scholars, not least of which are massive quantities of very rich social, cultural, economic, political and historical data' (Kitchin, 2014:10). However, we should continue to critically reflect on these tools particularly as they are often developed for commercial purposes.

5.4 QUANTITATIVE SAMPLING ON SOCIAL MEDIA

Sampling is discussed in detail in chapter 7, but it should be mentioned here that sampling is a basic tenet of quantitative research, as it involves selecting subsets from a larger population in order to make generalisations about the larger population. In the case of social media datasets, researchers often do not have access to a full dataset (for example, all the tweets on a given topic) from which to draw a smaller sample. The majority of sampling approaches on Twitter consequently follow a 'non-probabilistic, non-representative route, delineating their samples based on features specific to the platform' (Gerlitz & Rieder, 2013).

As explained in chapter 2, one of the main limitations of using social media datasets is that certain demographic factors may lead to skewed samples, for example, issues related to socioeconomic status and access, as well as age (more young people use social media), and thus representative samples of a broader population can be hard to draw from social media because it is often not possible to access every social media post containing a specific keyword or hashtag. Besides variance in adoption rates and usage strategies, highly vocal users who post often may skew a sample, which is already problematic because it does not represent a true archive of posts related to past events (Gaffney & Puschmann, 2014). Sampling data is challenging 'because in most cases the distributions are extremely skewed, for example, few extremely active users and a long tail of far less productive users' (Gigliotti et al., 2012).

Twitter data, in particular, raises several sampling issues, and this will be discussed further below. However, sampling issues on other platforms are equally problematic. Drawing a sample from a visual platform such as Instagram, for example, is difficult as the platform does not provide any mechanism for users to monitor the high volume of the global photo stream. One can select public posts based on location or query the most popular photographs, but the available feed will depend on the researcher's platform settings. The high volume of data generated on social media platforms, and the constant data streams on these platforms, makes it difficult to draw clear boundaries around the total population from which to sample. Moreover, platform limitations in terms of Twitter or Instagram APIs also raise several issues about how much data researchers can access. For example, Instagram has closed public access to their API making it impossible to draw a sample via 3rd party applications. Even though Twitter datasets are usually quite large, the representativity of these datasets are often called into question, as they often do not draw a sample from the total population of tweets. What is referred to as the Twitter 'firehose' would theoretically contain all public tweets posted, but some publicly accessible tweets are missing from the 'firehose'. An API is a data interface which is primarily to provide software developers with a data-only version of a site's content. API's allow developers a way to interact with a platform's content and are also used by researchers to access data via such third-party applications.

When researching Twitter, most researchers use the streaming API to query Twitter, which allows one to search the current 'stream' of tweets and does not allow for retrospective research on past events (see also the discussion in chapter 9). The streaming API gives regular Twitter users access to a random sample of 1 per cent of all traffic on the platform, and access to 100 per cent of all tweets (the 'firehose') where there is a high volume of tweets, requires purchasing this data directly from Twitter or a company. Most researchers have access to a 'gardenhose' sample, which represents about 10 per cent, or a 'spritzer' of 1 per cent, or in the past, they had 'white-listed accounts where they could use the APIS to get access to different subsets of content from the public stream' (Boyd & Crawford, 2014). However, Gerlitz & Rieder (2013) have argued that setting up a query in real time using the streaming API leads to a valid sample stream as all tweets appear in near real-time in the queue and that the streaming API can function as a 'big picture view of Twitter.'

The Representational State Transfer (REST) API allows access to the social graph data of a group of users that is, information follower-followee networks, but this is also limited, and the search API essentially mirrors the Twitter search function, but again is limited as this only allows one to search for up to a week back (Gaffney & Puschmann, 2014). Access to Twitter data thus takes place via one of these APIs and a number of tools are used by researchers to specify what kind of data they want to collect.

Mecodify, for example, is a bespoke Twitter analysis tool which is freely available on GitHub (see also the discussion of Mecodify in chapter 9). Mecodify crawls the Twitter search page via a built-in script and extracts the tweets pulled up by search queries. It then fetches all messages and relevant information about the users who tweeted via the Twitter Application Program Interface (API). Mecodify allows one to search for topical keywords or hashtags and then download the tweets and information about users in a .csv file. User data can be imported into another free open-source application, Kumu, which allows one to conduct a SNA to explore the network relationship between users or groups of users. There are many such freely available open-source data collection tools for Twitter, for example, Vicinitas, (https://www.vicinitas.io), KeyHole (https://keyhole.co) and Twitonomy (https://www.twitonomy.com) as also explained in chapter 9 of this book. These methods are defined by Giglietto et al. (2012) as a computational supported statistical approach and allow researchers to continue the trend of conducting hashtag studies, which remain popular due to the ease with which researchers with minimal technical skills can 'track and gather sizeable datasets of all tweets containing specific hashtags (and keywords) and provide a web interface to download the resultant datasets in user-friendly Excel or comma-separated values formats' (Bruns & Burgess, 2016:23). In the early days of Twitter research, several tools for gathering Twitter emerged and there are many such tools today in addition to the ones listed above. The availability of such free hosted services

> *or as software released under open source licenses, also contributed significantly to such methodological innovation and evaluation: the open availability and extensibility of the key early research tools instilled a strong "open science" methods in the international Twitter research community which gathered around these tools and methods* (Bruns & Burgerss, 2016:23).

But as Boyd and Crawford (2014) have shown, the size of a Twitter dataset holds little relevance if the data is skewed from the beginning.

> *It could be that the API pulls a random sample of tweets or that it pulls the first few thousand tweets per hour or that it only pulls tweets from a particular segment of the network graph. Without knowing, it is difficult for researchers to make claims about the quality of the data that they are analysing* (Boyd & Crawford, 2014).

Another issue related to sampling in Twitter research is highlighted by Tinati et al. (2014:3), who point out that

> *research on the role of Twitter in grassroots activism and its potential for enhancing participatory democracy, either pre-selects the important actors (elected politicians especially) and/or takes a sample of tweets or users within a defined area of activity, often a hashtag stream.*

They argue that this process of sampling tweets, whether randomly or purposively, does not allow researchers to trace which actors and which information emerges as important over time, but rather predefines which are important.

The most common Twitter sampling technique is topic-based sampling which selects tweets via hashtags collected through the API and based primarily on topical concerns. This can be limiting as it excludes tweets which do not contain hashtags as well as other everyday phatic conversation on the platform, or @replies and other forms of everyday interactions between users.

Sampling on other social media platforms such as Facebook faces similar challenges. First, the vast range of data available – from the text of an actual post to the metadata of the posts, time, date, and engagement with (likes etc) and comments on a particular post. Moreover, the richness of Facebook, similar to Twitter, means that researchers also have to take into account how to sample complex data which also includes links, shares, images, videos and other media. There are fewer automated web services available for studying Facebook. Netvizz is a data extraction and collection application which allows one to export data in the form of network and tabular files from Facebook pages, profiles and groups via the API (Rieder, 2013). Since its creation in 2009 by Bernhard Rieder, Netvizz has been widely used, but as of 2019 it was discontinued by Facebook and is no longer available. Facepager, freely available on GitHub, was made for fetching publicly available data from YouTube, Twitter and other JSON-based APIs including Facebook (Junger & Till, 2018). Facepager simplifies the process of gathering data without the use of programming languages.

While this chapter highlights many of the quantitative methods that involve automated processes as part of the computational turn; once data is sampled a very common approach is to conduct a quantitative content analysis, coding data in much the same way one might code traditional media texts. Other traditional social science methods can also be used to study social media, for example, online or face to face surveys of users to explore their motivations and experiences using specific platforms.

5.5   SOME RESEARCH METHODS FOR QUANTITATIVE SOCIAL MEDIA STUDIES

Researchers adopting a quantitative research approach for social media studies may use some of the following research methods.

5.5.1   Quantitative content analysis

Once the issues related to sampling are resolved, researchers can also conduct a quantitative content analysis on social media datasets. Content analysis is a research technique and specific analytical approach for the quantitative study of manifest media content. Coming out of the positivist empirical paradigm described earlier, 'the purpose of quantitative content analysis is to quantify salient and manifest features of a large number of texts and the statistics are used to make broader inferences about the processes and politics of representation' (Deacon et al., 1999, 116). Much like a traditional print media content analysis, a quantitative content analysis of social media data can show trends, patterns and absences over large volumes of social media texts. Once a sample of posts is drawn from the social media platform being studied and properly cleaned as explained in chapter 9, the next step would be to develop a codebook to analyse the data. A codebook is a document that contains information (labels) about each of the variables (features) in the social media dataset to facilitate reliable data analysis (Neuenhof, 2016).

For example, as in the author's own experience, when data was collected from the microblogging social network Twitter, the codebook would highlight key categories in which to categorise tweets. A point in case is a study on how users tweet about a controversial political topic, might code tweets into categories such as 'sharing information', 'hate speech', 'political propaganda', or a range of other mutually exclusive categories to help organise the dataset and highlight key themes across the data corpus. This would allow researchers to make generalisations about a dataset, for example, being able to argue that 50 per cent of tweets or posts covered a particular topic in a particular way.

Depending on the size of the sample, a codebook can be compiled either manually or using an existing compatible file with software such as Statistical Package for Social Sciences, Excel or any other suitable data analysis software (Neuenhof, 2016).

Figure 5.1 below illustrates some of the information in the social media dataset that can be included in the codebook.

```
                        01
                 Name of the variable

                        02
           What the variable respresents (label)

                        03
            Standard data code of the variable

                        04
                    Variable date

                        05
                    Missing data
```

Figure 5.1:   Some of the information in a social media dataset that can be included in a codebook

Similar to traditional content analysis, researchers must consider issues related to intracoder and inter-coder reliability. See the detailed discussion of validity and reliability in chapter 2.

5.5.2   Data mining and text mining

As explained in chapters 8 and 9, techniques of data mining refer to the practice of extracting meaningful information from Big Social Datasets, to reveal insights that would not otherwise be possible because of the size of the datasets. Algorithms are used to identify hidden patterns and to cluster or classify data elements.

In addition to classification and clustering methods, there are a variety of mining techniques detailed in several textbooks ... including association rules, Bayesian classification algorithms, rule-based classifiers, support vector machines, text mining, link analysis, and multi-relational data mining (Barbier & Liu, 2011:329).

Much of the large volumes of data available for analysis on social media platforms take the form of text. This section of the chapter explores the methodology often referred to as 'text mining', which has emerged as an important tool in quantitative scientific research. This section of the chapter provides a definition of this methodology, provides examples of how the method of text mining has been used and explores some of the challenges associated with this method. The chapter also briefly outlines some of the text mining tools that are available and argues that a mixed-methods approach may be most useful when using the quantitative methodology of text mining. As Ampofo et al. (2015:163) argue, 'the technology can be powerful but it is often a blunt instrument.'

Text mining is a term used to describe the process of extracting information from large volumes of textual sources in order to 'extract meaningful associations, trends and patterns in large corpuses of text' (Ampofo et al., 2015:164). Text mining uses automated computer software to extract information automatically and quickly from written texts or resources, to search for new knowledge or interesting patterns. Text mining is a variation of data mining, which is the process of searching for patterns in large databases; and uses automated software to conduct the analysis.

The analysis of text from social media datasets often involves identifying topic clusters via document analysis; often using Python code or automated software such as the Gephi modularity algorithm (Gerlitz & Rieder, 2013). This allows researchers to explore which hashtags co-occur and how hashtags are clustered together. Clustering algorithms can determine which elements in a dataset are similar to each other. This is sometimes referred to as an NGram analysis and refers to a set of co-occurring or adjacent words.

Social network sites such as Facebook and Twitter, have recently become a valuable resource for extracting knowledge for market research companies, to investigate consumers' attitudes towards brands, and also for sentiment analysis discussed in further detail below. He at al. (2013) used text mining approaches to analyse customer-generated unstructured content on the social media pages of three large pizza chains. This research was based on the notion that companies need to monitor the social media activities of their competitors to increase their competitive advantage and to use social media more competitively. The wide adoption of social media has led to a wealth of textual data which, argue He at al. (2013), contains hidden knowledge which business can use to leverage a competitive edge.

5.5.3 Sentiment analysis

Text mining is a key aspect of the methodology of sentiment analysis. Sentiment analysis is the exploration of users' online opinions and categorisation thereof as positive, negative, or neutral, in order to determine the sentiment of a particular text. This methodology is also sometimes referred to as emotional polarity analysis, opinion mining, review mining or appraisal extraction (Mostafa, 2013). Sentiment analysis is referred to as a natural language processing application which uses text mining and computational linguistics to identify the prevalent sentiment present in a text in an automated way. To perform a sentiment analysis a body of text is required, and there has to be a way of evaluating this textual body to determine the sentiments contained for example one study analysed hundreds of online movie reviews by using machine learning methods to search for words expressing positive or negative sentiment (Hollander et al., 2016). Machine learning refers to the process of researchers 'training' analysis software to increase its accuracy in identifying sentiments. Researchers thus 'actively participate in the creation of rules and algorithms to be used in determining sentiment classification' (Hollander et al., 2016:8).

In a lexicon-based approach, researchers use a dictionary containing thousands of words pre-determined to be either positive or negative, then capture the degree of sentiment for individual words in a textual body. 'For example, a tweet containing the word "good" would be assigned a positive score, a tweet containing the words "very good" would be assigned an even higher positive score, a tweet with the word "bad" would be assigned a negative score, and so on' (Hollander et al., 2016:16). Researchers also sometimes conduct sentiment analysis by looking for positive or negative emoticons.

Social media has been demonstrated to be a reliable indicator of public sentiment and Twitter has even been used to predict the outcomes of important events such as elections or stock market fluctuations. With the growth of social media and millions of users sharing their personal opinions, these platforms have become a rich source of data for sentiment analysis and opinion mining (Barbier & Liu, 2011).

The main limitation of the methodology of sentiment analysis is that expressions of negative sentiment may not always contain words pre-categorised as negative; or that words which typically convey negativity might not actually be expressing any sentiment at all. Automated software alone can thus not always reliably detect sentiment, and coding sentiment by hand is often much more accurate even if it is much more time consuming. Moreover, 'language is complex, contextual and ever changing. Machines, for all their processing power, are sometimes incapable of interpreting linguistic subtleties' (Hollander et al., 2016:16).

5.5.4   Social network analysis

Not all quantitative research of social networking sites like Twitter is based on words and the content of tweets – some researchers have used the social graph data available to explore online relationships instead of message content. Many of the early Twitter research was conducted by researchers with a computer science background and focused on the analysis of the network structure of the platform, but more recently, the growing size of the network and limits to accessing data, have made this kind of research less frequent (Giglietto et al., 2012). Similarly, studies of the Facebook network are rare and usually based on datasets provided by the platform itself, as analysing a large network structure is often computationally challenging (Giglietto et al., 2012). Moreover, after the Cambridge Analytica controversy, platforms such as Facebook have restricted access to platform data via their APIs, currently limiting the ability of researchers to conduct Facebook research and meaning that data has to be manually collected, which is very time consuming. As Bruns (2019) has argued, limited access to the Facebook API makes it difficult for social media researchers to investigate disinformation campaigns and to hold platforms accountable for the ways in which their policies might enable such campaigns.

The methodology of SNA has its origins in the disciplines of classical sociology, psychology and anthropology; as well as being influenced by computer science and sociometrics. SNA draws from network theory to analyse the patterns of social relations between individuals to theorise the social structure in a community or network. This is premised on the idea that networks have both structure and influence; and that the position of individual actors in a network can influence their ability to access resources such as capital and information; and that therefore well-connected actors have better access to information and other resources. Relational data is thus the focus of SNA investigations, which conceptualise social structures as a network with ties connecting members, focuses on the characteristics of these ties instead of the characteristics of individual members; and views communities 'as networks of individual relations that people foster, maintain, and use in the course of their daily lives' (Otte & Rousseau, 2002:442). The use of SNA methods in the field of media studies has grown alongside the rise and widespread use of social networking sites.

Network analysis of social media populations allows researchers to explore how users within sites like Facebook or Twitter are connected to each other. Network analysis can answer questions such as:

What patterns are created by the aggregate of interactions in a social media space? How are participants connected to one another? What social roles exist and who plays critical roles like connector, answer person, discussion starter, or content caretaker? What discussions, pages, or files have attracted the most interest from different kinds of participants? How do network structures correlate with the contributions people make within the social media space (Smith et al., 2009:255).

SNA thus uses automated software and computational methods to study the structure of social media users' connections, looking specifically at who is most connected or influential, and which groups of people are most closely connected. A social network is a social structure of people who are directly or indirectly related through a common relation or interest, and networks have few or many actors (nodes) and one or many types of relations (edges). Network graphs are collections of nodes (sometimes called vertices and referring to actors or users) that are connected by edges (connections or ties). Analysing a network structure can give insights into the behaviour of elements within the network or an understanding of how information flows through the network. Analysing social media networks explores the relationship between nodes and could be useful to, for example, highlight leadership dynamics in collective activism.

There are several metrics used to define and analyse social networks. These metrics are briefly outlined below. Density is an indication of the level of connectedness within the network, and researchers might also consider issues such as homophily, in other words, the degree to which users form ties with others who are similar/dissimilar; or propinquity, that is, the tendency for users to be closely tied to others who are geographically near. Network density refers to the number of connections in a network. In addition, several centrality measures are usually considered in SNA: degree centrality, closeness centrality and betweenness centrality. Centrality refers to metrics which attempt to quantify the influence of individuals or groups in a network. Degree centrality refers to the number of connections a user has. Closeness centrality is the distance of one actor to all others in the network; while betweenness centrality, for example, measures how important a user is by looking at their role in allowing information to flow from one part of the network to another. Betweenness centrality refers to the degree to which nodes (users) stand between each other – a node or a user with higher betweenness centrality would be more influential or have greater control over the network because more information would pass through them.

The development of specific SNA software has been a contributing factor to the growth of the method. NodeXL, for example, provides data analysis and visualisation features as an add-on to Microsoft Excel (see the case study in chapter 9). The tool was intended to make network analysis easy to perform, for researchers to easily represent 'the connections between content creators as they view, reply, annotate or explicitly link to one another's content' (Smith et al., 2009:255).

Gephi is an open-source software tool for graph and network analysis which 'provides easy and broad access to network data and allows for spatializing, filtering, navigating, manipulating and clustering' (Bastian et al., 2009).

However, while researchers have used data from Twitter and Facebook to analyse connections between messages and accounts,

> *the relations displayed through social media are not necessarily equivalent to the sociograms and kinship networks that sociologists and anthropologists have been investigating since the 1930s … the ability to represent relationships between people as a graph does not mean that they convey equivalent information* (Boyd & Crawford, 2014).

Data from SNA is usually represented through visualisations to represent the social network by means of graphs or diagrams, showing how each of the users or nodes in the network is connected to the other, and how they are clustered into groups or communities, either by follower-followee or by @ replies. There is also a range of open-source software, which is used to create these data visualisations, for example, Gephi and Kumu.

> *Visualization of social networks has a rich history, particularly within the social sciences, where node-link depictions of social relations have been employed as an analytical tool since at least the 1930s* (Heer & Boyd, 2005:32).

5.5.5 Geospatial analysis

Social media sites allow people to check in to specific geographic locations, and also implicitly tracks their location through their use of these applications. Users actively contribute their geospatial locations, leading to the convergence of geospatial information science and social media opens up 'exciting opportunities to study human movement from the perspective of their socio-spatial behaviour' (Buchel & Pennington, 2017).

Researchers can use the geographic locations shared by users on social media platforms to gain insights into communities, economic and political impacts of events, disease outbreaks etcetera. Researching the geospatial properties of social media is about

> *measuring geospatial footprints of online and offline communities, determining their volume, finding their proximity to other communities, overlaps and intersections, identifying spatial clusters, locating hotspots of activities, and making predictions about possible outcomes of events* (Buchel & Pennington, 2017).

This method relies on users to geotag posts or on being able to retrieve the metadata from posts including photographs, to determine the user's geographic location.

(i)   Drawing findings and interpreting results from quantitative social media data

Drawing findings and analysing and interpreting the results from quantitative social media datasets follow the same model as other quantitative research projects, even though the data takes a different form. Much of this kind of analysis begins with descriptive statistical analysis, which usually refers to the analysis of one variable at a time. This level of analysis measures the prevalence of a specific characteristic in the population based on the sample; identifies the general patterns in the sample and population; and evaluates the extent to which a characteristic varies across the sample and population (Jensen & Laurie, 2016). The main purposes of analysing quantitative data are to identify the typical and interesting patterns in your data, by giving structure and meaning to your data.

5.6   DECEPTION DETECTION TOOLS

With the rise of fake news, predominantly circulated on social media platforms and exacerbated by the tendency for people to use these platforms as their primary sources of news, fake news detection has become an emerging research area (see chapters 2 and 9). Because it is cheap and fast to provide news online and disseminate it via social media, a large volume of news articles with intentionally false information are produced online for a range of financial and political purposes (Shu et al., 2017). Fake news detection is defined as 'the task of categorizing news along a continuum of veracity, with an associated measure of certainty' (Conroy et al., 2015:1), with the primary purpose of highlighting news that is intentionally deceptive or false and misleading. Identifying fake news follows several steps. First a focus on the features of news content using automated software to analyse the lexical and syntactic features of a text, frequency of words and phrases; secondly the extraction of visual-based features using a classification framework (Rubin, 2017). More recently, conceptual tools dealing with language accuracy, objectivity, factuality and fact-verification have emerged as scholars have begun to develop software for deception detection. Rubin (2017:359) has argued that

> when analyzing social media for potentially deceptive content, it is important to apply methods that consider not just what is being said, but also how the message is presented, by who, and in what format and context. The hybrid approach should include text analytics, network analysis and world knowledge database incorporation to fully take advantage of linguistic, interpersonal, and contextual awareness.

CASE STUDY: RESEARCHING #ZUMAMUSTFALL ON FACEBOOK

This case study is based on previous research (Bosch, 2019) exploring how citizens use social media sites for protest movements in South Africa. When selecting to explore the role a specific hashtag plays, in this case #Zumamustfall, the first step would be to conduct a brief issue mapping exercise. The purpose of this exercise would be to determine which hashtag or platform to study and to informally see where the most, or the most interesting discourses take place. While Twitter is widely used for social activism, the affordances of Facebook make it a vehicle for more detailed debate and discussion, and for this reason, Facebook was selected as the platform for analysis. The next step was to select the unit of analysis on Facebook that is, page, group or post within one of these. The Zuma Must Fall and Zuma March public pages on Facebook were selected as the unit of analysis as these pages were most 'liked' by users: by 81 164 and 105 316 people respectively.

The next step was to draw a sample of content from this page and then to conduct a content analysis of the content. The automated tool Netvizz was used to quantitatively pull and summarise posts by the pages and from users. From this, the 50 most recent posts on each page were downloaded for further analysis, as a convenience sample of content, as each page contained thousands of posts. Another approach may have been to generate a random sample. The second step was to then develop a coding manual to analyse these posts. Coding categories included looking at posts by page and users, looking at the intention of and purpose of the posts (for example, information sharing about events or links to news articles, etcetera). The coding sheet also allowed for the collection about information such as which types of posts received the most engagement. This allowed us to see that, for example, photographs were 'liked' and shared more by users rather than links, status updates, or videos; and that the photographs most engaged with were photographs of the various protest events, and those with the highest engagement score (likes, reactions, shares) showed South Africans of various races standing together or embracing at these public events. The quantitative component of the analysis also took into account the engagement by people located outside of South Africa is evident in the geographic locations of people who liked the page. In the case of the Zuma Must Fall page, of the 105 316 individuals who follow the page by clicking 'like', 74 216 were located in South Africa, with many others in a range of other locations for example 1590 in Great Britain and 665 in the United States.

➡

The quantitative analysis also took into account the frequency of user engagement and analysing the last 50 posts on the Zuma Must Fall page revealed that 3 122 users were liking or commenting a total of 4 967 times. This sample did not exclude the possibility of multiple comments by single users, highlighting the potential problem of social media amplifying the voices of the most vocal users (Bosch, 2019). Following on this quantitative analysis, further research took a qualitative form, using qualitative content analysis and discourse analysis methods to further analyse the textual content. An analysis of the texts of the tweets revealed the potential for social media platforms in South Africa to play a role in providing a platform for citizen activism by building connections between citizens, and in helping movements such as Zuma Must Fall to raise broader awareness and gain momentum. This mixed-methods approach allowed for a holistic study of a Facebook page to explore its primary functions.

5.7   SUMMARY

This chapter explains and highlights some key issues related to adopting a positivist research worldview and quantitative approach for a social media study. Consequently, characteristics of both Big Social Data and 'small data' were explained while also focusing on challenges researchers face when sampling large datasets. In addition, some popular quantitative research methodologies were discussed, and fake news deception tools pointed out. A case study illustrates some main concepts of this chapter.

Learning activities (Test yourself)

1. Choose a topical hashtag and search for available tweets using this hashtag, then draw a sample for further analysis.

2. Find a public Facebook page or group with topical content for analysis, then explain how you will select your unit of analysis for a quantitative content analysis.

3. Develop a codebook for a quantitative content analysis of tweets on a specific topic.

4. Using the tweets dataset collected earlier, draw a sample and conduct a content analysis of your dataset. Write a short 1 500-word report to present your findings.

Further reading

Rogers, R.A. 2013. *Digital methods.* The MIT Press.

Scott, J. & Carrington, P. J. 2011. *The SAGE handbook of social network analysis.* London: SAGE Publications.

Sloan, L. & Quan-Haase, A. (eds.). 2017. *The SAGE handbook of social media research methods.* Thousand Oaks, Los Angeles: SAGE Publications.

Snee, H., Roberts, S., Hine, C., Morey, Y. & Watson, H. (eds.) 2016. *Digital methods for social science: An interdisciplinary guide to research innovation.* United Kingdom: Palgrave Macmillan.

CHAPTER 6

Using a Mixed-Methods approach in Social Media Research

Esther Emmanuel Awuah

Mixing methods in research answers questions that qualitative and quantitative research methods alone cannot answer – Esther Emmanuel Awuah

Learning Outcomes

After completing this chapter, the researcher should be able to:

- outline various types of paradigms or philosophical worldviews associated with the mixed-methods approach;
- explain several types of mixed-methods typologies as well as the types of mixed-methods designs;
- determine the most appropriate mixed-methods design according to various research problem scenarios;
- analyse the pros and cons of using mixed-methods research (MMR) as well as each mixed-methods design; and
- justify the rationale for using the mixed-methods approach (MMA) in social media research.

6.1   INTRODUCTION

In this chapter, the MMA, which reminds us of the perfect combination of Spaghetti, Bolognese Sauce and Parmigiana Reggiano, is presented. The three ingredients combined make up an excellent meal. Similarly, the right combination of qualitative and quantitative methods in a single study produces superior social media research results.

This chapter introduces the reader to various elements found within the MMA, and how a researcher can best combine them to suit their research study — in such a way that the research problems are addressed more effectively.

This approach is contextualised within the social media research field. An explanation of social media research will be provided, and the proper application of the MMA in this context explained. This chapter also discusses the various paradigms or worldviews that guide MMAs, as well as the various typologies and mixed-method designs. However, in this chapter, the focus is mostly on Creswell and Plano Clark's basic mixed-methods typology (convergent parallel, explanatory sequential, and exploratory sequential). Finally, the chapter concludes with a case study that illustrates how AfroConsult Limited (AfroConsult) a consultancy firm in Ghana used the convergent parallel design to gather data on social media platforms, which helped them inform their social media strategy, and consequently helped them to gain thousands of followers on LinkedIn and Twitter — to become one of the most engaging consultancy firms on social media in Ghana.

Investigating the use of the MMA in social media research has become a primary concern within the field of social sciences. Over the past few decades, it has become evident that the field of MMR is widely accepted amongst social science scholars and researchers. In their studies, Creswell (2016); Johnson and Onwuegbuzie (2004); Johnson, Onwuegbuzie and Turner (2017); McKim (2017); and Mertens et al., (2016:2) have recognised MMR as the 'third' research paradigm, alongside qualitative and quantitative research methods. This acceptance of MMR as an independent and legitimate field in social sciences is apparent, with the ever-increasing number of publications in the field of MMR, and the launch of the *Journal of Mixed Methods Research*, as well as the formation of the Mixed Methods International Research Association (Creswell, 2016:215). Since MMR is an increasingly important area in research, this chapter provides an exciting opportunity to advance research knowledge in social media research. Hence, in this chapter, the central aspects of the MMA which the reader should be aware of when carrying out research studies, and how the approach can be applied to the field of social media research, are critically examined.

In the following section, the MMA and its definitions as well as the definition adopted in this chapter are presented. In addition, the various facets of these definitions are illustrated in a figure that presents the relationship that exists between the qualitative and quantitative approaches, and the MMA.

6.2 THE MIXED-METHODS APPROACH

Using more than one method in natural and social science research is not a new phenomenon. It can be traced to as early as the 1950s to the work of Campbell and Fiske (1959) who used the triangulation method in their study. Further use of more than one method in research specifically the MMA is also evident in the earlier works of Rossman and Wilson (1985), Jahoda, Lazarsfeld, and Zeisel (1933) and Webb, Campbell, Schwarz and Sechrest (1966). Several researchers and scholars whose work spans many decades argue that using the MMA in research aids researchers to conduct more efficient research and enables them to understand social phenomena more holistically, as opposed to when researchers use the mono-method approach (see, for example, Jahoda, Lazarsfeld, & Zeisel, 1933; Webb et al., 1966; Rossman & Wilson, 1985; Mertens et al., 2011; Whitehead & Schneider, 2012:268; Mertens et al., 2016; Guetterman et al., 2017; McKim, 2017:202).

6.2.1 Defining the mixed-methods approach

It is essential to clarify exactly what is meant by the MMR. Several definitions have surfaced over the past few years. The approach is largely described as the process of conducting research by mixing qualitative and quantitative methods. There is also consensus amongst the following researchers (Teddlie & Tashakkori, 2009; Onwuegbuzie & Combs, 2011:1; Creswell, 2016:36; Johnson, Onwuegbuzie & Turner, 2017:112; McKim, 2017:202) that the MMA is a research method that considers numerous perspectives, and stances from both qualitative and quantitative methods, combines these perspectives in one study, and uses them to gather data and to draw research conclusions. This view is supported by Leech and Onwuegbuzie (2009:265), who describe MMA as a method that consists of the processes of gathering, examining, and interpreting quantitative and qualitative data in a single study. With this approach, strengths from one method can be used to compensate for the weaknesses of the other to produce superior research results.

An early definition by Greene, Caracelli and Graham (1989:256), suggests that MMA integrates at least one quantitative method that is designed to collect numbers and at least one qualitative method that is designed to gather words. Another definition of MMA is offered by Creswell and Plano Clark (2007:5) who define the approach as an investigation method that combines quantitative and qualitative approaches with the sole purpose of providing a better understanding of research problems than a single approach offers. All these definitions have similarities as they all describe MMA as a method that mixes both qualitative and quantitative methods to enhance a researcher's understanding of a research phenomenon.

However, for the sake of this chapter, Creswell's (2016:2) definition of MMA is adopted as a research approach that is used to gather both quantitative and qualitative data, which are integrated, analysed and then interpreted based on the collective strengths of both data sets, with the objective of understanding a research problem. This definition has some similarities with previous definitions mentioned above; however, it provides further useful information that through the MMA, researchers can utilise strengths from both qualitative and quantitative methods to produce superior results. From the above definitions of MMA, an overview of these definitions is provided in Table 6.1 below.

Table 6.1:   Overview of MMA definitions

Author(s)	MMA definitions
Onwuegbuzie and Combs (2011:1) Creswell (2016) Teddlie and Tashakkori (2009) Johnson, Onwuegbuzie and Turner (2017) McKim (2017)	• Combines QUAL and QUAN methods in one study • Gathers data and draws research conclusions
Leech and Onwuegbuzie (2009)	• Gathers and examines QUAN and QUAL data • Interprets both data sets in a single study
Greene, Caracelli and Graham (1989)	• Integrates one QUAN method (designed to collect numbers), and one QUAL method (designed to gather words)
Creswell and Plano Clark (2007)	• Investigation method • Combines QUAN and QUAL approaches • Provides a better understanding of research problems
Creswell (2016:2)	• Gathers both QUAN and QUAL data • Integrates, analyses, and interprets data • Research-based on the collective strengths of both data sets • Enhances understanding of a research problem • Produces superior results

Source: Author

The definitions in Table 6.1 all have some similarities, namely, the combination of qualitative and quantitative methods into one study, and the analysis and interpretation of the data sets in a single study. However, the definition offered by Creswell (2016:2) provides further insights into the definition, namely, combining the strengths of both qualitative and quantitative methods and producing superior research results. Further analysis of these definitions reveals the relationship that exists between the MMA and the qualitative and quantitative approaches. This relationship and the boundaries of the MMA are illustrated in Figure 6.1 below.

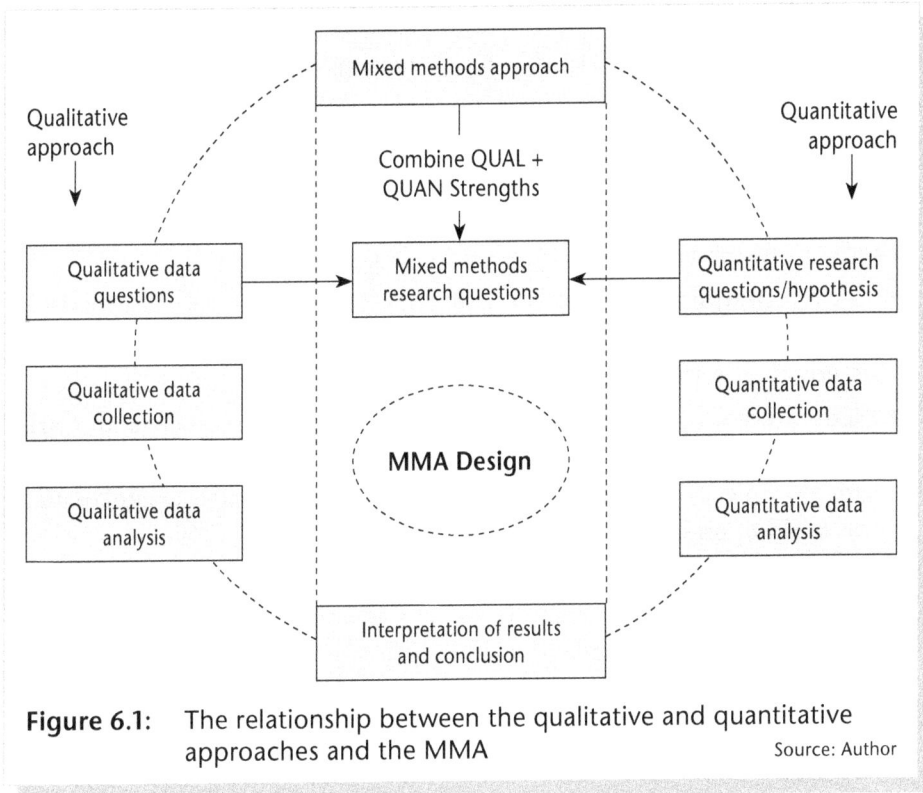

Figure 6.1: The relationship between the qualitative and quantitative approaches and the MMA   Source: Author

Figure 6.1 illustrates the relationship that exists between qualitative and quantitative research approaches, and the MMA. This illustration emanates from the definitions provided in this section. These definitions have described MMA in a variety of ways—however, there are clear similarities in these definitions, and these are summarised in Figure 6.1. In summary, the figure illustrates that the MMA combines elements from both the qualitative and quantitative research approaches, for example, the use of both qualitative and quantitative viewpoints, data collection, analysis and inference techniques. According to the definitions provided by Creswell and Plano Clark (2007), and Creswell (2016:2), combining these elements in one study increases the depth of understanding of a research phenomenon, and provides researchers with opportunities to compensate for inherent method weaknesses, thus producing superior results.

In the next section, the rationale for conducting a mixed-methods study, as well as the advantages and limitations of the MMA, are discussed.

6.2.2 Rationale for conducting a mixed-methods study

Previous mixed-methods studies have identified several rationales for conducting a mixed-methods study. Several researchers (Greene, Caracelli, & Graham, 1989; Collins, Johnson & Onwuegbuzie, 2004:22; Collins, Onwuegbuzie & Sutton, 2006; Onwuegbuzie & Combs, 2010:16; Plano Clark et al. 2015:302) have identified five rationales for conducting a mixed-methods study, namely:

- **Triangulation**: a researcher can converge and corroborate research findings from both qualitative and quantitative methods in a single study that is studying the same phenomenon.

- **Complementarity**: a researcher can elaborate, enhance and clarify research findings from one method with results from the other method, for example, using the qualitative method to provide further explanations or build upon initial quantitative results.

- **Development**: a researcher can use findings from one method to inform the other method, for example, using document analysis and interviews to improve a web-based survey.

- **Initiation**: a researcher can ascertain whether there are any contradictions in the findings. The results will be used to examine and reframe the research questions for the other method.

- **Expansion**: a researcher can expand the scope of their study (breadth, depth and range) by using different methods and ways of inquiry, resulting in more comprehensive results.

In addition to these rationales, there is further justification for choosing to use the MMA. The justification lies in the advantages of using the approach. One of the key considerations of every researcher before conducting a mixed-methods study is to understand whether an MMA is appropriate for the study in question (Creswell & Plano Clark, 2011:19) compared to using the mono-method design. This is only possible when a researcher understands the worldview perspectives of the approach, typologies, and designs, as well as the advantages and limitations of the approach. This understanding will enable researchers to choose the appropriate research design and conduct their research effectively. Hence, in the following section, the advantages and limitations of using this approach is discussed.

(i)   Advantages of using the mixed-methods approach

There are several advantages of using the MMA that have been identified in the literature (Creswell, 2007; Castro, Kellison, Boyd & Kopak 2010:356; Creswell, 2011:268–279; Creswell & Plano Clark, 2011:12; Johnson &

Onwuegbuzie, 2011:8; Malina, Nørreklit & Selto 2011:63; Molina-Azorin & Fetters 2019:279). Using the MMA has the following advantages:

- **Reduces the impact of weaknesses of both methods:** Both qualitative and quantitative approaches have weaknesses. As a result, using both approaches in data collection and analysis reduces the impact of these weaknesses on the research, and a researcher can answer questions that cannot be answered by quantitative or qualitative methods alone.

- **Increases a researcher's understanding of a research phenomenon:** Data collected with the aid of both methods adds deeper meaning and understanding of a research phenomenon. Words, images, and the narrative (qualitative approach) add more meaning to numbers (quantitative approach), and likewise, numbers add precision to words, pictures and the narrative. Consequently, the MMA can add more insights and comprehension that might have been missed when a single method is used. In addition, researchers can draw research conclusions with more superior results, and they can get a more comprehensive picture of a research phenomenon.

- **Increases value and credibility of the research results:** Using the qualitative and quantitative approaches provides additional evidence and support for the findings (for example) using one method to corroborate the findings of the other methods in one study that is studying the same phenomenon or using results from one method to develop and inform the other method. This leads to stronger research conclusions and increases the credibility of the research findings.

- **Can answer a broader range of research questions and provide evidence for theory:** When utilising only one method, researchers are confined to answer a limited range of research questions. Consequently, using both methods ensures that a broader range of questions is answered. Furthermore, researchers can produce more complete knowledge which is necessary for informing theory and practice.

- **Engages various stakeholders and involves them in research:** the MMA encourages stakeholder involvement in research for example stakeholders from both qualitative and quantitative methods are involved in a single study. Involving various stakeholders is vital in addressing challenging research phenomena.

(ii)   Limitations of the mixed-methods approach

There are several limitations identified in literature regarding the MMA (Johnson & Onwuegbuzie, 2004:15; Castro, Kellison, Boyd & Kopak 2010:356; Creswell & Plano Clark, 2011; Guetterman et al., 2017:13; Schutt, 2015:556). These are mentioned below:

- **Time consuming**: researchers use two methods. Therefore, it is more time consuming than when a single method is used. Data collection and analysis would also need more effort and time.

- **Expensive**: Using two methods increases the time involved in gathering and analysing data. This is highly costly. Hence, researchers would need to source for funding to carry out their research effectively.

- **A broader set of skills is needed**: researchers need to have skills in both qualitative and quantitative methods. If they do not have the expertise, they may need to collaborate with different researchers that have the required expertise or personally undergo training—which often is time consuming and expensive. However, collaboration may be challenging due to scholarly differences in methodological preferences and philosophical stances. Researchers may also have to learn about various methods and approaches and understand how to mix them appropriately.

- **More labour is needed**: it may be difficult for one researcher to carry out both qualitative and quantitative research, especially if two or more approaches are expected to be used concurrently. This would mean that researcher assistance is needed from other team members.

- **The field is still growing**: the field is still growing, there may not be complete answers as to how to solve problems of mixing paradigms, handling and interpreting conflicting findings, or how to qualitatively analyse quantitative data.

Reflecting on the suitability of the MMA for your social media study

Based on what you have read in this section, you have learnt that the MMA is a method that combines both qualitative and quantitative methods in a single study, to increase the understanding of a research phenomenon. Essentially, a researcher should be inclined to choose an MMA when quantitative or qualitative data alone are not sufficient to fully understand their research questions.

Think about this before choosing the best method for your social media study:

- Are you in need of different, multiple perspectives?
- Do you need to explain quantitative results?
- Do you need to confirm quantitative measures with qualitative ones?
- Do you need to better contextualise instruments, measures, or interventions?

Then, the MMA offers the perfect solution!

6.3   USING MIXED-METHODS APPROACH IN SOCIAL MEDIA RESEARCH

As explained in much detail in chapter 1, over the past few years, it has become apparent that social media has become an integral part in everyday life, with social media platforms playing an enormous role in the life of individuals, communities, businesses, politics, and the economy (McCay-Peet & Quan-Haase, 2017:13). Consequently, social media and their technologies have attracted much attention from users, as well as researchers who have begun to carry out research and publish works about social media use (Snelson, 2016:1). Ngai, Tao and Moon (2015:33) support this view and argue that social media have transformed the lives of several individuals globally and attracted much attention in the industry and academia. This interest has also arisen as a result of the increased production of user-generated content on social media platforms.

Social media can be defined as:

[V]arious forms of world-wide-web applications such as blogs, micro-blogging (for example Twitter), social networking sites (for example, Facebook), social bookmarking (for example, Digg) or video and image sharing (for example, Flickr), file-sharing platforms and wikis (for example Wikipedia collaborative encyclopaedia) (Fuchs, 2014:32; Poynter, 2010:160).

According to Davis et al., (2012). Through these web-based and mobile applications, individuals and organisations can create, engage, and share content in digital environments through multi-way communication. Shirky (2008) on the other hand describes social media as tools that allow individuals to share information with one another and take joint action independent from traditional institutions and organisations. All these definitions though possessing slight differences—agree that social media enables individuals and organisations to communicate with each other via world-wide-web applications. Due to the influence of social media, researchers have become highly interested in understanding the role and impact of social media in society (Snelson, 2016:1). Hence, the field of social media research emerged, and the body of literature is also growing steadily; however, trends in the research designs are not well known (Snelson, 2016:3).

In an attempt to discover the mixed-methods designs used by researchers in social media research, Snelson (2016) reviewed 55 mixed-methods publications from 2007 through 2013, where social media played a role in the research. Evidence from this review reveals that many of the studies involving the MMA followed a design that resembles Creswell and Plano Clark's basic mixed-methods typology (convergent parallel, explanatory sequential, exploratory sequential). A summary of the results of Snelson's mixed-methods study is presented in Figure 6.2 below.

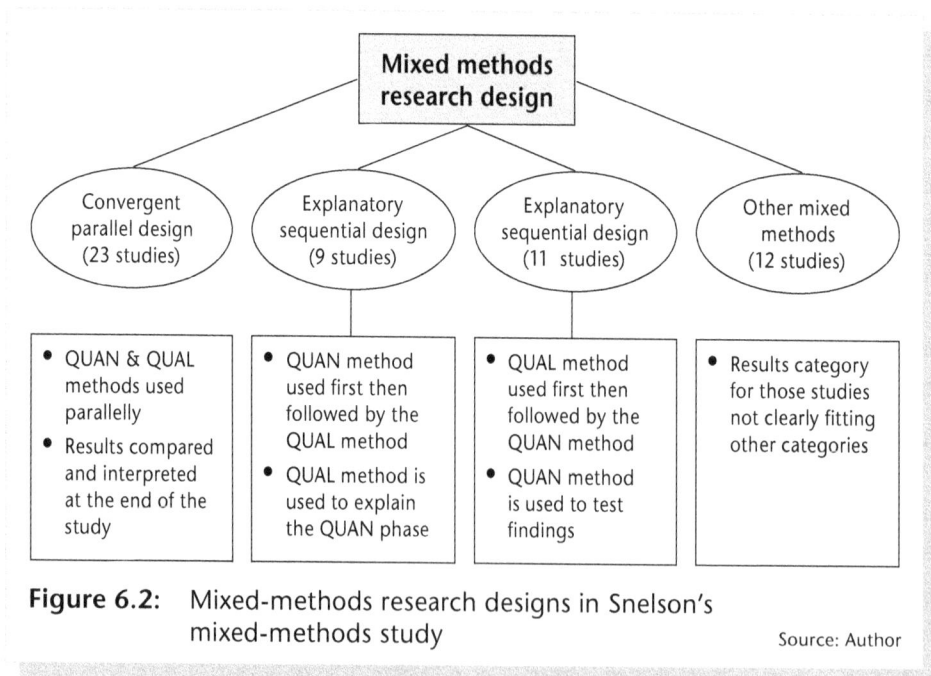

Figure 6.2:   Mixed-methods research designs in Snelson's mixed-methods study

Source: Author

Figure 6.2 above presents a summary of Snelson's findings. Most social media research studies that were reviewed in his study used Creswell and Plano Clark's basic mixed-methods typology. This approach seems to receive greater attention amongst scholars and researchers due to its straightforward design, which is easy to apply. This typology, as well as other typologies and designs, are discussed at length in the following sections; however, a discussion of the MMA designs that commence the paradigmatic perspectives in MMR are first explained in the following section.

6.4   PARADIGMATIC PERSPECTIVES IN MIXED-METHODS RESEARCH

There have been various debates in the literature about the use of the term paradigm. Several researchers and scholars have different opinions about what this concept is all about. Thus, different definitions have surfaced in literature. Johnson and Onwuegbuzie (2004:24) have defined paradigms as beliefs, values, and techniques that are shared by a group of individuals about the nature and conduct of research. Adams (2015:22) concurs with this definition and defines paradigms as a collection of views, values, and methods, which are collectively shared by the members of a certain group of people. Further examples can be seen in Morgan's (2007:52) work, where he reviewed several definitions and identified four different perspectives or descriptions of paradigms that can be identified in the literature.

- **Paradigms as worldviews**: ways of experiencing and ideas about the world, as well as beliefs about morals, values, and aesthetics.

- **Paradigms as epistemological stances**: distinctive belief systems that have an impact on how research is conducted (for example) how questions are designed and answered. This stance also focuses on an individual's philosophical worldviews.

- **Paradigms as common beliefs in a group of individuals in a specialty area**: common beliefs within a group or a community of researchers who agree about the meaningful questions in research as well as the procedures which are most appropriate for answering the questions.

- **Paradigms as model examples of research**: model examples that exist to guide how research is conducted.

This chapter will, however, not delve into too much detail as to which of the above-described paradigms is most appropriate. It is, nevertheless, emphasised that in this chapter, paradigms are both epistemological stances and models of examples on how research should be conducted. Researchers such as Creswell and Plano Clark (2011), Shannon-Baker (2016:321), and

Creswell (2014:35) advocate the use of paradigms in research, and they have published works that provide guidance in research. In this vein, Onwuegbuzie and Frels (2013:11) state that lack of philosophical direction in a mixed-methods study affects the quality of results. Similarly, Kivunja and Kuyini (2017:26) state that paradigms have an influence on what phenomenon should be studied, in what way it should be studied, and the interpretation of the study. Other researchers, however, opine that paradigms are not necessarily helpful in research, but harmful as they tend to force researchers to operate within certain belief constellations (Maxwell, 2011). However, in this chapter, the opinions of Creswell (2014:35); Creswell and Plano Clark (2011); Onwuegbuzie and Frels (2013:11); Kivunja and Kuyini (2017:26); Shannon-Baker (2016:321), that paradigms are a guiding light to research, and provide researchers with philosophical orientation for studies, guidance during the research process, for example, the choice of methodology and methods, and direction on how meaning can be constructed from data gathered during research, are supported. It is, therefore, advisable that researchers should state the paradigm in which they are placing their research.

Since MMR is still a growing field of research and researchers, especially novice researchers need enough guidance to conduct effective research, paradigms offer the ideal framework that guides research. For this reason, an overview of the various paradigms that researchers can apply in research and how they can be applied to guide mixed-methods studies are put forward. There are currently 13 philosophical stances for a mixed-methods inquiry that can be identified in the literature. However, there are three most recognised stances, namely, pragmatism (emphasis lies on the outcome and end product), transformative-emancipatory (emphasis lies on power, privilege, and the voice of marginalised groups) and the dialectical pluralism (argues for using multiple paradigms together) (Onwuegbuzie & Frels, 2013:9). These paradigms are discussed in the following subsections.

6.4.1 Pragmatism

Since MMR is an emerging field, the field must use a paradigm that considers insights from both qualitative and quantitative research. Pragmatism has been identified by several researchers as a philosophical companion for MMR (Johnson & Onwuegbuzie, 2006:16; Morgan, 2007:73), and as a foundation for the discipline (Tashakkori & Teddlie, 1998). Pragmatism helps to shed more light on how research approaches from both methods qualitative and quantitative can be mixed and designed appropriately. Furthermore, it is a flexible approach, which allows researchers to choose freely—the quantitative and qualitative assumptions that best suit their study needs and research purposes (Creswell, 2014:39; Johnson & Onwuegbuzie, 2006:17). It also focuses on the outcome or product of the research (Johnson & Onwuegbuzie, 2006), and the researcher can maintain subjectivity in their individual reflections and objectivity during data collection and analysis (Shannon-Baker, 2016:232). Pragmatism offers an optimal philosophical foundation for the MMA since it is flexible and allows mixed-methods researchers to use both quantitative and qualitative methods to collect and analyse data, rather than limiting them to only one method.

Therefore, methodologists should further discuss and consider pragmatism as a philosophical and methodological solution (Creswell, 2014).

6.4.2   The transformative-emancipatory approach

The transformative-emancipatory approach is a philosophical assumption held by a group of researchers. This perspective according to Mertens (2010) holds the assumption that research inquiry should be interlinked with politics and a political agenda that confronts social injustice, at all crucial levels. Similarly, Shannon-Baker (2014:38) posits that this perspective is typified by the deliberate collaboration with minority and marginalised groups, as it was established when there was an increased need to focus on national awareness on issues related to race, class, gender, and disabilities. Thus, the approach focuses on addressing the needs of marginalised groups and individuals (Creswell, 2014:23; Shannon-Baker, 2014) by focusing on the following:

- Studying the lives and experiences of various groups of people in society that have been marginalised, with the sole purpose of enhancing social justice and human rights.
- Analysing how the lives of these marginalised groups have been constrained by their oppressors and the strategies they use to resist, object to, and overthrow these constraints.
- Positively impacting the lives of research participants by providing a voice for them, raising their awareness and advancing an agenda for change.
- Positively impacting the institutions in which these individuals work or live.
- Allowing the research participants to assist in designing research questions, collecting data, and analysing the information—with the sole purpose of minimising biases.

Shannon-Baker is of the opinion that such studies should be carried out by using the triangulation approach for mixed methods. Furthermore, such kinds of research in marginalised communities require that the researcher builds strong ties with the community and understands the community and its people. Mixed-methods researchers would, therefore, need to plan and include the relationship-building phase as part of their qualitative phase in the sequential exploratory design (Creswell & Plano Clark, 2011), which begins with the qualitative approach and ends with the quantitative approach.

6.4.3   Dialectical pluralism

Dialectical pluralism is a philosophical stance and is the most recent of all the 13 philosophical stances in literature—as it builds on the dialectical approach (Onwuegbuzie & Frels, 2013). The dialectical approach argues for the use of two or more combined paradigms in a mixed research study (Tashakkori & Teddlie, 2010). Consequently, dialectical pluralism is inclusive in nature and allows the integration of two or more philosophical stances that may represent the qualitative (for example social constructionism) or quantitative (for example post-positivism) paradigms within a single study (Onwuegbuzie & Frels, 2013:12). Furthermore, Johnson (2012:752–753) posits that dialectical pluralism is a meta-paradigm (considers multiple paradigms including competing paradigms and gathers the key considerations into a workable whole), dialectically listens, considers various disciplines, stakeholders and theories, and continually assesses and improves research outcomes and the use process.

6.4.4   Post-positivism

While positivism remains the leading paradigm in quantitative research, post-positivist thinking is also on the rise, especially in the social sciences and education fields. Post-positivism is thus a mixed new paradigm consisting of both positivist and interpretive worldviews and is anchored in the belief that analytical facts alone are not enough to solve a study's research problem (Kelly, Dowling & Miller, 2018). Researchers adopting a post-positivism worldview argue for the triangulation of qualitative and quantitative research data (thus multiple data sources) and do not support the idea that there is one best way to uncover the 'truth' (Kelly et al., 2018).

Important takeaway

As a scholar or researcher of social media, you must understand the appropriate paradigm or philosophical stance that best informs your mixed-methods study, and the selection of an appropriate mixed-methods design. Factors such as objectives of the study and the phenomenon under investigation will help to inform researchers about the most appropriate paradigm and design to employ in a study.

Figure 6.3 below shows the relationship that exists between paradigms or philosophical views, research designs and methods. The next section connects these dots by discussing the various typologies and mixed-method designs researchers can utilise in their studies.

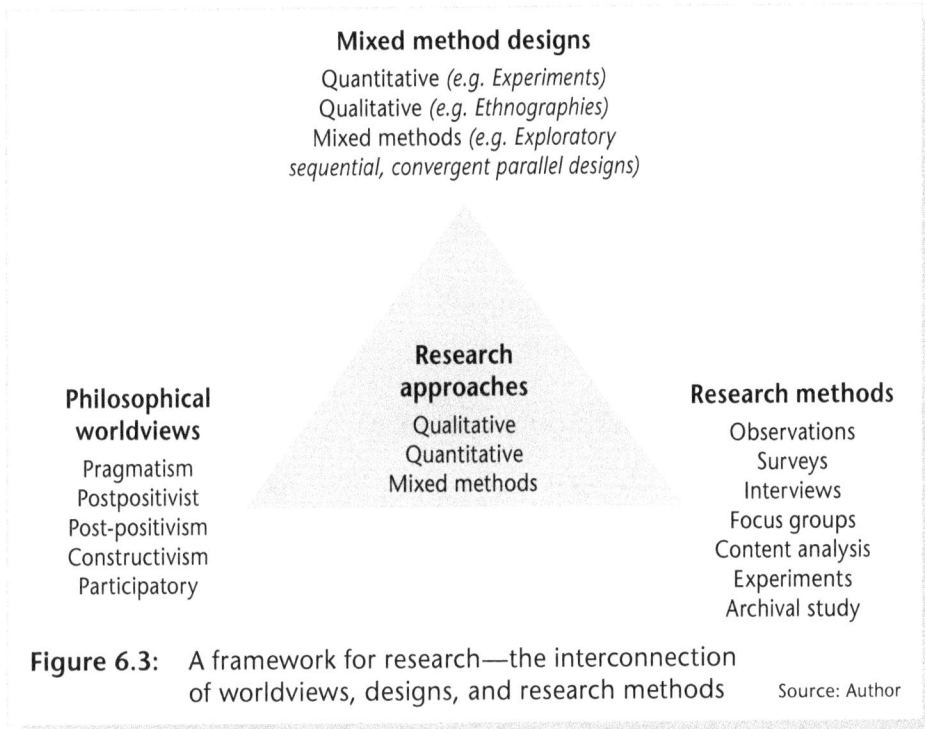

Mixed method designs
Quantitative *(e.g. Experiments)*
Qualitative *(e.g. Ethnographies)*
Mixed methods *(e.g. Exploratory sequential, convergent parallel designs)*

Research approaches
Qualitative
Quantitative
Mixed methods

Philosophical worldviews

Pragmatism
Postpositivist
Post-positivism
Constructivism
Participatory

Research methods

Observations
Surveys
Interviews
Focus groups
Content analysis
Experiments
Archival study

Figure 6.3:   A framework for research—the interconnection of worldviews, designs, and research methods   Source: Author

6.5   TYPOLOGIES AND DESIGNS OF MIXED-METHODS APPROACHES

There are several ways of looking at mixed-method designs. A number of academics have proposed looking at designs through the typological approach (Creswell & Plano Clark 2011; Johnson & Onwuegbuzie 2004; Leech & Onwuegbuzie 2009; Teddlie & Tashakkori 2006); while, Guest (2012) focuses on an alternative approach called Common Descriptive Dimensions, and Maxwell and Loomis (2003) emphasise the Systems Theory. However, in this chapter, the typological approach is adopted.

It is important to note that the MMR field is still in its adolescent stage. Hence, it is not surprising that novice researchers and scholars may find it relatively difficult to carry out MMR studies and to choose the appropriate mixed-method design for their studies. To simplify this process, several academics have developed several typologies that describe several mixed-methods designs, and how to apply them. Typologies are designed for the sole purpose of establishing order and simplifying complex phenomena in research (Guest, 2012:141). This is done by ensuring that categories established within typologies are well detailed, simple, and broad enough to describe the phenomena under study (Guest 2012:141). Some of the academics who have developed mixed-methods typologies are Creswell (2014); Creswell and Plano Clark (2011); Johnson and Onwuegbuzie (2004); Leech and Onwuegbuzie (2009); Maxwell and Loomis (2003); Onwuegbuzie and Collins (2007); Tashakkori and Teddlie (1998); and Teddlie and Tashakkori (2006). Within each typology, there are research designs which are crucial in providing guidelines on thoroughly conducting mixed-methods studies that is, to meet research objectives (Creswell et al., 2003:159).

The following sections provide four examples of typologies and mixed-method designs that apply to social media research.

6.5.1   The three-dimensional typology

Leech and Onwuegbuzie (2009) carried out a content analysis of various mixed-methods designs, which led to the development of their three-dimensional typology of mixed-method designs. They are of the opinion that most of the existing typologies can be summarised within their three dimensions, namely: (i) level of mixing—there are two ways of mixing designs, the partially mixed or fully mixed designs; (ii) time orientation—concurrent versus sequential (*are the quantitative and qualitative phases mixed at the same time or one after the other?*), and (c) emphasis of approaches—equal status versus dominant status (*do both quantitative and qualitative methods hold an equal level of importance or one of them holds a more dominant status?*). This three-dimensional typology yields the following eight MMR design matrices:

- **Partially mixed concurrent equal status designs**: (P1) refers to a study that employs partially mixed concurrent phases of quantitative and qualitative methods, with both methods having the same level of importance and status.

- **Partially mixed concurrent dominant status designs**: (P2) relates to a study that employs partially mixed concurrent phases of quantitative and qualitative methods, with one of the two methods having a greater status than the other.

- **Partially mixed sequential equal status designs**: (P3) pertains to a study employing partially mixed sequential phases of qualitative and quantitative methods, with both methods having the same level of importance and status.

- **Partially mixed sequential dominant status designs**: (P4) refers to a study that employs partially mixed sequential phases of qualitative and quantitative methods, with one method having a greater status than the other.

- **Fully mixed concurrent equal status designs**: (F1) refers to a study that mixes both the qualitative and quantitative methods equally within one or more or across the following four sections of a single study: the research objective, type of data and operations, type of analysis, and type of inference. The two methods are mixed concurrently at one or more stages of research.

- **Fully mixed concurrent dominant status designs**: (F2) pertains to a study that mixes qualitative and quantitative methods within one or more or across the following three sections of a single study: the research objective, type of data and operations, type of analysis and inference. The two methods are mixed concurrently at one or more stages or across the components, with one method having more importance and dominance.

- **Fully mixed sequential equal status designs**: (F3) pertains to a study that mixes both qualitative and quantitative methods equally within one or more, or across the stages of the study process, with both methods occurring sequentially at one or more stages or across the various stages of the study.

- **Fully mixed sequential dominant status designs**: (F4) refers to a study that mixes qualitative and quantitative methods within one or more, or across the various stages of the study process, with both methods occurring sequentially at one or more stages or across the various stages of the study. One method is given more importance and dominance.

The three-dimensional typology emphasises the level of mixing, time orientation and whether the methods have equal status, or one method has a dominant status over the other. The eight matrices provide a clear and concise guideline, and they simplify the selection of the appropriate design for the researcher.

6.5.2 The mixed-model designs and mixed-method designs

Similar to the three-dimensional typology, Johnson and Onwuegbuzie (2004) developed two typologies after analysing several typologies. There are two major types of mixed models (that is) the mixed-model designs (*qualitative and quantitative approaches are mixed within or across the stages of the research process*), and the mixed-method (*a quantitative phase and a qualitative phase are mixed in an overall research study*). These types of designs will be discussed in the following sections, beginning with the six mixed-model designs, then followed by nine mixed-method designs.

(i)   The six mixed-model designs by Johnson and Onwuegbuzie

When adopting the six mixed-model designs, the researcher must select the dominant paradigm aligned to their research objectives, whether the qualitative or quantitative objectives. The designs are shown in Figure 6.4 below.

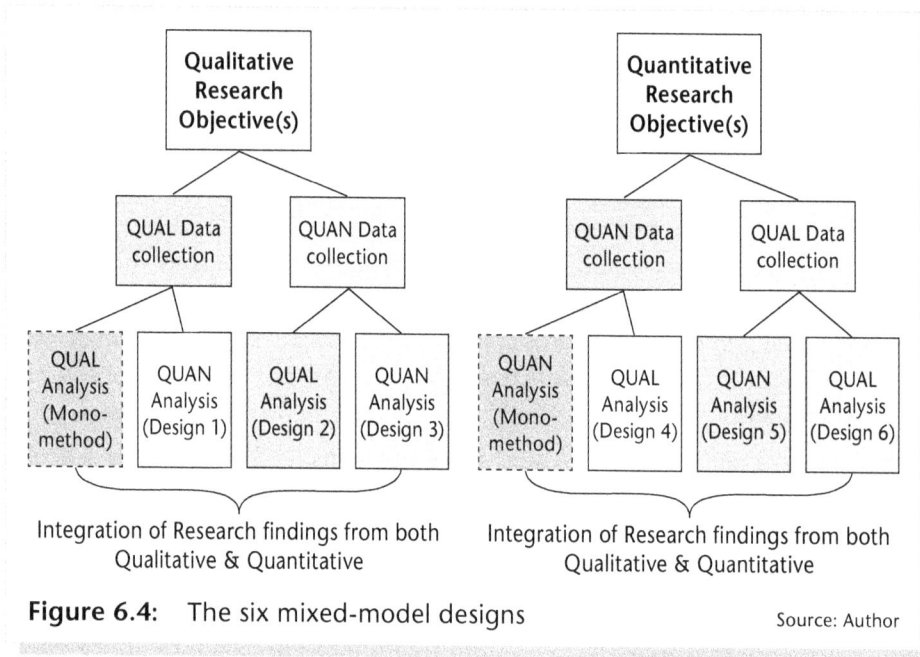

Figure 6.4:   The six mixed-model designs   Source: Author

In Figure 6.4, designs one to six are the six mixed-model designs; while the other two designs that follow the following steps: *Qualitative research objective(s), QUAL Data Collection and QUAL Analysis*; and *Quantitative research objective(s), QUAN Data Collection and QUAN Analysis* are mono-method designs. This figure shows a detailed research process and the combination of qualitative and quantitative methods across the stages of the research process. The mixing of these methods is called 'across-stage mixed-model designs' (Johnson & Onwuegbuzie 2004:20).

An example of how you can apply an across-stage mixed-model design to your study, with qualitative research objectives, a) you can utilise the qualitative data collection method by using the content analysis *(for example, analysing documents through the aid of a codebook)*, and b) use the quantitative method *(for example, using the basic descriptive statistics analysis)*. This would be the design 1 in Figure 6.4. The six mixed model is detailed and concise. It explains the steps a researcher can take during research in a way they can easily understand, and how to effectively apply the across-stage mixed-method design to a study. In the following section, an example of a mixed-method design, which mixes a quantitative and a qualitative phase in an overall research study, is presented.

(ii)   *The nine mixed-method designs by Johnson and Onwuegbuzie*

When selecting a mixed-method design, the researcher must consider and choose whether they will function within one dominant paradigm or not, and whether they want to conduct the research phases concurrently or sequentially. Furthermore, the researcher must ensure that the findings are mixed at a certain stage during the research process, for example, a qualitative phase might be conducted first, so that it informs the quantitative phase; or, the qualitative and quantitative phases are conducted concurrently, and the findings are mixed during the interpretation phase (Johnson & Onwuegbuzie 2004). This relationship is explained more in Figure 6.5 below.

The Concurrent Designs

Concurrent & Equal Status
(Design 1)

| QUAL Method | + | QUAN Method |

Design 1

Concurrent & Dominant Status
(Designs 2 & 3)

| QUAL Method | + | Quan Method |

Design 2

| QUAN Method | + | Qual Method |

Design 3

The Sequential Designs

Sequential & Equal Status
(Design 4 & 5)

| QUAL Method | → | QUAN Method |

Design 4

| QUAN Method | → | QUAL Method |

Design 5

Sequential & Dominant Status
(Designs 6, 7, 8 & 9)

| QUAL Method | → | Quan Method |

Design 6

| Qual Method | → | QUAN Method |

Design 7

| QUAN Method | → | Qual Method |

Design 8

| Quan Method | → | QUAL Method |

Design 9

QUAL stands for the qualitative method,
QUAN stands for the quantitative method,
+ stands for concurrent,
→ stands for sequential,
CAPITAL LETTERS signify for high priority or weight,
lower-case letters signify lower priority or weight

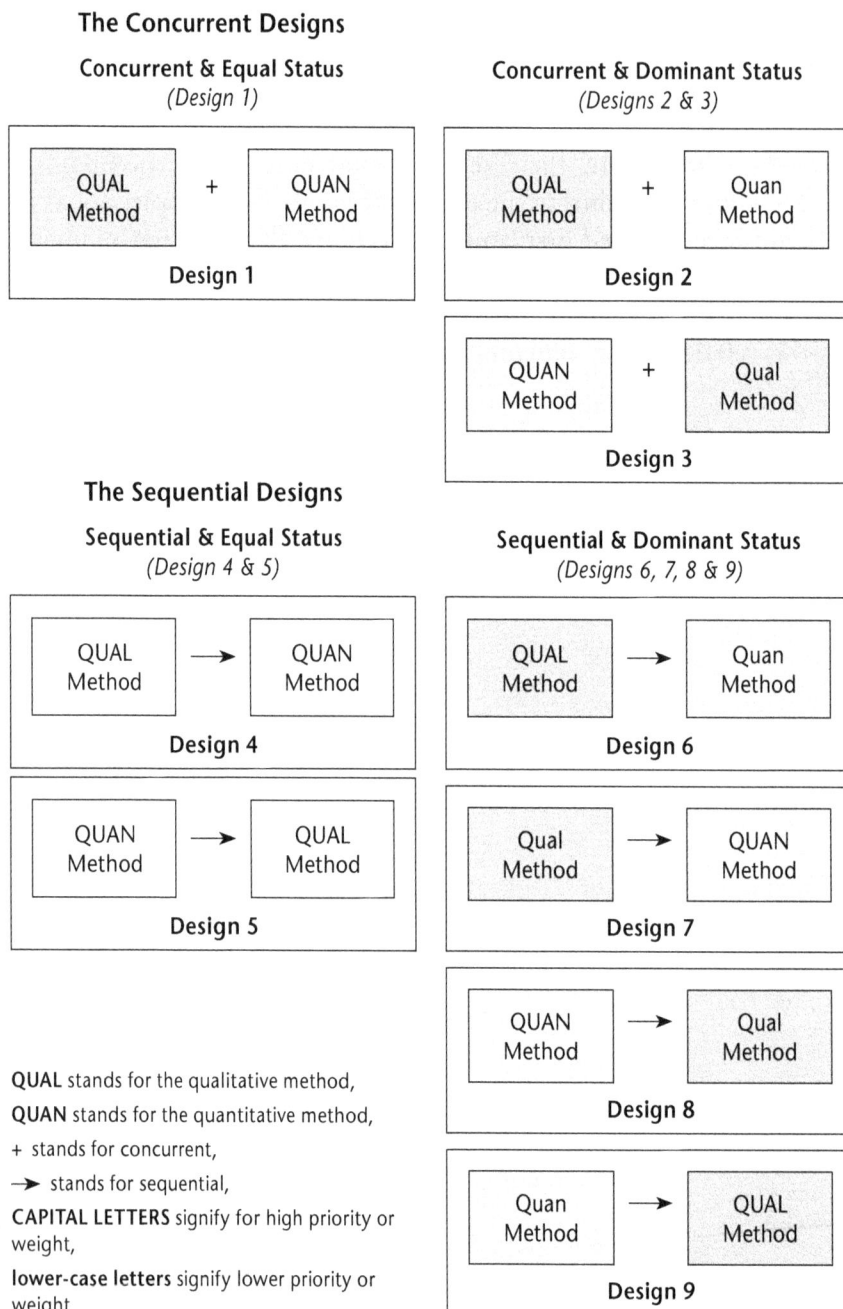

Figure 6.5:   The nine mixed-method designs

Source: Author

The mixed-method designs in Figure 6.5 lay emphasis on the choice and order of methods to be employed and the priority or status of their importance. This is a useful guide for researchers and follows a similar approach with Leech and Onwuegbuzie's three-dimensional typology.

6.5.3 The basic mixed-methods typology by Creswell and Plano Clark

There are four basic mixed-method designs proposed by Creswell and Plano Clark (2007) that researchers can apply to their mixed-methods studies. These are the convergent parallel design, the embedded design the explanatory sequential design and the exploratory sequential design (Creswell & Plano Clark, 2007), and these are discussed in the following subsections.

(i)   The convergent parallel mixed-method design

Creswell (2014:269) describes the convergent parallel mixed-method design as the most familiar design when it comes to the basic and advanced mixed-method designs. The key premise of this approach is that both qualitative and quantitative methods yield different types of information, with the qualitative method providing more detailed information of participants as well as their views; while the quantitative method produces numerical scores on instruments. With the convergent parallel mixed-methods design, researchers gather both quantitative and qualitative data from the same research phenomenon (for example) by measuring the same research questions or concept qualitatively and quantitatively, then the data is analysed separately, and findings are compared to see whether there are similarities or not. Figure 6.6 below illustrates this design.

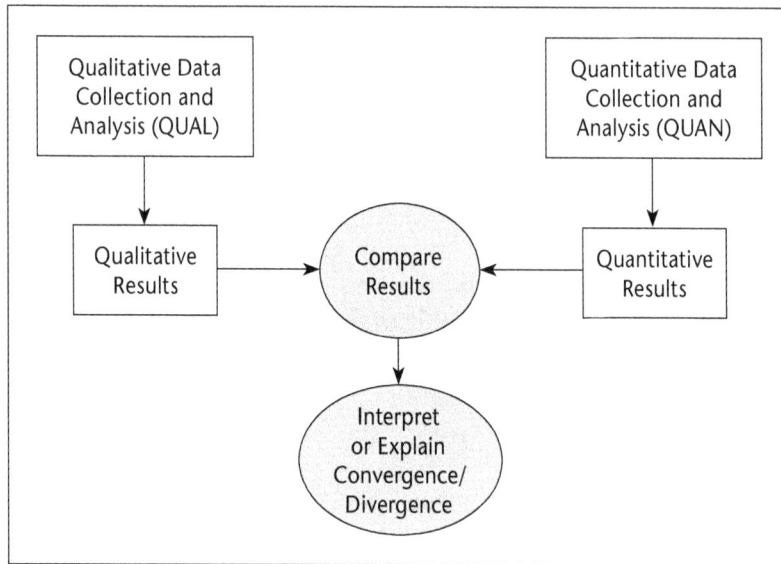

Figure 6.6:   The convergent parallel mixed-methods design

Source: Author

(ii)   The embedded design

The embedded design is a design in which either the qualitative or the quantitative data plays a supportive and secondary role to the method that plays the primary role in a study (Creswell et al., 2003). The researcher does this by embedding the supportive data within the method that plays the primary role (for example) a quantitative data can be embedded within a qualitative method (*quantitative design has less weight than the qualitative design*), or qualitative data is embedded within a quantitative method (*qualitative design has less weight than the quantitative design*). The idea behind this design is that a single data set or a mono-method design cannot fully answer a research problem, hence it is necessary to have both qualitative and quantitative data, to answer various types of questions (Creswell & Plano Clark, 2007).

(iii)   The explanatory sequential design

The explanatory sequential design, on the other hand, is described as a two-phase mixed-methods design (Creswell et al., 2003; Creswell & Plano Clark, 2007), whereby qualitative data is used to provide further explanation or build upon initial quantitative results (Creswell et al., 2003). Within this design, the quantitative method has more weight than the qualitative method and it begins with data collection and analysis of quantitative data, followed by the collection and analysis of qualitative data. Hence, the qualitative phase plays a more complementary role. Lastly, findings are integrated during the interpretation phase. Figure 6.7 below illustrates this research process.

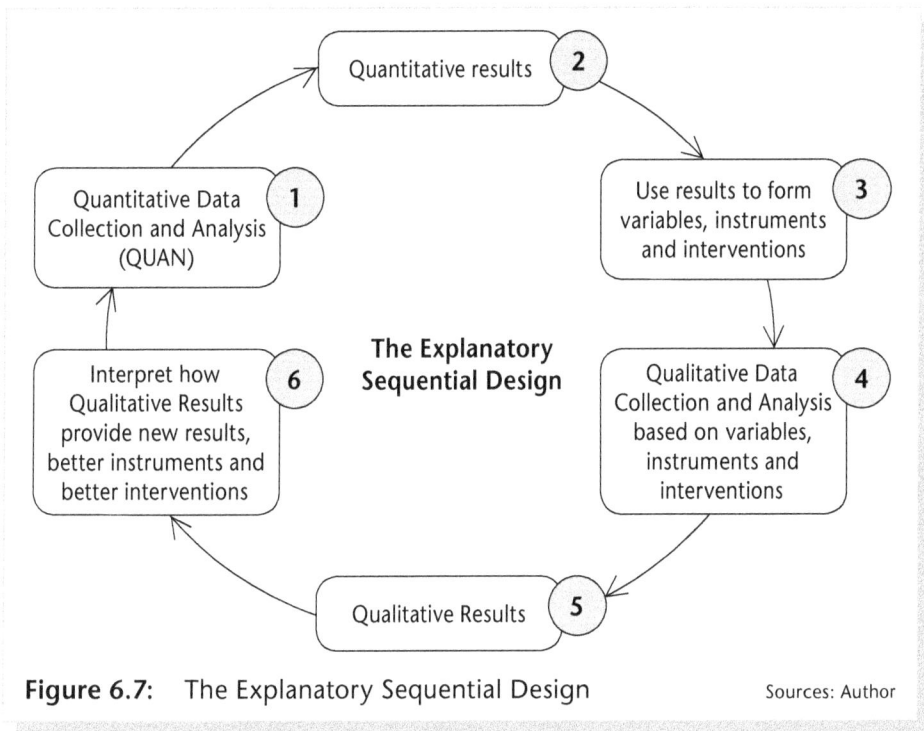

Figure 6.7:   The Explanatory Sequential Design   Sources: Author

(iv)   The exploratory sequential design

The exploratory sequential design has features similar to the explanatory sequential design. However, in this design, more weight is placed on the qualitative approach than the quantitative approach. It is also conducted in two phases, with the first phase being the qualitative data collection and analysis, followed by the quantitative data collection and analysis phase. This design assumes that exploration is needed (for example) if variables are unknown, and there are no theories to support the study or development of variables. Thus, the findings of the first phase help to inform the second phase, and findings from both phases are integrated during the interpretation phase. Figure 6.8 below illustrates this research process.

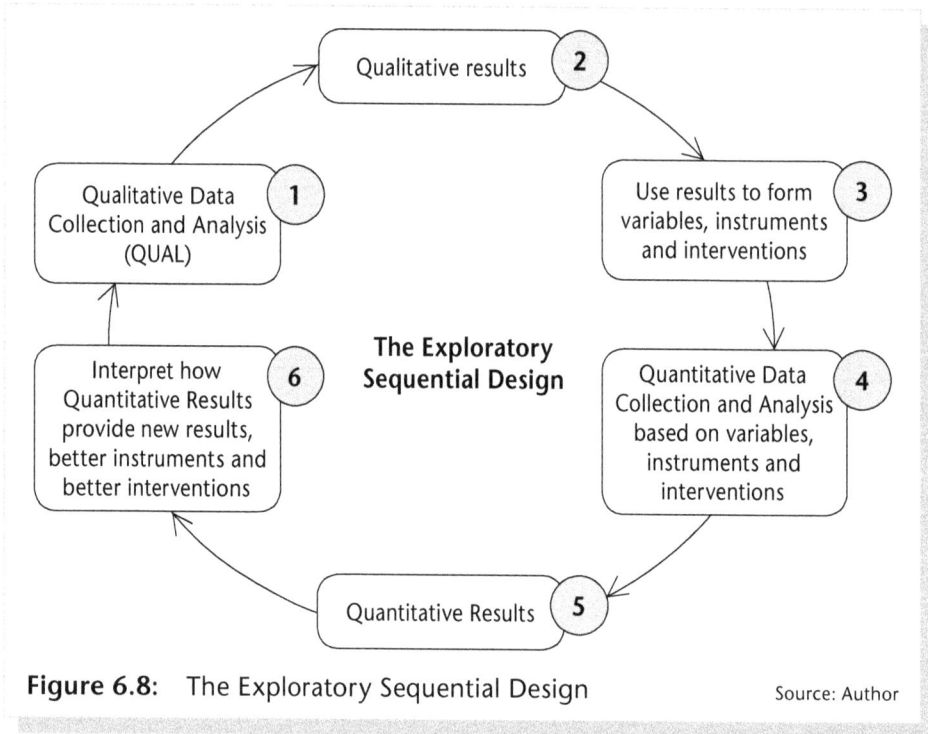

Figure 6.8:   The Exploratory Sequential Design   Source: Author

In addition, Table 6.2 below provides a summary of the components of the four designs discussed above.

Table 6.2:   Creswell and Plano Clark's basic mixed-methods designs

Designs	Exploratory	Explanatory	Convergent	Embedded
Purpose	A phenomenon that has not been studied clearly, is investigated to inform further research	Explains why, builds upon, and elaborates about a known phenomenon	One method provides more detailed information on participants and views while the other produces numerical scores on instruments	With two datasets, one data set provides a supportive, secondary role in a study that is based primarily on the other data type
Weight	The qualitative method has more weight	The quantitative method has more weight	Qualitative and quantitative methods have equal weight	Qualitative and quantitative designs have unequal weight

Designs	Exploratory	Explanatory	Convergent	Embedded
Timing	Sequential: QUAL design is used first then followed by the QUAN design (**QUAL → quan**)	Sequential: QUAN design is used first then followed by the QUAL design (**QUAL → qual**)	Concurrent: QUAL & QUAN designs are used at same time (**QUAN + QUAL**)	Concurrent or Sequential: (**QUAL (+)(→) quan**) (**QUAN (+)(→) qual**)
Merge Data	Merge data between the two phases	Merge data between the two phases	Comparison and analysis of separate datasets and interpretation	Embed one set of data (from the method playing the secondary role) within the larger dataset (the method playing the primary role)

Source: Adapted from Creswell and Plano Clark (2007)

Similar to Leech and Onwuegbuzie's (2009) three-dimensional typology, the basic mixed-method designs emphasise the choice and order of method to be employed, and the priority or status of the importance of the methods. This again is a useful guide for researchers who choose this design for their study.

Research by Snelson (2016), a review of 55 mixed-methods social media publications from 2007 through 2013, reveals that many studies involving the MMA followed a design that resembles Creswell and Plano Clark's basic mixed-methods typology (Creswell & Plano Clark, 2011; Creswell, 2014; Kong, Yaacob & Ariffin, 2018:152), with scholars using the convergent parallel (used in 23 studies), explanatory sequential (used in nine studies), exploratory sequential designs (use in 11 studies) (Snelson (2016). However, there was no evidence of the use of the embedded design in the research papers under study.

Table 6.3 below provides a summary of typologies and mixed-method designs for social media research.

Table 6.3   Summary of typologies and mixed-method designs for social
media researchers

Typology	Design	Author(s)
Three-dimensional typology	Consists of eight designs (*Four partially mixed and four fully mixed-method designs*). The premise of this typology is that mixing of mixed-method designs is carried out in three levels (i) level of mixing (*partially fully*), (ii) time (*concurrent or sequential*), and (c) weight (*equal status or dominant status*).	Leech & Onwuegbuzie (2009)
Mixed-model designs	Comprises of six mixed-model designs, with qualitative and quantitative methods mixed across the stages of the research process (for example), a study with qualitative research objectives can employ the quantitative data collection approach, followed by qualitative data analysis.	Johnson & Onwuegbuzie (2004)
Mixed-method designs	Consists of nine mixed-method designs, with a mixed-mixed method in which a quantitative phase and a qualitative phase are mixed in an overall research study, (for example) a qualitative phase might be conducted first so that it informs the quantitative phase; or, the qualitative and quantitative phases are conducted concurrently, and the findings are mixed during the interpretation phase.	Johnson & Onwuegbuzie (2004)
Basic mixed-method designs	This design comprises the convergent parallel design, the explanatory sequential design and the exploratory sequential design.	Creswell & Plano Clark (2011)

Source: Author

The table above provides a summary of the various typologies and mixed-method designs that have been discussed in this section. With various designs to choose from, it is crucial to know how to select the appropriate mixed-method design. In the following section, the process that researchers and scholars can follow in selecting a suitable design for their study is discussed.

6.6   CHOOSING THE APPROPRIATE MIXED-METHODS DESIGN IN SOCIAL MEDIA RESEARCH

Determining the most appropriate research design to employ when conducting research depends on several factors. These factors are analysed in this section. Before commencing your mixed-methods social media study, there are several questions that you need to ask yourself. These questions also act as a checklist, and when followed appropriately can help you choose a suitable design for your study.

- **What is your research problem?**

  The research problem (see chapter 2) determines which mixed method is most appropriate. Some problems are best addressed using MMAs and two different data sources. Thus, collecting only from one data source may not fully answer the research problem. Consequently, having a second database (for example, qualitative) may help in explaining any missing information from the first database (for example, quantitative).

- **What is your expertise in both quantitative and qualitative skills?**

  If you lack expertise with either the quantitative or qualitative method, then consider working in a team or getting trained in that method. If you lack expertise in a method (for example) using a quantitative survey or content analysis, then select a different method that does not emphasise that method.

- **How many available resources do you have at your disposal?**

  Having adequate funds and enough time to complete the study is crucial for your study. If you do not have enough funds or time to carry out the mixed-method study, then opt for a mono-method design, either the qualitative or quantitative method.

More questions that you need to ask yourself are illustrated in Figure 6.9 below. Creswell and Plano Clark (2011:80) describe it as the decision tree. These are further guidelines that will help you select the appropriate mixed-method designs. The decision tree focuses on three elements i) timing, ii) the weight of method, and iii) the mixing element.

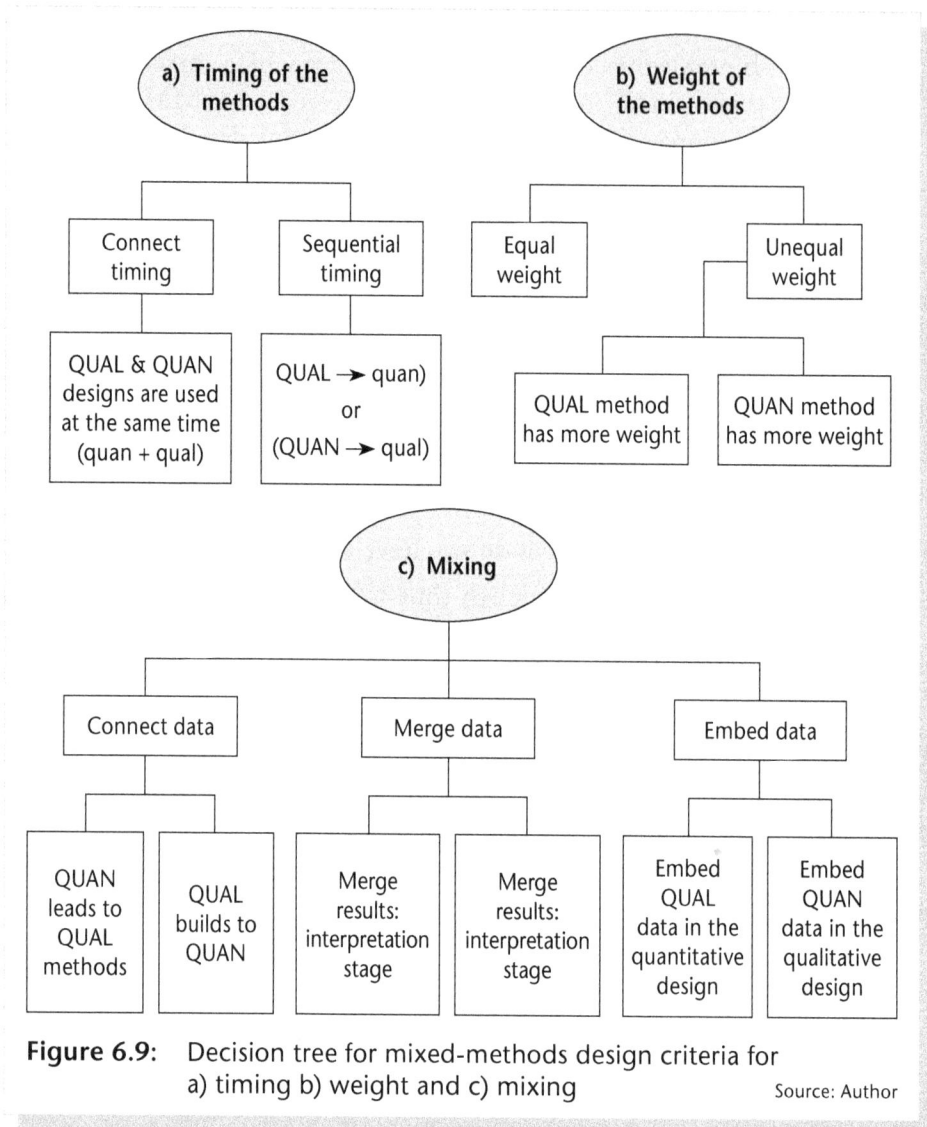

Figure 6.9:   Decision tree for mixed-methods design criteria for
a) timing b) weight and c) mixing

Source: Author

In the following section, an example of a mixed-methods study in social media research is provided by means of the case study of AfroConsult.

CASE STUDY: AFROCONSULT – MIXED METHODS IN SOCIAL MEDIA RESEARCH

AfroConsult is a new consultancy firm based in Accra, Ghana. It is the number one source for Risk Management, Project Management, and Business Consultancy. It recently won recognition at the annual Ghanaian Social Media Awards as one of the top three most engaged Ghanaian consultancy firms on social media (on LinkedIn and Twitter). The firm was established by two friends in November 2018, and to date (August 2019) it has managed to grow their followership on their social media pages a) LinkedIn: from 100 followers to 3 500 followers, and b) Twitter: from 80 followers to 2 100 followers—all won within a period of six months. The start-up firm has seen remarkable success within a few months after conducting a mixed-methods study in January 2019, which informed their internal social media strategy and enviably positioned them on LinkedIn and Twitter. This hypothetical case study illustrates how AfroConsult managed to gain this success.

A summary of their MMR study is provided below.

AfroConsult faced the following challenges when they commenced with their business a) fierce competition, and b) limited marketing resources. Consequently, they turned to social media so that they could a) market their expertise and showcase their services, and b) find customers and grow their business. So, they embarked on a MMR study to speak to their market so that they could improve their social media strategy with the following objectives in mind: a) grow their following on LinkedIn from 100 followers to 5 000 followers, and Twitter from 80 followers to 2 000 followers within a period of six months, c) Drive traffic from their social media pages to their company website, and increase their website traffic by 200 per cent, and d) Their long-term objective was to build long-term hip with their customers, retain new customers, and generate revenue. They produced the following five-stage MMR process:

Stage 1: Purpose of the study (see also chapter 2)

AfroConsult conducted this study in January 2019, over a period of four weeks. The purpose of their study was as follows:

- Research on who their target market and influencers are.
- Understand and listen to their target market and learn from influencers.
  - ○ Find out their communication habits and the type of content they engage with most.
  - ○ Find out about their disappointments and how they would want services to change in the following areas: Risk Management, Project Management and Business Consultancy.
- Identify the competitive advantages of its competitors.
- Identify the buzzwords that matter to their audience.

➡

Stage 2: Selection of mixed-methods design

The research team at AfroConsult developed a checklist that guided the selection of the appropriate mixed-methods design. With guidance from the mixed-methods design decision tree (Creswell & Plano Clark, 2011), and their own established checklist, they developed a final checklist that would guide them in selecting the appropriate design. Their checklist is as follows:

- **What will the timing of the qualitative and quantitative method be?**

  Concurrent, since they had an adequate number of people (4) in their research team, who would conduct the research.

- **What will the weighting of the qualitative and quantitative methods be?**

  Equal since they will conduct the data collection concurrently.

- **How will the methods be mixed?**

  The data will be analysed separately, and then the findings will be compared to see if they confirm or disconfirm each other.

- **Do you have enough expertise in both qualitative and quantitative methods?**

  All the people on the team had experience using the quantitative method. However, only one person had basic experience using the qualitative method (*interviews and content analysis*). To fill in this knowledge gap, one-week training in qualitative methods was planned—beginning on 3 December 2018 until 14 December 2018. So, the training took place before commencing with the study in January 2019. After the training, a decision was made to use quantitative online surveys and the qualitative content analysis of social media content on targeted pages. This decision was made because these were the methods that the members of the research team were most confident in.

- **Do you have enough funding and time to conduct the research?**

  Approximately US$1 750 was set aside for the following (development of a web-based questionnaire, internet charges, purchase of statistic software (SPSS), LinkedIn premium membership, and hiring an expert Statistician to assist with the data analysis stage. Four weeks were set aside for the entire process (data collection, analysis, and interpretation).

Stage 3: Data Collection

As a result of the above checklist, a decision was made to use the convergent parallel mixed-methods design, which would mean—concurrent data collection using both quantitative and qualitative methods.

Quantitative method

A questionnaire was developed with the aid of a short literature review, reviewed before commencing with data collection. There was a pre-test of the questionnaire and it went through several refinements following a rigorous process. Afterwards, they purchased the premium membership on LinkedIn to enable them to distribute their online survey via Messaging, to 250 users (*sample size*). The survey was also administered on Twitter via tweets and direct messages, and the target was 100 users (*sample size*).

The results were collected around the clock, which loaded automatically into the analytical tool of the web-based survey tool. This data was then transferred into the Statistical Package for the Social Sciences (SPSS), now officially known as the IBM SPSS Statistics software, manually for the data analysis stage.

Qualitative method

Through established key (search) words, the research team was able to identify key audiences and influencers in their field on LinkedIn (25 users) and Twitter (25 users). Once these were identified, the researchers began analysing the content on their profiles, specifically (their posts and their engagement such as likes, comments and shared posts). The team optically scanned through this content and activities. To ensure intercoder reliability, two coders carried out a pre-test of the codebook that was developed before the data collection process. After the pre-test, changes were made to the codebook accordingly. Thereafter, the content and activities on the target audiences' pages were analysed through the aid of the codebook. The data was coded using the deductive approach directly into SPSS by two coders and the data was prepared for analysis.

During the entire process of developing themes in the codebook and data collection, there was continuous validation of the accuracy of information.

Please note: there are ethical issues related to social media data mining, and researchers need to be well informed about these issues. One of the greatest challenges for social media researchers are ethical issues surrounding data subjects, such as ensuring the anonymity of and preserving the privacy of data subjects. Researchers must ensure that their identities are not identified in social media postings. More information regarding these ethical issues can be found in chapter 10 of this book.

Stage 4: Data Analysis

The data was analysed using the SPSS tool through the aid of a Statistician. The two databases were analysed separately and then converged together using the side-by-side comparison approach. The numerical data were analysed using descriptive statistics such as frequency counts; while inferences were drawn based on coding or themes (for qualitative data), and coding from data retrieved from the web-based survey tool (for the quantitative data).

A summary of these results is discussed in stage 5.

Stage 5: Comparison and interpretation of results

The researcher first reported the quantitative statistical results and then thereafter the qualitative findings eg themes were discussed, and then lastly comparison was made to either confirm or disconfirm the statistical results.

LinkedIn and Twitter Quantitative Results: Participant Demographics Only

Of the 250 people contacted via Messaging on LinkedIn, 138 respondents participated in the study. Seventy-three of the respondents were female and 65 were male. Of the 100 people contacted via direct messages and tweets on Twitter, 72 participated in the study. Forty-two of the participants were female and 30 were male.

Summary of findings from both Qualitative and Quantitative methods

In summary, AfroConsult Ltd a) Identified their target market and influencers successfully and they, *i) followed them on LinkedIn and Twitter, and ii) began engaging with them*; b) listened to their target market and received insights regarding their needs and disappointments, and eventually followed all their influencers, to receive key updates and information from them; c) Discovered their communication habits and the type of content they engage with most. This information enabled them to develop customised content that their target audience would appreciate and engage with. They also began marketing customised services to the right target audiences on LinkedIn; d) Identified the competitive advantages of their competitors and used this information to repackage their services and inform their service delivery; e) Identified the buzzwords that matter to their audience. This helped them to develop engaging content that contained the keywords and hashtags, which made it easier for their target audiences to find them on LinkedIn and Twitter; f) they managed to grow their followership on LinkedIn from 100 followers to 3 500 followers (*goal set was 5 000*), and on Twitter from 80 followers to 2 100 followers (*goal set was 2 000*), and g) They managed to grow their website traffic by 180 per cent, which was near the goal of 200 per cent that they had set.

In summary, the results from their mixed-methods study were used to inform their social media strategy, which was then implemented in AfroConsult's LinkedIn and Twitter pages.

6.7 SUMMARY

This chapter focused on the use of an MMA in social media research. It focused on discussing the typologies and designs of MMR and proposed the use of paradigmatic perspective as a guide for the MMR process. Since the field of MMR is growing and there is little guidance in carrying out effective research, there lies great potential in paradigms to provide a greater depth and breadth of information to guide and inform MMR. The chapter then explained how to choose the appropriate research design, and concluded with a case study of AfroConsult, which illustrated how this consultancy company based in Ghana positioned itself on social media and won thousands of followers after using the MMA to gather findings that informed and improved their social media strategy — to become one of the top three most engaged Ghanaian companies on social media.

Learning activities (Test yourself)

1. Can you define what MMA is in your own words?

2. In your own words, what would be your rationale for employing the MMA to your study?

3. Can you name four advantages and four limitations of the MMA?

4. Are paradigms and worldview perspectives the same? Explain your answer.

5. How many paradigmatic perspectives have been identified in the literature? Can you name three that are associated with the MMR approach? Do you think that there could be other perspectives that could be applied to a social media research study? Elaborate!

6. Describe two different types of typologies and their designs? Explain the importance of using typologies in MMR. Could these designs be adapted? What implications will the adapted designs have on the overall research design?

7. What is social media research? What led to the rise of this discipline?

8. What should you keep in mind when selecting the appropriate mixed-methods design for your study?

9. After studying Case study 6.1, answer the following questions:

   a. What challenges was AfroConsult facing before they embarked on the mixed-methods study?

   b. What strategy does AfroConsult use to grow its followership on LinkedIn and Twitter?

   c. What was the purpose of the study that they carried out? Please give three examples.

   d. Which mixed-method design did they choose to use in their study? How did they choose that design?

   e. What qualitative and quantitative methods did they use in their study?

Further reading

Bryman, A. 2007. Barriers to integrating quantitative and qualitative research. *Journal of Mixed Methods Research*, 1(1): 8–22.

Fetters, M.D, Curry, L.A. & Creswell, J.W. 2013. Achieving integration in mixed methods designs: Principles and practices. *Health Services Research*, 48(6Pt2): 2134–2156.

Guetterman, T.C., Fetters, M.D. & Creswell, J.W. 2015. Integrating quantitative and qualitative results in health science mixed methods research through joint displays. *Annals of Family Medicine*, 13(6): 554–561.

Sale, J.E., Lohfeld, L.H. & Brazil, K. 2002. Revisiting the quantitative-qualitative debate: Implications for mixed-methods research. *Quality and Quantity*, 36(1): 43–53.

Sandelowski, M. 2003. Tables or tableaux? The challenges of writing and reading mixed methods studies. In Tashakkori, A. & Teddlie, C. (eds.). *SAGE handbook of mixed methods in social and behavioral research*. Thousand Oaks, Los Angeles: SAGE Publications pp. 321–350.

Teddlie, C & Tashakkori, A. 2003. Major issues and controversies in the use of mixed methods in the social and behavioral sciences. In Tashakkori, A. & Teddlie, C. (eds.). *SAGE handbook of mixed methods in social & behavioral research*. Thousand Oaks, Los Angeles: SAGE Publications pp. 3–50.

Section C

WORKING WITH SOCIAL MEDIA DATA

Data

CHAPTER 7

Sampling For Social
Media Research

Braam van der Vyver

One of the most significant current challenges in large-scale online social networks is to establish a concise and coherent method aimed to collect and summarize data. Sampling the content of an Online Social Network (OSN) plays an important role as a knowledge discovery tool. – C.A. Piña-García, C. Gershenson & J.M. Siqueiros-García

Learning Outcomes

After completing this chapter, the researcher should be able to:

- describe the role of sampling in social media research;
- discuss how social media sampling can facilitate data collection;
- recognise all the methodological challenges of social media sampling;
- critically appraise the differences between social media sampling and conventional statistical sampling;
- analyse all the sampling methods in the book; and
- explain how validity and reliability can be achieved in social media sampling.

7.1   INTRODUCTION

As you would have noticed in the other chapters, in the age of Big Social Data, billions of people are using social media, such as Facebook, Snapchat, Twitter, and Instagram to, amongst other things, socialise, interact and create new content at a remarkable rate. Some of the data sets sourced from social media can be classified as Big Social Data, however, there is more to Big Data than postings on social media. For example, banks process billions of transactions every minute. The same goes for calls processed by mobile phone companies. New data is created with a wide array of devices, for example, bar code readers, smartphones, and tablets.

Most discussions on Big Data start with the question: how big is Big Data? In a report from the McKinsey Global Institute (Manyika et al., 2011:1) it is mentioned that '[b]ig data refers to datasets whose size is beyond the ability of typical database software tools to capture, store, manage, and analyse'. They quote the renowned blogger, David Smith's statement that Big Data is not just a description of raw volume. 'The real issue is usability' (Minelli et al., 2012:33).

Big Data often reflects a mixture of relationships that results in several possibly conflicting patterns in the data. The patterns often mask each other. Heimann and Danneman (2014:72) point out that:

> *This challenge ... is exacerbated by the large number of possible patterns in data that includes many variables and data that covers broad swaths of time, space, groups, and individuals. The second concern is that findings are often statistically significant but substantively tiny.*

Heimann and Danneman (2014:70) conclude that '[t]he conversation about social media data often becomes a conversation about Big Data and how Big Data is hard to analyze'. They purport that the technical aspects embedded in the definitions 'are less crucial than a deep understanding of the measurement and inferential challenges inherent in dealing with social media data' (Heimann & Danneman, 2014:70).

As mentioned, social media is a major contributor to Big Data. Schultz (2019) points out that research has shown that 300 million new users join social media networking sites each year. According to him, Twitter registered 474 000 tweets per minute while users are watching 4 333 560 YouTube videos every minute in 2019. Other mind-blowing statistics suggest that 300 hours of video are uploaded to YouTube every minute. Instagram users, on the other hand, upload over 100 million photos and videos per day. That is 69 444 million posts every minute! (Schultz, 2019).

The market leader in the social media sphere at the time of publication was still Facebook, where, according to Schultz (2019), every minute 510 000 comments are posted, 293 000 statuses are updated, and 136 000 photos are uploaded. Facebook users also click the like button on more than 4 million posts every minute. All this adds up to 4.3 billion Facebook messages posted daily and 5.76 billion Facebook likes every day (Schultz, 2019). In this tsunami of data, there is also a large complement of researchable information on marketing, political and polemic issues.

Lyon and Montgomery (2013:751) describe social media as a collection of non-hierarchical platforms that are not guarded by conventional gatekeepers. User-generated content can be accessed at low cost or for free and are driven by rapid responses from users. Social media users generate data that is of great value to researchers as well as decision-makers. Such data is viewed as a rich source for interpreting social dynamics (see also the discussion in chapter 1). Socially generated data, and especially Big Social Data, comes with many complexities. Capturing and sampling this data challenges the researcher to carefully consider the potentials and pitfalls that are embedded in Big Social Data.

There are two methodological approaches to Big Social Data analysis. The first is based on the Big Data approach in which all existing content is analysed. This approach does not involve any sampling. The second approach makes use of sampling. Sampling entails selecting a limited number of units from the total population so that inferences can be drawn from the entire population (Thompson, 2012:1).

Modern-day sampling has developed way beyond the automated selection of elements. Usability of sample data has become a major driver of data selection and query execution. Krippendorf (2018:21) declared that:

Ultimately, all reading of texts is qualitative, even when certain characteristics of a text are later converted into numbers. The fact that computers process great volumes of text in a very short time and represent these volumes in ways someone can understand does not remove the qualitative nature of the texts being analyzed and the algorithms used to process them.

This chapter explains how to sample social media data for qualitative and quantitative implementation. Different sampling methods, such as probability and non-probability type samples, are also discussed. The chapter also covers some of the challenges in social media data generalisation, for example, vague sample frames, over-emphasis of a single platform and sampling biases.

Sampling methods used for traditional media research and its applicability to social media are also introduced. Different methods of probability and non-probability sampling are then explained. Random sampling, systematic sampling and stratified sampling form part of probability sampling while purposive sampling, quota sampling, snowball sampling and convenience sampling are non-probability sampling methods that apply to social media.

Random sampling lends itself to quantitative analysis. It can be conducted in an automated manner with or without the use of one or more algorithms. The sampling error, if applicable, can be calculated and non-sampling errors, if applicable, can be identified.

Non-random sampling is better suited for hashtag analysis where a specific narrative is explored. With random sampling, there is a real possibility that important themes may be missed since they are not included in the sample. Where tweets or other postings are analysed, purposeful sampling increases the chances that relevant issues and themes will be detected and included in the sample. In the case of public opinion surveys, conventional random sampling of potential respondents is scientifically preferable. An alternative option would be to analyse social media discussions such as Twitter feeds. A stakeholder analysis will render the 'public' part of opinion while a thematic analysis will reflect the 'opinion' part. Where hashtags narratives retrieved from Twitter are researched, there is no doubt that a much richer set of themes/issues will be identified. It needs to be mentioned that the researcher's bias may be present and that the necessary measures to diminish such bias need to be taken.

7.2   DATA ANALYTICS

Before we get down to the *nitty-gritty* of Big Social Data, we must consider the practice of data analytics. The influential website, Investopedia, defines data analytics as the science of analysing raw data in order to draw inferences from the information (Frankenfield, 2019).

The next question that arises is why do data scientists, researchers, and marketers engage in Big Social Data analytics? Well, the answer is simple. Not only are we surrounded by Big Social Data sets, but these data sets are more accessible than ever before but that is not where it ends. The analysis of Big Social Data can contribute immense value to the value chain, a phrase coined by Michael Porter in 1985 that describes that set of functions that a company performs in order to deliver a useful product to its customers (Baltzan, 2017:29).

The potential applications of Big Social Data are virtually unlimited. Today it is used for customer segmentation, market basket analysis, credit risk modelling, market risk modelling, detection of fraud and/or money laundering and social media analytics to name but a few. For example, Facebook data in the form of posts, friends, activities, and pictures translates to personalised messages while Twitter postings reflect what issues are important to the user as well as what sentiments such user may harbour about the hashtagged topic. These are just two examples of the tsunami of researchable matter that is generated by social media.

The biggest problem that often comes with Big Social Data is the overwhelming volume. How does one achieve usability without drowning in a sea of data and that is where data sampling comes in? With sensible sampling, smaller data sets can be created which makes data analytics within a reasonable time frame affordable. Unfortunately, the basic principles of scientific sampling are very easily forgotten when a researcher gets access to really large data sets. Issues of sampling bias, if ignored, can result in faulty inferences just as easily with Big Social Data as with smaller versions. The only way to avoid these pitfalls is to stick to the basics and that is exactly what will be discussed in the next sections.

7.3   WHAT IS SAMPLING?

Sampling is compiling a dataset from a population in such a way that the best possible case for drawing inferences about that population can be established (Osborne, 2013:46). Sampling, in other words, is a process that is aimed at determining the exact number of units from a population that needs to be investigated in order to organise and describe the characteristics of the population and, if needed, to draw inferences about the population from this small subset of data. In the case of Big Social Data collections, this sample can consist of a collection of comments and/or responses. The sampling process also includes the determining of the sample size, for example, what number of percentages of the population should be investigated to reach justifiable conclusions. Although sampling can be carried out very accurately, there is no such thing as a perfect sample. Lohr (2010:3) reminded all researchers that even if it did exist, it can only be confirmed by measuring the whole population. This is out of the question for many social media research projects where user-generated contributions run into the millions.

7.4   WHY SAMPLING IS ESSENTIAL FOR SOCIAL MEDIA RESEARCH

While being cognizant of the arguments about sampling large social media datasets in chapter 5, the primary objective of sampling for social media studies is to obtain a small number of units or cases (the sample) from a much larger collection (the population) to allow the researcher to study the sample and produce valid generalisations about the population. Sampling from a population is the recommended method when a population is too large to investigate all the elements in the population or if it is impractical to do so.

Researchers utilise a variety of sampling methods that secure highly representative samples (for example, samples that are very much like the population). The researcher's aim is thus to collect the best available information about the characteristics of the population with the available sources like time, money and human resources at his or her disposal by studying the sample values only. The goal when sampling from a social media population is, therefore, to obtain as representative a sample as possible.

Although qualitative methods require much smaller samples than quantitative ones, Patton (2002:244) emphasises that there are no prescribed sample sizes for qualitative studies. This does not mean there are no guidelines in that regard. An important indicator that can assist in determining the sample size is saturation. Saturation or exhaustion refers to the point where additional data cannot contribute new information or insight (Kelly, 2006:372).

In the case of social media, samples can be drawn from Twitter every week until the interest in the topic diminishes, for example, when fewer tweets are posted. Alternatively, samples can be drawn as new themes or stakeholders are introduced. The Judicial Commission of Inquiry into Allegations of State Capture, Zondo Commission, can serve as an example where new information of new witnesses becomes available weekly. New samples can be drawn as new witnesses start to testify or new stakeholders are implicated.

7.5   SAMPLING SOCIAL MEDIA SOURCES

Researchers need to be aware of the following issues pertaining to sampling social media sources.

7.5 1   Why make use of social media?

Response rates to surveys (paper versions as well as online) used in quantitative research are steadily declining and have been since the advent of the internet. This trend was not only noticed among individuals but also among organisations (De Leeuw, 2005; Baruch & Holtom, 2008). Johnson and Owens (2003) investigated what lies behind this decline and found that confidentiality and privacy issues, exploitation of personal information, and scepticism to be the main reasons for this decrease. Twenty-eight per cent of non-respondents ascribed their unwillingness to participate to being too busy, 14 per cent did not consider the survey to be relevant, 12 per cent could not find the address where to return the completed questionnaire and 22 per cent mentioned that company policy prohibited them from participation (Baruch & Holtom, 2008). The decreasing response rates also challenge the validity and reliability of research projects affected by it. With it comes the risk that the credibility of the findings may be diminished.

Against the background of all the pitfalls that complicate survey research, social media has become a very attractive option for researchers. Social media data is freely available and can easily be collected from the various platforms. The pervasiveness and perceived richness of these data make them attractive sources for researchers whose objective it is to assess public opinion from the views of a selection of contributors. However, the ease with which this data can be obtained does not necessarily correlate with the potential quality of the findings (Heimann & Danneman 2014:65–66).

7.5.2 Advantages and disadvantages of sampling social media

Before social media arrived on the cyber scene, researchers had to rely on surveys to collect data for analysis. Once the internet was in full swing, online surveys have become very popular. The multivariate nature of survey data means that large permutations of independent and dependent variables can be covered. Unfortunately, surveys are only administered to 'cross-sections of randomly sampled individuals at different points in time' (Heimann & Danneman, 2014:70). Where surveys capture opinions at a specific point in time, social media research lends itself to monitor shifts in opinion by tracking these opinions of groups and individuals over space and time (Heimann & Danneman, 2014:70). Accordingly, '[s]ocial media is captured at the individual level and at an extraordinary rate' (Heimann & Danneman, 2014:70).

Analysing social media data is complicated by several factors that relate to the representation of populations as well by methodological issues regarding sampling, however, most of the social media platforms can serve as a base for the generation of sampling frames. The same sampling methods that are used for surveys can be used to constitute probability and non-probability samples as well as the recommended sample size using optimal allocation methods.

How accurately the population is represented in the sampling frame, for example, the quality of the sampling frame can be affected by at least three characteristics (Mecatti & Singh, 2014):

- Undercoverage: a part of the target population was eliminated from the sampling process. Undercoverage may occur if all the members of the population do not feature in the sampling frame. If researchers, for instance, had sampled responses from Facebook in 2012, the proposed sample would exclude approximately 34 per cent of online United States adults (Pew Internet & American Life, 2012). The same phenomenon would be detected if the reaction of the *Twitterati* (Twitter users) to South Africa's Constitutional Court's decision that outlawed corporal punishment in the household. Only 8.26 per cent of South Africans were registered Twitter users in the 2018–2019 period (Statscounter, 2019). The reaction of parents would have dominated the hashtagged responses since the youth are not active on Twitter.

- Overcoverage: elements that do not form part of the target population are unknowingly included in the sample. Overcoverage errors occur when units are enumerated in error (NCES, n.d.). The impact of the ineligible elements depends on what percentage they make up of the sample. An example is postings from fake news sites that end up in a sample of tweets issued by the news media.

- Multiplicities: Members of the target population are counted more than once. Many individuals have more than one Facebook or Twitter account.

If there is an increase in bias because the sample is erroneous and/or inaccurate, the probabilities increase that the findings of the population will be skewed (Hill, Dean & Murphy, 2013:302). As the percentage of uncovered elements in the population increases, so does the concern that bias will impact on the final outcomes of the study. Researchers designing a study should be able to explain what part of the population has not been covered by the sample and/ or to explain how the results are not affected by the exclusions. The validity of the sample may be evaluated by comparing the sampling frame with other sources defining the target population. With a non-probability sample, the linkages between the target population and the compiled sample are less clearly defined or even non-existent. The question, therefore, often arises if it really matters if the sample does not fully represent the target population? In the case of quantitative research, the answer is a definite yes. The presence of bias diminishes the value of the findings. The objective with quantitative research is to produce findings with small levels of bias, where small can be defined as meaningfulness in statistical terms (Batterham & Hopkins, 2006:50).

Sampling becomes even more complicated where the parameters of the sampling frame are not evident or when such a frame does not exist at all. Hill et al., (2013:203) cite the example of bloggers who regularly participate in the discourse on a particular topic or event, activists who frequent a specific website, or members of an interest group who share strong views on an international event. The parameters for such a sample are unclear or even non-existent. The only solution left is for the researcher to opt for non-probabilistic methods.

7.6   TYPES OF SAMPLING FOR SOCIAL MEDIA RESEARCH

Conventional sampling may also apply to social media studies and can be divided into two categories, namely probability and non-probability sampling.

7.6.1   Probability sampling

'Probability sampling is a scientific tool for obtaining a representative sample from a target finite population' (Kim & Wang, 2019:177). Probability sampling is the same as random sampling or representative sampling, however, random sampling differs from random assignment. Random assignment refers to the process of placing participants in an experiment into different groups (Trochim, 2006). The word random refers to the process implemented to select elements for the sample from a population.

A probability sample offers the guarantee that every element in the finite population has a known and calculable chance of being included in the sample (Durrheim & Painter, 2006:135). A randomisation technique or tool is used to choose those units that form part of the sample (Suresh, 2011:8). Random samples are more likely than non-random samples to render a sample that accurately represents the population. Such a sample enables researchers to make accurate assumptions or generalisations from the sample. With probability sampling, a relatively small sample can be used to draw inferences about a large population. Specified random sampling procedures are thus aimed at reproducible results with a guarantee that every element of the target population has a known nonzero probability of selection to be incorporated into the sampling frame.

Random selection is a mathematical process that will not be explained in this chapter. Suffice to say that random selection goes hand in hand with probability sampling. If a researcher implements random selection to obtain a sample, the researcher will be able to work out the sampling error which indicates how closely the sample is a true representation of the population.

To draw a simple random sample, a researcher starts with a list of every single unit or case of the population that he or she wants to research. This list is known as the sampling frame. Each element on the list is sequentially numbered before the process of random sampling can be executed (Schofield, 2006:31). To randomly select elements from the list, researchers can make use of a table or set of numbers that has been randomly generated.

These tables and lists are easily obtainable. Many research textbooks include such datasets as appendices to the book. A wide selection of free random number generators is available on the internet. Stat Trek is one such site that can be used to create a random number table of any required size. It can be accessed unlimited times and at no cost from chttp://stattrek.com/Tables/Random.aspx. Another option is Randomizer.org which is available at http://randomizer.org. The screenshot in Figure 7.2 is from Randomizer.

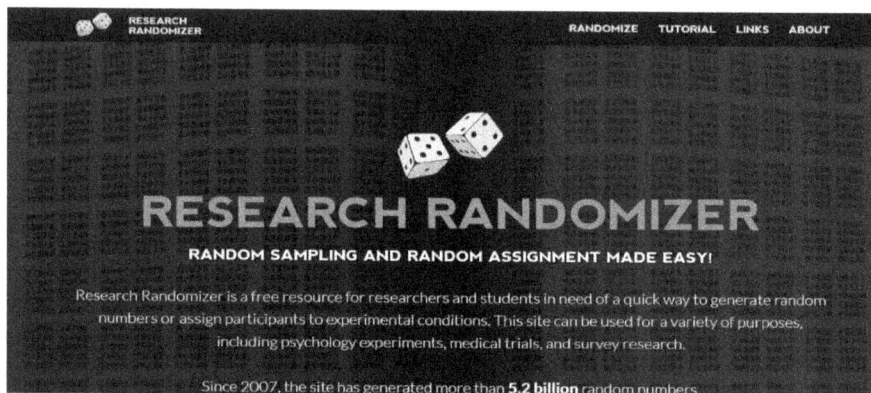

Figure 7.1:   A Screenshot from a research randomizer

Used with permission from Social Psychology Network   Source: https://www.randomizer.org/

A case in point is a dataset compiled by Golder, Wilkinson and Huberman (2007:7). This dataset consisted of messages and pokes sent by 4.2 million Facebook users who were members of one of 496 North American colleges and universities. Each user was assigned a randomised ten-digit identification (ID) number, while each of the 496 universities was assigned a randomised ID number between 1 and 500. The users were grouped by school.

A dataset constructed by way of probability sampling can be used to generate valid statistical inferences for finite population parameters. The following types of probability samples will be discussed: simple random sample, cluster sample, stratified sample, and systematic sample.

(i)   Simple random sampling

Although a simple random sample is the most basic form of probability sampling, it is also the foundation of more complex sampling methods. The prerequisite for simple random sampling (SRS) is that every subset of the population has the same chance of becoming the sample. Lohr (2010) distinguishes between SRS without replacement in which duplicates are not replaced and SRS with replacement in which duplicates are removed and substitutes are provided with a randomised technique.

The question immediately arises what prevents the researcher from investigating the whole population. The answer lies somewhere between the mammoth sizes of Big Social Data and the practicality of doing so. Facebook postings or tweets on a Twitter hashtag may run into millions. Even if the number of sampled units is restricted to unique postings/tweets the number can still run into the thousands. A researcher who, for example, has to advise a politician on the public opinion as reflected by the *Twitterati* may have to fall back on some form of sampling to assess the trends that are reflected in the postings. Lohr (2010:26) justifies sampling with an example of a medical technician that does not have to drain all the blood of a patient to measure their red blood cell count.

(ii)   Systematic sampling

A simple random sample can be quite cumbersome. Systematic sampling techniques are easier to carry out and offer the same benefits as random sampling. It also requires a list of every unit in the population. In this regard, Durrheim and Painter (2006:135) explain that once the list is in place the researcher simply calculates a fixed distance between the elements and then selects every kth element on the list. K represents the selection interval or the distance between the elements that are embedded in the sample. Before the sample can be drawn the researcher decides how many elements are needed in the sample. If the researcher wants to sample 2 500 Facebook postings from a population of 10 000 the selection interval, or k, would be four. The number of population elements is simply divided by the sample size that is, 10 000/2 500. The main benefit of systematic sampling is that the sample is more evenly spread throughout the population (Schofield, 2006:32).

There is one instance in which systematic sampling should be avoided. If the sampling frame of the population displays any pattern to it, bias can be introduced if systematic sampling is implemented. This phenomenon is called periodicity. Periodicity is defined as the tendency for a pattern to appear at regular intervals. Hayes (2019) explains that '[i]f the population has a type of standardized pattern, the risk of accidentally choosing very common cases is more apparent' (Hayes, 2019). If, for example, postings on a Twitter hashtag is sampled over 28 days and the researcher decides to conduct four observations, that is, on randomly chosen days. To decide on which days observations will take place, the researcher will have to determine a selection interval. The population size of 28 days will have to be divided by the sample size which is four days. The selection interval will thus be seven. If day two is randomly selected as a starting point it means that sampling will occur every seventh day until the time frame of the sample has run out. Sampling would thus be conducted on the following days: 2, 9, 16, and 23. Once the sample has been completed the researcher may discover that the whole sample was drawn on Saturdays and that certain members of the *Twitterati* are hyperactive on Saturdays. The end result is that the sample is dominated by a number of Twitter activists who made it their business to tweet from noon till night on a specific day of the week.

To secure a more representative sample, two prerequisites exist for the valid implementation of systematic sampling. First, it is of paramount importance that the elements that make up the sample frame must have been ordered randomly. In the second instance, the researcher must ensure that the first element of the sample is determined randomly. A random number generator can be utilised to ensure that the second objective is met. It may, however, be more complicated to meet the first prerequisite since social media postings appear in sequence according to the date and time they were posted. In the case of Twitter, the researcher can implement a random number generator to allocate random numbers to the tweets in a Twitter discourse.

(iii)   Stratified sampling

Stratified sampling is aimed at ensuring that the same range and diversity of the various groups that feature in the population are also present in the sample (Braun & Clarke, 2013:57). The relevance of stratification is determined by the problem statement and the research questions that drive the study. Variation, on the other hand, is driven by demographics, the nature of the topic, and/or the theories that guide the investigation.

In stratified random sampling, the researcher first decides on subpopulations that he or she wants to investigate in the population. Supplementary data is used to create the subpopulation categories. After the strata have been created, random sampling is used to populate the subpopulations. Durrheim and Painter (2006:136–137) pointed out that a researcher has a choice between two strategies. In proportionate stratified sampling, the same proportion of units are included for each stratum. If, for instance, 1000 tourists from Gabon and 10 000 from Nigeria visited South Africa in May 2019, a proportional sample would include 100 individuals from Gabon and 1 000 from Nigeria. Tourists from each of the two countries make up 10 per cent of the sample. The authors point out that if the researcher wants to analyse the data about the strata separately, he or she can oversample those strata on which they want to focus (Durrheim & Painter, 2006:136–137).

In general, stratified sampling generates more representative samples if the supplementary information on which the strata is based is accurate. In the case of a Twitter discourse, the tweets from professional journalists working for the conventional media can be separated from those that were posted by citizen journalists, that is, anybody that is not on the payroll of a media house or other media concern. These two strata represent different dimensions of public opinion.

The following two tweets illustrate the implementation of the strata. The first tweet is one from a renowned political journalist, Rebecca Davis. It was posted on the website of the Daily Maverick, a leading online newspaper. It points the user to an article she wrote about the Listeriosis crisis. See Davis (2018). The tweet reads:

@dailymaverick

Listeriosis outbreak: The blame games begin By REBECCA DAVIS

@becsplanb

https://buff.ly/2H7SrRW

The second one is from a citizen journalist. It reads:

> #Listeriosis ... My worry is homeless people picking up these polonys and eat them without knowing why we threw them away!

The tweet was republished on the website of Independent Online (iol), an online news site. See Mokati (2018) for the article. It is written in a more personalised style than the article of professional journalists.

(iv)   Cluster sampling

Cluster sampling is suitable for data sets where the whole population can be divided into clusters or groups. According to Lohr (2010:26), 'the observation units ... in the sample are aggregated into larger sampling units, called clusters.' A random sample is then drawn from selected clusters. These samples are put together to constitute the total sample.

Two types of cluster sampling exist, namely:

- Single-stage cluster sampling: *where all* the elements in each cluster are included in the sample; and
- Two-stage cluster sampling: where random sampling is implemented to selected clusters.

Durrheim and Painter (2006:138) explained that at the onset the population may be divided into more manageable clusters. These clusters can be reconfigured in multiple and progressive stages until the researcher is satisfied that researchable clusters have been compiled. In the previous example in which a distinction was drawn between professional journalists and citizen journalists, the professional journalists can be divided into those who tweet in an official capacity and those who tweeted in their personal capacity. The researcher can also cluster according to the media type that the journalist works for; that is, journalists working for the broadcast media versus those working for the print media.

The following requirements need to be met before cluster sampling can be instituted:

- Cluster elements should be heterogeneous. Ideally, the population should exist of distinct subpopulations made up of different types.
- Each cluster should form a small subset of the total population.
- Each cluster should be mutually exclusive. No elements of the one cluster should also appear in another cluster.

Brooker, Barnett and Cribben (2016:9) point out that clusters do not have to be formed before the analysis can start. The process can be implemented during analysis. In the case of Twitter, this mode of analysis is recommended by the authors when the researcher is not sure what to expect from the analysis. By not starting with a predetermined set of clusters he or she gets the opportunity 'to explore the overall topical makeup of the dataset to find out what kinds of things a user group tweet about, using a cluster map showing connected terms of interest' (Brooker et al., 2016: 9).

An example of cluster sampling meeting these requirements is found in Jing et al, (2015) where sampling was conducted on a fashion site on Pinterest. The authors pointed out that '[o]ne feature that is particularly relevant to Pinterest is the presence of certain object classes, such as bags, shoes, watches, dresses, and sunglasses' (Jing et al. 2015) These object classes were used as sampling clusters for their study.

7.6.2   Non-probability sampling

'A non-probability sampling method is any method of recruiting or obtaining units for analysis in which inclusion in the sample is not determined by a random process' (Hayes, 2005:36). Non-probability sampling entails sampling methods for which an element's likelihood of being included in the sample is unknown. Since the probability of selection is unknown, no method is available to calculate to what effect the sample represents the population. This is not a problem because quantified representation is not the objective of non-probability samples. This, on the other hand, does not mean that such samples are drawn arbitrarily or without any planned purpose in mind. The question then arises why a researcher would prefer to conduct a non-probability sample.

A non-probability sample can be administered in a pilot study which is conducted to gather information in order to design a questionnaire for a survey research project (Blackstone, 2012:79–80). It is also the preferred sampling method for exploratory research. This does not mean that it is only useful in the early stages of research. Non-probability samples are regularly used in comprehensive research projects. These projects are mostly qualitative in nature, where the researcher's objective is to gain an in-depth understanding of a phenomenon or a topic. Researchers who are interested in contributing by expanding or falsifying social theories may elect to use non-probability sampling.

The following types of non-probability sampling can be considered:

(i)   Purposive or judgemental sampling

Purposive sampling, sometimes also referred to as purposeful sampling or judgemental sampling, is a methodology in which elements of the population are selected for the sample 'on the basis of their fit with the purposes of the study' (Daniel, 2012:87) It forms part of a strategy in which particular settings, persons or events are selected deliberately in order to meet the research objectives. Daniel (2012:88) points out that it differs from availability sampling in that elements are not merely included in the sample because of their availability but because they meet certain inclusion and/or exclusion criteria. The benefits of purposive/judgemental sampling are that it is cost-effective, it can be executed quickly, it is convenient, and it can be tailored to fit the research objectives. The downside of it is that it is subjective, and it does not lend itself to generalisation.

In the case of a social media study, purposive sampling can be executed by way of the search function that is embedded in all the social networking platforms. An example is a search for and an analysis of all tweets that were posted by online news website News24 and its journalists. In many disciplines, researchers draw a social media corpus and then purposively sample the corpus based on specific criteria. For example, Du Plessis (2019) compiled a corpus of Facebook posts, Twitter tweets, blog posts and YouTube comments which she purposively sampled to investigate the LEGO brand's prosumer engagement with a grounded theory study.

For example, to obtain a purposive sample, a researcher uses as a point of departure certain perspectives that he or she plans to investigate and then searches for respondents who can contribute to the research objectives. If, for example, a researcher intends studying guests' satisfaction with accommodation facilities in Cape Town, he or she would ensure that each of the different types of accommodation is covered in the study. The same applies to the various types of guests that stay in these facilities. The types of accommodation can include a luxury hotel, family hotel, inn, guest house, and backpackers' facility. Guest types can range from business travellers, couples, solo traveller, family, and friends.

An example of a tourist's review of a facility in Delhi looks like this. It contains both quantitative and qualitative information.

'Perfect location if wanting to explore Parah Ganj and Old Delhi, reasonably priced, comfy room!'

Charlotte – July 5, 2016

Very good service 7.3 rating for service

Very good comfort 7.1 room quality and comfort

A review grid normally deals with location, cleanliness, service, and value for money. The rating options vary from one to five stars. Average scores are displayed as selection guidelines. Good performance scores also feature in the marketing plugs.

Another example deals with a survey done by the social media site, Trip Advisor, SA on the usability of reviews that were posted on the international booking website, Agoda. Anecdotal evidence of the survey is posted in a report, titled 'Can We Trust Agoda.com Review?', 767 travellers responded to this open-ended question. Purposive sampling would be the recommended sampling technique.

(ii)   Snowball sampling

Handcock and Gile (2011:1) point out that there are different views on the definition of snowball sampling. This tends to produce a plethora of inconsistent approaches regarding sampling strategy.

Qualitative researchers sometimes fall back on snowball sampling techniques to constitute one or more samples. This often occurs where the researcher has a clear idea of who they would like to include in the sample, but the target population is a hard-to-reach group. In survey research, such individuals would be approached to suggest other potential respondents. In that way, the researcher builds a growing sample similar to a snowball that increases in size as it rolls through the snow.

Snowball sampling is often used when a stigmatised group or behaviour is the topic of the investigation. Blackstone (2012:80–81) gave the example of

a researcher who wanted to study how people with genital herpes cope with their medical condition would be unlikely to find many participants by posting a call for interviewees in the newspaper or making an announcement about the study at some large social gathering.

If the researcher knows an individual who suffers from such a condition, he or she may invite the person to participate in the study and if the person agrees, also ask him to refer to other individuals who are also treated for it. Snowball sampling is therefore also referred to as chain referral sampling.

Snowball sampling is also not restricted to survey research. De Choudhury et al., (2010) conducted a comprehensive study on a large Twitter dataset with the use of snowball sampling. The team sourced the dataset of connected quality users from Twitter. First, a set of 500 genuine identifiable (not fake) authoritative users were identified. Those selected posted sensibly and reasonably frequently on a diverse range of topics. The dataset included politicians, musicians, environmentalists and other activists, techies as well as a wide array of opinion leaders. The list was compiled from the popular social media blog, Mashable that is available at the website (http://mashable.com/2008/10/20/25-celebrity-twitter-users/). This was followed by the compilation of an extended social graph of the users on which the 'friend' links of those who were selected were added. (This is where the snowballing comes in). Lastly, the team collected the tweets for all users whose names feature in the social graph every 24 hours. Tweets that were posted between October 2006 and November 2009 formed the sample frame. With the focus placed on trending topics, a set of 125 topics were randomly selected. The selection included 25 hashtags. The rest was made up of phrases or groups of words. For the purpose of analysis, the team combined the topics into themes. These themes were automatically assigned to trending topics with the open-source (free to use) toolkit called 'OpenCalais'. The final outcome was a study dealing with the impact of sampling on message diffusion.

Murphy, Hill and Dean (2013:1) opine that social media serves as the perfect intersection between survey research and snowball sampling. They explain that survey research is by definition 'a social interaction between a researcher and a (potential) respondent – a "conversation with a purpose"' (Murphy et al., 2013:1). According to them, the advent of the internet triggered the formation of new communication platforms to conduct such conversations. Murphy et al. (2013:3) describe the social media as 'the collection of websites and web-based systems that allow for mass interaction, conversation and sharing among members of the network.' They view LinkedIn as a platform that can be utilised to conduct snowball sampling among professionals in all spheres of public life. According to them, it lends itself to the targeting of members that belong to certain professional groupings.

PC Magazine identified LinkedIn as 'the most important cross-industry professional network around' (Duffy, 2013). There is a free version of LinkedIn available to anyone with an email address. In August 2019, LinkedIn's membership stood at 575 million users, with 260 million of them active on a monthly basis. 39 per cent of LinkedIn's users have signed up for LinkedIn Premium, the paid version of the platform (Osman, 2019).

Although LinkedIn communities are not representative of industries they may serve as platforms for snowball sampling (Goodman, 2011).

(iii)   Quota sampling

Quota sampling can be implemented by both qualitative and quantitative researchers but in most textbooks, it is classified as a non-probability technique. Quota sampling requires that a researcher identifies categories that are relevant to the purpose of the study and for which there is a high expectancy of some variation (Lohr, 2010:96). The researcher creates subgroups based on each category and then decides how many elements from each subgroup to include (Schofield, 2006:36). Each subgroup is then populated in accordance with the research design.

In the example of accommodation facilities for tourists in the Western Cape, a distinction can be drawn between self-catering units and facilities with a restaurant on the premises. An analysis of the online feedback on Trip Advisor may illustrate families tend to prefer self-catering options while solo travellers are more inclined to book into establishments which have a restaurant facility on the premises. To understand the rationale of their thinking, the researcher may decide to create four subgroups namely solo travellers who booked into self-catering facilities, families who booked into self-catering facilities, solo travellers who booked into establishments with restaurants, and families who booked into establishments with restaurants. Ten sets of responses from each subgroup can be analysed to make sense of their preferences. The difficult part would be to populate the subgroups with responses that match the prescribed characteristics (Yang, 2010:39).

(iv)   Convenience sampling

Convenience sampling a non-probability sampling strategy that is implemented by both qualitative and quantitative researchers. Convenience sampling refers to using datasets that are readily available (such as social media data). To draw a convenience sample, a researcher simply collects data from sources to which he or she has the most convenient access. Sections are based on certain practical criteria (Farrokhi & Mahmoudi-Hamidabad, 2012:785). This method, also known as haphazard sampling, is often used in exploratory research. The data collected mostly offer only anecdotal value. Krippendorf (2018:121) warns that there is an imminent risk that biases may cloud the analyses of such data.

Convenience sampling is very popular among journalists who need quick and 'dirty' information from a population of interest. The person-on-the-street interviews, also known as the voice of the people (vox populi in Latin – abbreviated as vox pop) that are often conducted by a journalist with a camera on his or her shoulder is an example of a haphazard sample being executed. Haphazard sampling cannot be used to generate scientific data, in fact, it offers only one benefit: convenience. This does not mean the results of this type of sampling do not find itself in the media. After a recent Constitutional Court ruling declaring corporal punishment at home unconstitutional, an influential news website, iol.co.za published an article with the heading: Twitter hits back over ConCourt ruling on corporal punishment in the home. Tweets from irate parents dominated the news report. The following tweet was republished in the news report:

Me: 'Mom the court has ruled that it is illegal to spank a child.' Mom: 'Is the court your mother?'

#ConCourt

Collecting data sets from social media can also be classified as convenience sampling. Its usability can be improved if it is supplemented with another sampling method. The sample frame is compiled from social media content while the implementation of another method to execute the sample adds more validity.

Convenience sampling is easy to execute but weak from a methodological point of view. Quota sampling is a form of convenience sampling in which there is an intervention to secure an improved representation of the population.

(v)   Sequential sampling

Sequential sampling is a non-probability sampling technique wherein the researcher picks a group of units or subjects in a given time interval, conducts his study, analyses the results then picks another group of subjects if needed and so on (Lohr, 2010:517). In sequential sampling, the sample size is not fixed in advance. Instead, data is evaluated as it is collected, and further sampling is stopped in accordance with a pre-defined stopping rule as soon as significant results are observed. The need for additional samples to obtain sufficient statistical power (quantitative methods) or the necessary saturation (qualitative methods) has provided justification to sequentially collect data until the sampling objective has been met (Albers, 2019). Thus, a conclusion may sometimes be reached at a much earlier stage than would have been with a more rigid sampling method.

Sequential sampling offers the following benefits:

- The researcher has unlimited options when it comes to sample size and sampling schedule. The sample size can vary from relatively small to excessively large depending on the nature of the project. The decision to extend the sampling process rests with the researcher. This method is ideally suited to longitudinal projects that carry over long periods of time. A Twitter analysis of activities at the Zondo Commission that ran for more than a year is an example of such a project. New witnesses appeared regularly before the Commission thereby introducing new themes and/or potentially implicating individuals that had not been named before.

- Due to the longevity of the process and the repetitive nature of this sampling method adjustments can be made between samples. The flexibility of the process may make it possible for the researcher to create conclusions and interpretations regarding the whole event or project.

- Although this sampling method does not aim to draw representative samples, sampling can be adjusted to accommodate new developments in the case that is under investigation. This may contribute to the researcher achieving a different type of representativeness of the samples.

- Due to the aforementioned disadvantages, results from this sampling technique cannot be used to create conclusions and interpretations pertaining to the entire population.

(vi)   Theoretical sampling

A less common form of sampling is theoretical sampling. According to Braun and Clarke (2013:57), it sometimes forms part of the process of the development of grounded theory. Sampling is conducted as an iterative process where the growing data analysis and the subsequent theory development determine the selection of new datasets to further the investigation (Coyne 1997). It may also occur that a specific criterion may warrant more sampling. Criterion sampling as Patton (2002) named it, will justify the sampling of more or even all of the data regarding that issue or event.

Braun and Clarke (2013:58) summarise that 'qualitative research sample selection involves theoretical and pragmatic influences, applied flexibly in a way which is justifiable in the context of your overall research design'.

When Van der Vyver (2017) collected tweets on the criminal trial of Oscar Pistorius, he purposefully sourced tweets that dealt with the defence that the legal team of Pistorius presented. He found a tweet from an esteemed law professor, Pierre de Vos, who tweeted to promote an opinion piece he wrote for the Daily Maverick to criticise the defence of Pretorius in which he claimed that he committed an involuntary act when he shot Reeva Steenkamp. The tweet simply contained a URL to the article and read:

> https://www.dailymaverick.co.za/article/2014-04-15-oscars-involuntary-action-thin-ice-mr-pistorius/#.U025SIUrgSQ

7.7   THE SAMPLING PROCESS

There are different views about which sampling process to follow, however, we propose that the following steps form part of the sampling process for a social media study:

Step 1: The first step is describing the target population. Hayes (2005:31) describes a population as the complete set of objects or units that the researcher is trying to make a certain inference about. The unit of analysis may be a person, group, institution, object, message, or any other entity that the researcher wants to use as a subject for research. The sampled population refers to the dataset from which the sample was eventually taken. For example, in the case of Facebook it will be the posts, for Twitter, the hashtagged tweets, and for Pinterest, the boards that users created.

Step 2: The second step in the sampling process is to identify a sampling frame. This is an accessible section of the target population and consists of a 'list, map or any other specification of sampling units … from which a sample may be selected' (Lohr, 2010:3). The sample frame can also be an entire corpus (text, images, videos) of social media posts during a specific period of time (see Bamman, Eisenstein & Schnoebelen, 2014).

Schofield (2006:28–29) points out that if the 'sample frame is not representative of the population to be described, then the sample will also be unrepresentative'. Not all individuals are included in social media samples. This is a result of the digital divide that is, the so-called gap between the haves and the have nots which means that not everybody has access to a device that can be used to connect to the internet and/or enjoy some form of connectivity.

Step 3: The third step in sampling is choosing a sample from the sampling frame using a suitable **sampling method**. This includes determining the **size of the sample**. A sample is a subset of the targeted population. A unit or element that can be selected for the sample is called a sampling unit. An observation unit, on the other hand, is a unit or element on which a measurement is taken, or observation is conducted.

Patton (2002:228) points out that 'different units of analysis are not mutually exclusive', however, each unit may require a different data collection method, a different type of analysis, and a different approach to generating findings and conclusions.

The size and the composition of the sample are the two most important parameters of it. According to Iarossi (2006:129), the objective of the study, the available budget and the required level of confidence and precision will impact decisions regarding sample size.

Sampling can also be conducted by following a time period strategy. One option is to implement continuous sampling on an ongoing basis. On the other hand, there is fixed-term sampling in which the process is conducted at predetermined time slots. The breaks in-between sampling sessions allow the researchers to inspect the sample and alter the sampling process and/or time frames provided that the research design allows for it.

Figure 7.2 below illustrates the sampling process recommended for a social media study.

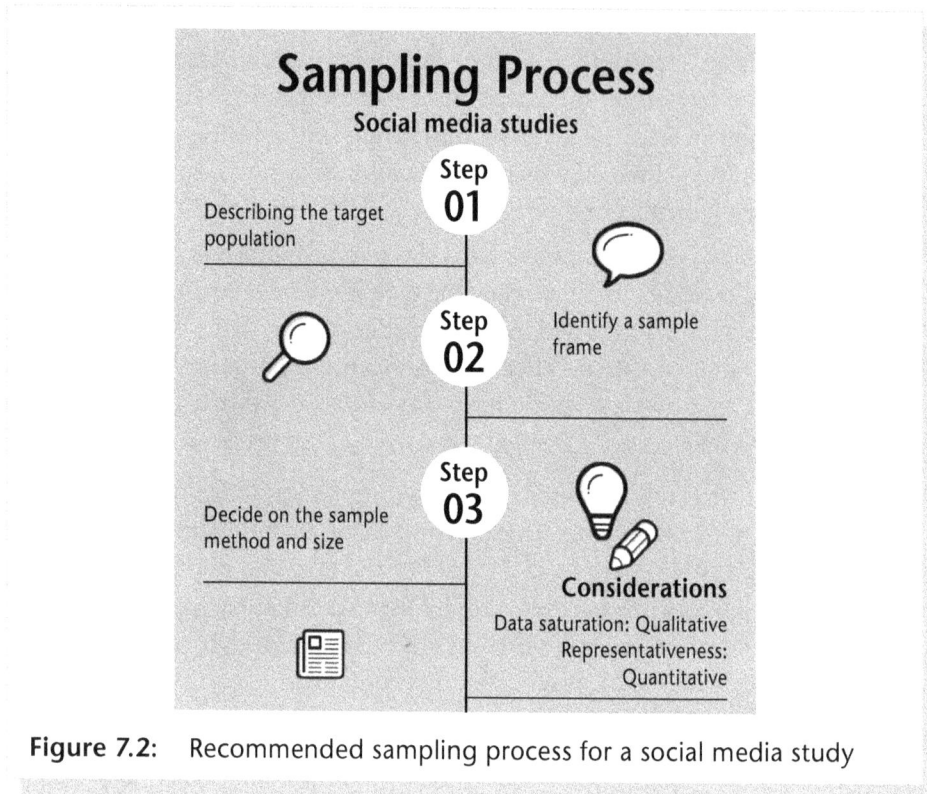

Figure 7.2:   Recommended sampling process for a social media study

The next section is dedicated to a discussion of the types of sampling for social media research.

7.8   MULTIMEDIA SAMPLING

Multimedia is any combination of text, sound, animation and video delivered by computer or other electronic or digitally manipulated means. It is a woven combination of digitally manipulated text, photographs, graphic art, sound, animation, and video elements. (Vaughan, 2008:1).

Video sharing websites such as YouTube and Instagram offer gargantuan amounts of user-contributed videos on the Web. To manage the ever-growing stock of videos, a wide array of content-based accessing, browsing, searching, sampling, and analysis techniques have emerged (Liujuan et al., 2013:61 Most of these techniques are computer-based and make use of algorithms. Since content searches bring up the material in chronological order, any sampling technique can, in theory, be implemented. In practice, however, the picture looks different.

Since multimedia information is represented in various forms, formats, and dimensions, searching such information is a lot more complicated than text-searching. To deal with this deluge of content it is essential to remove the duplicated information, to reduce the search time. Indexing and clustering can facilitate effective searching and retrieval (Saravan, 2016:27). While a number of software packages for multimedia retrieval are available on the internet, they are hamstrung by limited usability. Today, multimedia retrieval and sampling are conducted by way of content-based searches. Purposeful sampling seems to be the preferred method.

7.9   SELECTION BIAS

As pointed out in chapter 2, selection bias occurs when certain groups in the population are not represented in the sample. This could occur when some units in the population are sampled at a different rate than intended by the researcher. If researchers, for example, sampled tweets from *#End violence against women and children* over a weekend when a famous actress was severely assaulted by her boyfriend, the 'end violence against women' part of the hashtag would generate a much richer response than the 'end violence against children' part. Different stakeholders would participate in the discourse and a different array of themes would be generated than if it was the child of a famous actress who was the victim of the assault.

According to Lohr (2010:6), selection bias can be overcome by allowing a multiplicity of listings into the sample frame without adjusting for it in the analysis. If, for instance, the researchers working on the case of the ban of the Constitutional Court on corporal punishment in the household sampled from #Concourt as well as #Spanking, two different types of responses would in all probability be generated. The #Concourt hashtag would probably elicit more rational responses while #Spanking may draw more emotive responses. If Lohr's guideline is followed this distinction should be highlighted in the report.

7.10   THE ETHICS OF SOCIAL MEDIA RESEARCH

Researchers who make use of social network data may theoretically do so without the people who originally posted it knowing. Once the data is visible to all users of a social media platform, it is in the public domain, however, there remains disagreement about whether data sourced from social media platforms such as Facebook 'should be fair game for researchers, or whether repurposing such data for research violates the [rights] of content creators' (Hutton & Henderson, 2015:178).

The debate flared up when researchers at Facebook published the findings of a research project aimed at exploring emotional contagion through manipulation of Facebook's News Feed (Kramer, Guillory, and Hancock 2014). When it was discovered that Facebook did not obtain informed consent from participants, there was widespread criticism of the ethical violations committed during the experiment (Hill, 2014). Only after the dust had settled, Facebook inserted the word 'research' to a clause in their Data Use Policy regarding 'how we use the information we receive'. The document is one of three policy documents users are required to peruse and sign off before registering.

> *While Facebook considers this clause to be an acceptable proxy for gaining informed consent for individual studies, it betrays the expectation that participants engage in research knowing what information is collected, and for what purpose* (Hutton & Henderson, 2015:178).

Refer to chapter 10 for a more detailed discussion on social media ethics.

7.11   THE CREDIBILITY OF THE SOCIAL MEDIA STUDY

The following variables will determine the credibility of the research:

7.11.1   Validity

This variable describes the accuracy in which the findings reflect the data. Validity is closely related to truth value (Noble & Smith, 2015:34). It implies that the researcher recognises the existence of multiple realities. According to Creswell (2014:237), it is crucial for the researcher to declare his position and biases at the start of the study. All orientations, prejudices, and past experiences that may impact on the study must be placed on record. The researcher(s) must take that into account during the whole research process from design to data analysis. This will help any reviewer and/or reader to understand the predisposition of the reader as well as the viewpoints that guided the study.

If a researcher who, for example, embarks on a project to analyse public opinion reflected on Twitter regarding #PayBackTheMoney harbours strong views that ex-President Zuma should pay from his own pocket for all the security upgrades at his Nkandla homestead, it may impact on the selection of tweets such researcher uses to scaffold his findings. The researcher may need to engage another researcher to ensure that his or her prejudices are not reflected in the study.

7.11.2 Reliability

Joppe (2000:1) defines reliability as:

The extent to which results are consistent over time and an accurate representation of the total population under study is referred to as reliability and if the results of a study can be reproduced under a similar methodology, then the research instrument is considered to be reliable.

The first part of the definition clearly telegraphs that it is aimed at quantitative research. Although the reliability construct is better known for its role in evaluating dimensions of accuracy in quantitative research, it is not unusual to see it featured in other types of research too. If the idea of testing is viewed as a way of information elicitation, then the most important test of any qualitative study is the reliability of its findings. Eisner (1991:58) postulated that a good qualitative study can help us 'understand a situation that would otherwise be enigmatic or confusing.' Reliability is thus seen as a concept that reflects the quality of a quantitative study with a 'purpose of explaining' while the quest for quality in a qualitative study has the purpose of 'generating understanding' (Stenbacka, 2001:551).

Patton (2002) states that validity and reliability are two factors which any qualitative researcher must pay serious attention to. Lincoln and Guba (1985:290) make mention of the congruence of reliability and validity and suggest that the following question should guide the researcher's approach: 'How can an inquirer persuade his or her audiences that the research findings of an inquiry are worth paying attention to?' They list credibility, consistency, neutrality, dependability, and transferability as the essential criteria that determine quality (Lincoln & Guba, 1985). They are also of the opinion that the measurability that can be achieved for reliability makes it a better fit for quantitative research while dependability is more suited for qualitative research, Lincoln and Guba (1985:300). Stenbacka (2001:552) supports this viewpoint and reasons that since queries about reliability can only be solved by measurements, it is of no consequence to the assessment of the quality of qualitative research.

7.11.3   Generalisability

Generalisability is the variable that distinguishes probability samples from non-probability samples. Braun and Clarke (2013:280) state that the test for generalisability is 'whether the results generated in one study can be applied to wider or different populations'. True generalisability can only be achieved by way of sampling if every unit or case of the researcher's target population has an equal chance of being included in the sample and that cannot be achieved with social media sampling.

7.11.4   Consistency

Consistency relates to the level of 'trustworthiness' with which the methods have been implemented and requires the researcher to document a 'decision-trail'. This will confirm that the researcher's decisions are earmarked by clarity and transparency. 'Ultimately an independent researcher should be able to arrive at similar or comparable findings' (Noble & Smith, 2015:34).

7.11.5   Applicability

This variable deals with the question of whether consideration was given to whether findings can be applied to other contexts, settings or groups (Noble & Smith, 2015:34).

7.11.6   Neutrality (or confirmability)

Neutrality has been achieved when truth value, consistency and applicability were addressed. It is based on the acknowledgement that the methods that are undertaken and findings that are derived are intrinsically linked to the researchers' philosophical position, experience, and perspectives (Noble & Smith, 2015:34).

7.11.7   Diversity

Although diversity is a valued characteristic of a sample, it is according to Osborne (2013:45) 'not always possible to have broad dimensions of diversity represented in every sample for every research question'. Braun and Clarke (2013:56) explain diversity as a maximum variation or maximum heterogeneity. Not all researchers strive to obtain diversity in their samples. In some cases, the researcher aims to achieve typicality or homogeneity of perspective. It speaks for itself that it is a lot easier to achieve diversity with purposive sampling than with any of the random sampling techniques, provided that the researcher is well-acquainted with the stakeholder environment.

7.12   NEW METHODOLOGIES THAT FACILITATE SAMPLING

A researcher who wants to start a new project on social media will be confronted by a deluge of data. Data is the new differentiator. The question is how can this data be downloaded in a usable format? The first thought that would probably cross the researcher's mind is to copy and paste it manually, however, it is not practical to do it for large websites with thousands of pages. The only option may be web scraping.

Web scraping is a process of automating the extraction of data in an efficient and fast way (Patel 2018). Web scraping makes it possible to extract data from any website, no matter how large the dataset is. Web scraping is also the best option when websites contain data that cannot be copied and pasted. The mere fact that the data could be copied and pasted does not guarantee usability. Before the analysis can start the data needs to be converted to a usable format. The wide array of web scraping tools that are available to the researcher allows for him or her to save the data in a usable format such as CSV. He or she would then be able to access, analyse and implement the data the way you want.

nCapture is an example of a web scraping tool that can be downloaded for free. It works well with NVivo which is a licensed qualitative data analysis tool. The payment of an annual licensing fee is required for usage. See chapter 8 for more information.

7.13   CASE STUDY: THE OSCAR PISTORIUS TRIAL

The trial of Oscar Pistorius, Paralympic athlete and poster boy of the 2012 Olympic games, grabbed headlines all over the world. Pistorius was eventually found guilty of the murder of his girlfriend, model Reeva Steenkamp. During the trial, the social media was dominated by enthusiastic contributors who wanted to share an opinion on the case. On 11–12 September 2014 when Judge Masispa delivered the verdict, 700 000 unique tweets were posted (ROI Africa, 2014). The massive numbers challenged researchers to do quantitative as well as qualitative analysis of the content.

Van der Vyver purposefully selected tweets from professional as well as citizen journalists that were posted during the trial. He compared themes and presentation styles between the two main types of contributors. He only ended the process once the results were, in his view, saturated.

Mawson (2014) cited figures that were provided by Mike Wronski, Managing Director of research company, Fuseware, on the most mentioned individuals on Twitter during the first day of trial. The sample is thus defined as tweets posted on the first day of the trial, namely 3 March 2014.

It is interesting to note from the results for day one that three of the four most mentioned individuals are journalists covering the story (Mawson, 2014).

Table 7. 1:   Most mentioned individuals in the Twitter hashtags related to the Oscar Pistorius Case

Person	Number of mentions
Barry Bateman	2 849
Oscar Pistorius	977
Karyn Maughan	830
MandyWiener	440

Source: Mawson (2014)

These findings are a result of the metadata (retweets, likes, and conversations) that the tweets triggered.

7.14   SUMMARY

Before the advent of the internet, polling and surveys were the dominant ways of collecting data but they have become very time consuming and expensive. Social media platforms have increasingly replaced other modes of data sourcing such as surveys conducted by telephone and emails (Phan & Airoldi 2015). The compilation of questionnaires, the training of the field workers, the execution of it, and the analysis of the data requires time, a reasonable budget as well as diligence. With budgets shrinking at an alarming rate, researchers, especially early-career researchers are often forced to look for alternative data collection options. Social media platforms offer affordable data at the fingertips of a researcher but before a researcher can consider going that route, there are a number of advantages as well as constraints that he or she must take into account.

First, it is of paramount importance to note that sampling of social media data very seldom lends itself to random sampling. All of the contributors who post content do so on their own initiative. The sample therefore only represents a small and narrow segment of the population. It speaks for itself that the digital divide excludes many citizens who harbour strong views but do not have internet access. The results can, therefore, not be assumed to reflect the views of the public as a whole. The same warning applies to researchers who sample data from Twitter or any of the other social media platforms.

On the positive side, it can be assumed that those who post a comment feel strongly about the issue they are posting about. The hashtag # on Twitter, for example, serves as a billboard that invites interested parties to contribute. In the case of a telephone poll, many respondents tender opinions although they are not informed about the topic. It is a fact of life that people feel foolish when they have to admit that they have not heard of a certain topic, so they just proceed and guess a few answers. Respondents may also support the dominant opinion even though they hold a completely different view. These negatives are mostly not present when an individual makes the effort to post on social media.

Social media lends itself to a wide array of sampling methods. The researcher can select from an impressive collection of computational models to several very basic manual methods to sample the data. The decision on which sampling method to use thus rests with the researcher. As long as the selection can be justified within the context of the research problem, the validity of the sampling process will not be queried. A justifiable sampling process by no means guarantees the reliability of the findings which rather will depend on the accuracy with which the sampling is executed as well as the trustworthiness of the findings.

Learning activities (Test yourself)

1. Explain the differences between sampling for social media and sampling for surveys.

2. What are the main methodological challenges and issues that need to be taken into account for sampling for social media?

3. Can you think of a research problem for which sampling from the social media can form part of a suitable research design? If so, describe it.

4. Can a randomiser be used in social media sampling? Justify your answer.

5. How can a researcher enhance the trustworthiness of a qualitative social media study's findings?

Further reading

Babbie, E. & Mouton, J. 2001. *The practice of social research.* Cape Town: Oxford University Press.

Bar-Yossef, Z. & Gurevich, M. 2008. Random sampling from a search engine's index. *Journal of Applied and Computing Mechanics*, 55(5): 24:1–24:74.

Caci, B., Cardaci, M. & Tabacchi, M.E. 2012. Facebook as a small world: A topological hypothesis. *Social Network Analysis and Mining*, 2(2): 163–167.

Colleoni, E., Rozza, A. & Arvidsson, A. 2014. Echo chamber or public sphere? Predicting political orientation and measuring political homophily in Twitter using Big Data. *Journal of Communication*, 64(2): 317–332.

Dusek, G. A., Yurova, Y. V. & Ruppel, C. P. 2015. Using social media and targeted snowball sampling to survey a hard-to-reach population: A case study. *International Journal of Doctoral Studies*, 10: 279-–299. Available from: http://ijds.org/Volume10/IJDSv10p279-299Dusek0717.pdf [8 August 2019].

Haralabopoulos, G. & Anagnostopoulos, I. 2014. Real time enhanced random sampling of online social networks. *Journal of Network and Computer Applications*, 41:126–134.

Hester, J.B. & Dougall, E. (2007). The efficiency of constructed week sampling for content analysis of online news. *Journalism & Mass Communication Quarterly*, 84(4): 811–824. doi:10.1177/107769900708400410 [3 October 2019].

Lee, S.H., Kim, P.J. & Jeong, H. 2006. Statistical properties of sampled networks. *Physical Review E*, 73(1): 016102.

Neumann, W.L. 2007. *Basics of social research: qualitative and quantitative approaches.* 2nd ed.. Boston, MA: Pearson.

Tailor, G. R. (ed.). 2005. *Integrating quantitative and qualitative methods in research.* Maryland: University Press of America.

CHAPTER 8

Collecting Big Social (Media) Data

Ronesh Dhawraj

Big data is the artefact of human individual as well as collective intelligence generated and shared mainly through the technological environment, where virtually anything and everything can be documented, measured, and captured digitally, and in so doing transformed into data. – Sivarajah et al.

Learning Outcomes

At the end of this chapter, the researcher should be able to:

- distinguish among the varied types of Big Social Data;
- distinguish the different types of raw data, of which Big Social Data is one type;
- critically explain how and why social media can be regarded as Big Social Data;
- recognise which methodological tools are available to researchers to conduct sound research using Big Social Data;
- decide when and under what circumstances researchers can opt for a manual or automated approach of Big Social Data collection;
- critically analyse some of the checks and balances of Big Social Data collection to ensure 'trustworthiness' is achieved for a credible study; and
- become more confident when using Big Social Data for research.

8.1   INTRODUCTION

Technology continues to permeate every facet of contemporary life. The last decade has witnessed an unprecedented information explosion, a time like no other in history. Central to this drastic technological evolution is how social media has reconfigured the communication and information spaces (McCourt, 2018). Besides providing an important, low-cost communicative function for businesses, entertainment, crisis communications and the political world, social media platforms now provide researchers with a treasure trove of instantly-available information to understand the 'behaviours, attitudes and beliefs' of ordinary people – in real time (mostly) (Sloan et al., 2019:1). This rapid diffusion of social media avenues also means that vast accumulation of user-generated 'hidden knowledge' data is available to researchers (Saad et al., 2018:76) – representing an 'explosion of opportunity for research' according to Stieglitz et al. (2018:156). As much as researchers are encouraged to openly embrace this development as an opportunity to tap into gargantuan reservoirs of mostly free information, this deluge has also meant a quiet reluctance on the part of scholars because there is just *too much information*.

When social media and the concept of big data intersect, researchers become even more intimidated with the extent of available information; and the added encumbrance of dealing with unstructured and often noisy data (see chapter 5, section 5.3). Hopefully, with this chapter on social media data collection novice researchers and established scholars will feel less fearful of working with infinite amounts of data emanating from social media platforms. Using two explicit examples from his own experience (to be expanded in section 8.9 of this chapter), the author illustrates how best to handle complex, noisy and unstructured Big Social Data. However, to fully grasp the concepts of social media and big data, there is a need to first begin by giving a broad overview of the different types of Big Social Data and what this all means for communication researchers. Please note that scholars often use the terms big social data and social big data interchangeably.

8.2   TYPES OF RAW BIG SOCIAL DATA

This section should be read with the discussion of Big Social Data in chapter 5.

For purposes of clarity, Olshannikova et al., (2017:1–2) articulate that Big Social Data is commonly referred to as 'large data volumes that relate to people or describe their behavior and technology-mediated social interactions in the digital realm'. In simple terms, humans are increasingly using information communication technologies or ICTs to fuel social interactions for several reasons. For the authors, such digital interactions are executed for three prime reasons: to represent oneself digitally (basic profile data and user-generated content as part of a broader community are illustrations), to generate 'technology-mediated communication data' (one-to-one and one-to-many communication using technology as the main conveyor) and 'digital relationships data' (cultivating and maintaining a follower base in the form of Facebook friends and/or followers over Twitter and Instagram and other such platforms) (Olshannikova et al. 2017:12–14). Part of the raw Big Social Data package includes vanity metrics such as 'shares', 'likes', 'favorites', 'mentions', impressions', the use of hashtags, clicking on links to external websites, analysis using keywords, the concept of attracting new followers; and general comments left by people who seek to interact with social media posts. In an age of rapid technological leaps and increasing social media platform proliferation, questions also arise around 'meaningful social media data' versus mere 'vanity metrics' for research purposes (Barnhart, 2019). For purposes of this particular chapter, however, the discussion focuses on the omnipresence of data, the concept of Big Social Data, retrieving historical, real-time, and visual data; and some of the associated pitfalls related to each of these data types.

8.2.1   An era defined by a data explosion

Five years back, Dobre and Xhafa (2014) estimated that some 2.5 quintillion bytes of data were produced globally on a daily basis. To wrap one's head around this, one quintillion bytes is expressed as a single Exabyte; and it takes no less than one billion gigabytes to comprise a single Exabyte (Sivarajah et al. 2016:263). Earlier, Gantz and Reinsel (2012) had predicted that a serious data explosion before the end of the decade could result in 40 zettabytes – or 40 trillion gigabytes – being 'generated, imitated and consumed' by 2020. Desjardins (2019b) has since suggested that 463 Exabytes of data are expected to be created daily by 2025, equating to '212,765,957 DVDs per day'. Perhaps this is what Sivarajah et al. (2016:263) spoke of much earlier: A *data deluge* of unstoppable big data proliferation where the knowledge economy expands at even greater speeds over shorter periods of time.

On social media and social media data, Smith (2019) estimates that 30 per cent – or 3.5 billion – of the world's 7.7 billion population is online with some social media platform presence. In the United States, for example, numbers suggest that while Americans upload approximately 2.1 million photographs every minute for social media applications such as Instagram, another million users log onto Facebook every 60 seconds. Video-sharing sites such as YouTube equally receive their fair share of online attention with some 4 million online video views recorded in the US for every minute. With microblogging portal Twitter too, it is about volume: some 500 million tweets (or 6 000 tweets every second) are said to travel within the 'Twitter-sphere' in a 24-hour cycle (see also Desjardins, 2019a; Desjardins, 2019b; Kemp, 2019; Davies, 2019). Smith (2019), furthermore, estimates that each 'connected' person who elects to go online has an average of 7.6 social media accounts; and will generally spend approximately 142 minutes online daily. Please refer to Table 8.1 for an outline of the global Internet and general social media connectivity.

Table 8.1:   Global 2019 Internet and social media connectivity

Detail	Explanation
Internet	4.39 billion users, 366 million more than 2018 (9% increase between 2018 and 2019)
Social media	3.48 billion users, 288 million more than 2018 (9% increase between 2018 and 2019)
Mobile phone diffusion	5.11 billion mobile users, 100 million more than 2018 (2% increase between 2018 and 2019); 6 billion smartphones to be in circulation by the end of 2020
Social media using mobile devices	3.26 billion users, 297 million more than 2018 (10% increase between 2018 and 2019)
Social media usage	Average social media user spends 2 hours and 16 minutes daily on social media platforms daily, up from 2 hours and 15 minutes in 2018

Source: Katapally (2019), Smith (2019) and Kemp (2019)

Additionally, Table 8.2 provides a quick snapshot of five of the world's most popular social media platforms at the time of publication coupled with their respective follower base.

Table 8.2:   Leading global social media platforms and their user base

Platform	Typology	Users/followers
Facebook	Social networking, sharing of pictures, connecting with family, friends, and colleagues	2.37 billion
You Tube	Posting of videos	1.9 billion
TikTok	Sharing of short videos	1.5 billion
Instagram	Picture and video-sharing	1 billion
Twitter	Microblogging using the sharing of brief updates through text, image, video, live-streaming, and audio	330 million

Source: Vela (2020), Smith (2019) and Statt (2019)

8.2.2   Historical, real-time, and visual Big Social Data types

Big Social Data can either be synchronous or asynchronous. In other words, data can be posted in real time or be communicated much later than the original posting. When it comes to so-called 'historical data' or asynchronous data that is not in real time, a portal such as trackmyhashtag.com/historical-twitter-data can come in very handy (see Saylor, 2012). Although researchers will pay a small amount for the data, this 'raw' Twitter data will nearly-always include several elements to help the researcher such as Twitter user identification, time of the published tweet, the actual content of the tweet, tweet type (in terms of it either being a retweet or reply), the device used to send out the tweet, the quantitative velocity of the said tweet, a geo-tag attached to the tweet; and the number of 'likes' and retweets the tweet eventually accumulated. Several other organisations are offering a similar type of service; this though at most times is a monetised service. The bigger the data set request, the higher researchers will be expected to pay for the access. As far as real-time data is concerned, social media platforms are constantly churning our billions of gigabytes of user-generated information every second of the day. The synchronous nature of such data is invaluable to organisations, researchers and research institutions that will use these vast data sets to derive more nuanced readings of human behaviours. While there remain a number of open-source avenues to access this real-time data, most social media platforms have since monetised the analytics component.

Although data collection using visual data such as still imagery and moving video is still in its infancy, there are a number of tools available to researchers should they choose to pursue this academic route. For example, if the intention is to study the picture and video-sharing application, Instagram, a data collection tool such as Instaloader can be easily used (Creps, 2019). Both pictures and videos can be downloaded together with the accompanying hashtags, captions, and other relevant information. Other remarkable features of using Instaloader is that it is a free open-source software 'written in Python'; and provides several functionalities such as filtering important data such as comments, geotags, profile names and users' feeds (Barnhart, 2019; Creps, 2019).

While research on another video-sharing application, TikTok, is still in its early stages (see Yu 2019), due attention should nonetheless be paid to this Chinese-founded global phenomenon. The initial idea behind TikTok was the idea of a lip-sync application called Musical.ly; this was then bought by ByteDance in August 2018 (Statt 2019; Vela 2020). Boasting approximately 1.5 billion downloads as at late-2019 (Statt 2019), TikTok is a big data social media platform allowing users to post short and funny videos of between 15 and 60 seconds (Montgomery 2020). The application is also highly prized for being a light-hearted portal that connects with the younger generation, a much-sought-after demographic when it comes to online marketing audience segmentation (11 Reasons TikTok...2019). Today, TikTok is regarded as the 'biggest, most exciting social media platform out there right now' (Vela 2020) and is expected to overtake other popular big data social media platforms such as Facebook, Twitter and Instagram because users are increasingly searching for something new and less serious (Boxiner et al., 2019).

8.3   BIG SOCIAL (MEDIA) DATA MINING

Big Social Data is today regarded as a 'twenty-first-century phenomenon', a time like no other defined by vast reams of easily available information, with users now empowered more than ever to be online co-creators of that information (McCourt, 2018). But what happens after one has identified the Big Social Data one needs? What needs to happen next? This is where the concept of data mining emerges. Before any definition of social media data mining can be provided, it is essential to reflect on what the concept of *data mining* entails. According to Kudyba (2010), data mining becomes an obvious action where organisational data and organisational processes exist. Barnhart (2019) adds that the more data researchers can collect; 'better results' can be eventually reached through 'more informed decision-making'. When this data is needed to analyse the inner workings of said organisation, data mining is said to have resulted in the yielding of 'actionable information' to help the organisation function better (Kudyba, 2010). Priya (2017) supports this sequential nature of data mining, arguing further that the core objective of any data mining initiative is the generation of fresh perspectives and deeper insights that may not have existed previously. Interestingly, when the concepts of big data and social media 'collide', the term *social media mining* emerges. While bearing similarities to data mining, social media mining is more specific, confining itself to social networking sites such as Facebook and other digital media avenues like Twitter and Instagram which researchers can easily tap into to uncover a multitude of motivations for human behaviours, choices and patterns.

At the same time, there should be no confusion when it comes to terms such as *social media analytics* and *social media data harvesting*. Sathish et al. (2017:174), for example, argue that while social media analytics is the 'art of collecting (big) data from social media websites like Facebook, Twitter, YouTube, WhatsApp and blogs' to gauge 'the sentiments of the people', data harvesting is about categorising that content. Agreed, social media analytics could be used interchangeably with social media mining, data harvesting on the other hand in the main comprises of three main categories, namely *content data* in the form of user comments and online profiles; *behaviour data* which give social scientists a brief glimpse into how users interact with content through actions such as sharing online posts; and *network structure data* which more often than not include embedded hyperlinks and other visual cues within online content (Liang & Zhu, 2017:2). Therefore – according to Sathish *et al* (2017), Liang and Zhu (2017) and Patnaik and Barik (2018:262) – the terms *social media analytics* and *social media data harvesting* are not synonymous. Dhawraj (2019), additionally, asserts that *social media analytics* is used when deeper nuances of the data set are needed. Twitter, as an example, provides its own set of social media data analytics for users to understand how successful their accounts have been; and what content worked better than others (How to use Twitter analytics, 2019). During this *social listening* exercise, changes can be made to the overall strategy for future better message-targeting (Wronski, 2015). Patnaik and Barik (2018:264) could not have summed it up better, though, when they asserted that social media data analytics simply put is indeed about capturing, understanding and eventually presenting what one finds in a vast data set.

In the next section, the discussion moves to the different research methods and tools available to researchers, students, and scholars for their Big Social (media) Data collection journey.

8.4 AN OVERVIEW OF DATA COLLECTION METHODS AND TOOLS FOR BIG SOCIAL (MEDIA) DATA

At present, there is an expanding list of available Big Social Data collection tools, both free and paid. Some examples include Chorus (free), Mozdeh (free), Twitter Arching Google Spreadsheet (TAGS) (free), Webometric Analyst (free), NodeXL (paid) and Pulsar (paid) to name a few (see also chapters 2, 5 and 9). When selecting social media data collection tools, the research method should always be the main consideration. With Big Social Data research on a rapid rise in the last decade, several authors have since come to the fore to document its impact on various disciplines. Ahmed (2019), for example, used Twitter conversations to provide qualitative insights into health pandemics and epidemics. Since then, Ahmed (2019) has written extensively on his foray with social media data collection, going so far as extending Stieglitz et al's. (2018) earlier suggestions of popular research methods when dealing with social media data.

8.4.1 Collecting Big Social Data manually or with automated tools

When it comes to collecting Big Social Data for academic research purposes, it is perfectly natural for novice researchers to feel a sense of anxiety. However, to successfully vanquish this nervousness, having a clear strategy that ultimately determines what researchers want from the data becomes integral. A series of hard but practical questions need to be asked from the onset: what is the data about, what does the data need to tell one, is the collected data sufficient to resolve the main research problem and subsequent research questions of the project, how best can the data be 'cleaned' to ensure analysis of only the most important aspects; and what other 'organisation' of the data set is needed to enable the researcher to derive deeper and meaningful knowledge? Radford (2019), in this respect, advises that researchers need only be firm, decisive and confident at this crucial juncture of social media data collection. Part of the decision-making process is knowing when to opt for using either a manual data collection approach that entails physically capturing the data oneself or a second option of electing for the automated alternative (see also chapter 2).

In the past, websites and social media platforms permitted scholars somewhat unfettered access to data on their sites. This has slowly changed in the wake of the *Cambridge Analytica* data breach scandal and the introduction of more government regulatory red tape (see Robertson, 2018; Watkins & Sutton, 2018; McCourt, 2018). While researchers can still rely on using Application Program Interfaces (or APIs) provided by various platforms, most of the changes introduced since then include limited data access and payment for what is mined (Ahmed, 2019). Twitter, for example, in its 2015 API update now 'restricts' free access to a mere 1 per cent of published tweets within a seven-day window period. Facebook, too, prevents third-party applications from accessing 'user IDs' for public pages (Davies, 2019).

8.4.2 The manual approach

Before deciding whether the manual or automated approach would suit a research project more, Radford (2019) proposes researchers first take a conscious decision from the onset by focusing predominantly on the research design of the study. If, for example, researchers need to use data from sites such as Facebook or Twitter, there would be no issue with the researcher manually 'taking notes' of interactions between users on each platform as the data is already in the public sphere. Radford (2019), additionally, advises that this is perfectly legitimate because it is 'no different' to making observations 'as if you were standing on the street or any other public space'. Regardless of this boundless access, researchers still need to adhere to the respective platform's own privacy policies and regulations of the researcher's institution, McCourt (2018) warns.

When it comes to manually drag-netting information from users' private electronic emails (emails), direct messages (DMs) or 'private' social media posts, consent from the said user would, however, need to be obtained beforehand. While there is no single magic bullet to overcome the many bureaucratic hurdles researchers nowadays face, opting for the manual data collection approach sometimes vetoes the threat of any third party permission that needs to be sought and/or the added worry of paying for the data (Liang & Zhu, 2017:13–15). Also, although possible and sometimes preferred, manual data collection could result in incomplete data sets as also pointed out in chapter 2. It depends on how large the dataset is and also how experienced the researcher is. For reasons of practically guiding future researchers, though, two examples are provided in section 8.9 of how manual social media data collection could be achieved and the motivations behind each respective selection.

8.4.3 The automated approach

The automated approach becomes indispensable when handling Big Social Data, notably when voluminous amounts of data are the order of the day. Big Social Data produced from sources such as blogging, microblogging, social network services, sharing and video communication services, social news, gaming, crowd-sourcing services and mobile applications are a few examples of this (Olshannikova et al: 2017:15–19). Of course, it may happen that sometimes researchers prefer not to physically collect the data due to some other constraint and/or the sheer size of the data set; this is when the automated approach becomes available. Both Liang and Zhu (2017) and Radford (2019) provide three ways how this can be seamlessly executed through – what they call – 'web services', a 'do-it-yourself' option and through 'web scraping'. With 'web services', researchers automatically select the data they need siphoning off a site using 'services' such as 'Volunteer Science' or 'Export Tweet' which come with an in-built facility of legitimate data access without the regulatory hassles. If this fails, researchers can opt for the 'do-it-yourself' alternative where customised APIs can be built bottom-up to suit the intricacies of the research project. Some programming language examples include 'Python' and 'R'. 'Tweepy' can be used with 'Python' while 'twitteR' can be matched with 'R' for easy Twitter data downloading (Liang & Zhu, 2017:15–16; Ahmed 2019; Davies 2019). The distinct advantage of using such tools is the speed at which data can be accessed and downloaded. However, downsides such as API access application and programming literacy remain challenges.

With 'web scraping', researchers can 'scrape raw content' from multiple websites and platforms using a myriad of programming tools. A word of caution though, that electing to use 'web scraping' involves writing a brand new program to draw said data from the site; this then still needs to be recreated as 'structured data'. While there may be risks associated with 'web scraping' the data one needs, opting for such a facility can nonetheless be rewarding in terms of 'power and flexibility' in creating the ideal data set engineered around a researcher's customised requirements (Liang & Zhu, 2017; Ahmed, 2019; Davies, 2019; Radford, 2019).

Other options available to researchers when dealing with large Big Social Data sets – notably when it comes to storage – include using software tools such as NVivo Pro (to be clearly illustrated in section 8.9 of this chapter) and Leximancer, a text-mining software tool used to speedily analyse qualitative 'natural-language text data' in a number of formats and languages (see Biroscak, Scott, Lindenberger & Bryant 2017; Haynes, Garside, Green, Kelly, Thomas, & Guell 2019: 454–455).

8.5   MAPPING THE BIG SOCIAL DATA COLLECTION PROCESS

The data collection process is closely linked to the research design of a study (also outlined in detail in chapter 2). For easier reference, please see Figure 8.1 for a simple illustration of how the Big Social Data collection process possibly unfolds:

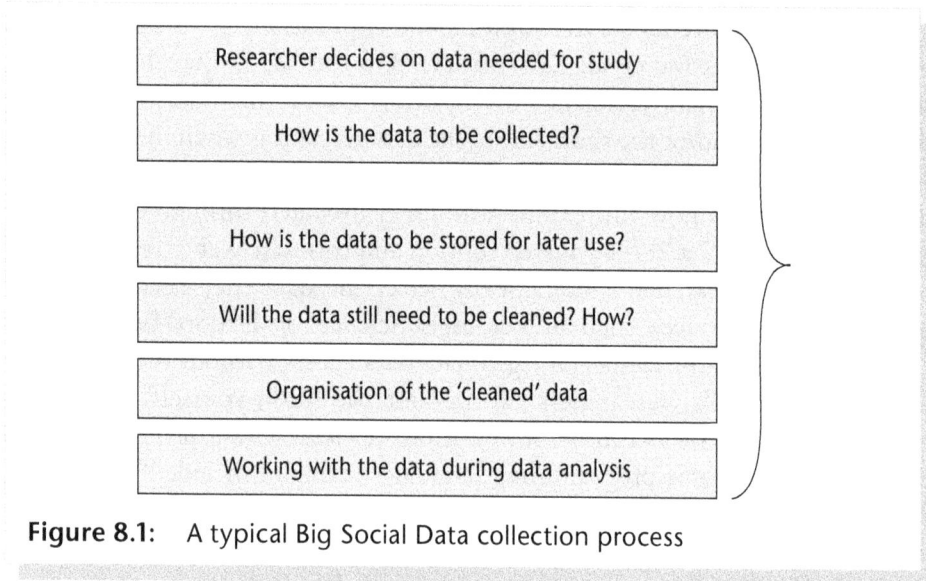

Figure 8.1:   A typical Big Social Data collection process

In the next section, the author addresses the matter of embellishing one's Big Social Data study with the all-important credibility factor.

8.6   'TRUSTING' THE COLLECTED BIG SOCIAL DATA

For any social media study to be credible and enjoy the confidence of the academic and professional world, researchers need to demonstrate the rigour of their research through criteria such as reliability and validity. A detailed discussion on quantitative and qualitative studies and how to achieve reliability and validity for a quantitative study and how to achieve trustworthiness, credibility, transferability and confirmability for a qualitative study is also outlined in chapter 2. Fortunately, Creswell (2007:17–19) simplifies this by suggesting that especially qualitative scholars need to address issues around 'trustworthiness, rigor and quality' whenever reference is made to reliability and validity. While internal validity (credibility) is concerned with how reliable the collected data is, external validity (transferability) can be regarded as a synonym for reliability and how final results can be generalised to wider research populations. Granted many scholars will disagree; arguing that it mostly pivots on whether the study is quantitative or qualitative in nature.

Creswell (2007:17–19), however, is the first to point out that while the aim of qualitative studies is not to generalise; the objective is to nonetheless provide 'unique impressions and understandings' applicable to a particular context.

In the example cited later in section 8.9 of this chapter – namely case study 2 – to secure the trustworthiness of the study Dhawraj (2019) relied on Bickman and Rog's (2008) assertion that generalisation would still be possible if the researcher could explicitly account for how the Grounded Theory was developed from start to finish. Replication was, thus, possible, as long as the researcher's perceived bias, personal perspectives and other 'recorded protocols' could be accounted for. Dhawraj (2019), however, relied on Sikolia et al's. (2013) proposal that the best way to evaluate the 'trustworthiness' of a Grounded Theory study – notably using Big Social Data – was to measure it against various criteria, namely credibility (internal validity), transferability (external validity), dependability (reliability) and confirmability. Firstly, when it came to *credibility (internal validity)*, various data sources were used including social media data (the corpus of African National Congress (ANC) and Democratic Alliance (DA) tweets); and detailed descriptions of the tweets were notarised using memos on NVivo Pro 12 which then supplemented theoretical sampling, theoretical coding and theoretical saturation. Secondly, the element of *transferability (external validity)* was safeguarded using the researcher's own detailed account of the data, including final interpretations. When it came to the third criteria of *dependability (reliability)*, extensive audit trails numbering some 50 pages captured over NVivo Pro 12 were generated. This substantial diarising of what was observed within the different data sets (including the corpus of social media data in the form of tweets) were also aligned with the fourth characteristic, namely *confirmability*, to buttress the overall veracity and 'trustworthiness' of the study (see Dhawraj, 2019).

As far as case study 1 is concerned (see section 8.9 in this chapter) where Dhawraj (2013) used Facebook conversations from former DA leader Mrs Helen Zille's page to gauge how she and her party reached out to potential voters in the 2009 general elections, the best way to secure the credibility of the data and study was to use several pilot studies. For example, a 26 per cent (25.92%) pilot study of Mrs Zille's 27 Facebook posts was used. This was then tested by the researcher and an additional coder using Holsti's (1969) *inter-coder reliability test*. The 'agreement level' hovered around 86 per cent (85.71%). The high confidence level of this test was further strengthened by ensuring Zille's 27 Facebook posts were categorised soundly; and into the correct categories (as part of the quantitative content analysis exercise). Both the researcher and the second coder safeguarded this (see Dhawraj, 2013).

The two examples cited (please see section 8.9 of this chapter) illustrate to future researchers that the *trustworthiness* of any study (using Big Social

Data notably) can be attained. The data collection method and data analysis processes are the final arbiters and ultimate determinants of how researchers go about guaranteeing the soundness of a study. Audit trails – as outlined in both case studies – are integral factors when it comes to research projects involving big data (sets) in the shape of social media web-based information. A researcher's full immersion in the process, coupled with a detailed report-back on his or her role needs to be accounted for.

8.7 LOOKING TO THE FUTURE OF BIG SOCIAL DATA COLLECTION

A critical reading of scholarship around Big Social Data collection reveals persistent deficiencies within the field. A cursory glance at published writing on the subject matter involving still and moving imagery analysis, for example, yields only limited results such as Hu et al. (2014), Pila et al. (2017) and Saad et al. (2018). Pearce et al. (2018) provide another example of this shortcoming within the discipline. In their research, Pearce et al. (2018) found that because APIs were easily available to help researchers with their data collection and data analysis journeys, this ironically continued to disadvantage the probing of multi-platform analysis and concomitantly moving beyond the exclusive focus on text only. To remedy this, the authors proposed what they labelled a *visual cross-platform analysis (VCPA)* model to give due recognition to still and moving imagery; and to also account for multiple social media platform probing. A vital argument for their model is perched on the idea that while there will always be value in deriving patterns from online vanity behaviour metrics such as 'likes', 'retweets' and 'shares' from textual analysis, still imagery and video by their very nature played an equally 'important communicative role' in the examined data set (Pearce *et al*, 2018:16). Therefore, these two key elements could no longer be subjugated at the expense of elevating other parts of whole data sets. Optimal utilisation of their *VCPA model* (and other subsequent ones) which encourages cross-platform analysis, however, is still sadly in its early days.

8.7.1 Retrieval of visual data, still and moving

Of course, the main debate confronting the retrieval and use of still, moving and audio Big Social Data remains around applicable ethical rules over publicly available information. Underpinning this assertion is the argument that online social media users volunteer information on various social media platforms knowing full well it is accessible to global audiences, organisations, political parties, and other such entities. It would then beg the question of why there would be a fuss if and when researchers needed to dip into these information-rich platforms to deepen science's understanding of human behaviours? When it comes to YouTube videos, Hu (2019), for example, argues that it is not always possible for researchers to obtain written or informed consent from people who voluntarily post material on a public platform such as the video-sharing portal. The author further says that because no legal prescripts govern this type of research, it does not automatically mean the researcher's own ethics cannot come into play. If videos contain the voices and faces of minors (those aged 18 and under) as a clearer illustration, what ethical recourse should researchers pursue? Will parents of minors who voluntarily post videos to a globally accessible site need to be contacted to provide consent before researchers can use the material for study purposes? Researchers, too, are bound by strict timelines. Seeking prior consent becomes unfeasible with the added bureaucracy becoming yet another unnecessary distraction.

When it comes to still photography, here too one cannot shy away from various copyright-related issues. In case study 1 by Dhawraj (2013) – to be expanded in section 8.9 – while users' comments on a public profile like politician Mrs Zille can be easily used for deeper academic probing, the researcher is constrained because he cannot simultaneously use screen-grabbed 'still' images of those comments because of the online user's image attached to that comment. Simply put, it would border on unethical conduct on the part of the researcher. Other notable issues researchers face when using still and moving imagery and audio files originate from the fact that such data is sometimes cumbersome to deal with, it needs huge amounts of storage space, and going through each piece of audio or video file is an arduous process. With videos, for example, researchers would normally assign content analysis themes to each piece of dialogue and/or video frame. When it comes to audio files such as interview transcripts, again file sizes and storage space become determining factors. To be illustrated in case study 2 (in section 8.9), Dhawraj (2019), for his thesis used computer programme NVivo Pro 12 to store the interviews. The programme was also used when analysis of the transcribed interviews was needed. Permission from the two interviewees, however, for the interview material to be used was secured beforehand.

Markham (2012) says that another means of tackling the ethical dilemma associated with still pictures is to 'blur' or 'de-identify' the face of online users when explicit consent cannot be obtained. This becomes even more applicable when the research deals with 'sensitive contexts' such as 'health issues' and societal 'stigmatized identities' that may or may not compromise another person's right to privacy (Haimson, Andalibi & Pater, 2016).

8.8   CASE STUDIES

Seeing that many social media studies deal with communication science and political communication in specific, two case studies entailing how politicians leveraged social media for the 2009 and 2016 South African election campaigning periods are provided as examples of how best to collect and use social media data for study purposes. In case study 1, Facebook conversations for South Africa's main opposition party, the DA, were dissected to gauge just how that political party used the social networking site for election campaigning in the 2009 general elections. The microblogging site, Twitter, provides the backdrop for *case study number 2* to show how it was leveraged by the ANC – South Africa's governing party since 1994 – and the DA for party-political campaigning in the 2016 local government elections. By providing these real-world examples, it is hoped that some guidance can be provided to novice researchers who at times may feel deflated and possibly intimidated when confronted by large, chaotic and wholly unfamiliar web-based data sets.

8.8.1   Case study 1: Mastering the art of a Facebook election campaign

For case study 1, Dhawraj (2013) attempted to understand the DA's thinking behind using the social networking site, Facebook, as a *de facto* campaigning and political public relations (political PR) campaign tool for South Africa's 2009 national and provincial elections. Although Dhawraj (2013) used the DA's 286 media releases and former party leader Mrs Helen Zille's 2009 campaign speeches as part of the broader research arsenal, the main thrust of his research involved dissecting how then party leader, Mrs Helen Zille, had leveraged Facebook to get out her message to bolster her brand. After thoroughly examining all elements of the party's 2009 election campaign, Dhawraj (2013) deduced that while Facebook facilitated public opinion on the DA as a party, its former leader's charismatic spearheading of the campaign had made her and her personal Facebook page quantitatively more popular than the actual party page. Posted messages gleaned from Ms Zille's Facebook account attested to this too. The leader became synonymous with the party's anti-ANC messaging for the duration of the 2009 election campaign. As a result, the DA, at the time, went on to increase its vote-share under Mrs Zille's leadership, including electorally winning the Western Cape for the first time (see Moakes, 2011; Southall & Daniel, 2009:119–120). Symbolically, the Western Cape had also become the only South African province out of eight that was now not under an ANC government post-1994 rule (Schulz-Herzenberg, 2009:29).

When it came to accessing and collecting the required data, namely the DA's 286 media releases and Mrs Zille's campaign speeches, these were not difficult to acquire as political parties tend to have such election documentation freely available in multiple spaces over the World Wide Web (WWW). A key aspect of Dhawraj's (2013) research, however, was accessing Ms Zille's public posts on her Facebook platform. This, too, did not prove difficult because all 27 posts made between 1 January 2009 – 30 April 2009 (the measurement parameters) were easily downloadable from her Facebook page. What did prove a little cumbersome, though, was capturing the hundreds of user comments Ms Zille's 27 election posts had generated at the time. To counter this 'information deluge', intense thematic content analyses were used to capture online sentiment around the DA leader. In this regard, a manual data collection process of the relevant Facebook posts from Ms Zille's account was followed; no automated tool was thus used to acquire this data. Importantly, for this particular exercise, no prior permission was needed for using users' online comments in response to Ms Zille's public Facebook posts as supporters of the DA had publicly posted their comments for all to see. In other words, all the posts on the DA's Facebook page were in the public sphere (public domain). Instead of complicating the research data collection phase, a conscious decision was, thus, taken to use simple screenshots of individual user messages for the thematic content analysis phase. This made working with the 'data' a simple and easy process.

When using data from social media platforms for academic research purposes, it is also important to remember that there really is no hard and fast rule. The aim is to keep it simple and uncomplicated at best to ensure proper organisation during both the data collection and all-important data analysis steps of the research cycle. If screenshots of online conversations work, use this function unashamedly and unabashedly. Also, this is rich, information-laden data that is mostly free. Researchers need only remember that online conversations disappear without warning (Wigston, 2010). Therefore, one must be at least ten steps ahead to ensure the necessary data is indeed captured and stored in a safe place for later use. Of course, if the research problem and subsequent research questions call for deeper analysis from the data, mere screenshots might not be suitable. In such a case, using APIs and other data extraction tools might suffice. Liang and Zhu (2017:9), for example, recommend using *graph.facebook.com* for accessing the Facebook API and api.twitter.com for enabling Twitter's API. Sloan et al. (2019:4) also recommend the COSMOS tool (see http://socialdatalab.net/) for the 'simplest' retrieval of Twitter data for 'non-technical' researchers. Ms Helen Zille's 27 Facebook posts were eventually reconciled with a specially-created coding rubric for Dhawraj's (2013) study to find resonance with what the former DA leader had said in her campaign speeches and media releases in the lead-up to the 2009 general elections. Each post gradually made its way into thematic descriptive content categories to either support or reject the overall conclusions.

Fortunately, it was during this study where Facebook was observed and confirmed as an additional media outlet for the DA's 2009 election campaign drive. Around this time, Twitter had not taken off as successfully as Facebook. Its utility only began seeping into the national political psyche from the 2011 municipal elections onward when political leaders from across the political divide began using the microblogging site to either attack each other or to make ad hoc political assertions in the run-up to said poll. By the time the 2014 national and provincial elections arrived, both Facebook and Twitter had become indispensable communication tools for South African election campaigning (see Dhawraj 2013). At the time, some nine million South Africans were said to be active on Facebook and five million on Twitter. When coupled with easy web-enabled smartphone access, the 2014 polls thus became known as the country's first social media and 'digital elections' (Social media fires up…2014). This is one of the main motivations why Dhawraj (2019) sought to capture these developments within an altogether new study: just how was Twitter being used for election campaigning purposes in the 2016 elections? Sub-section 8.9.2 below is exactly what the researcher aims to detail: just how did the DA (and South Africa's ANC) use Twitter for campaigning in the 2016 Local Government Elections (LGE)?

8.8.2 Case study 2: Tweeting a whole local government election

For case study 2, Grounded Theory was used to generate a conceptual framework to understand how the ANC and DA used microblogging site, Twitter, for the 2016 local government election campaigning cycle (see chapter 4 for a discussion on Grounded Theory). Moreover, Dhawraj (2019) sought to prove that Twitter could indeed be classified as an *urban electioneering platform* which political parties could harness for party-political campaigning in notable urban constituencies. An integral element of the research was tweets sent out by each party during the campaigning, election, and post-election periods, namely 1 May 2016 to 31 August 2016. South Africa's fifth municipal elections were held on 3 August 2016. Additionally, both the ANC and DA's 2016 election manifesto served as a key data source for the study. These widely available party documents were needed to provide congruence that political parties could leverage Twitter as a party-political election tool with which election issues could be claimed (party-political issue ownership).

For the (social media) data collection phase of Dhawraj's (2019) study, quick-thinking and speed were needed to counter the grim reality that historical Twitter data could not be easily retrieved after a seven-day window period (Liang & Zhu, 2017). If this window had been missed, all sorts of other complications coupled with costs in US dollars would have entered the research process. Seeking simplicity with minimal bureaucratic red tape to retrieve the necessary data sets, namely the ANC and DA's tweets from 1 May 2016 to 31 August 2016 and without being coerced into using Twitter's API, the researcher, again, boldly decided to physically capture each party's tweets every week for four months. These were then saved as public display format (PDF) files in a folder on his laptop for later use. It should be noted that saving the ANC and DA's tweets in this manner neither altered nor lessened the value of the said data. Together with the text, images and other crucial data of individual tweets could be 'frozen' using PDF files. Please see Figure 8.2 for an example of how the files were stored (see also chapter 9 for a detailed discussion on data storage):

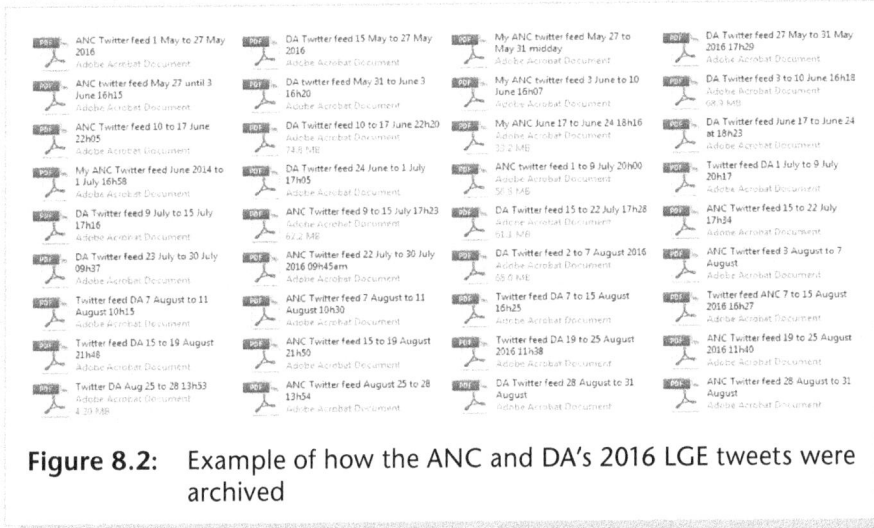

Figure 8.2:   Example of how the ANC and DA's 2016 LGE tweets were archived

There are many associated advantages of pursuing this type of manual data collection route. Firstly, control over the entire research cycle was vested in the researcher's hands without the need to pay a third party in foreign currency for data retrieval. Secondly, third parties could not guarantee access to the full data set – even after payment. By manually capturing every single tweet sent out by the ANC and DA using the measurement parameters (1 May 2016 to 31 August 2016), the researcher was assured that each of the approximate 14 000 tweets was included in the final data set. For example, when the researcher approached US-based research company Twitonomy to help retrieve historical election data for the ANC and DA dating back to the 2016 elections, a representative had advised they would only be able to go far back as three months. Still, curious to see what other 'data analytics' Twitonomy could offer the research project, the researcher was encouraged by his doctoral co-supervisor to take a month's trial priced at US$19. At the end of the single month's subscription, the researcher felt vindicated by electing to use the manual approach of collecting the 14 000-strong corpus of tweets as Twitonomy offered no novel service to enrich the existing data set. Therefore, thirdly, there was also no need to enable Twitter's APIs to get the required data. In this sense, unfettered access to what the ANC and DA tweeted during the 2016 election measurement period was guaranteed; and the required 14 000-strong corpus of tweets were collected.

➡

The single biggest disadvantage of doing things in this manner, however, was of course that it became very time-consuming (see chapter 2 on manual data collection). Capturing the data manually each week for four months did become monotonous, cumbersome and at times difficult to remember amidst one's other personal, work and study commitments. In such instances, key pieces of data could have been missed. There was indeed one such incident that crept into the equation where the researcher had been travelling a lot due to political parties campaigning all over the country. The researcher had to be thoroughly disciplined by creating 'to-do lists' every now and again where even airports transformed into data collection sessions using 3G cards. Of course, it could be argued that such pressure is unwarranted because technology has moved rapidly; such data retrieval could be easily done using other means. For the researcher, however, personal control of the research project with minimal external disruptions always took precedence. There was also the realisation that should the physical capturing of the tweets not been done studiously, the weak South African currency rate against the dollar-priced external retrieval services could have been another element that could have impacted and weighed down the bigger project.

A vital element of Dhawraj's (2019) study was the use of computer software application, NVivo Pro 12, which helped better organise the collected data. After acquiring a license at a discounted student rate priced in US dollars, the software program became the main storage site for the ANC and DA's 14 000 tweets, related 2016 election manifestos; and two semi-structured interviews were conducted to verify the study's overall findings. These data sets were, additionally, 'backed up' onto other hardware such as memory sticks to prevent file corruption – an unplanned stark reality of using any web-based service as Wigston (2010) warns. Figure 8.3 is an example of how these files were stored on NVivo Pro 12.

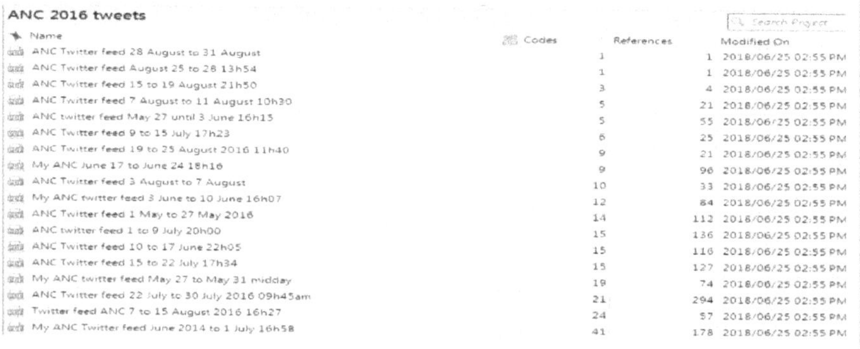
ANC 2016 tweets

Search Project

Name	Codes	References	Modified On
ANC Twitter feed 28 August to 31 August	1	1	2018/06/25 02:55 PM
ANC Twitter feed August 25 to 28 13h54	1	1	2018/06/25 02:55 PM
ANC Twitter feed 15 to 19 August 21h50	3	4	2018/06/25 02:55 PM
ANC Twitter feed 7 August to 11 August 10h30	5	21	2018/06/25 02:55 PM
ANC twitter feed May 27 until 3 June 16h15	5	55	2018/06/25 02:55 PM
ANC Twitter feed 9 to 15 July 17h23	6	25	2018/06/25 02:55 PM
ANC Twitter feed 19 to 25 August 2016 11h40	9	21	2018/06/25 02:55 PM
My ANC June 17 to June 24 18h16	9	96	2018/06/25 02:55 PM
ANC Twitter feed 3 August to 7 August	10	33	2018/06/25 02:55 PM
My ANC twitter feed 3 June to 10 June 16h07	12	84	2018/06/25 02:55 PM
ANC Twitter feed 1 May to 27 May 2016	14	112	2018/06/25 02:55 PM
ANC twitter feed 1 to 9 July 20h00	15	136	2018/06/25 02:55 PM
ANC Twitter feed 10 to 17 June 22h05	15	116	2018/06/25 02:55 PM
ANC Twitter feed 15 to 22 July 17h34	15	127	2018/06/25 02:55 PM
My ANC twitter feed May 27 to May 31 midday	19	74	2018/06/25 02:55 PM
ANC Twitter feed 22 July to 30 July 2016 09h45am	21	294	2018/06/25 02:55 PM
Twitter feed ANC 7 to 15 August 2016 16h27	24	57	2018/06/25 02:55 PM
My ANC Twitter feed June 2014 to 1 July 16h58	41	178	2018/06/25 02:55 PM

Figure 8.3: Screenshot showing how the ANC's tweets were stored on NVivo Pro 12

While NVivo Pro 12 assisted in storing the varied data sets of the doctoral study, the software program also greatly assisted when it came to 'cleaning' the data before any data analysis could be executed. Data cleaning as a process, as also explained in chapter 9, mainly involves eliminating any superfluous material from the data set, including repeat and irrelevant tweets. When dealing with large volumes of 'noisy' often unstructured social media data, data cleaning becomes an automatic exercise for further data refinement. Data cleaning also ensures better organisation (Baruffa, 2018; Ryklief, 2018). In this case, the 'refined' data was initially arranged according to monthly tweets to achieve this 'better organisation'. Providing easy access to each saved PDF file within the broader corpus, the researcher could sift through the data without any hindrance while notarising what needed to be included and which tweets needed to be excluded. The 'memo' facility within NVivo Pro 12 – and a crucial element of Grounded Theory – served this function. Please see Figure 8.4 as an example.

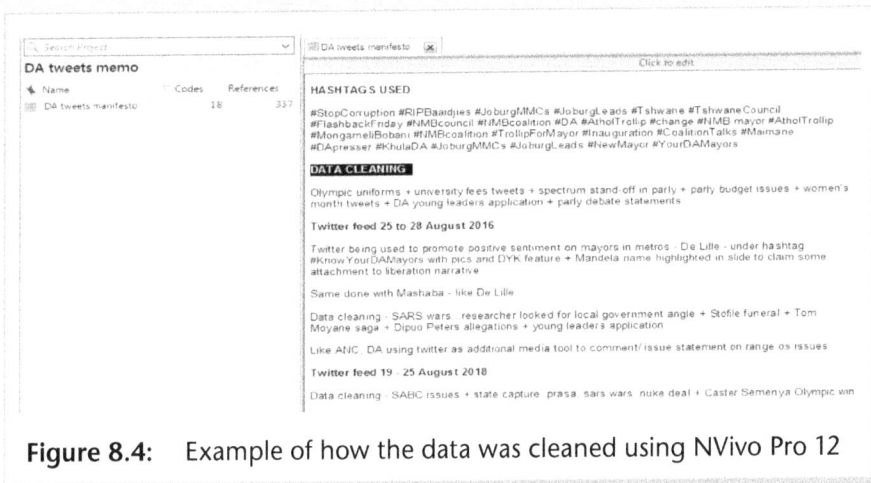

Figure 8.4:   Example of how the data was cleaned using NVivo Pro 12

The other main reason for choosing to use a software program such as NVivo Pro 12 is its ability to simplify the work of the researcher when it came to coding. Here too, data organisation over the program made it much easier and more manageable to work with the extensive corpus of ANC and DA tweets. Although there are many advantages to using the NVivo Pro 12 software during the social media data collection and organisation phases, the programme still required the researcher to be fully immersed in the data analysis cycle. Codes and sub-codes were then notarised using the software's 'branch' facility, making the researcher's life easier when it came to visualising the bigger research project. Please see Figure 8.5 as an example of how this data organisation helped the researcher to code the thousands of tweets over NVivo Pro 12.

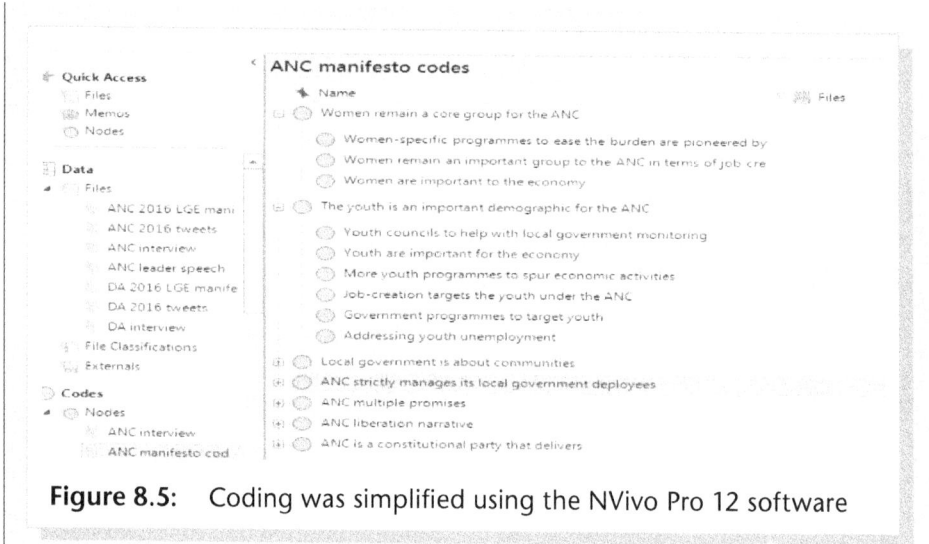

Figure 8.5:   Coding was simplified using the NVivo Pro 12 software

Another example of how NVivo Pro 12 simplified the researcher's data analyses exercise was how key words prefixed by hashtags could be easily isolated to give deeper meaning to the data set. Dhawraj (2019), in his study, surmised that subject-driven hashtags were important conversation-drivers and simultaneous agenda-setters, especially for the DA' 2016 election campaign in targeted South African 'battleground' metropolitan areas. Please see Table 8.3 as an example of this point.

Table 8.3:   How dominant DA hashtags were highlighted over NVivo Pro 12

Hashtag	In-text mentions	Corpus percentage
#khulada	1963	1.01%
#voteforchange	1219	0.63%
#imvotingda	704	0.36%
#da	507	0.26%
#msimangaformayor	360	0.18%
#keepmakingprogress	310	0.16%
#mashabaformayor	301	0.15%
#trollipformayor	264	0.14%
#electiondebate	233	0.12%
#jobsnotjets	222	0.11%
#mayorsforchange	191	0.10%
#sabccensorship	185	0.09%
#dafinairally	110	0.06%
#electionday	99	0.05%
#daforjobs	98	0.05%
#manifestoforchange	98	0.05%

Source: Dhawraj (2019)

When examining the ANC's use of hashtags for the party's 2016 election Twitter campaign, Dhawraj (2019) deduced that unlike the DA, the ANC did not optimally leverage these (hashtags) to drive election-related conversations for itself; and/or amongst its follower base. Please refer to Table 8.4 for an illustration of this.

Table 8.4:   How dominant ANC hashtags were highlighted over NVivo Pro 12

Hashtag	In-text mentions	Corpus percentage
#ancthankssa	1967	1.33%
#voteanc	793	0.62%
#anctgmkhize	688	0.54%
#anceverywhere	659	0.52%
#asinavalo	534	0.42%
#siyanqoba	475	0.37%
#zuma	415	0.33%
#ancfriday	408	0.32%
#ancdpramaphosa	313	0.25%
#anc	238	0.19%
#mantashe	219	0.17%
#ancinthestreets	209	0.16%
#thisismyanc	169	0.13%
#ancsgmantashe	134	0.11%
#ancsg	100	0.08%

Source: Dhawraj (2019)

An added advantage of NVivo Pro 12 is a data visualisation function that converts mostly quantitative information in easy-to-use and easily understandable graphs, tables, and word clouds. This makes the often-complex research more user-friendly.

In section 8.9, the researcher provided two detailed accounts of how social media data collection need not be a frightening experience altogether. Using Facebook and Twitter as examples from his post-graduate scholastic journeys, it was shown that research using user-generated content on public platforms can be harnessed effectively. Researchers need only be clear and unambiguous with their research design, overall research problem, the research questions and subsequent research objectives.

8.9   SUMMARY

This chapter sought to demonstrate how contemporary researchers collect Big Social Data for academic research purposes. An already fast-changing chaotic world is poised to get even more chaotic as rapid leaps in technology further shape the online world. As the WWW changes, so too does the expectation that more social media platforms will enter the online space to facilitate more user-driven content generation. As an academic field of study, there remains a reluctance for researchers to probe social media and the large volumes of unstructured data they generate. Fuelling this unwillingness is a sense of defeatism and the idea that dissecting social media data should best be left to the information technology (IT) specialists. There is also a sense of impatience and trepidation when it comes to understanding social media and related online jargon such as those found in computer software programming. Not many researchers from the humanities will, therefore, actively venture into a field where special computer programmes and APIs are needed to filter huge chunks of data from websites – including additional regulatory challenges that may emerge. With this said, there is an urgent need for more scholarship on social media data collection. Researchers also need to push the constraining boundaries and want to choose to go beyond the low-hanging fruit of simple textual and/or single platform analysis. Gradual mindset shifts are being effected but an overhaul will still need many years of rigour, perseverance and hard-core courage.

As illustrated in this chapter, conducting research using Big Social Data is not a difficult task. Two clear examples were given to show just how methodical it is. When coupled with sound research design, unambiguous research questions and focused research objectives, research projects using vast social media data sets do become easier. Researchers should never feel overwhelmed, especially when unconventional data sets and novel data collection methodologies are to be used. Equally, the volume and 'unstructured' nature of the data should never sow seeds of confusion in a researcher's mind. Technology has leap-frogged by great strides in the last decade; there will always be some computer software programme that can assist researchers 'manage' the data, and streamline the final analysis process. In case study 2, for example – cited in this chapter – the author illustrated how NVivo Pro 12 was optimised when it came to the data collection phase. The software also formed an all-important element in the value chain within the data analysis cycle. Technology exists to aid and enable the researcher and never to disable their efforts.

Learning activities (Test yourself)

1. List the different types of Big Social Data available to researchers.
2. What are the six distinguishing factors of big data?
3. Please explain how and why social media can be regarded as Big Social Data.
4. What are the three types of Big Social Data?
5. What are some of the methodological tools available to researchers to conduct sound research using social media data?
6. During social media data collection, under what circumstances will researchers decide when to use a manual or automated approach?
7. What are some of the challenges when working with still and moving imagery and audio?
8. What are some of the checks and balances to ensure social media data collection and the subsequent analysis is a trustworthy exercise?

As part of an online exercise, you are encouraged to attempt using different APIs to retrieve online data from both Facebook and Twitter. See section 8.9 for a brief discussion on how this can be done (graph.facebook.com can be used for Facebook and api.twitter.com can be used for microblogging site Twitter). Jot down what you observe after this exercise. What types of information does the API raise?

As an added activity, now try using the 'manual' approach of sifting data from Facebook and Twitter. Choose a political party page of your choice, follow or like the page or handle; and then begin to conduct visible data from each site – manually. How was the process? Were there any challenges? What were some of the advantages of doing social media data collection in this manner?

Further reading

Adu, P. 2016. Perfecting the art of qualitative coding. Available from: https://www.qsrinternational.com/nvivo-qualitative-data-analysis-software/resources/blog/perfecting-the-art-of-qualitative-coding [15 June 2018].

Adu, P. 2019. *A step-by-step guide to qualitative data coding*. Oxford: Routledge.

Ahmed, W. & Bath P.A. 2015. Comparison of Twitter APIs and tools for analysing tweets related to the Ebola virus disease. In iFutures: iSchool Postgraduate Research Conference, 7 July 2015, University of Sheffield, Sheffield. Available from: http://eprints.whiterose.ac.uk/87868/ [11 October 2015].

Ahmed, W. 2015a. Using Twitter as a data source: an overview of current social media research tools. Available from: http://blogs.lse.ac.uk/impactofsocialsciences/2015/07/10/social-media-research-tools-overview/ [5 March 2016].

Ahmed, W. 2015b. Challenges of using Twitter as a data source: An overview of current resources. Available from: http://blogs.lse.ac.uk/impactofsocialsciences/2015/09/28/challenges-of-using-twitter-as-a-data-source-resources/ [10 October 2015].

Ahmed, W. 2016a. Echosec: Location-based social media search – potential for academic research and industry. Available from: https://wasimahmed1.wordpress.com/2016/02/22/a-review-of-echosec-location-based-social-media-search-potential-for-academic-research-and-industry/ [23 February 2016].

Ahmed, W. 2016b. How hashtag activism and twitter diplomacy converged at this-is-a-coup. Available from: http://blogs.lse.ac.uk/impactofsocialsciences/2016/01/07/how-hashtag-activism-and-twitter-diplomacy-converged-at-thisisacoup/ [22 March 2016].

Ahmed, W. 2017. Communicating science through social media: Tools and techniques. Available from: https://www.slideshare.net/was3210/communicating-science-through-social-media-tools-and-techniques [15 May 2017].

Ahmed, W. 2018a. More room for greater depth and detail: Implications for academic research of Twitter's expanded character limit. Available from: https://blogs.lse.ac.uk/impactofsocialsciences/2018/02/09/more-room-for-greater-depth-and-detail-implications-for-academic-research-of-twitters-expanded-character-limit/ [9 February 2018].

Ahmed, W. 2018b. Amplified messages: How hashtag activism and Twitter diplomacy converged at #ThisIsACoup – and won. Available from: http://blogs.lse.ac.uk/impactofsocialsciences/2016/01/07/how-hashtag-activism-and-twitter-diplomacy-converged-at-thisisacoup/ [15 April 2018].

Al-Qurishi, M., Al-Rakhami, M., Alrubaian, M., Alarifi, A., Rahman, S.M.M. & Alamri, A. 2017. Selecting the best open source tools for collecting and visualizing social media content. Available from: https://www.researchgate.net/publication/282914403_Selecting_the_Best_Open_Source_Tools_for_Collecting_and_Visualizing_Social_Media_Content [28 August 2019].

Bringer, J.D., Johnston, L.H. & Brackenridge, C.H. 2004. Maximizing transparency in a doctoral thesis: The complexities of writing about the use of QSR*Nvivo within a grounded theory study. *Qualitative Research*, 4(2): 247–265.

Data never sleeps 7.0. 2019. Available from: https://www.domo.com/learn/data-never-sleeps-7 [14 August 2019].

Desjardins, J. 2019. Why big data keeps getting bigger. Available from: https://www.weforum.org/agenda/2019/07/why-big-data-keeps-getting-bigger [14 August 2019].

Duca, D. 2019. Social scientists working with LinkedIn data. Available from: https://ocean.sagepub.com/blog/social-scientists-working-with-linkedin-data?utm_source=twitter&utm_medium=SAGE_social&utm_content=sageoceantweets&utm_term=487297a6-1264-4b13-afeb-d6e16af2ac2f [27 June 2019].

Gandomi, A. & Haider, M. 2015. Beyond the hype: Big data concepts, methods, and analytics. *International Journal of Information Management*, 35(2): 137–144.

Günther, W.A., Mehrizi, M.H.R., Huysman, M. & Feldberg, F. 2017. Debating big data: A literature review on realizing value from big data. *Journal of Strategic Information Systems*, 26(3): 191–209.

Herrman, J. 2019. How TikTok is rewriting the world. [O]. Available from: https://www.nytimes.com/2019/03/10/style/what-is-tik-tok.html [3 April 2020].

Hutchinson, A.J., Johnston, L.H. & Breckon, J.D. 2010. Using QSR-NVivo to facilitate the development of a grounded theory project: an account of a worked example. *International Journal of Social Research Methodology*, 13(4): 283–302.

Janes, D. 2017. What in the world is TikTok? A beginner's guide to the fast-growing social media app. [O]. Available from: https://www.oprahmag.com/entertainment/a29399102/what-is-tik-tok/ [3 April 2020].

Johnston, L. 2006. Software and method: reflections on teaching and using QSR NVivo in doctoral research. *International Journal of Social Research Methodology*, 9(5): 379–391.

Khan, S.N. 2014. Qualitative research method: Grounded theory. *International Journal of Business and Management*, 9(11): 224–233.

Kudyba, S. 2010. *What is data mining?* Available from: https://www.youtube.com/watch?v=R-sGvh6tI04 [28 August 2019].

Liang, H. & Zhu, J.J.H. 2017. Big data, collection of (social media, harvesting). *The International Encyclopedia of Communication Research Methods*: 1–19.

Mukurunge, T. & Bhila, T. 2019. Social media and political party campaign: Case of Lesotho June 2017 election. *International Journal of Trend in Scientific Research and Development*, 3(1): 1116–1122.

Oussous, A., Benjelloun, F.Z., Lahcen, A.A. & Belfkih, S. 2018. Big data technologies: A survey. *Journal of King Saud University – Computer and Information Sciences*, 30(4): 431–448.

Oweis, N.E., Owais, S.S., George, W., Suliman, M.G. & Snasel, V. 2015. A survey on big data, mining: tools, techniques, applications and notable uses. Available from: https://www.researchgate.net/publication/282845795_A_Survey_on_Big_Data_Mining_Tools_Techniques_Applications_and_Notable_Uses [5 April 2019].

Pater, J.A., Haimson, O.L., Andalibi, N. & Mynatt, E.D. 2016. 'Hunger hurts but starving works': characterizing the presentation of eating disorders online, in *Proceedings of the 19th ACM Conference on Computer-Supported Cooperative Work & Social Computing*, NEW YORK, NY, 1185–1200.

Perez, S. 2019. It's time to pay serious attention to TikTok. [O]. Available: https://techcrunch.com/2019/01/29/its-time-to-pay-serious-attention-to-tiktok/ [3 April 2020].

Pila, E, Mond, J.M., Griffiths, S., Mitchison, D. & Murray, S.B. 2017. A thematic content analysis of #cheatmeal images on social media: Characterizing an emerging dietary trend. *International Journal of Eating Disorders*, 50(6): 698–706.

Robertson, J. 2018. Cambridge Analytica shuts operations after Facebook scandal. Available from: https://www.bloomberg.com/news/articles/2018-05-02/cambridge-analytica-shuts-all-operations-afterfacebook-scandal [3 May 2018].

Sage Publishing. Putting big data to 'good' use. 2017. Available from: https://www.youtube.com/watch?v=VuXEyFX0fSg&feature=youtu.be&utm_source=twitter&utm_medium=SAGE_social&utm_content=sageoceantweets&utm_term=586afadf-b104-429b-a663-0cb06a5af84a [25 June 2019].

Shleyner, E. 2018. Social media metrics that really matter – And how to track them. Available from: https://blog.hootsuite.com/social-media-metrics/ [9 March 2019].

Varela, M.E. & Parikesit, G.O.F. 2017. A quantitative close analysis of a theatre video recording. *Digital Scholarship in the Humanities*, 32(2): 276–283.

Wigston, D.J. 2010. *An introduction to quantitative content analysis*. Honours (BA) tutorial letter 101 for HCMMPRB, University of South Africa, Department of Communication Science: 62–77.

Wilk, V., Soutar, GN, Harrigan, P. 2019. Tackling social media data analysis: Comparing and contrasting QSR NVivo and Leximancer. *Qualitative Market Research: An International Journal* 22(2): 94–113.

CHAPTER 9

Analysing Social Media Data

Wasim Ahmed and Charmaine du Plessis

Raw data is both an oxymoron and a bad idea; to the contrary, data should be cooked with care. – Geoffrey Bowker

Learning Outcomes

After completing this chapter, the researcher should be able to:

- describe the data cleaning process to prepare and store a social media dataset for analysis;
- differentiate between quantitative, qualitative, visual and audio social media data analysis methods and tools;
- differentiate between a qualitative, quantitative and mixed methods approach to analysing social media data; and
- critically analyse different types of social media data while recognising various challenges.

9.1   INTRODUCTION

This chapter provides an overview of social media data analysis from a quantitative, qualitative and mixed-method approach (MMA) respectively. Figure 2.2 in chapter 2 provides some insight into where data analysis fits into the research process. Data analysis follows data collection and entails making sense of and assigning meaning to social media data which are often noisy, unstructured and without any context.

However, before data analysis can start, data must first be adequately cleaned and stored for proper interpretation. An overview of several software applications as well as tools for other platforms is provided while our chapter also touches on how visual and audio social media content can be analysed and the methods and tools available for this. Finally, we outline several tips and challenges that researchers may need to overcome when researching and analysing social media.

With the rise of digital technology and new means of online digital communication more and more of our daily interaction is taking place in the online world. Interactions in social media generate a vast amount of data, also referred to as Big Social Data, that can be studied by academic researchers from a wide variety of disciplines such as sociology, history, communication science, computer science, political science and literature studies, among many others. Professionals, furthermore, analyse social media data to make business decisions. However, gaining access to social media data provides a key challenge for researchers and for certain platforms such as Facebook and WhatsApp since it will require the consent of users within a group to permit a researcher to study the content (see chapter 10).

However, one platform, Twitter (see chapter 1), is unique in the sense that it provides free access to a sample of its data, making it possible for researchers to retrieve data for research purposes. As opposed to a Facebook group, content on Twitter is almost completely public and can be accessed by anyone with an Internet connection provided that a user's profile was not made private. Because Twitter provides access to its data via an Application Programming Interface (a means to connect to Twitter to retrieve data), several pre-built and easy to use software applications have been developed for the analysis of social media data deriving from Twitter. Although, it must be noted that data access to these platforms may change in the future due to potential privacy and/or commercial reasons.

Important to note is that this chapter must be read together with chapters 2, 4, 5 and 8 as these chapters are interconnected. While content analysis and social network analysis are considered as data analysis methods, they are also research methods (see Bengtsson, 2016; De Bruin & McAuliffe, 2018). Qualitative, quantitative content and social network analysis are consequently discussed in chapters 4 and 5 as research methods respectively and not repeated in this chapter. It should also be mentioned that although there are many qualitative data analysis methods available to the social media researcher and professional, we focus only on thematic analysis in this chapter because it is widely used for qualitative social media studies.

9.2   DATA CLEANING AND STORING

In chapter 8 it was explained how social media data can be collected. By now you know that raw social media data is unstructured, scattered and 'noisy' posing some challenges for social media researchers wanting to prepare data for analysis. Social media data is not only vast but also sensitive in that people's conversations and information were extracted (see chapter 10). A social media researcher is also faced with different types of data, namely user profiles, different media content (images, text, videos, sound, animated gifs), statistics such as likes, shares, number of followers as well as user comments. Each type of data must, therefore, be approached, cleaned, and organised in a different way (Wang, 2014).

As was also explained in chapters 2, 5 and 7 social media datasets contain a large volume of data that can also be full of spam or fake profiles. While it is not always possible to detect fake profiles without using advanced analytics techniques (Zheng et al., 2015), the researcher must put in a great deal of effort to improve data quality by adequately cleaning and organising the data before analysis.

Data cleaning is the process of preparing data for analysis by removing all irrelevant and incorrect parts and identifying incomplete areas that would need more data. This first step is important to avoid inaccurate or biased results, to limit exposure of sensitive or private information and to allow for better data interpretation (Wang, 2014). Figure 9.1 depicts the data cleaning and storing process for social media data.

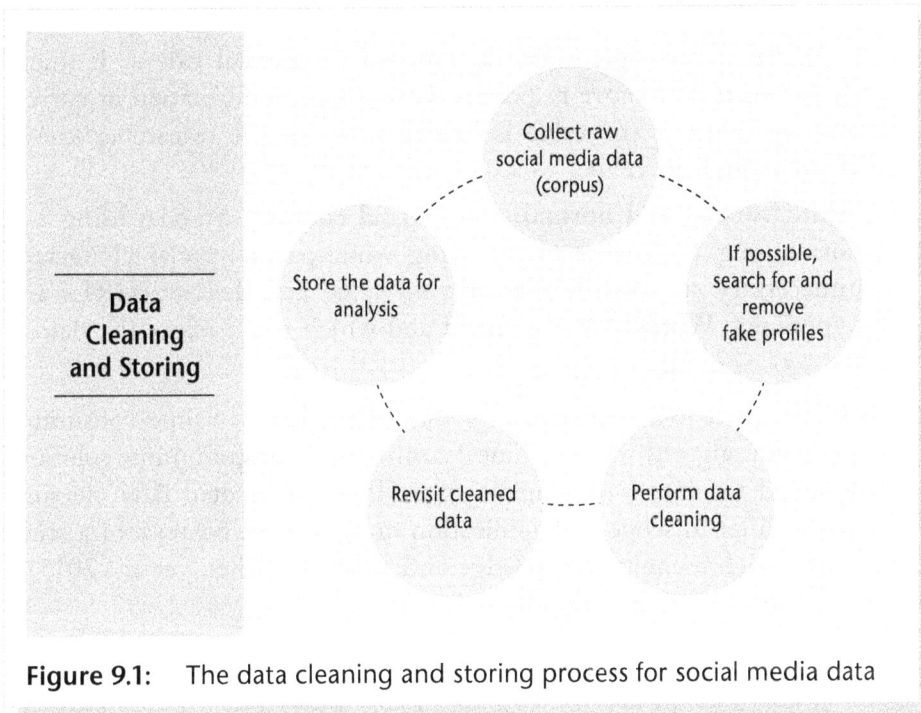

Figure 9.1: The data cleaning and storing process for social media data

Data cleaning of social media deals with the following issues (Wang, 2014; Zheng et al., 2015; Krystyanczuk & Chatterjee, 2017):

- **Spam**: Social media attracts much spam in the form of links which can be promotional but also malicious attempts. Although spam detection software and algorithms can assist, spamming has become more sophisticated to avoid detection. It is also important for the researcher to understand what spam entails.

- **Duplicate data**: Since social media users share and repost information, duplicate posts can skew statistics and the study's results and must be removed from the dataset.

- **Data discrepancy**: It is important to avoid inconsistency of data by checking for spelling errors, synonyms or abbreviations. These issues in the data could result in undetected duplicate information and compromise the integrity of the data.

- **Incomplete data:** Data may be incomplete because of missing information due to access restrictions or errors that might have occurred during data collection (for example, a communication failure). Some examples of incomplete data are missing numerical values. It might be necessary to remove responses with missing information or correct missing values if the value is known or when the researcher knows where to find the value.

- **Standardising and normalising textual content**: Standardising and normalising text refers to removing whitespaces, special characters, unnecessary stop words that add no value and deleting URLs and hyperlinks. Words that are joined and which could affect the dataset must also be split.

While it is possible to do data cleaning manually (albeit in a time-consuming manner), many algorithms, machine-learning and programming solutions were designed to clean social media data. These automated data cleaning frameworks differ in scope and application must suit the purpose of a study and require much technical knowledge and expertise (Zheng et al., 2015) – see also the section further reading.

OpenRefine (previously known as Google Refine) is open-source software that could help social media researchers who do not have the skills to handle advanced cleaning algorithms or programming languages to clean messy social media data (OpenRefine, 2019).

As also mentioned in chapter 2, social media researchers still have difficulty in accessing social media data storage facilities that are mostly commercial and expensive.

After cleaning a social media dataset with machine-learning or programming tools, the clean dataset can be stored in a database application for safekeeping and future use. Examples of database applications are MongoDB, HBase or Cassandra (Krystyanczuk & Chatterjee, 2017). Datasets that were manually cleaned or in other suitable ways, can be stored by using cloud solution applications such as Google Drive or similar solutions depending on the size of the dataset. OpenRefine allows researchers to store cleaned data to a central database, namely Wikidata (OpenRefine, 2019). However, a cloud computing environment always poses some security and privacy risks which are beyond the researcher's control and should be approached with the utmost caution (Tabassam, 2019).

Once data is ready for analysis, the analysis can either be performed quantitatively, qualitatively or with a MMA (depending on the research problem – see chapter 2) and are explained in the subsequent sections.

9.3   QUANTITATIVE DATA ANALYSIS OF SOCIAL MEDIA DATA

When a social media researcher adopts a quantitative data analysis approach to analyse social media data, the researcher follows a systematic approach and transforms collected or observed social media data into structured numerical data. A quantitative social media study often describes an event by answering the 'what' and 'how many' questions (see chapters 2 and 5). The measurement is objective, deductive (guided by the data) and supported by statistical, mathematical, or numerical analysis and computational techniques (see Sloan & Quan-Haase, 2017).

Social media data analysis tools provide basic statistical data (metrics) and data visualisation about, for example, the number of social media mentions, post reactions, shares followers and clicks or finding influencers or analysing real-time hashtags (see chapter 2). More advanced methods, on the other hand, provide insight into areas such as social networks, sentiment and relationships, amongst other things (see chapter 5).

However, for a social media researcher to make any valid statistical claims about a large social media dataset, it is important to account for any limitations in the data, where the data originates from, as well as potential bias in interpretation (see chapter 7). In addition, researchers must account for the complicated methodological processes involved during the data analysis process. Also, important to remember is that the accessibility of a volume of data does not make it ethical to extract, store and use by default and a researcher must also account for ethical implications of using the data – see chapter 10 (Boyd & Crawford, 2011).

9.3.1 Use of Twitter across disciplines in a quantitative approach

Twitter has found use across a broad range of areas and disciplines ranging from teaching, scholarly communication, health research, crisis and risk communication, marketing, libraries, and politics and political uprisings (see also chapter 1). All the disciplines and areas utilising Twitter data will generate vast amounts of data that can be tapped into for both professional and academic purposes. Table 9.1 below highlights how a researcher can tap into data from Twitter and the infrastructural affordability provided by the platform across different disciplines.

Table 9.1: Various uses of Twitter across different disciplines

Uses of Twitter	Infrastructural Affordability
Teaching	Twitter allows students and teachers to create free accounts and allows users to share information and course materials via a designated hashtag.
Scholarly communication	Communities may form on Twitter and allow users who are connected to share recently published papers. Specific hashtags may form for certain modules which can be utilised by the class.
Health research	Data from Twitter around major health scares can be retrieved in almost real time which can be utilised by health authorities.
Crisis and risk communication	Natural disasters such as flooding have the potential to generate bursts of social media posts which may be geo-tagged, and which would allow the ability to allocate resources in real time.
Marketing	A wide range of organisations has exploited the potential of Twitter for marketing purposes that is, commercial organisations, non-commercial, and governmental organisations. Twitter has also been utilised for monitoring consumer views and opinions, and as a tool for customer support. Includes the use of Twitter for internal communication.
Libraries	Twitter has been utilised across libraries for announcements, special events, opening times, book arrivals, and exhibits.
Politics and political uprisings	Twitter is an independent social media service provider and allows the freedom of speech permitting a wide variety of political discussions.

Table 9.1 above highlights Twitter's use across a wide range of disciplines, for example, Twitter has been increasingly researched for its ability to provide insight into health and a recent study from our group (Ahmed & Lugovic, 2019) as well as a PhD thesis (Ahmed, 2018) has noted that Twitter can be utilised to provide public, unfiltered insight into a range of health topics such as infectious disease outbreaks that could be vital information on potential misunderstandings or geographical information on the incidence of a disease outbreak.

9.3.2 Overview of social media data analysis tools and methods for a quantitative analysis

There are several software tools which can be used by professionals and academics for the analysis of social media data and which permit different types of quantitative analysis. Our focus in this chapter is Twitter (see section 9.3.1) because there is no other platform that has made its data available to researchers at this scale (Ahmed, 2017). Provided below, firstly, we will look at tools which have access to the free Twitter Search Application Programming Interface (API) which can retrieve tweets going around a week or so back in time. For tweets going back even further tools such as Track my Hashtag (n.d.) should be explored which provide historical Twitter data for a fee that may be reasonable for academics. Many further commercial tools are outlined which can be used for historical data, but which may have a higher cost.

(i)   Mecodify

For researchers who do not have knowledge of coding or lack some technical skills, Mecodify (Al-Saqafis, 2016) is an open-source tool with a user-friendly interface that can assist with analysing social media data. Examples of a wide range of published work where researchers used Mecodify can be accessed at http://www.mecodem.eu/outputs/publications/. Examples of working papers can be accessed at http://www.mecodem.eu/outputs/working-papers/.

This open software programme can, amongst other things, generate tables and graphs for purposes of data visualisation, assist with network analysis, analyse Twitter hashtags, identify influential Twitter users and be used for comparative studies, for example, comparing Twitter activity with real events. Data extraction was at the time of publication only limited to Twitter, but plans were underway to expand to other platforms that use APIs to extract social media data (Al-Saqafis, 2016).

(ii)   NodeXL

NodeXL (Smith et al., 2009) is a plugin for Microsoft Excel and it allows users to retrieve data from platforms such as Twitter, YouTube, Wikipedia, and Flicker among others and runs on Windows operating systems. NodeXL can be accessed at https://nodexlgraphgallery.org/Pages/AboutNodeXL.aspx.

Users of other devices such as Apple can instead use a virtual machine to access NodeXL. Users can use the data importers to retrieve data and once data has been captured it is possible to:
- generate time series graphs;
- use graph layout algorithms to generate visualisations;

- generate metrics by group clusters and for the overall graph; and
- identify most used hashtags, URLs, Domains, Word-Pairs, Replied-To, mentioned and influential users using metric such as Betweenness Centrality.

NodeXL has thousands of academic citations and has also been utilised within commercial research. NodeXL has a limited free version, a Student and Academic license and a commercial license. NodeXL draws upon the methodology of social network analysis which is a useful way of understanding the connections between a set of social media users. NodeXL also maintains an online gallery of social network graphs known as the NodeXL graph gallery (http://www.nodexlgraphgallery.org/) and certain datasets will be available to be utilised for research purposes. It is also important to note that NodeXL can also use non-social media data as long as the data represents connections between entities.

One of the key benefits of NodeXL is the ability to visualise social media discussions. Figure 9.1 below provides an example of the visual nature of graphs and the ability to highlight users.

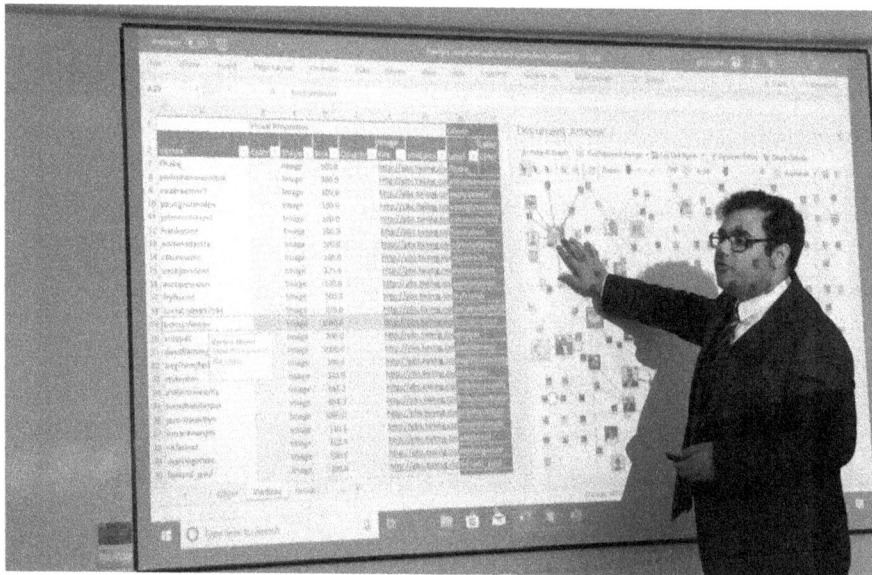

Figure 9.2:   Dr Wasim Ahmed is pointing towards the centre of a social network graph highlighting an influential Twitter user at a Researching Social Media event at Sheffield Hallam University

(iii)   Mozdeh

Mozdeh is an application designed for Windows operating systems (a desktop computer is advised) and was formed by the Statistical Cybermetrics Research Group (n.d.) at the University of Wolverhampton. In Mozdeh it is possible to search Twitter through the Search AP and to retrieve Twitter. Mozdeh can be accessed here: http://mozdeh.wlv.ac.uk/. Once a user has utilised Mozdeh to retrieve data, it is possible to:

- remove spam;
- search tweets;
- find gender differences;
- generate time-series graphs;
- create social network graphs;
- identify word frequencies; and
- remove random samples of tweets.

Mozdeh can be utilised for long-term Twitter data capture as long as the search remains active and the computer is switched on.

(iv)   Chorus

Chorus (Brooker, Barnett, & Cribbin, 2016) is a tool which uses Twitter's Search API and traces its roots to Brunel University. Chorus contains two programmes: 1) a tool known as 'Tweetcatcher' which will retrieve Twitter data and 2) Tweetvis which can analyse Twitter data. Once a user has downloaded tweets in Chorus using Chorus Tweet catcher, it is possible to perform the following on the data:

- The ability to visualise tweets over time in the Timeline Explorer
- Among others, Chorus permits the ability to examine metrics such as:
  - frequency of tweets;
  - sentiment;
  - collocated words;
  - semantic novelty; and
  - homogeneity.

Chorus can be obtained by completion of a download form for non-commercial purposes which can be accessed here: http://chorusanalytics.co.uk/.

(v)   Netlytic

Netlytic (n.d) is an online tool which has access to data from platforms such as Twitter, YouTube, and Facebook. Netlytic is available in a free version which handles a maximum of n=10000 units. Netlytic was created by *The Social Media Lab*. Once Netlytic has been utilised to retrieve data it allows the following to be performed:

- view location of social media posts on a map;
- produce social network graphs;
- identify popular topics; and
- identify emerging themes.

Netlytic can be accessed here: https://netlytic.org/.

(vi)   Twitter Archiving Google Spreadsheet

A web-based tool known as TAGS (Twitter Archiving Google Spreadsheet) (n.d.) allows the ability to retrieve data from Twitter's Search API. Once data has been retrieved in TAGS it is possible to:

- examine metrics such as number of tweets, retweets, and unique tweets among others;
- further explore tweets within TAGS Explorer; and
- search tweets.

TAGS can also retrieve data automatically in varying intervals and an advantage of the tool is that it is cloud based and does not depend on keeping a computer running to retrieve tweets.

(vii)   Twitonomy

Twitonomy (n.d) is a commercial tool which utilises the Search API and the tool is web-based and has limited free functionality. Twitonomy allows users to search using keywords and user accounts among other operators and allows users to perform some of the following:

- The ability to produce visual insight into tweets based on hashtags, mentions, replies, retweets, and tweets.
- The tool provides specific insight into Twitter users based on metrics such as tweets sent per day, the number of retweets, users mentions links, replies, hashtags, tweets retweeted and favourited.
- Twitonomy's free version allows the ability to produce these metrics listed above for free on user accounts.

As mentioned above Twitonomy has a premium version which allows keyword search ranging from $19 a month or $199 for the year at the time of writing at the time of publication. Twitonomy can be accessed here: https://www.twitonomy.com/.

(viii)   Pulsar Social

Pulsar Social (n.d.) provides the ability to pull in data from a wide range of social media platforms such as Twitter, Facebook, Instagram, and blogs.

Pulsar is a web-based tool which is fully commercial with prices starting at USD600, however, for bespoke projects the fee could be lower. When a user has retrieved data, Pulsar permits:

- the ability to filter data;
- image and video analysis;
- the option to manipulate and explore data;
- data visualisation;
- sentiment analysis; and
- viewing Twitter locations on a map.

Pulsar provides users with the ability to set up queries which run frequently to retrieve data from several social platforms. Pulsar Social can be accessed here: https://www.pulsarplatform.com/.

(ix)   SocioViz

SocioViz (n.d.) is a tool which is available for free and is web-based. It is based on social network analysis and has access to the Twitter Search API and can pull in data from Twitter. Once users have retrieved data it allows the following to be performed:

- the ability to analyse topics, terms, and hashtags;
- identify opinions, influencers, and contents; and
- the ability to export data.

SocioViz is not-for-profit and is available freely. SocioViz can be accessed here: https://socioviz.net/.

(x)   Visibrain

Visibrain (n.d.) is web-based and has access to platforms such as Twitter, Facebook, Instagram, Blogs, and Online Press. Visibrain has access to Twitter's Firehose API and once a user has pulled in Twitter data, it is possible to perform some of the following:

- the ability to generate time series graphs;
- the ability to examine metrics such as most occurring retweets, tweets, locations, hashtags, and keywords;
- the ability to pinpoint audience type, device, and content; and
- exportability to Gephi for graph visualisation.

Visibrain has several different tiers which can start from $365 for around 10,000 Twitter mentions. Visibrain can be accessed here: https://www.visibrain.com/en/.

(xi) Webometric Analyst

Webometric Analyst (n.d.) is a tool which can pull in data from various online sources such as YouTube, Mendeley, Twitter, Tumblr, Flicker among other web sources. Once a user retrieves data from Webometric Analyst it is possible to perform some of the following actions on the data:

- generate network graphs;
- create network diagrams;
- generate image reports; and
- extract images from a series of Tweets and/or Flicker posts.

A key feature of Webometric Analyst is its ability to repair data from Mozdeh (a powerful Twitter capture tool) henceforth if Mozdeh ever crashes Webometric Analyst can recover this data and repair files that have been affected. Webometric Analyst can be accessed here: http://lexiurl.wlv.ac.uk/.

9.3.3 Advanced data analysis statistical and programming-based tools

Some tools were outlined above which do not require much technical or programming knowledge above, however, there are also a set of further advanced data analysis statistical and programming-based tools that may be of interest to readers such as:

- R (https://www.r-project.org/)
- SPSS (https://www.ibm.com/uk-en/analytics/spss-statistics-software)
- KNIME (https://www.knime.com/)
- Weka (https://www.cs.waikato.ac.nz/ml/weka/)
- Tableau (https://www.tableau.com/en-gb)
- Gephi (https://gephi.org/)
- Leximancer (https://info.leximancer.com/)

The packages above should be researched when identifying which software tool to use as they may provide beneficial features. Table 9.2 provides an overview of further tools (adapted from Ahmed, 2019).

Table 9.2: An overview of further tools

Tool	OS	Download and/or access from	Platforms*
Audience	Web-based	https://audiense. com/	Twitter
Brand24	Web-based	https://brand24. com/features/#4	Twitter, Facebook, Instagram, Blogs, Forums, Video
Brandwatch	Web-based	https://www. brandwatch.com/	Twitter, Facebook, YouTube, Instagram, Sina Weibo, VK, QQ, Google+, Pinterest, Online blogs
Chorus (free)	Windows (Desktop advisable)	http:// chorusanalytics.co.uk/ chorus/request_ download.php	Twitter
COSMOS Project (free)	Windows and MAC OS X	http://socialdatalab. net/software	Twitter
Echosec	Web-based	https://www. echosec.net	Twitter, Instagram, Foursquare, Panoramio, AIS Shipping, Sina Weibo, Flickr, YouTube, VK
Followthehashtag	Web-based	http://www. followthehashtag. com	Twitter
IBM Bluemix	Web-based	https://www. ibm.com/cloud- computing/bluemix	Twitter
Keyhole	Web-based	https://keyhole.co/	Twitter, Instagram, Facebook
Mozdeh (free)	Windows (Desktop advisable)	http://mozdeh.wlv. ac.uk/installation. html	Twitter
Netlytic	Web-based	https://netlytic.org	Twitter, Facebook, YouTube, Really Simple Syndication (RSS) Feed
NodeXL	Windows	https://www. smrfoundation.org/ nodexl/	Twitter, YouTube, Flickr, Wikipedia

➡

Tool	OS	Download and/or access from	Platforms*
NVivo	Windows and MAC	http://www. qsrinternational.com/ product	Twitter, Ability to import
Pulsar Social	Web-based	http://www. pulsarplatform.com	Twitter, Facebook topic data, Online blogs
Social Elephants	Web-based	https:// socialelephants.com/ en/	Twitter, Facebook, Instagram, YouTube
Symplur (Healthcare focus)	Web-based	https://www. symplur.com/	Twitter
SocioViz	Web-based	http://socioviz.net	Twitter
Trendsmap	Web-based	https://www. trendsmap.com	Twitter
Trackmyhashtag		https://www. trackmyhashtag. com/	Twitter
Twitonomy	Web-based	http://www. twitonomy.com	Twitter
Twitter Arching Google Spreadsheet (TAGS) (free)	Web-based	https://tags.hawksey. info	Twitter
Visibrain	Web-based	http://www.visibrain. com	Twitter Facebook Instagram Blogs Online Press
Webometric Analyst (free)	Windows	http://lexiurl.wlv. ac.uk	Twitter (with image extraction capabilities), YouTube, Flickr, Mendeley, Other web resources

9.3.4 Quantitative data analysis

There are no predetermined steps to analyse quantitative social media data and will differ from study to study depending on different scholarly views, epistemologies and/or machine-learning or other techniques adopted. Quantitative data analysis is concerned with analysing very large social media datasets often at speed. Important to note is that a related set of machine-learning methods are popular for this purpose. These methods involve training a model to code a subset of data which the machine then automatically codes. Other machine-learning methods may be more exploratory in nature and would uncover key topics by mining large sets of data. Tools and programming languages such as Weka (https://www.cs.waikato.ac.nz/ml/weka), R (https://www.r-project.org) and Python (https://www.python.org/) could be explored for quantitative data analysis. Sentiment analysis is another quantitative method concerned with identifying positive, negative, and neutral social media posts at speed (see chapter 5). The SentiStrength algorithm (http://sentistrength.wlv.ac.uk/) could be explored by readers interested in conducting sentiment analysis on social media data.

Recommended further reading on machine-learning tools

What are machine-learning tools?

https://www.trustradius.com/machine-learning

Best tools

https://www.altexsoft.com/blog/datascience/the-best-machine-learning-tools-experts-top-picks/

Open-source tools

https://towardsdatascience.com/10-must-try-open-source-tools-for-machine-learning-1c4420ef40df

---

9.4   QUALITATIVE DATA ANALYSIS OF SOCIAL MEDIA DATA

Similar to traditional qualitative studies, data analysis is also a fundamental step in qualitative social media research. How meticulously social media data is analysed, will affect the outcome of a qualitative social media study (Flick, 2013). Qualitative data analysis can be done in several ways using different qualitative data analysis tools as also explained in chapters 4 and 8. There is hence no 'one-size-fits-all' approach when doing a qualitative data analysis which depends on a study's research design and question(s).

In this section, we will discuss qualitative data analysis in the context of social media, initial essential steps for qualitative data analysis of social media data, the main approaches of qualitative data analysis and the steps of thematic analysis.

9.4.1   Qualitative data analysis in the context of social media

One of the most recognised definitions of qualitative data analysis is by Flick (2014:5) which reads as follows:

Qualitative data analysis is the classification and interpretation of linguistic (or visual) material to make statements about implicit and explicit dimensions and structures of meaning-making in the material and what is represented in it.

Meaning-making refers to revealing the intent of the original author (which can be subjective or social), the particular event or circumstances. Thus when it comes to vast social media data, qualitative data analysis will organise and reduce raw data by removing irrelevant information to identify and reveal important patterns in the data to arrive at informed conclusions based on rich and meaningful results (Cresswell, 2013; 2014).

The aim of the analysis could, amongst other things, be to (see Flick, 2014):

- describe or explore a social media phenomenon in much depth;
- explore a specific social media case in detail; or
- compare different social media cases.

To ensure the validity and reliability of the results, the researcher must carefully document all steps and procedures of the qualitative data analysis as also highlighted in chapter 2, section 2.8.11.

9.4.2   Initial essential steps in qualitative data analysis of social media data

Qualitative data analysis of social media data requires a more specialised approach although the process is similar to other qualitative studies (Veek, 2013). Social media data that was collected represents a corpus (consisting of posts, comments, images and/or videos) and from this corpus, only applicable data must be used for the analysis (Hu & Lui, 2012).

Due to the vast amount of social media data, a clear focus and objectives must guide the analysis, but it is also important to allow for the discovery of new information which could be found in unexpected ways. The analysis must start with searching for key terms iteratively (repeatedly) by first concentrating on broad terms and then narrowing down to specific terms or combining terms. The researcher must also be guided by data saturation and know when enough data is available for the analysis to replicate the study. A rule of thumb for data saturation in a qualitative social media study is reached when new information is not discovered and further coding is no longer practicable (Fusch & Nesch, 2015).

Social media data is not static but with millions of new posts every day. A social media data set will thus look different at another time and will have a different outcome. Social media data should thus be narrowed down to specific periods. A researcher doing a social media study must report that the data is only applicable to a specific period and provide reasons why the study focuses on that period (see Hand, 2018).

Once social media data has been properly cleaned and organised, the same data analysis process is followed as for traditional qualitative data such as for content analysis or thematic analysis. Data is coded according to themes or categories which can be done manually or with software (Veek, 2013).

9.4.3   Three main approaches to conducting a qualitative data analysis

There are three approaches to conducting qualitative data analysis, namely a deductive, inductive or hybrid approach. Which one of these approaches to adopt for analysis, however, depends on the study's objectives (see chapter 2). The three approaches are explained as follows (Tjora, 2019):

(i)   Deductive qualitative data analysis approach

A deductive qualitative approach is theory-driven and considers a theoretical framework/structure which the researcher previously prepared. For example, the researcher may use the social media study's research question(s) to group the social media data into different themes or categories for analysis.

(ii)   Inductive qualitative data analysis approach

With an inductive qualitative approach, the social media data guides the analysis since not much is known about the topic. The data hence determines the themes or categories for the analysis. For example, this approach is very useful when doing a Grounded Theory study using social media data. The inductive approach is more time-consuming than the deductive approach and is useful when building new theories.

(iii)   Hybrid qualitative data analysis approach

A hybrid approach is followed when a researcher uses both an inductive and deductive approach for the data analysis to achieve particular objectives. The researcher can, for example, first consider the study's research questions when doing a deductive analysis of social media data but also allow for themes or categories to emerge from the data afterwards with inductive coding (Fereday & Muir-Cochrane, 2006).

9.4.4 Thematic analysis

Thematic analysis (TA) is an umbrella term for a set of approaches to conducting a qualitative data analysis when a study focuses on identifying themes (patterns of meaning) in qualitative data (Clarke et al., 2019).

TA is widely adopted by qualitative researchers doing social media research. Once social media data is adequately cleaned and organised with suitable qualitative data analysis software (see section 9.3), the purpose of a TA is to develop different themes to explain the shared meaning. A TA thus identifies patterns in the meaning across a dataset (Hawkins, 2018).

There are also different versions of TAs that allows for some theoretical flexibility, but which may differ in terms of how to develop themes (Guest, MacQueen & Namey, 2012). For example, themes can also be developed by using a coding framework or codebook (Brooks et al., 2015) or by using secondary sources (Clarke & Kitzinger, 2004).

The chapter, however, focuses on the reflexive TA approach as proposed by Braun and Clarke (2013) and Clarke et al. (2019) because the approach is 'theoretically-flexible' and can be used within different frameworks to address a range of research questions. Also, the reflexive approach can be used in conjunction with any of the different TA approaches below when doing a thematic analysis.

(i)   Different approaches for conducting a thematic analysis

A TA can be done following different approaches (orientations). As mentioned in section 9.6.4, qualitative data analysis can be done deductively, inductively or follow a hybrid approach depending on the purpose of the study. These approaches are also applicable to a TA.

In addition to the above three approaches, a TA can be done semantically. This means that coding and theme development are based on the exact (straightforward) content of the data (Anderson & Clarke, 2017). Another approach is to develop themes in a latent way and to report on assumptions and concepts that are implicit in the data (the hidden meaning of concepts in the data) (see Frith & Gleeson, 2004).

A researcher may also follow a critical realist (essentialist) approach and report on the implicit (unspoken) reality that is reflected in the data (Everson-Hock et al., 2010). Lastly, a researcher may follow a constructionist approach and report on how the data create reality (Brown, 2008).

(ii)   Steps followed in a thematic analysis

The following steps guide a TA as was originally put forward by Braun and Clarke (2006). However, because their ideas and thinking have since evolved, the steps proposed below also reflect their latest work (see Braun & Clarke, 2013; Clarke et al., 2019).

Before following these steps, as mentioned in section 9.2, social media data should already have been cleaned and properly organised. The researcher should also have identified the TA approach that will be followed as explained in section 9.4.5.1.

Figure 9.3 below depicts the different steps of a TA that could be applied in different contexts (reflexive).

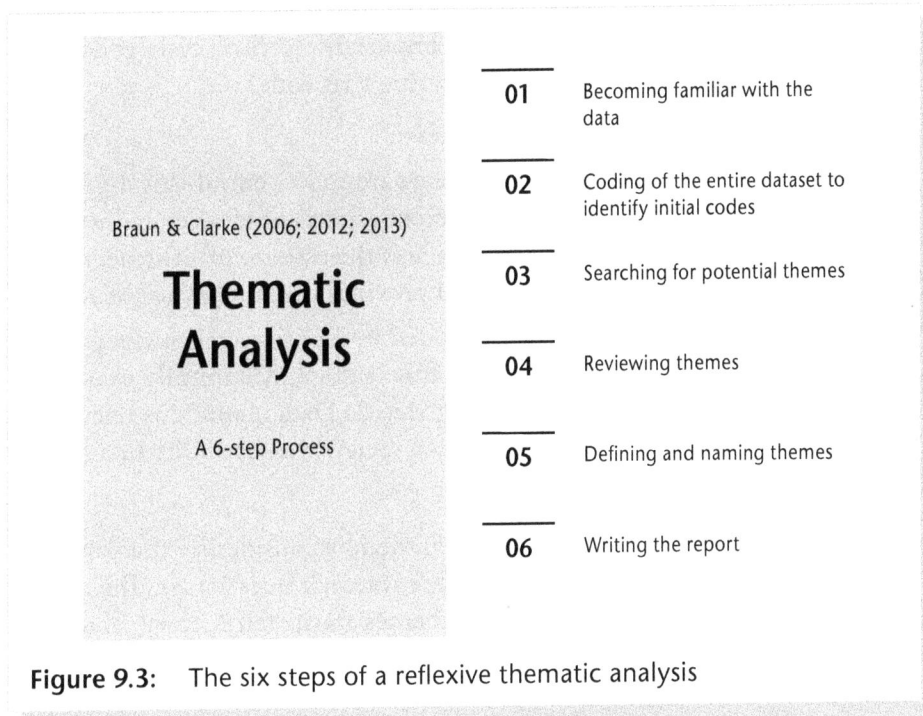

Braun & Clarke (2006; 2012; 2013)

Thematic Analysis

A 6-step Process

01 Becoming familiar with the data

02 Coding of the entire dataset to identify initial codes

03 Searching for potential themes

04 Reviewing themes

05 Defining and naming themes

06 Writing the report

Figure 9.3: The six steps of a reflexive thematic analysis

The six steps are explained as follows (Braun & Clarke, 2013:174–179):

Step 1: Becoming familiar with the data

This first step requires the researcher to become familiar with the data by reading and re-reading the content. The more the researcher reads through the data, the more acquainted he or she will become with the content. The main idea behind the first step is to obtain a good understanding of the depth of the data while taking notes and obtaining some ideas for initial coding.

Step 2: Coding of the entire dataset to identify initial codes

Following step 1, during the second step the researcher must label the data (with codes) to identify those features that will assist in addressing the study's research question(s). For example, the entire dataset must be coded after which all the codes and data extracts are collated for analysis later.

A code includes a single idea about a segment of data that the researcher captures with different labels that relate to the study's research question(s). Codes thus act as 'building blocks' that eventually combine to become themes and thus link data with theory. A theme can be developed by combining multiple codes. Also important is that each code must correspond with a data quotation reflecting that code.

Step 3: Searching for potential themes

A theme describes a pattern that reappears around a 'centralising organising concept' in a dataset and captures different aspects of ideas contained in it. The centralising organising concept depicts the essence of a theme, reflects the core of what the theme entails and provides consistency to the theme.

During step 3 initial themes are generated by identifying broader patterns of the meaning of potential themes. This is done by carefully examining all codes which were identified during step 2. Data quotations relevant to each potential theme must be collated to review the feasibility of a theme.

Step 4: Reviewing themes

During step 4 all initial themes are reviewed by considering the dataset to ensure that they will address the study's research question(s). The quality of the themes is thus checked. The themes must 'tell a story' about the data and are now further refined, combined, split, or even discarded. For example, it might become evident that some themes must rather be combined or split into more themes.

Step 5: Defining and naming themes

During step 5, all themes are now defined and named to determine 'the story' behind each. This means that each theme must be analysed in detail to determine what the single focus is as well the scope. All themes must also be given an appropriate name that reflects a unique meaning. The researcher must be careful to not have overlapping or repetitive themes. However, themes may build on one another.

Step 6: Writing the report

During the last step, the researcher must write the report in narrative format and report on each theme. It is important to place the discussion within the literature in a convincing manner together with quotations from the data in support of all arguments.

9.4.5 Adopting a mixed-method approach for a thematic analysis

It is also possible for researchers to combine computational data analysis techniques with a TA or another qualitative data analysis to reap the benefits of both statistical and rich qualitative data. We recommend the four phases as put forward by Andreotta et al. (2019:1766–1781) and depicted in Figure 9.4 below.

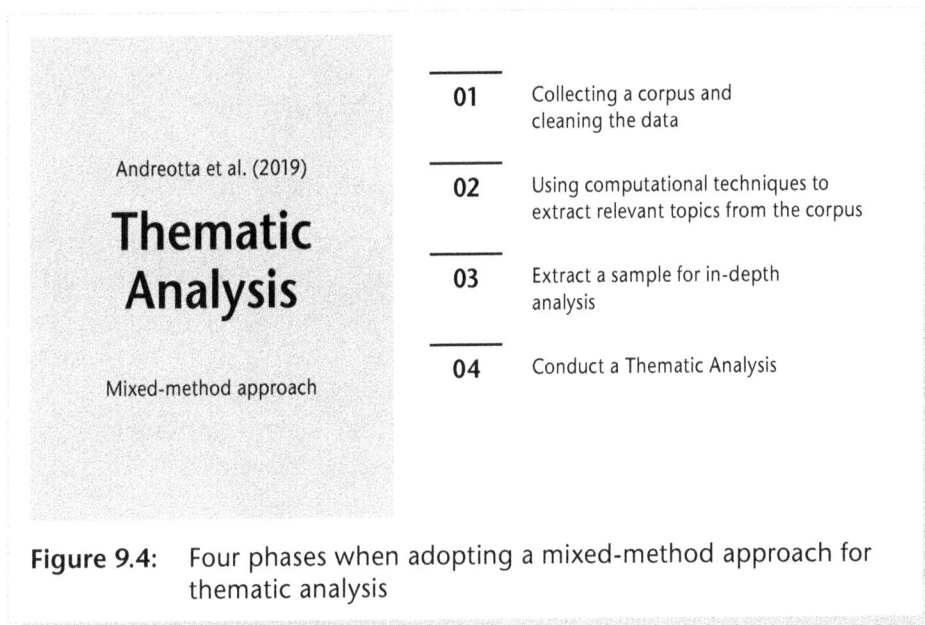

Andreotta et al. (2019)

Thematic Analysis

Mixed-method approach

01	Collecting a corpus and cleaning the data
02	Using computational techniques to extract relevant topics from the corpus
03	Extract a sample for in-depth analysis
04	Conduct a Thematic Analysis

Figure 9.4: Four phases when adopting a mixed-method approach for thematic analysis

These four phases are explained as follows:

Phase 1: Collecting a corpus

As mentioned in chapter 2, social media data represents a corpus consisting of text, images, videos or other graphical information. It is explained in detail in chapter 8 how to collect social media data with automated software or computational techniques (see also section 9.3.2). A corpus is first collected in line with the purpose of the study (see chapter 2) and thereafter cleaned (section 9.2). Phase 2 is the next step.

Phase 2: Using computational techniques to extract relevant topics from the corpus

During phase 2 computational techniques are used to reduce the corpus and to extract relevant topics. To achieve this, the corpus is divided into batches and for each batch, relevant topics are extracted. It then becomes important to assess the relevance and quality of these topics and to group similar topics evident in the different batches. Thereafter the most relevant topics are identified to address the study's research question(s) followed by selecting the most applicable topics.

Phase 3 Extract a sample for in-depth analysis

During phase 3 the researcher extracts a manageable sample from the topic descriptions for qualitative analysis (see also chapter 7). For example, instead of analysing 30 000 tweets, the researcher may only analyse a final sample of 300 tweets.

Phase 4: Conduct a thematic analysis

During phase 4, a TA is conducted on the final sample by following the different steps as explained in section 9.4.5. The researcher may also conduct a qualitative content analysis as explained in chapter 4.

9.4.6   Software for qualitative data analysis

There are numerous computer-assisted qualitative data analysis (CAQDAS) tools available for qualitative social media data analysis. NVivo, ATLAS.ti and QDA Miner are highlighted in this chapter as some of the best software that could assist with initial data organisation and coding. It is important to remember that text does not constitute the most important social media data but includes images, videos, art and emoticons. Qualitative data analysis software must thus be able to organise and handle diverse forms of social media data (Veek, 2013).

(i)   NVivo

As also discussed in chapter 8, NVivo (QSR International, n.d) is utilised within the social sciences as a tool to work with qualitative data. Nvivo has also developed a method to extract Twitter data using the NCapture plugin. Once data is retrieved, among others, it is possible to perform a number of analyses on the data such as:

- the ability for users to filter on username and number of followers;
- to code data using content or a TA; and
- the ability to analyse Twitter sentiment.

A further important aspect to note is that NVivo permits the ability to import data from various other sources. For example, if a user had used another tool to pull in data from Twitter or Facebook it would still be possible to import this data into NVivo for further analysis. TAGS can be accessed here: https://tags.hawksey.info/.

(ii)   ATLAS ti.

Atlas ti. is a powerful and widely used qualitative data analysis software to categorise and code social media data. The software can analyse large bodies of textual, graphical, audio and video data and assist the social media researcher to arrange, bring together and manage social media data in a systematic, yet creative manner. In addition, the software can analyse documents in various formats, for example, txt, doc, docx, odt, and pdf and can perform several semantic operations to understand the meaning of the data. The software also has various tools for visualisation and theory building, for example, word clouds (Archer, Janse van Vuuren & Van der Walt, 2017).

(iii)   QDA Miner and WordStat

With QDA Miner and WordStat by Provalis Research, the social media researcher will be able to not only to collect but also analyse a large amount of social media data obtained from Twitter, public Facebook pages and RSS feeds). The software can identify keywords and themes from the data, extract topics and categorise data according to pre-established topics and is suitable for both a deductive and inductive analysis (Provalis Research, 2020).

9.5   RISE OF VISUAL SOCIAL MEDIA: METHODS AND TOOLS

The increase in social media usage over the last 10 years has seen a shift to more visual content shared by users and platforms such as Instagram have emerged to become extremely popular. For academic and professional researchers wishing to study visual content, it can be difficult to know how to retrieve visual data and how to analyse it for insight. There are several tools and methods available to researchers which are described in this section (see also chapter 8 for a discussion on collecting visuals).

The Webometric Analyst tool, outlined earlier, can be used to retrieve images from Twitter and it can also produce lists of most frequently downloaded identical images. A further tool is known as Instaloader (https://instaloader. github.io/) and can download images (or videos) alongside captions and other metadata from Instagram.

Both tools above can be used to pull in data from Twitter and Instagram respectively, however, these tools do not analyse images.

9.5.1   Visual data analysis

Researchers currently have access to excellent software to assist with a visual analysis of images and videos obtained from social media. For example, NVivo for Windows can import videos directly from YouTube and play, code and annotate the video using a timeline (Zamawe, 2017). On the other hand, the qualitative software Atlas.ti can assist with the visual analysis of still images by creating code prefixes and code families (grouping of related issues) (Archer et al., 2017).

In addition, researchers have developed qualitative methods of analysing images and videos such as using thematic content – see, for example, the work of Pila et al. (2017) who analysed #cheatmeal images on Instagram and the case study in chapter 4 relating to conducting a content analysis of a video on YouTube. Social media visuals can also be analysed using multimodel analysis such as visual semiotics. A multimodel approach considers both text and visuals (see chapter 4 for a discussion on visual semiotics).

There are also services such as the Google Cloud vision AI which allows the ability to gain insight into images and using pre-trained models to detect emotion and understand the text (Fang, 2019).

9.5.2   Visual cross-platform analysis

Pearce et al. (2018) encourage a visual cross-platform analysis of social media data (as opposed to analysing only images on a single social media platform) to widen the scope of a social media study. They argue that a multimodal approach can assist with such analysis and could combine the analysis of text, audio and images. In this regard, Poulson, Kvåle and van Leeuwen (2018) see social media as 'semiotic technology' and suggest that a wide range of semiotic methods and approaches must be applied for a social media study.

9.5.3   Audio data analysis

Several types of software can transcribe, and code audio obtained from social media for analysis, for example, NVivo and Atlas Ti. Audio files can be imported in wave (Waveform Audio File), mp3 (MPEG-1 Audio Layer 3) and WMA (Windows Media Audio) formats for analysis. In addition, completed transcriptions can also be imported (Archer et al., 2017; Zamawe, 2017).

It is also possible to conduct an audio analysis with deep learning techniques. Deep learning is a subsection of machine learning (artificial intelligence) and can perform an analysis based on deep learning algorithms (programmed formulas) without any human involvement (Shaikh, 2017).

See this interesting case study demonstrating an audio data analysis: https://www.analyticsvidhya.com/blog/2017/08/audio-voice-processing-deep-learning/

This chapter is not concerned with audio analytics but those who are interested can read more about this kind of analysis at https://www.microsoft.com/en-us/research/project/audio-analytics/.

9.6   CURRENT CHALLENGES AND TIPS WHEN UTILISING AND ANALYSING SOCIAL MEDIA DATA

There may be unique challenges to utilising and analysing social media data for academic research that social scientists may not have encountered previously. In this section, we document several challenges that may be faced when making use of social media data such as Twitter.

There may be specific legal issues and social media companies may have their terms and conditions that must be adhered to (see chapter 10 for a detailed discussion on social media ethics). On Twitter, for example, sharing of Twitter data is prohibited and instead, academics and professionals should look to share the unique identifier which is associated with each tweet which will allow users to retrieve data using unique identifiers only. Furthermore, if it has not been possible to record or disclose the unique identifiers then by sharing the time-period data has been captured alongside the keywords utilised it may be possible for other academics to retrieve the same data.

There may be several ethical considerations to take into account when making use of social media data because when data is retrieved in large quantities it will be difficult to obtain informed consent from all users within a dataset because of the sheer volume of data that is retrieved. Moreover, there will be ethical considerations in how social media posts are reported in an academic publication. As a rule of thumb, if data has been retrieved without the consent of a user then it may be advisable to anonymise both the post and the user handle. NatCen in the United Kingdom published a report detailing the views of the public for social media research which may be useful to refer to (Beninger et al., 2014) – see also chapter 10.

It must also be noted that there may be challenges over retrieving data from social media platforms such as Twitter. This is because if we are to search for a specific keyword such as 'South Africa', only data that contains this keyword will be retrieved. However, there may have been discussions that were about South Africa but may not have specifically mentioned 'South Africa' in their tweets. A general suggestion would be to brainstorm all potential keywords very carefully to ensure the most relevant data is retrieved as excluding important keywords could introduce a systematic bias leading to a biased sample. Data should then be filtered carefully to remove any potentially spamming keywords.

Social media platforms generate vast amounts of data but some of this may consist of spam and academics often must develop methods of removing spam from datasets (see chapter 2). This can occur because spammers like to 'link-bait' on popular hashtags (for example, posts which are created for users to click them and take them to non-relevant websites) – see chapter 11. Popular topics on social media such as Twitter are likely to receive a lot of spam. Moreover, sometimes it is difficult to know whether an account is fictitious or not. On Twitter, users may create automated accounts known as 'bots' which can be used for legitimate purposes or for illegitimate purposes such as to artificially retweet, like or follow accounts. Users can also purchase packages to gain retweets to game the system and it may be difficult to spot this. The amount of potential gaming and manipulation of social media data is currently unknown but as retweet and follow packages can be located via Google suggest they may be very popular.

A further issue that will be faced relates to the cost of social media data because social media organisations often profit for the resale of data. A classic example is Twitter data which can cost a lot of money when trying to retrieve data via the Twitter Firehose API which is 100 per cent of tweets. Moreover, another limitation of Twitter's Free Search API is that if a user has not set up data retrieval or retrieved data from the previous seven or so days then it will not be possible to retrieve this data. However, the Firehose API will provide data going back in time but it may be expensive to do so and it will depend on both the query and the time the data is retrieved.

A further factor to affect social media data is that it will not be representative of the offline population. For example, even Facebook users will not be representative of Internet users and Facebook data will not be representative of Facebook users. This is because not all users will post about certain topics on Facebook.

There are likely to be several further issues that researchers will identify in the future but that are currently unknown. This is because as the field is currently still evolving there could be methodological issues around utilising social media data that we currently do not understand. Henceforth, researchers using social media platforms should be careful with the inferences with the data (see chapter 2 on methodological issues and limitations).

The case study below explores the NodeXL data analysis tool.

9.7 CASE STUDY: NODEXL DATA ANALYSIS TOOL

If a group of political scientists in South Africa wanted to develop an understanding of the network shape, influential hashtags, co-occurring words and during the 2019 South African elections many tools, methods, and techniques could be utilised. The researchers could search the NodeXL graph gallery, mentioned earlier, for network graphs related to the topic. They would find many graphs that have been uploaded which are related to the election. Figure 9.5, below, is a social network graph of all tweets which have mentioned 'South Africa' which have been tweeted over the 11-hour, 17-minute period from Tuesday, 07 May 2019 at 08:08 UTC to Tuesday, 07 May 2019 at 19:26 UTC.

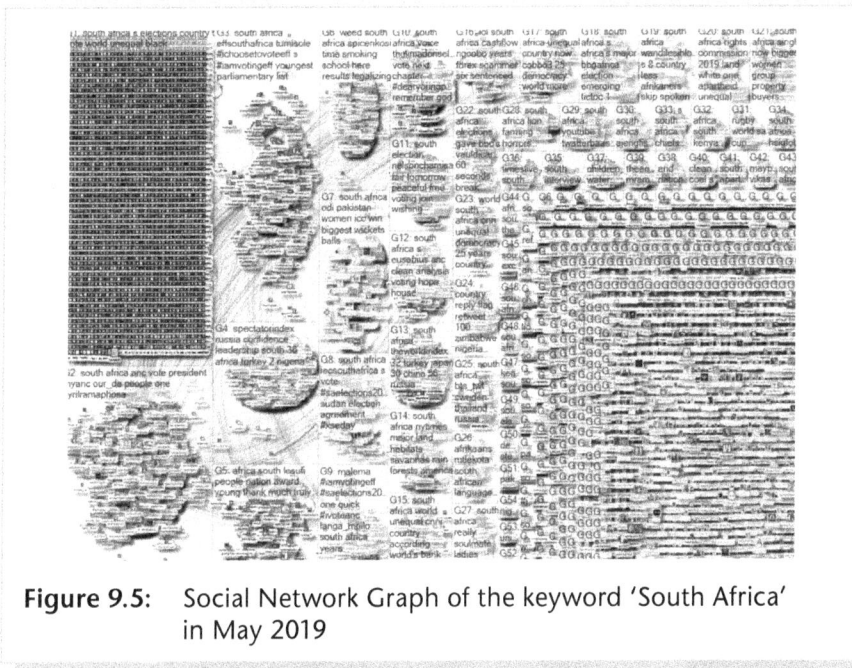

Figure 9.5:   Social Network Graph of the keyword 'South Africa' in May 2019

The graph in Figure 9.5 has clustered a Twitter discussion into several different groups and has attached labels to them on the top left-hand side. G1 refers to Group 1, and G2 refers to Group 2, and so forth, and the ordering of the groups is decided by the size of the group and the largest group is labelled as 'Group 1'. The network graphs often look more complicated than they are. They simply highlight all the different types of clusters formed by users who mention one another. More guidance on interpreting social network graphs can be found elsewhere (see the six types of Twitter networks by Smith et al., 2014). The analysis also reveals several popular hashtags which in this case consisted of the following:

- #iamvotingeff
- #ichoosetovoteeff
- #saelections2019
- #ivoteanc
- #saycaward

- southafrica
- dearyoungperson
- onesaforall
- uphephela
- africa

The most frequently occurring co-words consisted of the following:

- south, africa
- africa, elections
- africa,s
- world's,unequal
- 25, years

- middle,class
- africa,world's
- black,middle
- class,voters
- n,c

Within NodeXL it is also possible to view the network by zooming in either within the desktop version or by using the NodeXL graph gallery's interactive explorer. Figure 9.6 below, displays an interactive version of the social network graph shown previously as Figure 9.5 and by hovering the mouse over a node it displays the tweet that the user has sent.

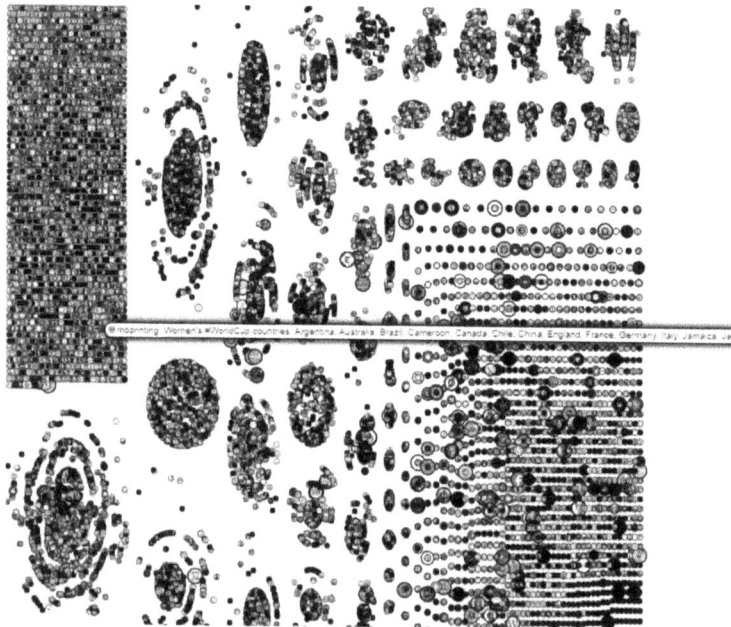

Figure 9.6:   Interactive Explorer in NodeXL

9.8   SUMMARY

This chapter provided an overview of social media data analysis from a quantitative, qualitative and MMA respectively and explained the importance of data cleaning. Different social media data analysis tools were highlighted while a case study illustrated one of these tools, NodeXL. In addition, the chapter also clarified conducting a qualitative TA and a visual data analysis. The chapter concluded with some tips on how to overcome current challenges.

It is important to conduct social media research with ethical guidelines in mind (see Ahmed, Demartini & Bath, 2017). Furthermore, different universities will have their policies regarding social media research. This could involve anonymising tweets reported in research and/or obtaining institutional research ethics approval before collecting research data when conducting social media research (see also chapter 10).

Since its inception, social media platforms have transformed in the features they offer based on public interest and demand. A once textual online world became a visual online world with the rise of image-sharing platforms. This highlights how sharing information might change and social media researchers may need to look towards new methods, tools, and techniques to study this data.

Learning activities (Test yourself)

1. Table 9.3 below is a self-test on how to achieve certain goals utilising NodeXL which was outlined earlier. The exercise aims to test knowledge of how to best utilise the feature of NodeXL. Before completing this activity, it may be worth re-reading the section on NodeXL.

Table 9.3:   Learning Activity on Using NodeXL

Goals	How would achieve the goal?
Determine dominant external media narratives shared on social media during an evolving news event. And establish different discussions that are taking place based on an emergent new development.	
Ascertain users who are concerned with an evolving news event.	

See Ahmed and Lugovic (2019) for the completed version of this table available at https://www.emerald.com/insight/content/doi/10.1108/OIR-03-2018-0093/full/html

2   List the main differences between a quantitative, qualitative and MMA to social media data analysis.

3.   Explain with reasons which qualitative data analysis approach a researcher would adopt for the following scenarios:

  • A researcher who is conducting a Grounded Theory study, collects social media data with the NViVo software and then uses the social media data to build a theory.

  • A researcher is conducting a social media study on crisis communication and collects and analyses data that reflect social media users' responses to the crisis. The researcher uses the study's research questions to group social media data into different themes.

  • A researcher is conducting a study on self-identity in social media. The researcher first uses a theoretical framework to develop themes and then considers the data to add more themes.

Further reading

The following sources are recommended for further reading since they illustrate qualitative and quantitative data analysis in different settings:

Chuma, W., Bosch, T., Wasserman, H. & Pointer, R. 2017. Questioning the media-democracy link: South African's journalists' views. *African Journalism Studies*, 38(1):103–127.

Clarke, V. & Braun, V. 2016. Thematic analysis. In Lyons, E. & Coyle, A. (eds.). *Analysing Qualitative Data in Psychology*. 2nd ed. London: SAGE Publications, pp.84–103.

Connelly, L. M. & Peltzer, J. N. 2016. Underdeveloped themes in qualitative research: Relationships with interviews and analysis. *Clinical Nurse Specialist*, January/February: 51–57.

Dey, N., Borah, S., Babo, R. Ashour, A.S. 2019. *Social network analytics: Computational research methods and techniques*. London: Academic Press.

Howitt, D. 2012. *Introduction to qualitative methods in psychology*. 2nd ed. (Chapter 7: Thematic analysis). Harlow, Essex: Pearson Education.

Kawash, J. 2014 (ed.). *Online social media analysis and visualization*. Switzerland: Springer International Publishing.

Langdridge, D. 2004. *Introduction to research methods and data analysis in psychology* (Chapter 14: Transcribing, coding and organising textual data). Harlow: Pearson.

Osborne, J.W. 2013. *Best practices in data cleaning: A complete guide to everything you need to do before and after you collected your data.* Thousand Oaks, California: SAGE Publications, Inc.

Riccardi, F., Mizrahi, T., Garcia, M., Korazim-Kőrösy, Y., & Blumsack, A. 2017. *Using Atlas.ti in qualitative research for analyzing inter-disciplinary community collaboration.* SAGE Research Methods Cases. Doi:10.4135/9781473995895.

Rohm, A., Kaltcheva, V.D. & Milne, G.R. 2013. A mixed-method approach to examining brand-consumer interactions driven by social media. *Journal of Research in Interactive Marketing*, 7(4): 295–311.

Sorensen, L. 2018. Populist communication in the new media environment: A cross-regional comparative perspective. *Palgrave Communications*, 4(48), Available from: https://www.nature.com/articles/s41599-018-0101-0 [19 June 2020].

Sponder, M. 2012. *Social media analytics: Effective tools for building, interpreting, and using metrics.* New York: McGraw-Hill.

Tan, E., Guo, L., Chen, S., Zhang, X. & Yihong, E.Z. 2012. Spammer behavior analysis and detection in user generated content on social networks, *Proceedings of the IEEE 32nd International Conference on Distributed Computing Systems*, ICDCS'12, Washington, DC, 305–-314.

Section D

IMPLICATIONS OF
SOCIAL MEDIA RESEARCH

Implications

CHAPTER 10

Ethics In Social Media Research

Fortune Tella

Ethics is knowing the difference between what you have a right to do and what is right to do. – Potter Stewart

Learning Outcomes

By the end of this chapter the researcher should be able to:

- discuss the ecosystem of ethics in social media research;
- explain breaches to confidentiality, privacy, etcetera in the conduct of research on social media;
- recognise how to handle ethical issues in social media research utilising Big Data;
- identify and assess ethical challenges in social media research;
- apply and appraise ethical practices in social media research; and
- formulate recommendations for protecting the confidentiality of users.

10.1 INTRODUCTION

Advancements in internet technology, especially because of the Fourth Industrial Revolution (4IR), have changed how individuals receive and send information on the internet, particularly on social media platforms. As mentioned in other chapters, social media users generate vast amounts of Big Social Data daily and the researcher thus faces numerous ethical challenges when using this data for research purposes.

Furthermore, these rapid technological developments have created interactional and conversational opportunities for social media users who have become data targets for social media networks, third-party organisations and researchers. The use of data mined from users for marketing and research purposes has led to ethical misconduct by social media networks, third-party organisations, and researchers.

Social media thus offers researchers a lot of data and content opportunities. Furthermore, the social media space has enabled researchers across different disciplines to carry out some particular types of research which will be difficult to do in traditional research. Also, researchers have used social media to access data from underrepresented population groups. Research conducted on social networking sites (SNSs) can be cheaper and more convenient.

The use of social media as a channel for conducting research, recruiting research participants, and accessing Big Data, has attracted attention, especially on matters of ethics. The unfortunate issues of privacy, confidentiality and anonymity breaches on social media platforms, have led to an increased call on social media networks, third-party organisations and researchers to be more responsible in protecting the data of users. Recently, the Federal Trade Commission (FTC) of the United States of America (USA) fined Facebook USD5 billion for its role in the breach of the privacy of users by Cambridge Analytica (Davies & Rushe, 2019). Davies and Rushe (2019) in a news report published by *The Guardian* newspaper, the founder and CEO of Facebook, Mark Zuckerberg is quoted to have stated:

> *We have a responsibility to protect people's privacy. We already work hard to live up to this responsibility, but now we're going to set a completely new standard for our industry* (Davies & Rushe, 2019).

It is important to remember that when discussing ethics and the appropriateness of ethics in social media research, the role, knowledge and understanding of the ordinary social media patron or user, must be explored and assessed. Some social media users are ignorant of how their data (for example personal information and sent and received messages) are used for research purposes. The appreciation of privacy issues by such users is quite muted. Also, the private data versus data in the public domain debate has created a challenging situation for social media patrons on the ownership of social media content. As a result of this lack of understanding and consensus on ownership of social media content, the consent of users is sometimes taken for granted, and in some research circumstances, the consent is not requested or obtained at all. Some researchers resort to using such content in ways that expose users to danger by compromising on the confidentiality and anonymity requirements of research. Digital tools have also made it possible for users' data and social media activities to be traced even when these activities have been anonymised and de-identified. Even though some legal remedies are available to social media patrons, the remedies do not necessarily offer comprehensive protection to patrons.

The knowledge and awareness of social media patrons concerning ethics, and researchers' commitment to upholding ethical guidelines in social media research, are important matters that must be addressed and discussed.

The figure below outlines the ethical issues addressed in this chapter.

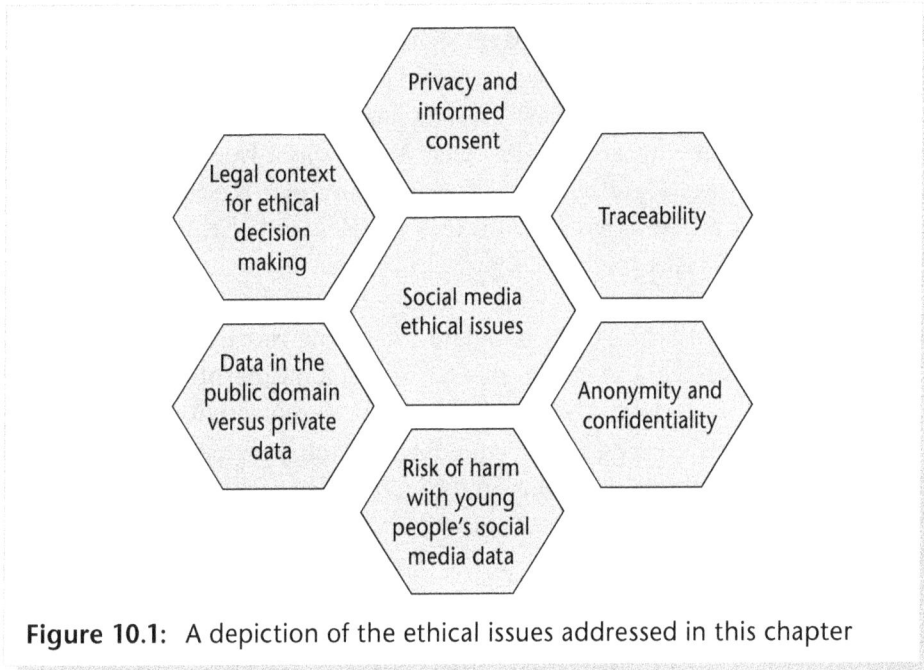

Figure 10.1: A depiction of the ethical issues addressed in this chapter

10.2 THE MEANING OF THE CONCEPT OF ETHICS

Before embarking on a discussion of the ethics in social media research, an overview of the concept of ethics and associated meanings is important.

Although there are different views about what exactly ethics in research entails it is best described as revolving around standards of conduct that differentiate between right and wrong and good and bad (Shamoo & Resnik, 2009).

To provide a thorough perspective on ethics and what role it plays in social media research, reference is made to the principles of ethical practice, as suggested in the well-known work of Kitchin (2007), for online research. Kitchin (2007) posits that any research involving human beings must focus on autonomy, justice, and beneficence. Autonomy refers to the right of every research participant to be able to decide to take part in research and those who are unable to make their own decisions to be protected (Kitchin, 2007).

The aspect of justice stresses that research participants should be treated fairly during the research (Kitchin, 2007). In essence, the methods deployed by the researcher must be transparent and honest in dealing with participants. Further, the researcher's identity must be made known to the participants.

Beneficence involves a demand for researchers to assess and evaluate properly all sorts of harm or risks (for example, physical, social, medical or psychological) on research participants (Kitchin, 2007).

Ethics in social media research has attracted the attention of public interest groups and human rights bodies. Groups such as the British Sociological Association, British Educational Research Association, European Society for Opinion and Market Research, Association of Internet Researchers (AOIR) and the Norwegian National Committees for Research Ethics (NESH) all have ethical guidelines for the conduct of online research and use of data (Penneck, 2018:2; Consumer International, 2018). The various guidelines do not necessarily offer a single template for online researchers to use. It is thus important for researchers to gain an understanding of the key ethical considerations that apply to their social media research activities.

This chapter on ethics in social media research provides an interesting discourse on research responsibility and the integrity required of researchers. It also forays into some dilemmas and debates on ethics in respect of social media research. The popular view is that social media research, whether for educational or commercial reasons, must be guided by ethics to ensure that the user enjoys some form of protection on social media.

10.3   DATA IN THE PUBLIC DOMAIN VERSUS PRIVATE DATA

The chapter first considers the topical issue of the public versus private data debate. The issue has gained attention on the internet and social media spaces. To facilitate a thorough understanding of the issues involved in the debate, the chapter first explores the concept of ownership of social media data and then proceeds to provide the various schools of thought on public versus private data. It then touches on the theme of ethics and concludes on available ethical remedies researchers can rely on to overcome or manage the private versus public data conundrum.

10.3.1   What data do you own, what data is not yours?

The private versus public data debate has existed for some time. There seems to be no end in sight as to whether information sent and received on social media by users should be considered private or public.

When social media patrons or users sign on and agree to the Terms and Conditions (T&Cs) of social networking services, clauses governing the T&Cs are emphatic on the ownership of data and content uploaded or posted on social media platforms. The service providers, considering the T&Cs mentioned before, have taken the stance that they have the right to declare and describe the data as public, even though the user who created it did not have the intention to make it public (Williams, Burnap & Sloan, 2017). In essence, social networking services have the legal right to publish such data (Innes et al., 2016). As a result, the user's privacy, anonymity and confidentiality can become compromised.

What you own or what is not yours can also be assessed based on the responsibility of the user in determining what content to post or upload. Whereas the user does not have control of the architecture of the social media ecosystem, the user does have control over the content he or she uploads and the activities he or she associates with on SNSs. The private/public data debate can be viewed from the position of form and source. The user can control the form (for example, the message or content) and can so avoid the apprehension of sensitive content assuming the label of public data. Conversely, the provider controls the source (for example, the channel or platform) and has certain leverage in describing the data as public especially when viewed against the T&Cs.

10.3.2 The schools of thought on data in the public domain versus private debate

The answer to the question of when data can be considered 'in the public domain' and what should be treated as private data is quite controversial. Some authors have argued that when messages are posted online or on social media platforms (which are public spaces) then such messages/comments can be described as public data (Whitehead, 2010). They assert that since the social media (SM) data of users is 'published text', SM users have consented to have their data used for research or any other form of enquiry. The proponents of this contention assert that messages from users posted in the public space should be considered public. Furthermore, if the information or data can be accessed online without any user registration requirement, then the data on such sites are public data (for example, news websites, corporate sites, etcetera).

The private data school of thought, however, holds the position that if the user is required to use passwords and usernames in order to access and use a website then the posts of the user are private. In such a scenario, the user's posts and comments will then qualify as private (AOIR, 2012; Holmes, 2009). They argue that even though online conversations and interactions occur in the public domain, the nature of the conversations and the view of the users make them private. Although this school of thought supports the user owning the posts, realistically, the social network provider's T&Cs make it difficult for the user to describe posts on his or her platform as private.

The SM architecture adds to the private versus public data dilemma. The social network provider controls the architecture. Users are sometimes unable to control activities such as 'tagging', comments and sharing that are part of the SM architecture. It is important to state that even though the provider exerts strong control over the data, the provider must still apply discretion and can be compelled by a legal regime to institute measures that give the user control over content and data that correctly fits the label 'private'.

10.3.3   Ethical issues pertaining to private and public data

Researchers take particular care when interpreting private or public data. It must not be taken for granted that the T&Cs agreed to by users offer researchers a blanket to use content and posts of users without due regard for ethical considerations necessary for privacy and confidentiality protections.

Table 10.1 below outlines ethical considerations that can assist SM researchers:

Table 10.1: Questions to guide the decision-making process of social media

How does a researcher handle public content/comments posted on a research participant's site by other users who are not part of the study participants?

How should data be published to prevent participants from being traced?

What should be considered public data?

How should data such as video and audio of participants posted on their timelines be interpreted?

Source: Henderson et al. (2013)

The questions in Table 10.2 below will assist researchers to make the right ethical judgements.

Table 10.2: Recommended questions to assist the social media researcher in applying ethical judgement in research

Does the use of user data/posts/content expose the user to danger?

Does the use of content considered sensitive and private appropriate to be interpreted as public for research purposes?

Can self-regulation help researchers to be ethically responsible when using and analysing user data?

If researchers reflect on these questions combined with institutional ethical guidelines on SM research and their own awareness and knowledge of good conduct, the conundrum of what is considered private and what public can be addressed.

10.3.4   Ethical remedies available to researchers

Based on the questions posed in the previous section, researchers must appreciate the need to be ethically responsible when conducting SM research.

When engaging in judgements about public data versus private data, researchers can overcome potential challenges by having regard for the considerations depicted in Table 10.3 below:

Table 10.3: Public versus private data ethical consideration

	Ethical consideration	Interpretation
1	Integrity	A researcher's ethical judgement must be influenced by what is right and what is wrong (McFerran, Aquino & Duffy, 2010). The researcher must value integrity which, in turn, can help him or her determine when to treat the SM data of the user as public or private.
2	Discretion	Researchers must exercise proper discretion in balancing the rights of users and the benefits of the research (Gelinas et al. 2017; Kaiser 2009). This discretion must be a top priority in determining private or public data.
3	Self-reflective attitude	The researcher needs to have a self-reflective attitude towards good ethical conduct. This means that the researcher must see him- or herself in the role of the user whose SM content is the subject of the SM research. Such an attitude will remind researchers to be careful and circumspect in how they use a user's data for research (Markham & Buchanan, 2012). A self-reflective attitude should guide the researcher in treating private or public data in ways that do not offend, discriminate, slander, dehumanise, or embarrass the user.
		As part of self-reflective measures, researchers should further consider good governance practices in the use of both private and public data. Such an approach by researchers could protect users against privacy and confidentiality breaches. Good governance measures applied on data will indicate that researchers are committed to openness, transparency, and trustworthiness (Clark et al. 2015).
4	Competent ethics committee	Institutions and researchers must be interested in the well-being of research participants or subjects. It is in view of this that institutions should establish ethical committees to ensure proper ethical conduct by researchers. When such committees are in place, there should also be processes in place that ensure that researchers submit to the ethical guidelines of conducting research on both traditional and SM (Townsend & Wallace, 2016; Benton et al., 2017). Beyond this, ethics committee members must be competent in ensuring that research conducted in the SM space is properly done and the researcher abides by the ethical guidelines. They must also be in a position to provide suggestions and recommendations in overcoming SM ethics dilemmas (Benton et al., 2017). The ethics committee must put in place measures that ensure that researchers do not use private or public data in ways that pose risks to the privacy and well-being of users. The ethics committee must also enforce measures such as holding researchers accountable for failures in the use of private or public data. (Clark et al. 2015).

The interests of the researcher and the user can be well served if the researcher is benevolent in his or her approach to the research rather than having malevolent intentions.

10.4   THE CONCEPT OF PRIVACY IN SOCIAL MEDIA RESEARCH

The SM environment encourages users to engage in activities that may lead to information disclosures that other parties could potentially use for activities which the user had not consented to. It has been argued that in situations where the data of users are freely accessed, and used for research purposes irrespective of the intent and desire of the user, the privacy of users can be compromised and violated (Donath, 2007; Bahri et al., 2018; Choi & Sung, 2018).

An interesting thought on privacy is that users must have opportunities to self-manage personal data. Suggestions such as users' 'self-declared' stand on privacy have been advanced for the protection of user data. Some SM platforms such as Facebook and Twitter have privacy and security features that are expected to provide some assurances to users (Külcü & Henko, 2014; Kayes & Iamnitchi, 2017). These features, however, do not offer sufficient guarantees in the protection of the user's privacy.

The next section, therefore, first explains what privacy means in the context of SM whereafter the discussion progresses to privacy protection behaviour on social media, the challenges to privacy protection of users, the actions users can take to ensure privacy protection, and the expected role researchers must play in privacy protection.

10.4.1   What privacy means in the context of social media

The SM environment has in recent times attracted negative attention as a result of privacy-related matters such as privacy breaches by corporate entities and theft of personal information by unscrupulous individuals. Social media platforms, to a certain extent, recognise the rights of the internet user to privacy. For example, Facebook and other SNSs have policies in place that provide some level of protection to users. However, to be able to understand privacy and how it should be managed, an explanation of privacy is important.

What then is considered privacy in the context of SM? According to Cutillo, Molva and Önen (2011:1) privacy in the context of SM means 'the ability of a person to have control over how the person's personal information is obtained, managed, processed, and shared by and to any other entities'. This definition and the other associated benefits of SM have motivated people to join SNSs. Users willingly make available their personal information, sometimes ignorantly, to both known and unfamiliar people.

From this explanation of privacy, the individual user is supposed to be in control of the information posted on SM such as the personal profile, posts and online activities connected to the user. Since the user retains control of the personal information, the consent of the user must be an important thought for any researcher to consider in the conduct of SM research.

10.4.2 Privacy protection behaviour on social media

Researchers need to have knowledge of users' specific privacy behaviour on SM when making decisions about SM research that will involve such users. In this regard, Wisniewski et al. (2016) describe the privacy behaviours of users as including holding on to contact information, sharing of information to selected individuals on a friends list, restricting other users from accessing personal information, obstructing applications, limiting the availability to chat, preventing other users from accessing or viewing a user's timeline or wall, requesting a friend to remove a post or image, untagging from a post of image, and changing one's news feed.

In order to provide a good understanding of how privacy settings on SM platforms, particularly Facebook, are used, Wisniewski et al. (2016) list six categories of privacy management strategies which are explained in Table 10.4 below.

Table 10.4 Privacy management strategies

Category	Description
Privacy maximisers	These are SM users who maximise almost all the privacy features available on SM platforms.
Self-censors	These users' approach to privacy is to self-censor by being careful about the kind of information that they upload to SNSs. They use minimally the available privacy features on SNSs.
Selective sharers	This category of users though shares a lot more information and protects their privacy by sharing information selectively to customised friends list.
Privacy balancers	Users in this category show moderate levels of behaviour towards privacy management.
Time savers/consumers	These users demonstrate passive behaviour towards privacy as they are interested in reading the posts of other users. They are careful in interacting with other users.
Privacy minimalists	The minimalists use only a few common privacy features. They, however, are open in their disclosure.

Source: Wisniewski et al. (2016)

SM researchers must take note of these privacy management categories of users and consider these categories in their research decision-making activities.

10.4.3 Challenges to privacy protection of users

Billions of people populate SM platforms and when users' personal information is compromised and used, either benevolently or malevolently, they can suffer negative consequences (Krasnova et al., 2010; Van Slyke et al., 2006). Recent reports in the media and governmental actions have confirmed that the personal information of users is being compromised and the privacy of users is being breached. Culprits include social networking services, internet service providers, third parties and other users including researchers (Luo et al., 2009; Lewis, 2015).

10.4.4 Privacy protection

SM users expect providers to be transparent on privacy matters related to the use of SNSs. The user is interested in the intent of website use and privacy policy of the provider (Moreno et al., 2013). A number of SNSs seemingly have in place provisions that offer some privacy protection to users. Facebook, YouTube, Twitter, and LinkedIn provide the user with control of some privacy settings.

Several studies conducted indicate that even though most users are aware of these privacy protection controls, they do not activate these controls (Ellison, Steinfield & Lampe, 2007; Tufekci, 2008). It is argued in this chapter that the privacy controls can serve a worthy cause only if users can be prompted to activate the controls are reminded of their security.

Many SM users still do not understand or know how their personal information is used for research. Many users are more interested in the SM benefits than the accompanying privacy matters. It is accordingly important that SM users take an active interest in protecting their personal information on social media and seek an understanding of privacy issues on SM.

10.4.5 Researchers and privacy protection

The SM environment presents researchers with enormous research opportunities. Researchers can access rich data to help answer the research question (see chapter 9). The ecosystem of SM, however, is noted for being sensitive to ethics and law. Researchers sometimes ignore or abuse these ethical and legal considerations. Respect, transparency and disclosure are important ethical considerations for any researcher interested in the privacy of the SM user (Avalon & Toch, 2013; Henderson, 2013; Bender et al., 2017).

10.4.6   Respect for privacy

Researchers must respect the right of users to privacy. Users have a right to protect their personal information. When a user's personal information is exposed, such user may suffer both physical and emotional harm (Avalon & Toch, 2013; Cutillo, Molva, & Önen, 2011).

One important ethical issue for SM researchers is the use of images posted on SM. Ethical concerns have been expressed when using images posted on SM. The nature of privacy settings on some SM platforms, tend to lead researchers to interpret images of users shared publicly, as public material that can be used for research (Hargittai, 2010; Highfield & Leaver, 2015). The use of publicly accessible images must be examined against the potential harm to the owners or authors of the images. Researchers must apply the appropriate ethical judgement when using such images. The issues of privacy, informed consent, copyright, and authorship must be properly considered and assessed before such images are used for research. For guidance, researchers should check for specific provisions in national legal frameworks concerning the use of SM images for research (Highfield & Leaver, 2016). In any decision to use such images in presentations and publications, researchers must comply with ethical responsibility such as respect for privacy, informed consent or clearance from ethics review committees (Burns, 2015; Tiidenberg, 2015). In addition, the researcher must demonstrate knowledge of the ethical issues associated with the SM platforms selected for research. An ethics review committee the researcher is associated with must approve the researcher's evidence of knowledge of these ethical issues before the research can commence (Lunnay et al., 2015). In his or her application, the researcher must demonstrate competence in conducting safe and ethically responsible research that respects and attaches importance to the privacy of the user (Lunnay et al., 2015).

10.4.7   Transparency

In most ethical codes governing professional bodies, professionals are required to be transparent in their engagement with people. Researchers must show an active interest in 'privacy literacy' to promote transparency in the use of data mined from SM users. This will enable users to make appropriate and relevant decisions when using their SM platforms (Rivers & Lewis, 2014).

Researchers who conduct SM research, similarly, must be transparent with users. This means that they must be honest and truthful when they want users to participate in their research. The purpose, benefits and risks associated with their research, must be made known to the user (Beninger et al., 2014). Researchers must avoid exaggerating information about users who participate in their research. These transparency measures, however, can be problematic especially in situations where data of users are mined. Some SM situations require researchers to aggregate trends, provide reasons for SM groups or extract the meaning of multimedia tagging and the use of algorithms for distinct interpretations of user behaviour on SM platforms (Jing, Zhang & Ma, 2006; Dubinko et al., 2007). The approach to applying transparency measures must be well balanced and ethically considered.

10.4.8 Disclosure

To gain the confidence and trust of users, researchers must disclose their identity and presence on SM, for example, when joining Facebook groups for research purposes. Researchers must also make these disclosures when they intend to use SM data. Researchers must not be seen 'snooping' or 'prying' in order to observe and report on users especially when users expect their activities not to be monitored. However, some observational research approaches may exempt researchers from disclosing their identities and presence on SM (Moreno et al., 2013). For example, researchers may be recording the behaviour of users and hence making the researcher's identities known can compromise the objectives of the research. In order to be ethically cautious and responsible, data from such types of research must be presented in a way that will not expose users to harm, reputational damage or some other risk (Moreno et al., 2013).

The privacy of SM users is strongly cherished, and researchers must be guided by the right ethical judgements when using SM data of users.

10.5   INFORMED CONSENT IN SOCIAL MEDIA RESEARCH

The nature and size of SNSs make them attractive for the conduct of research and recruitment of research participants (Hutton & Henderson, 2015). However, much research using SM data in the public domain ignores the informed consent of users (Hutton & Henderson, 2015). Many SM studies also use traditional research methods (see chapter 4), and the theme of consent thus remains important. While many SM studies use observational data, researchers in some instances are expected to obtain the informed consent of research participants in order to undertake a SM research activity. It is possible and practical in some SM research projects to establish measures to obtain the consent of users. For example, SM studies that involve online surveys, interviews (private chats), and focus group discussions (set up via SM, for example, Facebook) should obtain the informed consent of users in some form which can also be automatically built into the data collection process (Hutton & Henderson, 2015; Williams, Burnap & Sloan, 2017). However, exceptions can be made for observational research on SM as obtaining the informed consent of users can compromise research objectives and findings. Furthermore, in some research scenarios, obtaining consent may be difficult (Beninger et al., 2014). Research that involves data mining does not provide avenues for researchers to interact with the research subjects to obtain their consent. Also, the researcher may not be able to ascertain the identity of research subjects and this may impact on obtaining consent for the study (Bull et al., 2010).

The case of informed consent is thus not a one-size-fits-all for all SM platforms. For example, Twitter's T&Cs are emphatic that users' public posts can be made available to third parties and there is no need for the informed consent of the owner of the posts (Williams, Burnap & Sloan, 2017).

We, therefore, need to understand the meaning of informed consent before examining informed consent within the context of the SM experiences of the user. The vulnerability of the SM user is an important area of discussion which was elaborated on before focusing on how researchers can be ethically correct in taking decisions on informed consent.

10.5.1   Informed consent defined

Informed consent has become entrenched in research practice over the years. Researchers must fulfil this requirement to ensure the protection of the rights of research participants.

Informed consent originally emerged from the field of medicine (Nunan & Yenicioglu, 2013). Several ethical guidelines including informed consent are borrowed from the medical profession.

Informed consent is defined as a 'procedure for ensuring that research participants understand what is being done to them, the limits to their participation and awareness of any potential risks they incur.' (SRA, 2003:28).

Researchers are expected to conduct research within certain legal and regulatory boundaries. Aside from these boundaries, one other particular demand for research is the aim of the research interests of participants and the general well-being of society. In striking a balance between these interests, researchers must decide on how to make information about participants available and the amount of data to provide. They must also consider whether participants, research themes, and settings, deserve special treatment. All these play critical roles when the researcher makes informed consent decisions.

10.5.2   Informed consent and the experience of the social media user

As mentioned, much SM research using available data on SM platforms ignores the informed consent of users (Hutton & Henderson, 2015).

Users usually are unaware that their data may have been used for research or will be used for research.

Typically, whenever human subjects are used for research, consent must be obtained from the participants or respondents (Sleeper et al., 2013; Kleinig, 2010). Even though informed consent is desirable, where SM research is concerned, it is impractical and not always possible for the researcher to reach out to all SM users who might be the subject of a research study because of the volume of the data involved, including anonymous profiles. Another case in point is that the data required for SM research is easily accessible and in the public domain (for example, Twitter) as users largely make such data available without any form of coercion from a researcher. The challenge for the researcher lies in whether the issue of informed consent of the SM user must be treated the same way as the informed consent of traditional research participants or respondents?

Research shows that SM users are not so willing to share their SM activity data for research (Leon et al., 2013; Ayalon & Toch, 2013). For example, disagreement still exists as to whether it is ethically right to use data from public sources such as Twitter for research. The T&Cs caveat some SNSs use to protect commercial and operational rights whenever the informed consent principle is compromised is not appropriate. For example, Facebook's privacy and ethical policies, particularly, the 'Data Use Policy' provides a legal excuse for Facebook to indicate informed consent given by the user to have user data and information mined for research.

SNSs are, nevertheless, useful in many ways. However, as they are largely motivated by commercial interests, as against the social interests of the user, the issue of ethics will always be at the centre in any discourse on SM use. SNSs can gather rich user data and with the help of software analysis tools, SNSs providers can predict user behaviour, preferences, character and attitudes. As already discussed, these predictions are made most of the time without the consent of the user. The Facebook newsfeed experimental project is an example of the online community expressing angst as a result of Facebook embarking on this project without the permission of users (Jouhki et al., 2016). The vulnerabilities users are exposed to are a source of concern to the SM usage community.

10.5.3 The vulnerability of the social media user

The opportunities afforded by SNSs have resulted in SM users consciously and voluntarily providing intimate personal information. Users have been releasing excessive information about their identities. As SM providers are becoming known for all types of empirical studies that revolve around the behaviour and attitude of users, it remains important to address faithfully the issue of ethics.

The architecture of SM promotes activities such as tweeting, sharing, posting, liking and following. The disclosures emanating from the sharing, tweeting and posting activities of users, are being used in research and generating discussions amongst researchers. Past disclosures such as comments that criticise groups or old photos of some users have gone viral and exposed these users to abuse, harm, discrimination, cyberbullying and blackmail (Leon et al., 2013; Ayalon & Toch, 2013).

The four affordances that Boyd (2011) speaks about provide a good perspective on the vulnerability the SM user is exposed to:

- Scalability: The SM activity of users is easily visible.

- Replicability: The user's identity and data can be copied and duplicated.

- Persistence: The online engagements, conversations and other activities of the user can be automatically recorded and stored permanently.

- Searchability: Personal data information is retrievable through a sophisticated search.

It must be mentioned that users' SM activities often reveal their behaviour and this behaviour can be studied for both commercial and research purposes. However, the studies on the behaviour may be interpreted in ways detrimental to the interests of the user. If users are aware that their activities and the interpretation thereof can potentially expose them to harm, users will be more careful in what they expose and demand to be proactively interested in their consent being obtained.

It is clear that SM users are under surveillance and as such, there is a need to have in place, ethical guidelines that will ensure that the consent of users is sought and obtained before research is undertaken.

10.5.4 Being ethically right on informed consent

As mentioned, not only will it be challenging but, in many cases, impossible for any researcher interested in Big Data on SNSs to obtain consent from every user. Some users might have left the SM platform in the meantime or simply not respond to direct messages requesting their consent.

It is important to know if users will welcome the idea of their data or SNSs activities being used for research without their consent or without being informed of the implications of the use of users' data and SNSs activities. Research activities that involve obtaining information and/or data of the SNSs activities can provide rich data on the different phenomena connected to communication, messaging, access to and dissemination of information, symbolism and semiotics.

There might be a need for a new regulatory framework on how SNSs broadly obtain consent from users (Custers et al., 2013). The usual practice of SNSs obtaining consent of users at the registration point of the websites needs to be reconsidered. It is arguable that consent given in this manner should not be categorised as permanent. Opportunities for consent renewal must be made available to the user. The SNS landscape is continuously changing as are concerns for ethical breaches. If it becomes possible for consent to be renewed, these SNSs will be careful of creating data gaps that encourage ethical breaches.

The user is at risk of providing a certain form of consent, for example, 'secured consent' which Hutton and Henderson (2015) explain allows users to give consent just once to all possible research activities on user data over a period of time. This approach, though useful to the researcher, can be detrimental to the user if the data is used in situations contrary to the wishes of the user. Some researchers have argued that user consent should be obtained every time the user's data and information is to be used for research purposes (Sleeper et al., 2013).

Researchers must take note that, although users have already given their consent to the T&Cs of the SNSs services, they might have done so to use SNSs. Also, users usually do not have a choice, lack understanding of the consequences of the T&Cs, and usually consent is packaged as a 'take-it-leave-it' offer (Regan, 2002; Dutton & Blank, 2013). Internet enthusiasts and users who are interested in SNSs might be more interested in signing up to use and not pay attention to how their data and content are used or abused. Researchers must embrace the idea that the user in the future might want to change the consent given to the SNS provider. The researcher might have a justifiable cause for relying on the T&Cs the user consented to, and thus use the personal information of the user (Sleeper et al., 2013). The researcher, however, must also be rational in appreciating the right of the user to change consent. It is incumbent on the researcher to get the consent of the user even when the personal information was made available consciously and voluntarily.

10.6   THE CONCEPT OF ANONYMITY

Privacy breach concerns have resulted in many internet and SM users taking steps to ensure anonymity online. According to Rainie et al. (2013) in a study they conducted for the Pew Research Centre, 86% of internet users have taken action to remove or hide their digital footprints from the Internet and SM. The actions taken include avoiding using the names of users, masking internet protocol, and encrypting messages. Further, 55% of users have also taken remedial measures to avoid being observed on the Internet by governments and regulatory bodies.

Saunders et al (2015:617) offer this definition for anonymity:

Anonymity is one form of confidentiality – that of keeping participants' identities secret. However, confidentiality also includes keeping private what is said by the participants, something only achievable through researchers choosing not to share parts of the data.

The subject of anonymity has become topical for SM owners, users and researchers. The desire for some users to remain anonymous has led to the creation of SNSs such as *Whisper* and *Secret* which have made it possible for users to have anonymous experiences online. Anonymity is also connected to researchers de-identifying or non-identifying online research participants (Correa et al., 2015).

In SM terms and what the SM architecture allows, anonymity opportunities for the user manifests in (1) hiding of physical characteristics (2) providing pseudonyms such as avatars or usernames and (3) full anonymity where users remain unknown (Keipi et al., 2015:719).

From the aforementioned, it is trite that both SM users and researchers find anonymising identity useful.

The key areas of focus discussed in this section are:

- usefulness and drawbacks of online anonymity; and
- anonymising to keep ethical breach in check.

10.6.1   Usefulness and drawbacks of online anonymity

The anonymity opportunities of SNSs can either bode well or be problematic for users. For users who want to have their identities hidden, Kang et al. (2013) point out some advantages to users of being anonymous, namely, users:

- can avoid being disliked by others;
- can protect loved ones;
- can have control over personal image;
- have the freedom to be expressive;
- have control over personal information;
- are protected against legal suits.

Despite the benefits associated with an anonymous profile there are drawbacks that the user will be exposed to if the identity is rendered anonymous. Some of these drawbacks include:

- Bad reputation: a user can be maligned and castigated which will cause the user's reputation to suffer.
- Irresponsible behaviour: a user can use the anonymous identity to engage in abhorrent behaviour.

- Disconnected from real friends: Since the user's identity is anonymous, the user might lose some friends.

- Inconsistent self-image: The confidence of a user might be weakened as the user's persona will not be a true reflection of the user's identity.

Whichever way one looks at the issue of anonymity, it is critical to establish positive and negative attributes for the SM user.

10.6.2 Anonymising to keep ethical breach in check

In making use of SM data for research, researchers need to consider anonymising information or data that can identify users (Rainie et al., 2013).

So, how can researchers use anonymity to ensure that the user and the personal data of the user are not abused? Table 10.5 below provides some guidelines.

Table 10.5: Ways for anonymising social media users' data

1	Data sets derived from the personal information and content of users should be anonymised especially in cases where the user has not given consent to the use of the personal information and content (Beigi et al., 2018).
2	The data gathered directly or indirectly from users should be reconstructed. Changes can be made on the data but care must be taken to ensure that the original meaning of the research work is maintained and not diluted (Benton, Coppersmith & Dredze, 2017).
3	Researchers can use the paraphrase technique and other creative ways in presenting any information connected to a user. This will ensure that the user is not identified through the user's online activities (Benton et al., 2017).
4	In situations where consent is not obtained and to avoid ethical breaches, researchers are admonished and encouraged to de-personalise users' data (Keipi et al., 2015; Goga et al., 2015). This involves removing or deleting all items that identify users (for example, names, contact information, gender etc.).
5	In instances where researchers use extracts from the content of users, researchers must pseudonymise the identity of users (Keipi et al., 2015; Beigi et al., 2018; Saunders et al., 2015).
6	When other researchers intend to use data from a research that de-identified SM research participants, the researchers must agree not to take actions that will re-identify the participants (Benton, Coppersmith & Dredze 2017; Saunders et al., 2015; Jamieson & Güez, 2018). The researchers who de-identified the user data can either decide not to grant other researchers access to the data, or the researchers can include a 'Terms of Use' policy to ensure that their data is not ethically breached by other researchers. The policy must be forcefully enforced (Li, 2013).

While it is important to anonymise user information and data, the process may not be entirely successful. There are limits to the process of anonymity. There are digital tools that can trace anonymised and de-identified information of users to their established identities on SM (Li, 2013). Researchers must serve notice on users who participate in SM research that there are possibilities that information directly or indirectly elicited from them can be traced to them.

It must be pointed out that not all research is the same and a one-way approach to anonymising data is, therefore, not practicable. The anonymity strategy for each research must be contextualised for that specific research.

10.7 CONFIDENTIALITY IN SOCIAL MEDIA RESEARCH

The protection of the confidentiality of research participants is critical for the integrity of any research. Mehmood et al. (2017) add that the hallmark of any research is the protection of the confidentiality of research participants. Confidentiality ensures that participants are not susceptible to risk or harm.

As previously discussed in the anonymity section of the chapter, personal identity items such as name, age, school, residence and conversation extracts of users that might have been de-identified, can be re-identified and traced to users (Li, 2013, Penneck, 2018). Such breaches can weaken the confidentiality assurances given by researchers to research participants (Kaiser, 2009; Penneck, 2018). Researchers must be able to navigate confidentiality dilemmas in such a way that the user's identity is not compromised or breached. Embarrassment, vulnerability, and disclosures are just some of the unfortunate occurrences of confidentiality breaches (Gibson, Benson & Brand, 2013).

As it is important to provide clarity on confidentiality and how it is understood in the SM ecosystem, the next section considers, first the meaning of confidentiality whereafter threats to confidentiality are explained. In order to be clear on confidentiality decisions that researchers must take, we consider the confidentiality dilemma researchers face in conducting SM research. Lastly, we discuss the benefits of a confidentiality agreement.

10.7.1 What does confidentiality mean for social media studies?

According to Saunders et al. (2015:617) 'confidentiality ... refers to all information that is kept hidden from everyone except the primary research team.'

Confidentiality is not a stand-alone ethical principle. Privacy is an important consideration in any decision on confidentiality (Leiker, 2011). It also involves a decision by a researcher to protect the privacy of a research participant in respect of information and personal identity. It is a promise by the researcher not to divulge information that breaches the privacy of the research participant or respondent.

10.7.2   Threats to confidentiality

The confidentiality established between the researcher and research participants is based on trust. Just like anonymity, confidentiality is not always guaranteed, especially in respect of SM research. Confidentiality can be threatened in the following ways (Saunders et al., 2015; Kaiser, 2009; Gibson, Benson, & Brand, 2013):

- Exposure of identity/views of a user.
- Anonymised data is re-identified leading to privacy breaches.
- The researcher uses user information or images without the informed consent of the user.
- Terms of use regarding user information are breached by other researchers.

10.7.3   The researcher confidentiality dilemma

Researchers can encounter decision-making challenges regarding the confidentiality of users or participants, especially in observational SM research. Should the researcher remain truthful to the personal information of users? Or should they protect the privacy of participants (Kaiser 2009)? In order to be clear on how to deal with the dilemma, a further question to be asked is: would the data if linked/traced to participants lead to harm or risk to participants? If the answer is yes, the next question to ask is: will anonymising reduce or remove the harm or risk? If yes, then the ethical consideration or choice must be in the interest of the participant.

It should be noted that if the confidentiality of the research participant is betrayed, there could be implications for the future research projects of the researcher. Participants will not trust the word or promise of researchers. However, in an observational study, the researcher can be exempted by institutional review boards (IRB) from ethical check if the SM study is to observe public behaviour (Moreno et al., 2013; Whiteman, 2012: 97). It is thus important for researchers interested in an observational study of posts, tweets, and other SM activities, to obtain the approval of IRBs before undertaking such studies. It is imperative for such researchers to apply anonymisation strategies to protect the privacy of users.

10.7.4   Benefits of the confidentiality agreement

When researchers apply good ethical judgement in respect of confidentiality, the following benefits will manifest (Crow & Wiles, 2008; Moreno et al., 2013):

- Trust will be established between the researcher and participants.
- The participant is reassured that participant data or information will not be abused or exposed.

- The rights of participants are respected.
- Participants will not be unduly perturbed by thoughts of breach of trust.

From these, researchers must note that research can only be done if would-be participants volunteer. Most would-be participants will volunteer if they are assured of their confidentiality.

10.8   TRACEABILITY IN SOCIAL MEDIA RESEARCH

Traceability issues raise potential dangers to SM users. Users and their data (for example, texts, images, and symbols) are traceable on SM. Criminal-minded users can trace an SM user by accessing data that such user advertently or inadvertently made available on social media. This is a concern especially when viewed from a privacy and private data perspective. Therefore, it is important, to begin with, a definition of traceability and then move on to the traceability challenges researchers face, before discussing how researchers can overcome traceability challenges.

10.8.1   Defining traceability

Traceability in digital technology means that electronic communication (that is, typed communication) carried out on the Internet by a user can be traced due to physical trace or data-trace which can get stored or electronically recorded (Jungherr, 2015). A user's SM activities, such as posting, tagging, image uploading, and commenting can be stored or archived. The user may be ignorant that SM architecture allows for this activity to take place. This can be a potential risk to users especially when such electronic communication can be accessed, used for research, and published. Such users might not be in support of their electronic communication on SM platforms to be made available for whatever reasons to the public.

10.8.2   The researcher and traceability challenges

Researchers are expected to obtain the informed consent of research participants or respondents before the commencement of research (Mehmood et al 2017) but which, as already mentioned, is not always possible when conducting SM research. Assurances of confidentiality and anonymity are given to participants, but which is not the case when using observational SM data. Most ethical clearance certificates for research provide for informing participants that when they make information available for the purposes of research, their personal information and identities should be protected (Mehmood et al 2017; Kaiser, 2009; Gibson, Benson, & Brand, 2013).

These assurances and the trust research participants bestow on researchers encourage participants to take part in the research. However, these assurances are not fool-proof and can be breached, especially on SM (Donath, 2007; Bahri et al., 2018; Choi & Sung, 2018).

Online and SM activities are digitally recorded, networked, searchable and available (Schroeder, 2014). Hence the personal information of research participants is not entirely secure and protected (Bahri et al. 2018; Choi & Sung 2018). The information is accessible and a commitment to confidentiality and anonymity by researchers is not sustainable (Donath 2007; Bahri et al. 2018; Choi & Sung 2018).

Especially the traceability of user information poses an ethical challenge to researchers. Researchers face the difficulty of how to use and present data collected from participants (Kaiser, 2009; Gibson, Benson & Brand, 2013). How effective and protective can the researcher's anonymising of user data prevent digital tracing of users' data? It has been suggested that measures such as paraphrasing data of users may help in minimising the threat of digital tracing of user data. However, as already discussed in the section on anonymity, it is possible to re-identify anonymised data and information of users. For example, other users or hackers can use certain techniques to trace comments to particular user profiles (Henderson & Johnson, 2013:8).

10.8.3 Overcoming traceability challenges

The researcher will always be confronted with of the challenge pertaining to a breach of confidential information and data of users. There are no strict technological measures that can stop the occurrence of user data or information used in research from being accessed through tracing (Schroeder, 2014). The following, however, can help in dealing with the traceability of user data (Greenwood, & Rashid, 2013; Jamieson & Güez, 2018):

- Care must be taken to protect the personal identities of recognisable SM user profiles in reports published by researchers.
- Social media datasets may be encrypted, and password protected.
- Researchers must avoid storing research data of users in cloud storage environments due to security concerns.
- Various datasets emanating from research should be stored separately, encrypted and password protected. This can make the re-identification process of such data cumbersome and complicated for people interested in tracing the data to users.

These measures at least show that the researcher is committed to good ethical conduct. Researchers must abide by confidentiality and anonymity assurances given to research participants. If the measures can be implemented, instances of de-anonymising and re-identifying of user data, particularly for research will minimise.

10.9   THE RISK OF HARM WORKING WITH YOUNG PEOPLE'S SOCIAL MEDIA DATA

The subject of harm to children and adolescents on SM brings to the fore a dispassionate discussion of themes such as invasion of privacy, ethics and legal considerations.

The Internet and SM offer users, including children and young people, many opportunities and benefits. Such opportunities include self-expression, networking and interaction (Holloway, Green & Livingstone, 2013). However, SM platforms also have become avenues for causing harm to young people and children. Cyberbullying, sexual grooming, harassment and exposure to harmful content are some of the negative acts targeted at young people and children (Marwick & Boyd, 2014). These acts can pose research challenges to researchers using SM datasets of children and adolescents.

We examine how young children and young people use SM and explore the ethical issues researchers must deal with and conclude on challenges researchers face when using children and young people.

10.9.1   Young people's use of social media

Eminent SM scholar, Ellison Boyd (2014) describes perfectly the SM eco-system experience on young people. Boyd (2014:213) asserts that:

> *Networked publics are here to stay. Rather than resisting technology or fearing what might happen if youth embrace social media, adults should help youth develop the skills and perspective to productively navigate the complications brought about by living in networked publics. Collaboratively, adults and youth can help create a networked world that we all want to live in.*

Social networking services have enabled young people to develop and share content meaningful to their and their peers' experiences. They connect and interact with known people such as friends and family as well as people they meet online (Holloway et al., 2013; Staksrud, Ólafsson, & Livingstone, 2013).

The motivation for young people to use SM is largely driven by the need to be self-expressive and have a degree of autonomy in their communication engagements and interactions (Robinson et al., 2014b; Humphry, 2014). Young people can access new ideas (both good and bad) that can help their self-expressiveness (Holloway et al., 2013; Staksrud et al., 2013).

One issue that has gained traction on SM is the potential risks young people are exposed to when they are used in SM research (Marwick & Boyd, 2014; Staksrud et al., 2013). Researchers are often in a dilemma on how they should engage young people in obtrusive and unobtrusive research. As young people may not be able to understand the consequences of informed consent, it is recommended that parents or teachers could act on behalf of young people in providing consent. This can, however, be challenging when the research involves young people who might be distances away from the researcher. Obtaining consent from all young participants might be herculean (Henderson et al, 2012; Sharkey et al., 2011).

As stated in section 10.4.4 of this chapter, some SM users, particularly young people do not take adequate measures to protect their information (Ellison, Steinfield & Lampe 2007; Tufekci 2008). Researchers must show interest in the SM awareness of users. Users who are literate on SM use and ethics will likely take appropriate steps to be ethically responsible on SM (Rivers & Lewis 2014). Knowledge in staying safe and secure is important for all SM users. Table 10.6 summarises steps users can take to stay safe on SM.

Table 10.6: Staying safe on social media

Security measures	Enforcement guideline
Strong password	The password of the user must be strong and long.
Different password	Users should consider using a different password for each SM account (for example, Facebook, Instagram, Twitter etc. of a user must have a different password).
Password-protect phones	It is important that users protect their SM apps on their phones with a password.
Caution against links clicking	As hackers are always a threat on SM sites, users must be cautious in patronizing suspicious content.
Know privacy policies	Users must know the privacy policies of SM platforms and alter their privacy settings to control who accesses their accounts.
Act against unwholesome content	If someone harasses or threatens a user, the user must block such an individual or draw the attention of the SM company for the individual to be penalised.
Be alert to protecting your reputation	When on SM platforms, users must exercise the right discretion in posting texts, pictures, audio files and videos. Contents that can cause irreparable damage to the reputation of users must not be posted on SM platforms.

10.9.2   Ethical considerations for researchers

Researchers must be responsible for the use of SM datasets of young people. The following recommendations can help researchers manage the challenge associated with using young people or their data for research:

- As already emphasised in the section on confidentiality and anonymity, the issue of SM users' rights protection when using observational data, must consider the guidance provided for by the IRB. Researchers must seek a certain form of exemption from IRBs in order to use observational research data of users including young people (Moreno et al., 2013; Whiteman, 2012).

- Researchers must categorise consent. Consent can be categorised to cover consent for study participation and consent for the use of extracts or quotes etc. This can improve the understanding participants will have about the study (Sharkey et al., 2011). Sharkey et al. argue that the consent of young people should be an ongoing exercise. It should not be a once-off activity and should be sought and obtained during the collection, analysis, and reporting stages of the research.

- Researchers must take the responsibility of explaining the research objectives and the role of young people in the research, for example, when interviewing teenagers about their use of SM. Young people must understand the purpose of research and how the results will be used.

- The right measures must be applied by researchers in anonymising information and ensuring the confidentiality of young people (Livingstone & Brake, 2010). Researchers must reconstruct research narratives connected to the research data of children to ensure that all forms of identities connected to these young people are removed. Much care and expertise should be deployed in ensuring that content that can harm young people cannot be traced to young people (Livingstone & Brake, 2010).

10.9.3   Challenges when using young people for social media research

The approach to obtaining informed consent from young people can be plagued with some difficulty. Researchers can experience the refusal of parents in the approval of informed consent. Some parents may object to the participation of their children in the research. Researchers must, therefore, decide carefully how to navigate through such difficulties and be committed to ethical rightness in deciding the way forward.

The use of email to send informed consent forms to parents or other guardians has some limitations. Some of the forms may not be returned and the young people may access the forms meant for their parents to fill on their behalf. Researchers may consider the use of a phone (audio or video phone calls) to discuss informed consent issues with parents or guardians (Parsons, Sherwood & Abbott, 2016). In all cases, informed consent should be documented whether written or electronically recorded.

It is quite established that young people must be protected in SM research (Parsons, Sherwood & Abbott, 2016). The personal information and data that can expose them to harm must be handled well and not compromised (Oswald, James & Nottingham, 2016).

10.10   THE LEGAL CONTEXT FOR ETHICAL DECISION-MAKING OF RESEARCHERS FOR SOCIAL MEDIA RESEARCH

Privacy, confidentiality, anonymity, traceability, private and public data and children's use of SM present potential legal challenges and opportunities to both users and researchers. As already stated, privacy and informed consent policies are designed mainly to satisfy the interests of SM service providers. Many users have experienced challenges in privacy and informed consent challenges.

Social networking services require users to agree to the T&Cs that regulates the use of their platforms. These T&Cs are a contract and form presented on a 'take-it-leave-it' basis which gives SM networks the upper-hand in the management of data. In this section, the legal regime and framework of SM use are discussed and assessed to ascertain how these can improve or enhance good ethical conduct by researchers. The themes covered are the legal framework's influence on good ethical conduct, data protection agencies, and data protection controls. Other important thematic areas covered are copyrighting data sets, legal and ethical alertness on SM content, and addressing the legal shortfalls in data protection of users.

10.10.1   Legal frameworks influence on good ethical conduct

Several countries have legislation that offers some form of protection to the personal information and data of SM users. As of May 2018, over 100 countries have laws that specifically seek to protect the personal data of citizens (Consumers International, 2018).

10.10.2 Data protection agencies

Personal data of users are managed by national bodies such as the United Kingdom Data Service, Data Protection Commission of Ghana, National Information Technology Development Agency of Nigeria, Information Regulator of South Africa and FTC of the USA. Regional and continental bodies such as the European Union (EU) have specific data protection policies such as policies on privacy (Weller & Kinder-Kurlanda, 2016). The EU Charter for the Fundamental Human Rights seeks to protect the personal data of EU citizens (Fuster & Gellert, 2012.). The EU has over the years called for more transparency and responsibility in the ways SM operators and third-party organisations use and manage the personal data of online users (Ur & Wang, 2013). For example, the EU has called for the institutionalisation of a policy christened 'right to be forgotten' which is geared towards the permanent removal of data from databases upon the request of a user (Ur & Wang, 2013; Mantelero, 2013).

Researchers must apply the right controls, ethical standards, and national data policies in conducting SM research. The following are ways researchers can be ethically responsible in their SM research activities:

(i)   Data protection controls

In conducting SM research, data protection policies and laws must guide researchers to put in place access controls to research data and information. Weller and Kurlanda (2016:168–169) suggest that researchers can create access categories for research data. Such categories will involve:

- access to data that will be available to everyone without the need to register;
- access will be given only when the researcher has allowed it;
- data can be accessed only after the expiration of an embargo or data accessible to restricted environments; and
- access to data will be afforded after the signing of user agreements.

These access control measures may offer a legal cover to researchers. Other researchers interested in SM datasets must identify with the ethical and legal principles of protecting research participants and their information (Weller & Kurlanda, 2016).

(ii)   Copyrighting datasets

It is important for researchers to pay attention to copyright issues connected with their research and datasets. SM researchers should even consider licensing datasets. For example, licensing opportunities are available on Creative Commons. This approach will ensure that datasets and the SM studies of researchers can be attributed (Weller & Kurlanda, 2016).

(iii)   Legal and ethical alertness on social media content

Researchers must have knowledge and understanding of important legal and ethical issues useful for conducting SM research, also when using Big Data. For example, researchers must have knowledge of and understand the laws governing the use of images, videos, audios, and texts (Henderson et al., 2010; Alm, 2014). The knowledge of how much content must be used will help researchers in their research work. For example, there have been instances where SM users have posted content or images of other users or friends or tagged them in conversations without their consent (Henderson et al., 2010; Alm, 2014). If researchers use such content for their research, legal and ethical questions could be raised to judge their conduct.

(iv)   Addressing the legal shortfalls in data protection of users

The legal solutions do not necessarily have to be enforcement solutions. Suggestions have been made for judicial, legislative, and administrative solutions (Livingston, 2011). These solutions also have their challenges. The legal systems in most countries are deficient on matters connected to the protection of user information and data (Radin, 2004). The legislative action could restrict the SNS industry and ultimately affect their operations and growth (Jerome & Kollipara, 2010). The legislative measures may improve user rights but users' bargaining ability against excesses of the industry may be curtailed.

Effective remedies on privacy, informed consent, anonymity, traceability, harm to young people and confidentiality could revolve around the altering of deficiencies in the SM architecture and ecosystem. Specific remedies could be applied to the deficiencies that work against the data protection rights of users (Livingston, 2011).

10.11 CASE STUDY: THE GRAPHIC COMMUNICATIONS GROUP LIMITED

The case study below illustrates the public versus private data debate as discussed in section 10.3 above.

On 8 August 2019, Starr FM, a local radio station in the capital city of Ghana, Accra, reported that one of Ghana's leading media companies, Graphic Communications Group Limited (GCGL) had issued a directive on the use of SM by employees (Starr FM, 2019). The Starr FM report indicated that the directive forms part of a new SM policy instituted by GCGL to ensure responsible behaviour on SM platforms by employees of GCGL.

➡

The directive, as explained by GCGL, is to provide an opportunity for employees to first post opinions or views on the official SM accounts of GCGL whereafter they can post such opinions on their own SM accounts. The Communications Manager of GCGL, in an interview with Starr FM, explained that the directive aimed to prevent employees from engaging in activities that can potentially damage the brand of the company (StarrFM, 2019). The manager stated:

If you put it there, you can put it anywhere. Nobody really cares but it must be first on our platforms so that the benefit of you being followed now gets to the organisation because that's where you get your daily bread.

From the manager's statement, it is clear that the motive for the directive was also to drive traffic to the SM accounts of GCGL. The news report also indicated that management had received reports that the SM activities of some employees were distasteful and affecting the brand of the company.

Some employees of GCGL reacted to the directive and called for it to be scrapped:

We just don't understand this; it is bad, Graphic is a leading brand in Ghana and we are preventing our own from sharing their personal views on social media. It is distasteful and must be reversed by management – a staff member to Starr FM.

As is evident in the case study, there is always an ethical dilemma when considering how to treat the SM data of users. It must, however, be emphasised that any research-related decision on user data or activities on SM must be considered within the boundaries of ethics, data policies and rules, as well as discretion.

Source: StarrFM (2019).

10.12 SUMMARY

This chapter provided a holistic discussion on ethics and its relevance to SM research. The various concepts in ethics were discussed and the role of the researcher in conducting ethical research on SM was explained. The ethical issues in SM research explored in this chapter included private versus data in the public domain, privacy, informed consent, anonymity, confidentiality, traceability, the risk of harm working with children and legal context for ethical decision-making.

SM users are sometimes oblivious to the fact that their SM activities can result in the invasion of privacy and breach of their right to informed consent.

Researchers are, therefore, expected to be ethically right when using SM information and data of users.

Anonymity is an important ethical consideration for researchers. While anonymity can ensure good ethical practice, the integrity of research data must not be compromised. Conversely, researchers must take steps to secure and protect the confidentiality of users.

Social media use is important in the lives of young people. The appropriate ethical measures must, however, be used to ensure that children are not exposed to harm and danger.

In this regard, legal frameworks supported by both data protection agencies and SM providers are a prerequisite for the data protection of users. Attention to legal remedies on anonymity, privacy, informed consent, and confidentiality among others must be taken seriously.

Learning activities (Test yourself)

1. What kind of measures would you recommend to researchers in interpreting private/public data?
2. How should researchers handle sensitive information about SM research participants?
3. What ethical judgements will you say are right for informed consent?
4. As anonymity is prone to abuse, propose ways for dealing with the abuse?
5. How responsible should researchers be in ensuring the confidentiality of study participants?
6. What recommendations do you have for researchers who do not take the required steps in protecting the confidentiality of users?
7. Describe how user data and information can be traced to SM.
8. Describe strategies that researchers can use to ensure that children are not exposed to harm in collecting, analysing and interpreting research data of children and young people.
9. Describe roles researchers can play in ensuring the legal rights of study participants in a SM research project.

Further reading

Vinerean, S, Cetina, I, Dumitrescu, L & Tichindelean, M. 2013. The effects of social media marketing on online consumer behavior. *International Journal of Business and Management*, 8(14): 66–79.

Scott, S.V. & Orlikowski, W.J. 2014. Entanglements in practice: Performing anonymity through social media. *MIS Quarterly: Management Information Systems*, 38(3): 873–893.

Ghazinour, K. & Ponchak, J. 2017. Hidden privacy risks in sharing pictures on social media. *Procedia Computer Science*, 113: 267–272.

CHAPTER 11

Researching the Hyper-Connected Society: Implications of New Media Data for Social Media Research

Ashiya Abdool Satar

The contemporary pervasive consumption of and dependence on digital devices, forces us to redefine our ontological status starting from the space we occupy, in-between the organic and the inorganic and between the real and the fictitious. Our knowledge of reality is the knowledge of a subject living on ontological thresholds. As Jason Farman[1] states: the virtual is not the opposite of the real, instead it is a component of experiencing the real. – Daniela Carpi

Learning Outcomes

After completing this chapter, the researcher should be able to:

- **explain** the implications, both positive and negative, of social media usage on the individual, society, and organisations, which, more than likely, provide an important focus in social media research;
- **assess** the challenges of a hyper-connected society, in terms of:
  - moral challenges, such as hashtag publics, armchair advocates, and slacktivism
  - the impact of social media on commerce
  - the effects of social media in the workplace
  - separating psychosocial from platform-driven behaviour, concerning the various effects of social media usage on the individual, that is, self-expression in networked communication channels, identity formation and projection, and social media addiction.
- **evaluate** the implications of online and offline Big Social Data on research findings, in terms of:
  - digital ontology and epistemology
  - limitations and opportunities of data extraction interfaces
  - data selectivity: implications of data exclusion in research samples

---

[1] Farman, J. 2012. Mobile Interface Theory: Embodiment and the Mobile Interface. (London: Routledge) 22.

- **critique** the pros and cons of the slacktivist culture of digital micro-activism through the perusal of a case study citing real-world examples of digital activism;
- **formulate** feasible solutions to balance the pros and cons of a slacktivist culture apparently burgeoning in the hyper-connected society; and
- **synthesise** the arguments put forward in this chapter to critically analyse and evaluate the **influence** of hyper-connectivity on society and how social media research can help us understand this better.

11.1 INTRODUCTION

New and emerging communication technologies bring with them increased possibilities in social networking, social media platforms, and connected devices that generate new forms of data. Social media also continues to play an important role in defining **how** many of us communicate and interact today. However, although social media sites enhance social connection and interaction across geographical spaces, the power of these media in shaping our views of reality and engineering, amongst others, social, civic, educational, informational, recreational, entertainment, and political spaces cannot be understated. Notwithstanding the paramount importance of these influences that affect our living, learning, and working spaces, even more pertinent is the influence of social media on personal identity and the psychological health of the individual. As such, social media researchers need to be aware of these challenges and implications of social media in the hyper-connected society as foci of social media research. This chapter is vital in unpacking some of the various focal areas of social media research, concentrating on the positive and negative influences of social media. No social media research study is complete without understanding the influence these media have on the world as we know it and experience it. Therefore, this final chapter presents the researcher with various avenues and possible areas of social media research, where you are made aware of some of these crucial issues apparent in the information age (which is rapidly moving towards the 4IR).

To contextualise the deliberations related to the implications of new media data in the modern hyper-connected society, the chapter begins with a discussion of the effects of social media. This introductory section highlights the implications of social media in cultural, political, commercial, and organisational contexts, and also covers its influence on the individual (Burgess, 2014:282). In doing so, this section covers topics such as social mobilisation (Steinberg, 2016: 413; Airike; 2013a) in terms of hashtag publics (Bruns et al., 2016:22), slacktivism (Dennis, 2018a; Dennis, 2018b; Airike, 2013b; Riley, 2013), armchair advocates (Steinberg 2019:415; Airike,

2013a), and many other issues related to the implications of social media and the networked audience, broadening the scope of the discussions on topics related to psychosocial and platform-driven behaviour (Mole, 2017; Gardner, 2019:1157) such as, *inter alia*, digital personas (Subrahmanyam et al., 2008).

Social media research involves online research, which has significant implications for the research process, more so with data collection, sampling, and generalisation of findings. Therefore, this last chapter outlines the strengths and weaknesses associated with different forms of Big Data, with a particular focus on Big Social Data. A discussion of data access, digital exclusion, and the effects on targeted populations, samples, and general aspects of the online research process related to new media data is also presented in order to understand the implications that these elements may have on research findings.

Consequently, the discussions hone in on the implications of Big Data, online and offline (Agratchev, 2012), and move to deliberations on the possibilities and limitations of APIs and other technical interfaces, the effects of skewed digital access on data extraction and its implications on new media data (Richterich, 2019:1005; Hutchinson, 2016:2; Ruths & Pfeffer, 2014:1064; Mahrt & Scharkow, 2013), as well as the influence this has on samples drawn from social media data and subsequent research findings (Clement, 2020; DOMO, 2019; Cooper & Mann, 2016: 14). In other words, research that is based on Big Data (and by implication Big Social Data) affects the underlying epistemologies and ontologies of research (Brooker, Dutton & Greiffenhagen, 2017:611, Boellstorff 2016: 388; Crawford & Finn 2015:492; Berry, 2011:1). The chapter ends with a case study outlining the slacktivist /activist dilemma and key learning activities that allow the reader to synthesise the information put forth in this chapter.

11.2 UNDERSTANDING THE NETWORKED AUDIENCE: EFFECTS OF SOCIAL MEDIA

It is estimated that approximately 2,82 billion people worldwide used social media sites in 2018, which is an average of 33 per cent of the global population (Clement, 2020; DOMO, 2019; Statista, 2019; Baer, (2018; McNair, 2018). These numbers show a marked increase from eMarketer's (McNair, 2018) estimates of 2017 that indicate that '74.7% of mobile internet users used their device to access social media.' In fact, Chaffey (2020), Clement (2020), and Statista (2019) indicate that social network penetration is growing exponentially, and statistical estimates for January 2019 suggest that 45 per cent of the global populace accessed some form of social media, while the data approximation at the end of January 2020 showed an increased global usage of social media by 4 per cent – thus reaching 49 per cent, which accounts for around 3.8 billion users. The burgeoning mobile device market, which can be attributed to the affordability of erecting cellular network infrastructure in emerging economies, is driving this trend further upward. Statistical data indicate that there is a positive correlation between social media interactions and mobile device usage (Cooper, 2020; Statista, 2018). What is interesting to note is that social media use in emerging markets in Africa, Latin America, Asia-Pacific and the Middle East has risen immensely in the last few years, thanks to increasing access to and use of mobile technologies (Chaffey, 2020; McNair, 2018). Southern Africa shows a 36 per cent mobile social network penetration rate, Middle Africa 6 per cent, Western Africa 12 per cent and Northern Africa 37 per cent, with Eastern Asia showing a penetration rate of 70 per cent (Clement, 2020; Statista, 2018). These figures are projected to grow as the 4IR agenda progresses.

What this means is that more of the world will be connected – perhaps 'virtually', which is great. However, this connectivity is somewhat 'flawed', as is explained hereunder.

The world is becoming more connected through smart devices, applications and tools, which are all driven by the rapid advancement of the Internet. But, at the heart of all this hyper-connectedness are 'people' – living beings – whose lives have been affected by the sheer magnitude of the digitally connected and networked world, which has associated implications, as discussed in the subsequent sections.

11.3 IMPLICATIONS OF A HYPER-CONNECTED ERA: IMPACT ON INDIVIDUALS, ORGANISATIONS AND SOCIETY

Globalisation and communication have a reciprocal relationship. Both these phenomena exemplify the modern world as the need to communicate across geographic and spatial boundaries served as a catalyst for globalisation (Nayyar; 2016:40; Benfield, 2009). What is most exemplary in the development of communication in these times is the means and modes created to collaborate and interact with others digitally, which behoves great benefits for society in terms of opening up spaces for knowledge-sharing, learning, community development, and social interaction, irrespective of physical distance (Nayyar, 2016:40). However, with such great benefits come equally daunting drawbacks. First, research indicates that hyper-connectivity changes the way that people interact and inhibits healthy social bonding that is formed through face-to-face interactions (see Price-Mitchell, 2019; Benetoli, Chen & Aslani, 2018; Drahošováa & Balcob, 2017). Moreover, Nayyar adds that 'greater technology enablement of work (and the resulting fragmentation of jobs) threatens the security of jobs traditionally considered as skilled in the developed world'. What is even more worrying is that nowadays, many of us interact online and, as Elwell (2014:246) states, '[e]verything we do online has an audience.' The problem is that we do not always know who (or what) is at the other end of the screen, what the reach of our interaction is, and what is, or can be, done with the messages that we post or interactions we are involved in online (no matter how innocent these interactions may seem!). So, point number one for consideration in the use of social media is that you have an audience!

The social media audience ranges from, inter alia, followers to friends (and foes, unfortunately!), researchers (yes, the honourable and the not-so-honourable ones!), marketers (the apparent and discrete ones!), and data-mining organisations (that use automated web crawlers to track your hyper-interactions – sounds petrifying, hey?).

It is getting harder for us to 'disconnect' from technology as we always want to remain 'in the loop' of things, whether it be staying up to date with the latest celebrity gossip, the newest consumer trends, or sharing personal experiences with our digital acquaintances. Elwell (2014:246) explains that our audiences

interact with the episodes and story-worlds we create for (and of) ourselves in ways that affect those stories. We comment, like, post, and blog not simply to be read or seen, but to be responded to; to be interacted with.

This is a time where we have become so obsessed with being almost 'mindlessly' connected to our devices and networked spaces that we have created a digital reality for ourselves. Is this really that bad? After all, seeking connections with others is an innate human need and social media makes it possible to associate with spatially dispersed others instantly and in real-time.

11.3.1 Moral challenges of social media

McKeon and Gitomer (2019) and Gaitho (2018) reveal that social media interactions have made it possible to uncover various social ills, such as unethical political (think about corruption and tenderpreneurship in South Africa) and organisational actions (such as Johson & Johnson's testing of beauty products on animals), dangerous cultural practices (such as genital mutilations in West Africa), as well as environmental issues (deforestation of the Amazon rainforest, for example). Nevertheless, although we have access to an almost infinite supply of information and knowledge, the instant nature of social media interactions also makes it possible to rapidly spread false news to many people. This means that it becomes possible to entrench traditional stereotypes (such as the objectification of women, for example), feed personal biases (such as cultural and religious intolerance, for instance), spread an atmosphere of general malaise and despondency (constant information about death, disease and destruction) and mobilise unscrupulous groupings (such as cults) (see also the discussion on challenges researchers face in chapter 2). These issues make us think about the limits of connectivity. How much connectivity is enough? Where do we draw the line with sharing and consuming information from the Internet and, especially, networked sites? Are we becoming more passive in our approach to 'real' societal change through our 'virtual advocacy' through social media platforms?

(i)   *Social mobilisation and the #Hashtag Publics: do birds of a feather flock together?*

Social media, by virtue of the Internet, has made it possible for people with similar views, despite how marginal these views are, to mobilise and share their opinions through various multimedia items such as memes, videos, audio, and text, etcetera to create visibility of their issues and to gather support for their ventures without the need to secure a dedicated follower base (Gaitho, 2018). In this respect, Bruns et al. (2016: 20) refer to the Twitter hashtag (#) as a key feature for garnering support and interactions on a variety of issues ranging from crisis reporting (#HurricaneSandy), celebrity news (#BabyKapoorKhan), sporting updates such as the rugby world cup (#RWC2019), or political news (#SAelections2019, #CanadaElection2019), etcetera, that have the ability 'to facilitate the creation of ad hoc or hashtag publics.' Bruns et al. (2016:21) and Airike (2013b) explain that the hashtag has gained so much prominence that other social media sites, such as LinkedIn, Facebook and Instagram, as well as traditional news sites, use the functionality to enhance engagement of certain topics, posts, news items, and or media. Any Twitter user can create a hashtag and start a trending discussion that allows the general tweeting and non-tweeting public to follow the discussions on specific events, issues and/ or topics. Although many researchers tend to focus on the political uses of the hashtag in mobilising publics (see Auman-Bauer, 2019; Perez-Rivera et al., 2019; Anderson et al. 2018; Chadwick & Dennis, 2016; Boynton et al., 2014), there are various other uses of hashtag data (see Bruns & Moon, 2019; Chae, 2015; Filo et al., 2015).

Application programming interfaces (APIs) make it easier to gather hashtag data streams on Twitter and have, therefore, become a prominent form of data extraction for research purposes, overshadowing other forms of less 'organised' information on Twitter, Therefore, Bruns et al (2016:21) argue that

> there is a strong need to put hashtag use into better perspective also by comparing the patterns of user engagement around topical hashtags with the broader patterns of activity relating to these topics outside of the hashtags themselves – however methodologically difficult such work may turn out to be,

to expand the depth and breadth of research in this field. Some of the challenges associated with relying on hashtag data are briefly outlined below (Bruns & Burgess, 2015:23; Campbell, 2013):

- Hashtag hijacking – some hashtaggers use trending topics to promote their own interests and pages. Therefore, their conversations might not revolve around the focal topic. Hashtags are thus hijacked.

- Engagement and conversations around the hashtagged topic provide an easy-to-follow thread of conversations around a topic but do not necessarily mean that the tweets in this collation (based on the common hashtag functionality) are related to the focal issue. So, in essence, the collation of Tweeters assimilating around a hashtag cannot really be referred to as a 'community' rallying for a particular cause or concerned about a specific issue/topic.

- Then again, tweets that are relevant and related to trending topics might not contain the hashtag and will thereby be excluded from the data set during the extraction of hashtagged topics.

- Highly visible and trending topics might use more than one hashtag, which might filter data through different streams. For example, some of the hashtags used during the recent elections in South Africa included tags such as #SAelections, #IWantToVoteBut, #2019Elections, #IdiotsVoteSoYouBetter,#VoteWisely. Researchers need to be aware of this and should consider the existence of multiple hashtags in their data extraction techniques.

- Generic hashtags such as #SouthAfrica or #Australia, for example, are effective in collating tweets around a trending topic, but may also include tweets that are outside the scope of the topic under research, related to specific elections or crises in these areas at a specific point in time.

- Hashtags are formed for entertainment purposes as well, such as, #firstworldproblems or #tuesdaymotivation or #TBT or Throwback Thursday, that gather Twemes (Twitter memes) that are sometimes unrelated to the main topic, are followed for their distraction and enjoyment only and not for forming an ad hoc public.

(ii)   Armchair advocates

Armchair advocacy refers to people who advocate for changes in society through digital micro-activism, using various social media platforms. In other words, these are people who try to change the world from the comfort of their homes, by staying behind their computer screens and lament the problems of the world (Armchair politician or advocate for change, n.d.; Bentley, 2013). Armchair advocacy is a great way to bring social ills to the fore and to harness attention around and support for these issues. As noble as the intentions of armchair advocates are, the problem that arises when we remain passive advocates for change and only bemoan the sad state of the world by complaining about issues that plague our world (such as poverty, war, inequality, or smaller concerns such as mobile data prices) without actually doing anything concrete about it. We do this either to vent our frustrations, join the popular voice on the matter, or articulate our deep sentiments about the topic without offending anyone or being held responsible for awakening the masses. We just want to rant, unfortunately, without trying to contact either the correct people or the appropriate means for instilling change! Think about the informal WhatsApp groups created in many communities dedicated to ranting about municipal bylaws not being enforced, service delivery issues and so forth. Many of these complainants are simply 'keyboard warriors' who complain but have not taken any steps to promote change in any way. We need to ask ourselves if we want to wear the 'crown of complaints' or 'be the agents of change'? All we have to do is to ask these questions:

- How can I make a difference?
- What can I do to improve the situation?
- Who can help me to initiate change?
- Why does this matter?

See, we can move from armchair advocates to agents of change with a very simple change in strategy, intention, and purpose!

Steinberg (2016:413); Airike (2013a); & Bentley (2013) add that there are various groups, organisations and individuals who genuinely want to make a difference in communities. Therefore, it is important to rally support from the right people through voicing genuine concerns via the correct social media channels, considering the growth in social media following through mobile technologies across the globe. However, although it is not enough to simply 'like', 'retweet', 'comment', or 'share' important issues via social media platforms, these actions have the potential to reach a diverse audience, across the world, almost instantaneously in a way that can mobilise support and resources for a cause. So, armchair advocacy does NOT have to mean passively reproaching the disordered condition of society on networked sites, but rather it can be used to direct societal well-being, through small meaningful steps such as harnessing support for an online petition, such as the very successful #DataMustFall campaign in South Africa that was started to pressurise cellular phone companies to lower the astronomical prices of mobile data in the country (see Karombo, 2019; Shapshak, 2019; Koopman, 2018). This is an example of successful online activism, that 'has both amplified the voices of marginalized individuals and shifted national conversations on important legal and social issues' (Steinberg, 2016:413) that has been gradual, but significant changes in securing better data prices in South Africa. Utilising the power and reach of social media platforms, the initiators of the #datamustfall campaign, Amandla.mobi, have organised various influential online petitions and campaigns, ranging from a call for tax-free sanitary wear in South Africa, to an appeal for better law enforcement in one of Cape Town's townships (Cele, 2018). This is how you steer the advocacy ship from the comfort of the armchair to the flagship that drives the winds of change.

(iii)   Slacktivism or digital social work– to like or not to like?

So, social media is a catalyst in bringing societal concerns to the fore and giving voice to the marginalised! This is wonderful news! However, there is a downside to all of this online activism, unfortunately. We are seeing a growing move towards passive online activism: 'slacktivism' (previously referred to as 'clicktivism') (Dennis, 2018b). Slacktivism replaces the popular term of yore 'clicktivism' and encapsulates all forms of passive digital micro-activism, such as, inter alia, 'liking', 'commenting', 'posting', 'sharing' and 'retweeting' that exonerates the social media activist of all responsibility to 'act' and 'participate' in enacting 'actual change'. Well, I feel strongly about the gruesome culling of whales in the Faroe Islands and vehemently oppose this action. But, what can I do? Yes, let me sign this online petition (https://www.change.org/p/her-majesty-margrethe-ii-stop-the-slaughter-of-dolphins-pilot-whales-by-the-people-of-the-faroe-islands). At least I have made my voice heard, right?

Perhaps! Slacktivist activities feed the psychosocial need for acceptance, belonging, and purpose, but can deter one from the actual work that needs to be done to enact social change (Dennis, 2018b:27; Airike, 2013b). Therefore, although it can be argued that online activism plays an important role in amplifying the visibility of perturbing problems in society, such as poverty, discrimination, the digital divide, displaced rain, civil conflicts, animal rights, etcetera, does it really bring about meaningful action and required changes? (Airike, 2013b; Riley, 2013).

Nonetheless, Dennis (2018a:10; 2018b:25) and Airike (2013b) argue that academic discussions related to digital activism are usually based on rigid technological determinism and neglect to analyse social media in association with other media, thereby providing a skewed picture of the influence of online activism as slacktivists still have an impact (even if simply creating awareness of the problem!).

We need to ask ourselves how do we motivate others and inspire ourselves to become active advocates of change and not just engage in slacktivist activities (such as changing profile pictures and following a cause on Facebook)?

11.3.2 Impact of social media on e-commerce

The penetration and effects of social media usage are felt at the organisational level too. Aral, Dellarocas and Godes (2013:6) add that understanding how social media features enable and constrain social and economic phenomena is critical to understanding the effects of social media on society. Social media features affect consumers' utility by influencing the degree to which adoption by consumers' peers affects their own utility for the product.' In terms of commercial activities, Delgado (2018) explains that retail power has now shifted to the consumer, thanks to networked communications. Consumers are now more informed about the products and services that they wish to purchase, and popular brands need to focus on developing relationships with consumers to secure sales based on a continuum from awareness to relationship building that culminates into the successful purchase of their products. You might ask where does social media and Big Data fit into all of this?

Social media applications make it possible for consumers to share information and experiences about different products based on first-hand experiences. As such, consumers know what to expect from a product or service even before engaging in the transaction, which influences their decisions to purchase the products before they interact with your organisation. Therefore, organisations, now more than ever, depend on Big Data and Big Social Data to provide information on consumer attitudes, behaviours and preferences through their online interactions and conversations (such as the influences that tweets, photo-tagging, or likes have on their brand) (Aral et al., 2013:3). However, Agratchev (2012) adds that online analytics should preferably be used in conjunction with offline data on consumer behaviour as shoppers' affective online interactions with the brand, the product and the organisation cannot be gauged accurately through web analytics. Offline data analytics captured by physical stores can provide richer data on shoppers' preferences based on the influence of factors such as emotions, location, demographics and weather on buying behaviour (See Rishika et al., 2013).

Many organisations go a step further and market themselves through relationship-building exercises on social media platforms (such as chatbots and avatar interaction, tagging and sharing functionalities, peer referral functions and blogging features), but function on the side of caution when integrating social media sharing functionality on their online company sites as social media sharing can have some negative effects on the reputation of a company and its brand.

11.3.3 Effects in the workplace (i.e. training and development, recruitment etc.)

In terms of social media integration in the organisation, especially considering the important role of Big Data in organisational development, Delgado (2018) explains that this would entail the intersection between Big Data and social media. To achieve this, organisations will need to hire, amongst others, data analysts, computer scientists, brand management specialists, customer relationship managers and other skilled staff who can translate tagged data into meaningful measures to optimise business.

Apart from benefitting the bottom line, digital networks can benefit individuals in the workplace as well. Organisations should consider implementing the strategic use of social media networks in the workplace as they promote knowledge-sharing, specifically in terms of the dissemination of specialised knowledge (Gaitho, 2018; Subrahmanyam et al., 2008:422). Alampi (2012) expands on the benefits of sharing expert knowledge via social media platforms with specific reference to scholarly research. She emphasises the role of social media, not only in marketing academic research but also in creating networks of collaboration, with students and peers across the globe, in the co-construction and development of knowledge that would benefit communities. However, as is the case with any online sources, Alampi (2018) urges researchers to saunter on the side of caution as social media sites contain much fake information and sensationalised content.

Moreover, working professionals can also use social media sites, such as LinkedIn for example, for creating a personal brand and establishing a network of collaboration between peers. Rein and Lee (2019) explain that some companies now recruit staff through interaction with their LinkedIn profiles. However, on the flip side, as is the case with all online activities, creating a social media identity can lead to cyberbullying, stalking, stolen identities, and misuse of personal information. However, although hackers 'steal' and misappropriate personal data, we, as social network users, need to be privy to the information that we share as we can cross the public-private domains when interacting online. By sharing private information in the public domain, we could jeopardise our personal and professional reputations.

11.3.4 Untangling psychosocial from platform-driven behaviour – the effect of social media on the individual

Social media has become so entangled with our 'offline' lives that digital expressions shared on social networking platforms have a profound influence on our personal and professional personas (Adami & Jewitt, 2016:264). Therefore, as researchers (and social media consumers) we need to be cognisant of how we use these sites to create meaning and self-expression through a mixture of text, images, and audio, how we use the interactive functionalities of these networks, and what effect these virtual expressions and interactions have on our overall well-being.

The initial factor to be aware of is that we interact with 'virtual personas' online. Although many of us use social networking sites to connect with offline acquaintances, we tend to expand our network of connections to online 'friends' and 'followers' (who are mostly unknown to us in real life) as well.

This complex dance between the 'online' and 'offline' worlds, thus leads to various psychosocial issues. Gaitho (2018) and Subrahmanyam et al. (2008:421) identify some perturbing effects of social media usage, namely, cyberbullying, poor social bonding, psychological and physiological problems, such as anxiety, addiction, and depression.

(i)   Self-expression, social connectedness, or groupthink?

Gardner (2019:1164) and Burgess (2014:281) explain that the (r)evolutionary nature of the social media environment inspires newfound motivations and inspirations for networked participation and user-created content on these 'constantly-evolving' platforms. Burgess (2015:284) refers to this phenomenon as 'the emergence of what we might call a 'platform paradigm' – a way of organising our thinking about the social media landscape as much as it is a way of organising the burgeoning business of connecting users with their creative content and each other,' where content is becoming more audience-centric. As a result of this audience-centred approach to digital expressions, we notice that as our lives become more entangled with the online world through round-the-clock connectivity (and as much as you might think that the Internet of Things (IoT) simplifies the complexity of mundane activities, it actually complicates matters further!), so too is our self, intertwined with the virtual (and digital photography and the rise of the 'selfie' adds fuel to this proverbial fire!) (Crano, 2019:1125). Crano (2019: 1133) adds that: '"Selfieness", thus amounts to an ideology of self-production, self-promotion, and even self-consumption', to such an extent that we lose ourselves in the digital crowd and crave the acceptance of the virtual others. Strange? Paradoxical? Yes – but, still true, unfortunately!

Elwell (2014:233) laments the death of the Web 1.0 of yore, in terms of the anonymity that it offered us, as it enabled us to keep our analog ('real' – offline) and digital ('virtual' – online) personas separate. Sure, modern technology, Web 2.0, 3.0, 4.0, 5.0 and 'beyond' (considering that by the time you read this text, we may be outside the limits of the Web 5.0 era) provides amazing opportunities for interaction, development, and networked living (see Digital Evolution, n.d.; Huss, 2019; Smith, 2018; Khanzode & Sarode, 2016; Flat World Business, 2011

– for amazing information on the evolution of the Web) – but, the concern with the blurred lines of the online and offline realms of self-identity overshadows the profound capabilities of these advanced applications to some extent. This quandary of interactions that traverses the bounds of the 'virtual' and the 'real' creates a need to 'fit in', 'be popular', and 'outdo others' and leads to cyberbullying (such as online harassment, acts of defamation of character and reputation, and/or unethical coercion to carry out involuntary actions), which has become a huge problem amongst the youth, working professionals, and marginalised groups (Subrahmanyam et al. 2008:421). The problem with cyberbullying is false information is spread instantaneously (and anonymously) on various platforms, which can spiral out of control and lead to detrimental effects on the bullied persona. This shows how self-expression on networked sites can harness groupthink and the dangerous mobilisation of bullies.

To take this discussion of the detrimental effects of digital self-expression further, Barboni et al. (2018:2) explain how female politicians are harassed online. The authors analysed the social media conversations of high-profile politicians in Chile, South Africa, and the United Kingdom between September and November 2017. The findings of their study revealed that while politicians (and political hopefuls) can interact with their audiences almost instantly on social media platforms, thereby opening up the public sphere and enhancing inclusive political discourse, digital spaces also provide a fertile ground for the harassment of female politicians, specifically. Essentially, the self-expression of female political leaders and their need to connect with their communities on social media platforms provided a breeding ground for feeding bias and stereotypical views of women in political positions. Can you think of other examples of negative social connectedness and groupthink? How different is this from the offline convergence of bullies? What would you say have the most profound effects, cyberbullying, or harassment in our physical spaces? Why?

(ii)   Is that you? Digital persona and digital self-portraits: who is behind that screen?

The world of social media allows us as individuals to produce a self-narrative across various platforms, using various media, which is an aide in the construction of our identities (Adami & Jewitt, 2016:265). Think of your own, or others', profiles on Instagram, Facebook, Twitter, Snapchat and LinkedIn, or any other networking sites, for example, and how different or similar these digital profiles are to each other and the individual. Also, think of the different types of media used in the portrayal of the self in the profiles and the narrative provided within the sites and to what extent they match the reality of the individual in question. Elwell (2014:240) refers to this form of personal storytelling as 'transmediated self-identity' that traverses between the 'real self' and the 'virtual' self. Elwell goes on to explain that '[w]e no longer 'go online', rather the Internet is of a piece with the infosphere where we already are and of which we are increasingly a part'.

We cannot explain this actuality better than Adami and Jewitt (2016:265), who said:

> [W]e can see evidence of this … in bloggers' (re-)use of badges, sort of visual avatars, functioning not only as a form of embodiment and self-expression of identity, but also for the construction of a sense of shared belonging within a sub-culture specific community.

The problem with all of this blurring of the online and the offline self, as Smith (2016:325) points out, is that we cannot differentiate between what is real and pretentious, leading to a distorted sense of self.

(iii)   The networked audience: traversing the continuum of addiction

A profound negative effect of social media usage is that it leads to addiction. In simple terms, addiction, as referred to within the context of this study, pertains to the overdependence on social media. For a more theoretical definition of the term, we refer to Dwyer and Fraser (2019:1045), who describe addiction

> as a 'chronic relapsing disease' of disordered compulsion – that is, an illness in which an individual 'loses control' over their substance use as a result of physiological changes due to use of alcohol or other drugs.' This definition does not satisfy the social scientist who questions the ontological frame of such a description that situates addiction as a stable, unified, pre-existing disease entity.

Although there is dissension between experts on the existence of internet and/or social media addiction, there is a growing body of knowledge on the topic (see Dwyer & Fraser, 2019; Alampi; 2018, Walton, 2017; Subrahmanyam et al., 2008).

We argue that social media addiction is real, and the effects traverse a wide spectrum of social and psychological issues. For one, overreliance on social media reduces motivation, leads to poor concentration and focus, diverts attention, and creates a more accessible platform for criminal groups and cults to lure children and adolescents to carry out unsavoury acts, such as crime, prostitution, and drug abuse, for example. What is more, is that obsession with artificial acquaintances and online interactions that essentially '[lack] the intimacy identified with conventional friendships, where people actually know each other, want to talk to each other, have an intimate bond and frequently interact face to face', negatively impacts personal relationships and the ability to 'bond' with family and friends in the offline sphere

(Walton, 2017). While some people use the social media space to create friendships and initiate conversations to combat loneliness (this is especially true for retired persons who find themselves alone, but can also be valid for other groups of people), other users feed their egos with the attention garnered on social media sites (this is apparent in how celebrities, for example, use these platforms). Imagine being one of these celebrities (such as the reality television family 'The Kardashians', for example) who ceaselessly thrives on the adoration of the virtual masses to gratify the ego. What will you do when these sites are shut down for a day? Mind you, this has happened for many sites at some point, such as the time in the earlier part of 2019, when there was a global error with the WhatsApp and Facebook applications and no one could log into these sites (see Liao, 2019 for example). We know, you might say that you would be okay, and life goes on! However, Dwyer and Fraser (2019:1044) and Walton (2017) state that the jury is out on this matter; and many researchers are starting to see that social media withdrawal and overreliance, both lead to feelings of anxiety, depression, and a plummeting sense of self and the only cure is to brave the bounds of abstinence from social media for a few weeks and then to 'connect' again responsibly and sensibly.

11.4 IMPLICATIONS OF BIG DATA AND BIG SOCIAL DATA (ONLINE AND OFFLINE) ON RESEARCH FINDINGS

Considering the prominent role of Big Data in research, it has been discussed at length in the preceding chapters. Therefore, this being the last chapter, it seems fitting to end with a concise review of the implications of Big Data (and of course, its compatriot – Big Social Data) on research findings. Mole (2017), Olshannikova et al. (2017), Mahrt and Scharkow (2013:21), and Agratchev (2012) explain that we are witnessing exponential growth in Big Data to solve societal problems in both the online and offline realms, so much so that marketers (and other Big Data and Big Social Data analysts) use online and offline data to provide a holistic picture of consumer behaviour (for example, in the emerging field of 'applied Big Data for offline retail' where technology-driven in-store analytics [such point-of-sales metrics] supplement online analytics of consumer behaviour). Due to the immense size of the data points and the potential to collect data of varying elements within the spectrum of a phenomenon that can be collected from online and offline analytics, this trend seems to be spreading beyond marketing and retail analytics (Sebei, Hadj Taieb, & Ben Aouicha, 2018). Wondering what the difference between online and offline data is? Let me provide a concise description of each dataset.

Online data is generated from web-based applications, such as the clickstream from websites, emails, interactions on social media platforms (such as tags, for example), and other forms of online communications to collect information related to various forms of behavioural and demographic data that would provide a detailed picture of your target audience and their peculiarities (Lotame Solutions, 2019). Nowadays, online data is also generated by the IoT (for example, smartwatches, smart refrigerators, etcetera), and artificial intelligence (AI) (for example, customer service bots on social media). Offline data, on the other hand, refers to the collection of data from offline sources, such as in-store heat-mapping data that provides information on consumers' in-store movements within a specific store, and in-store purchases (in the case of retail marketing), for example (Van Rijmenam, 2013; Agratchev, 2012). Essentially, Big Social Data is a subset of the Big Data folio, if not already a huge element thereof that drives, amongst others, market, social, and journalistic research (Leetaru, 2019; Olshannikova et al., 2017).

A salient feature of Big Social Data, however, is that data appears and disappears instantly – a Tweet, a post, or a shared image can be seen now and be out of the datasphere less than an hour later. Therefore, social media researchers need to keep track of and interpret this data much faster, which can be done through the use of advanced applications, software programs, and/or API and AI interfaces, for example (Olshannikova et al., 2017). These emerging trends in data generation and collection change the way that 'we look at' and approach social media data. In other words, as researchers, we need to consider the ontology and epistemology of Big Data and Big Social Data research – all of which influence the research approach, design, and the findings.

11.4.1 Digital ontology and epistemology

Brooker et al. (2017:615), Boellstorff (2016:397), and Berry (2011:2) explore deliberations about the emergent paradigm in digital theory, with a particular focus on the ontological and epistemological turn in Big Data and particularly Big Social Data research. As discussed thus far, the modern world has traversed to the digital sphere 'where the relations between online and offline can have positive impacts on everything from inequality and belonging to climate change but can also have negative impacts in these domains' (Boellstorff, 2016:397). Therefore, we need to become aware of the nature of reality in this digital age, that is, the ontological outlook of the digital interactions that we are interested in, as well as the epistemological stance on the data gleaned from online sources as we saunter between the 'digital' and the 'real' (Brooker et al., 2017:615; Boellstorff; 2016:387). In this respect Berry (2011:12) speaks of developing 'a humanistic understanding of technology' as 'code becomes central to understanding in the digital humanities, and serves as a condition of possibility for the many computational forms that mediate our experience of contemporary culture and society.' These insights raise questions such as

(Brooker et al., 2017:615, Boellstorff, 2016: 387; Crawford & Finn, 2015:495):

Can Big Data be viewed and approached the same way as traditional research gleaned from more face-to-face methods? Can we assume that the discrete coding of Big Social Data research provides insight into 'reality'? What new modes of collective knowledge can Big Data and Big Social Data enable? Should virtual worlds be understood in their own terms? Or, should the virtual world be understood as an extension of the actual world? How can we separate human activity from non-human agents like bots in our research?

11.4.2 Possibilities and limitations of data acquisition and extraction: APIs and other technical interfaces

Gardner (2019:1158), Richterich (2019:1021) and Adami and Jewitt (2016:266) explain that Big Data and Big Social Data analytics are based on application programming interfaces (APIs) and algorithms. Even more interesting is that an increasing number of APIs are algorithmic. This means that specialised codes, programmes, and applications are used to sort and organise the large amount of data (textual, visual and/or audio) generated via digital platforms, and sift 'through data silos and open up huge possibilities for data integration' (Intellipaat, 2019).

Oslen (2018) explains,

[d]ata is always being generated by digital technologies, whether we are using apps on our phones, interacting on our social media, or shopping for products. All of this information combines with other data sources and becomes Big data.

So, what is driving this need for Big Data analytics?

Society's (as consumers) need for automation and customisation (also think beyond your tagging interactions on Facebook and Twitter, such as IoT) to simplify their lives can be considered as the key driving force for Big Data analytics. Intellipaat (2019) explains that 'people need everything instantly in a customized manner', from your preferences on your Facebook account, the preferred locations on Google maps, to your saved beneficiaries on your banking app – everything has to 'read my mind' and 'know my preferred choices'. APIs and algorithms do the 'brainwork' (well sort of! humans create these codes, programs, and applications, but you know what I mean!). Algorithms and APIs automate the entire procedure to make it simpler and accurate. For example, whenever you like, search or browse anything, an algorithm (for example, Google uses PageRank and Facebook uses EdgeRank to automate your preferences on their sites) processes the amount of data you generate and gives you the outcome you need (Intellipaat, 2019, Harper, 2018).

Despite how intelligent APIs and algorithms are, Barboni et al (2018:5) argue that they cannot interpret the 'affective' elements of online conversations, such as emotions, moods, and attitudes. Therefore, researchers should not only rely on Big Data analytics to reach conclusions but should also utilise human verifiers to review the sentiment contained in individual social media posts, to achieve higher levels of accuracy in research findings. Adami and Jewitt (2016:265) also point out that visual data are often overlooked in social media studies. They add that 'images are a large part of the artefacts produced and shared online', that could provide valuable insight into the human condition. Even Big Data analysis has been starting to see the valuable data that images shared online provide, but lean more towards quantified analytics, such as the number of shares and tags, for example. As much as quantitative data provides important information for digital images, what is lacking is the qualitative review of images shared and interacted with. Adami and Jewitt (2016:265) add that

> *when employed qualitatively, while content analysis can evidence represented themes and topics, subjects, objects and events, it cannot account for expressive, interpersonal, stylistic and overall social meanings, which in images are chiefly produced through resources such as colour, lighting, camera angle, frame, placement, or pictorial detail.*

Therefore, social media researchers are encouraged to use the quantified methods of Big Data and Big Social Data analytics in conjunction with qualitative techniques to uncover the full spectrum of meanings associated with visual data shared online (see also the discussion on content analysis in both chapters 4 and 5).

11.4.3 Data selectivity: implications of data exclusion in research samples

Now that you are familiar with the work of Big Data and Big Social Data analytics, you may question how data is mined from these digital systems. Indeed, increased automation in data analytics and data mining comes with newfound challenges. Cooper and Mann (2016:14), Hutchinson (2016:3); Crawford and Finn (2015:492), and Ruths and Pfeffer (2014:1064) explain that there are limits to the datasets mined via Big Data and Big Social Data analytics tools in terms of data selectivity and exclusion that should be considered in your research (see also the discussion on methodological challenges in chapter 2 and sample bias in chapters 5 and 7).

Hutchinson (2016:3), Cheliotis, Lu and Song (2015:586), and Crawford and Finn (2015:495) discuss some platform-specific sampling problems, such as:

• The representativity of samples of social media posts in relation to the population of posts on a platform (such as Twitter, for example) despite the volume of data retrieved.

- There is a possibility of skewed demographics, as we:
  - Firstly, cannot verify the information posted on social media profiles.
  - Secondly, we need to be privy of the privacy and confidentiality of social media users, so access to personal information could be limited in some instances.
  - Thirdly, APIs and algorithms, by design, are selective of data mined, depending on the query strings used.
  - Finally, non-human bots can be included in the data sample through search-extraction tools.

- Web crawlers and APIs, by design, delimit the types of data retrieved, which bring into question the reliability of data mined through digital analytics.

- It is highly unlikely to produce random samples of social media data, as we do not know the actual population of the data (of social media posts concerning a topic or phenomenon). Therefore, it is difficult to calculate the measurement error of social media data (particularly due to the influence of algorithms and APIs on generating data samples)

- When studying a particular event or phenomenon, people affected by these events and actualities might:
  - not have access to the Internet, or
  - if they have access to the Internet, may not be part of the social network platform being studied, or
  - they may be part of the social network platform under study, but might not contribute to the discussions on this topic, or
  - might contribute to the conversations on the topic of interest but may neglect using the key phrases and hashtags that link the conversations to the phenomenon under study.

Therefore, Cheliotis et al. (2015: 586) and Crawford and Finn (2015:495) advise social media researchers to use multiple extraction applications (such as by querying the Twitter Stream and Search APIs separately to identify sampling bias, for example), as well as different collection methods (such as a combination of data from different social media sites and/or a mix of social media data and traditional media data, where appropriate and feasible) to gain a holistic picture of the research problem. Finally, they recommend that researchers question their datasets and determine the populations (human and bots) that are represented in the data set/s and those that are excluded.

11.5   Case Study: Want to be an Activist? Oh no! Is Slacktivism The Solution? Not Quite?

We have all heard of the popular online campaigns such as **#HerNetHerRights**, **#BlackLivesMatter**, and **#IAmNotNext** (see Andrews, 2019; Kgabane, 2019; Kahla, 2019; Walker, 2019; Anderson et al., 2018) to name a few, that have moved us in a way that has touched the core of our souls – to the extent that we feel ashamed to be part of a species (we refer to the human race here!) that enacts indescribable harm to our 'kin and kind'. These online campaigns can essentially reenact our humanity and ignite our feelings of empathy, compassion and camaraderie. Other online campaigns, such as **#Standup4HumanRights, #Standup4Refugees, #AnimalRights, #SaveThePlanet,** amongst others, make us feel 'despondent' and 'really bad' because we feel incapable of even helping our 'kith and kin', leave alone assisting our fellow beings (see Eluère, 2019; Siapera et al., 2018 – to see some of the crises the world's displaced populations face). The campaigns that we have mentioned here only touch the surface of the problems that the world faces (actually only those afflictions that traditional and online media have so bravely brought to the fore – which would otherwise remain confined to the communities that experience these difficulties!). So, what can we do to make a difference?

The research into hashtag politics, hashtag trends, and hashtag movements are popular forms of online activism that interest social media researchers, as these movements help us to (try to) understand society and societal needs a bit better – particularly when people face social and cognitive dissonance in their world. However, these social media trends cannot be taken at face value, as these trends, more than likely, tend to depict deeper motivations and meanings, which the social media researcher needs to be aware of (particularly when collecting and analysing data and drawing conclusions). Thus, the following case study shows you two sides of online activism through the analysis of various hashtag movements.

Online activism is becoming a popular form of 'protest', but, unfortunately, puts us at the forefront of critics (some valid and some not-so-valid disparagements) citing a mushrooming culture of slacktivism and armchair advocacy (as was discussed earlier in this chapter). In this section, we wish to provide a practical example of an online campaign to make you rethink the slacktivist and armchair advocacy debates and to make you question your role in the slacktivist culture.

➡

Figure 11.1: The 'click', 'share', 'tweet' (and repeat) cycle of the slacktivist culture

(Photo credit: Elijah van der Giessen – Flickr – CC BY 2.0
https://www.flickr.com/photos/evdg/14393883018/sizes/z/)

But, first, we provide some important (yet, often overlooked) information about online activism (Netivist, n.d.; George & Leidner, 2019; McAuley & Rivera, 2019; Schradie, 2019; Eland, 2016; Rees, 2015; Fuentes, 2014; Joyce, 2010), such as the online activism continuum that ranges from advocacy to action:

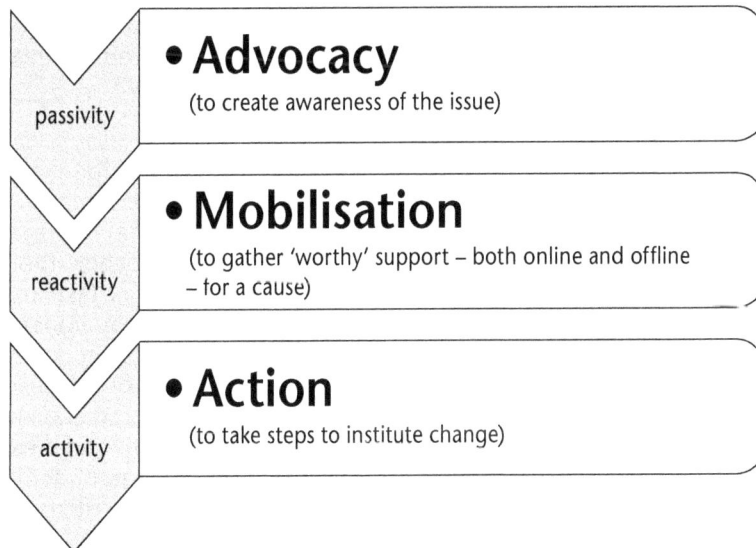

Figure 11.2: The online activism continuum

To make you understand the three points on the online activism continuum outlined above (namely, advocacy, mobilisation, and action), we provide examples of digital activism that traverse the line from passivity to activity in Table 11.1 below.

Table 11.1:   The online activism continuum: examples of digital activism that traverse the line from passivity to activity

Advocacy	Mobilisation	Action
Armchair advocacy	Online petitions	Military action instituted:
For example:	Such as:	For example:
• Post-it Forward (Tumblr)	• Change.org	• #Kony2012
• www.dontforgetburma.org (WordPress)	• MoveOn.org	
Hashtag activism	Offline organisation	Political change
Such as:	For example:	For example:
• #BringBackOurGirls	• OccupyWallStreet	• The Umbrella Revolution
• #PrayforParis	• FeesMustFall	

When we speak of the online activism continuum, we need to be aware that each phase of activity has varying degrees of dependence on the Internet. Also, depending on the particular campaign and/or cause being advocated for, there will be some level of offline advocacy, action, and interaction required at each phase of the online activism continuum. Look at the brief outline of each phase of the continuum depicted in Figure 11.2, as well as a concise discussion of the examples depicted in Table 11.1 (you will need to refer to this information when analysing the two parts of the case study provided below):

- **Advocacy**

    Advocacy, in the form of multimedia blogs and microblogs, for example, is the first step in creating awareness of an issue; and the Internet and, particularly, social media, provide a way to disseminate information quickly, easily, and widely. The problem with online advocacy, though, is that false information can also be disseminated just as fast and as extensively as factual information. This means that online campaigns could advocate for both positive and not-so-positive consequences in our living and working spaces. The key point to consider in terms of advocacy is strategic communication, such as planned messages, targeted audiences, and the most effective platforms for disseminating messages and creating awareness with a view of moving beyond the passive stage of activism. Disarrayed and untargeted online 'activism' is what invites criticism and feeds the slacktivist culture and perpetuates armchair advocacy.

➡

For example, the **#BringBackOurGirls**, and the **#PrayforParis** campaigns remained in the confines of passive 'virtual' resistance (in the form of joining the hashtag conversations to share in the grief, changing profile pictures to display solidarity for a cause, or (re)tweeting, liking, sharing posts and memes to spread the message far and wide) that created great awareness of these atrocities (see Chiluwa & Ifukor, 2015; Garber, 2015; Reines, 2015; Taylor, 2014;), but did not go any further along the continuum of online activism, as these campaigns were not targeted to institute some form of real action that would mobilise people and organisations, for example, that would put pressure on the terror group Boko Haram to bring back the abducted Nigerian girls or to institute concrete plans to encourage a culture of tolerance and diversity in Paris after the terror attacks in the French capital. In the same way, some (perhaps many) online campaigns such as www.dontforgetburma. org (that was created to promote awareness of the atrocious human rights violations in Burma) and Post-it Forward (that aimed to destigmatise mental health issues), which, critics might argue, provided a platform for a good 'rant' to feed the desideratum of the proverbial armchair advocate, but lost their momentum after a short while, in such a profound way that the matters advocated for and the conversations enacted around these issues have, sadly, become almost obsolete (see Holmes, 2015; Burma Campaign UK, 2007).

- **Mobilisation**

The continuum of online activism that we have put forth provides three broad, but useful categories of the process towards effective change. Although the process is not linear, we can see the process unfolding in a way that reprises these three elements of activism. Mobilisation, thus, belongs to the second phase of this process that exemplifies a form of lobbying to garner a collective voice on an issue. This is the phase where your targeted communications help you to 'organise' collective reaction, such as signing a petition online and/or offline protest action.

Noteworthy campaigns in this respect would be **Change.org** and **MoveOn.org** for example, that are leading advocacy groups who move a step further from simply creating mass awareness of a particular cause or issue, and gather support and funds for various problems, such as, inter alia, suicide prevention, animal rights awareness, etcetera. The problem arises when we think that societal problems can be solved with petitions (such as **Resist the Muslim Ban** and **Save Katarina the Orangutan**) and protests (for example, **OccupyWallStreet** and **FeesMustFall**) only (see Change.org, 2019; InfluenceWatch, 2019; MoveOn.org, 2019; DaSilva, 2018; Hodes, 2017, BusinessTech, 2016; Dermody, 2016; Levitin, 2015; Mui, 2012). No doubt, these are powerful ways to show our resistance to the status quo and oppose unfair actions, but does it bring about change? Do these petitions and protests actually result in policy changes, societal development, and social justice? Mobilisation requires long-term vision with coordinated leadership to enact meaningful action, public participation, and deep conversations about crucial societal issues. So, we have reached the point of 'gathering support', 'becoming visible', and 'being heard' – what is next?

- **Action**

  The final stage of online activism is action. This should be the ultimate goal of activism: inspiring some form of change. Good examples of online campaigns that led to actual change are the:

  - #**Kony2012** campaign that not only initiated wide-scale awareness of the atrocities that Uganda guerrilla leader, Joseph Kony enacted against children by enlisting them in the army, but it also increased pressure to increase U.S. military presence in the area to remove Kony's oppressive hold over the area and initiated various rehabilitation programs for the child soldiers that Kony created (see Invisible Children, 2019; BBC, 2018; Dailey, 2012; Grandoni, 2012), and

  - **The Umbrella Revolution** that led to gradual but significant political change in Hong Kong concerning the delegitimisation of the Communist Party rule and movement towards the institution of the Hong Kong Human Rights and Democracy Act (see Leung, 2019; Vines, 2017; Tsung-gan, 2017; Hong Kong: from the Umbrella Movement, 2015; Yuen, 2015).

What you can notice from these campaigns is the sustained and tireless efforts of activists to enact some form of change: slow, but effective. The key points to note at this stage of activism are:

- consistency;
- tenacity;
- organised leadership;
- planned action; and
- sustainable advocacy.

We believe that the distinction between a 'slacktivist' and an 'activist' is quite clear now. You also understand that activism involves varying degrees of online and offline activities (depending on the campaign or the issue being advocated for). Now for a hypothetical case study to make you think about online activism (use the continuum as a guide). Alishia is interested in promoting recycling in her community in Johannesburg, South Africa. She wants to start with the hashtag #**Ash'sRecyclingInitiative** on Twitter, Facebook, and Instagram. Her idea is to create a website with links to all the social media platforms that she will use.

Now, help her to organise her campaign below. For example:

- What would she do as a slacktivist?
  - How can she be as unstructured as possible?
  - Think of multiple hashtags that she could use and why?

- Obviously, she wants all her friends to pay attention and share her posts. So, will she use memes as an attraction? (Great slacktivist approach)
- What about an online petition? That would garner greater attention. What do you think?
- What would she do as an activist?
  - Which influential groups, individuals, organisations will she target?
  - How will she raise funds to institute the recycling initiative in her area specifically?
  - What actions are needed to institute changed behaviours? Liaisons with municipal leaders via Twitter? YouTube videos about the effects of undisciplined waste management, that would be linked to an online petition? Online and/or offline protests to pressure the municipality to institute new bylaws related to recycling?
- Think about all of these points (in conjunction with all the information provided in this chapter) and then have fun populating the table below.

Table 11.2: Are you a slacktivist or an activist Alishia?

	Slacktivist			Activist		
	Activities	Name the Platform	Online/ Offline	Activities	Name the Platform	Online/ Offline
1. Advocacy						
2. Mobilisation						
3. Action						

11.6   SUMMARY AND FUTURE INSIGHTS

This chapter provided some deeper insights into the implications of the hyper-connected society in terms of its effects on the individual, organisations, and society. Unquestionably, networked communications media provide unfathomable opportunities for human development and interaction, but these amazing boons come with equally alarming costs. These implications extend to the social media researcher who relies on automated data-mining applications, programs and interfaces, which are (should I say surprisingly?) developed by humans, that exclude certain data by design. Well, humans are not perfect and technology has its flaws, so we, as social media consumers and researchers need to become aware of these imperfections and try to address these issues through the utilisation of varying research methods and methodologies.

The most interesting aspect of working with digital data is the question of how we view reality in these digital spaces (digital ontology) and how we make sense of this data (epistemology). This is a fairly current debate on the topic that we have brought to the fore in this chapter to make you think about the changing nature of communications in the networked society. Hyper-connectivity has advanced to such a stage where almost every aspect of our personal (offline) lives intertwines with an online application of some form, and we actually fear being 'disconnected' – we fear that we might become 'invisible'. All this has detrimental effects on our social, psychological and physiological well-being, to such an extent that we even opt for a passive form of resistance against social ills by becoming 'slacktivists' – to inspire the 'feel-good' element of our 'human selves' (we refer to this term deliberately as our 'virtual' personas have almost become 'robotic', 'impersonal', and 'unfeeling' much the same as the technologies that we 'use'). The future of this hyper-connected maze of interactions and activities is looking more virtual and less real, we are afraid. Therefore, we urge you, as researchers and facilitators of discourse and interactions to promote 'real' action and collaborations, despite the pervasive nature of the networked society.

Learning activities (Test yourself)

1. Do you think that our hyper-connected lifestyle is good or bad? Why do you say so?

2. We have highlighted some of the moral challenges of social media usage. What other moral challenges of the networked society do you foresee as social media develops and expands?

3. What are the perceived effects of our digital expressions to unknown online personas? Would you say that the same is true for people that we know and interact with online? Why?

4. Would you say that 'armchair advocacy' is an assertive attempt at advocacy? Why would you say so? Provide some examples to support your view.

5. So how would you advocate for 'real' action, beyond the digital micro-activism of social media tools and functions, such as, inter alia, the popular 'like', 'share', and 'retweet'?

6. We all love some form of slacktivist culture – to follow a worthy cause or sign a trending petition. However, what do you think you need to do to avoid being classified as a slacktivist? Do you think the 'click of a mouse' can transcend the boundaries of the slacktivist culture? How?

7. How would you approach a social media research study after reading this chapter? What aspects (for example, problem formulation, sampling, approach, perspective, findings, interpretation) of your study would you frame differently? Make notes related to these aspects.

Further reading

Bimber, B., Flanagin, A.J. & Stohl, C. 2012. *Collective action in organizations: Interaction and engagement in an era of technological change.* Cambridge: Cambridge University Press.

Boynton, G.R., Cook, J., Daniels, K., Dawkins, M., Kopish, J., Makar, M., McDavid, W., Murphy, M., Osmundson, M. & Steenblock, T. 2014. The political domain goes to Twitter: Hashtags, retweets and URLs. *Open Journal of Political Science*, 4(1):8–15.

Cohen, J.E. 2012. *Configuring the networked self: Law, code, and the play of everyday practice.* New Haven, CT: Yale University Press.

Crawford, K. 2013. Hidden biases in big data. *Harvard Business Review.* Available from: http://blogs.hbr.org/cs/2013/04/the_hidden_biases_in_big_data.html. [25 August 2019].

Dixon, D. 2012. Analysis tool or research methodology? Is there an epistemology for patterns? In Berry, D. (ed.). *Understanding digital humanities.* London: Palgrave Macmillan, pp. 191–209.

Geiger, R.S. 2011. 'Lives of bots' in Lovink, G. & Tkacz, N. (eds.). *Critical point of view: A Wikipedia reader.* Amsterdam: Institute of Network Cultures, pp. 78–89.

Geiger, R.S. 2014. Bots, bespoke, code and the materiality of software platforms. *New Media and Society*, 17(3): 342–356.

Gillespie, T. 2010. The politics of 'Platforms'. *New Media and Society*, 12(3): 347–364.

Gillespie, T. 2014. The relevance of algorithms. In Gillespie, T., Boczkowski, P.J. & Foot, K.A. (eds.). *Media technologies: Essays on communication, materiality and society.* Cambridge, MA: MIT Press, pp. 167–194.

González-Bailón, S., Wang, N., Rivero, A., Borge-Holthoefer, J., & Moreno, Y. 2012. Assessing the bias in communication networks sampled from Twitter. *ArXiv 2012*. Available from: https://arxiv.org/abs/1212.1684 [19 June 2020].

Morstatter, F., Pfeffer, J., Liu, H. & Carley, K. M. 2013. Is the sample good enough? Comparing data from Twitter's streaming API with Twitter's Firehose' *Proceedings of the Seventh International AAAI Conference on Weblogs and Social Media, ICWSM 2013*. MA, United States, 400-408. Available from: https://asu.pure.elsevier.com/en/publications/is-the-sample-good-enough-comparing-data-from-twitters-streaming-

Tufekci, Z. 2014. Big questions for social media big data: Representativeness, validity and other methodological pitfalls *Proceedings of the Eighth International AAAI Conference on Weblogs and Social Media, ICWSM 2014*. MA, United States, 505-514. Available from: https://arxiv.org/abs/1403.7400

Riva, G., Wiederhold, B.K. & Cipresso, P. (eds.) 2016. *The psychology of social networking: Personal experience in online communities*. Berlin: DeGuyter Open.

Vromen, A. 2017. *Digital citizenship and political engagement: The challenge from online campaigning and advocacy organisations*. Basingstoke: Palgrave Macmillan.

References

CHAPTER 1

Adami, E. & Jewitt, C. 2016. Special issue: Social media and the visual. *Visual Communication*, 15(3): 263–270.

Anderson, K.E. 2020. Getting acquainted with social networks and apps: It is time to talk about TikTok. *Library Hi Tech News*, 37(4): 7–12.

Arthurs, J., Drakopoulou, S. & Gandini, A. 2018. Researching YouTube. *Convergence: The International Journal of Research into New Media Technologies*, 24(1): 3–15.

Ash, J. 2015. Sensation, affect and the GIF: Towards an allotropic account of networks. In Hillis, K., Paasonen, S. & Petit, M. (eds.). *Networked Affect*. Cambridge: MIT Press, pp. 119–134.

Azionya, C. & Sitto, K. 2018. Understanding the characteristics of writing online content. In Prichard, M. & Sitto, K. (eds.). *Connect: Writing for online audiences*. Cape Town: Juta, pp. 13–38.

Berthon, P., Pitt, L., & Campbell, C. 2008. Ad lib: When customers create the ad. *California Management Review*, 50(4): 6–30.

Biel, J.I. & Gatica-Perez, D. 2013. The YouTube lens: Crowdsourced personality impressions and audiovisual analysis of vlogs. *IEEE Transactions on Multimedia*, 15(1): 41–55.

Bolter, J.D. 2014. Augmented Reality. In Ryan, M., Emerson, L. & Robertson, B.J. (eds.). *The Johns Hopkins guide to digital media*. Maryland: Johns Hopkins University Press, pp. 30–32.

Bosch, T. 2017a. What are social media? Introductory definitions. In Fourie, P.J. (ed.). *Media studies: Social (new) media and mediated communication today*. Cape Town: Juta. pp. 39–58.

Bosch, T. 2017b. Researching audiences in the age of social media. In Fourie, P.J. (ed.). *Media studies: Social (new) media and mediated communication today*. Cape Town: Juta. pp. 59–80.

Boyd, D.M. & Ellison, N. 2008. Social Network Sites: Definition, History, and Scholarship. *Journal of Computer-Mediated Communication*, 13: 210–230.

Breslin, J.G., Passant, A. & Decker, S. 2009. *The social semantic web*. Heidelberg: Springer.

Bresnick, E. 2019. Intensified play: Cinematic study of TikTok mobile app. Available from: https://www.researchgate.net/publication/335570557_Intensified_Play_Cinematic_study_of_TikTok_mobile_app. [14 April 2020].

Burger. M. 2017. Participation in the digital age: Public self-expression and public identity 'work'. In Fourie, P.J. (ed.). *Media studies: Social (new) media and mediated communication today.* Cape Town: Juta. pp. 380–398.

Businesstopia. 2018. *Models of communication.* Available from: https://www.businesstopia.net/communication. [6 September 2019].

Calero, A. 2015. *How to use 360-degree video in your social media marketing.* Available from: https://www.socialmediaexaminer.com/how-to-use-360-degree-video-in-your-social-media-marketing/. [30 August 2019].

Carah, N. 2014. Curators of databases: Circulating images, managing attention and making value on social media. *Media International Australia*, 150(1): 137–142.

Carr, C.T., & Hayes, R.A. 2015. Social Media: defining, developing, and divining. *Atlantic Journal of Communication*, 23(1): 46–65.

Cassinger, C. & Thelander, A. 2017. Brand new images? Implications of Instagram photography for place branding. *Media and Communication*. 5(4): 6–14.

Chaffey, D. 2020. Global social media research summary 2020. Available from: https://www.smartinsights.com/social-media-marketing/social-media-strategy/new-global-social-media-research/. [27 April 2020].

Clark, R.C., & Mayer, R.E. 2016. *E-learning and the science of instruction: Proven guidelines for consumers and designers of multimedia learning.* 4th edition. New Jersey: John Wiley & Sons.

Cornelissen, J. 2020. *Corporate communication. A guide to theory & practice.* 6th edition. London: SAGE Publications.

Couldry, N., & Van Dijck, J. 2015. Researching social media as if the social mattered. *Social Media and Society*, 1(2): 1–7.

Degenaar, A. 2019. The effectiveness of the organisation Loving Thy Neighbour's support to the non-profit sector [Personal interview]. 6 May, Potchefstroom.

Dunlap, J.C., & Lowenthal, P.R. 2016. Getting graphic about infographics: design lessons learned from popular infographics. *Journal of Visual Literacy*, 35(1): 42–59.

Eppink, J. 2014. A brief history of the GIF (so far). *Journal of Visual Culture*, 13(3): 298–306.

Du Plessis, C. 2017. Using social media for branding. In Fourie, P.J. (ed.). Media studies: Social (new) media and mediated communication today. Cape Town: Juta. pp. 351 – 378.

Du Plessis, C. 2018. Blogging. In Prichard, M. & Sitto, K. (eds.). *Connect: Writing for online audiences*. Cape Town: Juta, pp. 181–205.

Engelbrecht, R. & Ngcongo, M. 2018a. Developing an online profile and persona. In Prichard, M. & Sitto, K. (eds.). *Connect: Writing for online audiences*. Cape Town: Juta, pp. 39–58.

Engelbrecht, R. & Ngcongo, M. 2018b. Storytelling for social media platforms. In Prichard, M. & Sitto, K. (eds.). *Connect: Writing for online audiences*. Cape Town: Juta, pp. 206–230.

Featherstone, R.M. 2014. Visual research data: An infographics primer. *Journal of the Canadian Health Library Association*, 35(1): 147–150.

Flatow, D., Naaman, M., Xie, K.E., Volkovich, Y. & Kanza, Y. 2015. On the accuracy of hyper-local geotagging of social media content. *Proceedings of the 8th ACM international conference on web search and data mining*, 127–136. Available from: ACM Portal: ACM Digital Library. [07 October 2019].

Fourie, P.J. 2017. Social media and mediated communication in postmodern society. In Fourie, P.J. (ed.). *Media studies: Social (new) media and mediated communication today*. Cape Town: Juta. pp. 1–37.

Freberg, K. 2019. *Social media for strategic communication: Creative strategies and research-based applications*. London: SAGE Publications.

Fuchs, C. 2017. *Social media: A critical introduction*. 2nd edition. London: SAGE Publications.

Golder, S.A., & Huberman, B.A. 2006. Usage patterns of collaborative tagging systems. *Journal of Information Science*, 32(2): 198–208.

Grieve, R. 2017. Unpacking the characteristics of Snapchat users: A preliminary investigation and an agenda for future research. *Computers in Human Behaviour*, 74(1): 130–138.

Griffin, E.M., Ledbetter, A., & Sparks, G. 2015. *A first look at communication theory*. 9th edition. McGraw-Hill Higher Education.

Grusin, R. 2009. YouTube as the end of new media. In Snickars, P. and Vonderau, P (eds.). *The YouTube Reader*. Stockholm: National Library of Sweden.

Handley, A. & Chapman, C.C. 2011. *Content rules. How to create killer blogs, podcasts, videos, ebooks, webinars (and more) that engage customers and ignite your business*. Hoboken: John Wiley.

Highfield, T. & Leaver, T. 2016. Instagrammatics and digital methods: studying visual social media, from selfies and GIFs to memes and emoji. *Communication Research and Practice*, 2(1): 47–62.

Hillis, K. 2014. Virtual reality. In Ryan, M., Emerson, L. & Robertson, B.J. (eds.). *The Johns Hopkins guide to digital media*. Maryland: Johns Hopkins University Press, pp. 510–514.

Holmes, D. 2005. *Communication theory. Media, technology and society*. London: SAGE Publications.

Jenkins, H., Purushotma, R., Clinton, K., Weigel, M. & Robinson, A.J. 2006. *Confronting the challenges of participatory culture: Media education for the 21st century. An occasional paper on digital media and learning*. Chicago: MacArthur Foundation.

Jordan, K. 2018. Validity, reliability, and the case of participant-centered research: reflections on a multi-platform social media study. *International Journal of Human-computer Interaction*, 34(10): 913–921.

Kane, G.C. 2017. The evolutionary implications of social media for organizational knowledge management. *Information and Organization*, 27(1): 37–46.

Kannan, S. & Shreya, N. 2017. Understanding emoticons: Perception and usage of emoticons in WhatsApp. *Artha-Journal of Social Sciences*, 16(3): 49–68.

Kanter, B. & Fine, A. 2010. The Networked Nonprofit: connecting with social media to drive change. San Fransisco: Jossey-Bass.

Kaplan, A.M. & Haenlein, M. 2010. Users of the world, unite! The challenges and opportunities of Social Media. *Business Horizons*, 53(1): 59–68.

Kerpen, D. 2011. *Likeable social media. How to delight your customers, create an irresistible brand and be generally amazing on Facebook (and other social networks)*. New York: McGraw-Hill.

Koch, T., Gerber, C. & De Klerk, J. J. 2018. The impact of social media on recruitment: Are you on LinkedIn? *SA Journal of Human Resource Management*, 16(0): 1–14.

Kumar, A., Bezawada, R., Rishika, R., Janakiraman, R. & Kannan, P.K. 2016. From social to sale: the effects of firm-generated content in social media on customer behaviour. *Journal of Marketing*, 80(1): 7–25.

Laestadius, L. 2017. Instagram. In Sloan, L. & Quan-Haase, A. (eds.). *The Sage handbook of Social media research methods*. Los Angeles: SAGE Publications. pp. 573–592.

Lange, P. G. 2009. Videos of affinity on YouTube. *In Snickars, P. and Vonderau, P (Eds.). The YouTube reader.* Stockholm: National Library of Sweden.

Lee, S. H., & Boling, E. 1999. Screen design guidelines for motivation in interactive multimedia instruction: A survey and framework for designers. *Educational technology*, 39(3): 19–26.

Lindgren, S. 2017. *Digital media & society.* London: SAGE Publications.

Lipschultz, J.H. 2018. *Social media communication. Concepts, practices, data, law, and ethics.* 2nd edition. New York: Routledge.

Littlejohn, S.W., Foss, K.A. & Oetzel, J.G. 2017. *Theories of human communication.* 11th edition. Long Grove: Waveland Press.

Loving Thy Neighbour. 2019. *About us.* https://www.lovingthyneighbour.org/aboutus.

Mahoney, L.M. & Tang, T. 2017. *Strategic social media: From marketing to social change: From marketing to social change.* 1st edition. Chichester: Wiley-Blackwell.

Manning, J. 2014. Definition and classes of social media. In Harvey, K. (ed.). *Encyclopedia of social media and politics.* Los Angeles: SAGE Publications. pp. 1158–1162.

McCay-Peet, L. & Quan-Haase, A. 2017. What is social media and what questions can social media help us answer. In Sloan, L. & Quan-Haase, A. (eds.). *The Sage handbook of Social media research methods.* Los Angeles: SAGE Publications. pp. 13–26.

McDowell, L.J. & De Sousa, P. 2018. 'I'd Double Tap That!!': Street art, graffiti, and Instagram research. *Media, Culture and Society*, 40(1): 3–22.

Muir, C. & Verwey, S. 2018. Crafting content in a collaborative economy. In Prichard, M. & Sitto, K. (eds.). *Connect: Writing for online audiences.* Cape Town: Juta, pp. 5–12.

Murthy, D. 2017. The ontology of Tweets: mixed-method approaches to the study of Twitter. In Sloan, L. & Quan-Haase, A. (eds.). *The Sage handbook of Social media research methods.* Los Angeles: SAGE Publications. pp. 559–572.

Oberlo. 2020. 10 TikTok statistics that you need to know in 2020. Available from: https://www.oberlo.com/blog/tiktok-statistics. [19 April 2020].

Page, R. 2014. Blogs. In M. Ryan, L. Emerson, & B.J. Robertson (eds.). *The Johns Hopkins Guide to digital media.* Maryland: Johns Hopkins University Press, pp. 42–45.

Pennington, D. R. 2017. Coding of non-text data. In Sloan, L. & Quan-Haase, A. (eds.). *The Sage handbook of Social media research methods*. Los Angeles: SAGE Publications. pp. 232–250.

Powers, J. H. 1995. On the intellectual structure of the human communication discipline. *Communication education*. 44(3): 191–222.

Purchase, H. 1998. Defining multimedia. *IEEE MultiMedia*, 5(1): 8–15.

Quesenberry, K. A. 2019. *Social media strategy: Marketing, advertising, and public relations in the consumer revolution*. 2nd edition. Lanham: Rowan and Littlefield.

Russell, M.A. & Klassen, M. 2019. *Mining the social web: data mining Facebook, Twitter, LinkedIn, Google+, Github and more*. 2nd edition. Beijing: O'Reily.

Safko, L. 2010. *The social media bible: tactics, tools, and strategies for business success*. 2nd edition. New Jersey: Wiley.

Salmons, J. 2017. Using social media in data collection: designing studies with the qualitative e-research framework. In Sloan, L. & Quan-Haase, A. (eds.). *The Sage handbook of Social media research methods*. Los Angeles: SAGE Publications. pp. 178–196.

Schaefer, N. W. 2018. *Social media explai*ned. 2nd edition. Schaefer marketing solutions.

Scholz, J., & Smith, A.N. 2016. Augmented reality: Designing immersive experiences that maximize consumer engagement. *Business Horizons*, 59(2): 149–161.

Shifman, L. 2014. Memes in digital culture. Cambridge: MIT Press.

Siapera, E. 2012. *Understanding new media*. London: SAGE Publications.

Smiciklas, M. 2012. *The power of infographics: Using pictures to communicate and connect with your audiences*. Pearsoncmg. Available from: http://ptgmedia. pearsoncmg.com/images/9780789749499/samplepages/0789749491.pdf. [7 September 2019].

Smith, N.A., Fischer, E., & Yongijan, C. 2012. How does brand-related user-generated content differ across YouTube, Facebook, and Twitter? *Journal of Interactive Marketing*, 26(1): 102–113.

Snickars, P. & Vonderau, P. (Eds.) 2009. *The YouTube reader*. Stockholm: National Library of Sweden.

Statista. 2020. Most popular social networks worldwide as of January 2020, ranked by number of active users. Available from: https://www.statista.com/statistics/272014/global-social-networks-ranked-by-number-of-users/. [19 April 2020].

Stewart, B. 2017. Twitter as method: using Twitter as a tool to conduct research. In Sloan, L. & Quan-Haase, A. (eds.). *The Sage handbook of Social media research methods*. Los Angeles: SAGE Publications. pp. 251–265.

Talhouk, R., Mesmar, S., Thieme, A., Balaam, M., Olivier, P., Akik, C. & Ghattas, H. 2016. 'Syrian refugees and digital health in Lebanon: opportunities for improving antenatal health', *Proceedings of the 2016 CHI Conference on Human Factors in Computing Systems*, 331–342. Available from: ACM Portal: ACM Digital Library. [07 October 2019].

Taljaard, E. 2019. Understanding the Loving Thy Neighbour context. [Personal interview]. 26 August, Pretoria.

TikTok. 2019. TikTok transparency report. Available from: https://www.tiktok.com/safety/resources/transparency-report. [19 April 2020].

Uricchio, W. 2009. The future of the medium once known as television. In Snickars, P. and Vonderau, P (Eds.). *The YouTube reader*. Stockholm: National Library of Sweden.

Van Dijck, J. 2013. *The culture of connectivity. A critical history of social media*. New York: Oxford University Press.

Vaynerchuk, G. 2013. *Jab, jab, jab, right hook. How to tell your story in a noisy social world*. New York: Harper Collins Publishers.

Vitak, J. 2017. Facebook as a research tool in the social and computer sciences. In Sloan, L. & Quan-Haase, A. (eds.). *The Sage handbook of Social media research methods*. Los Angeles: SAGE Publications. pp. 627–644.

Vonderau, P. 2014. Video. In Ryan, M. Emerson, L. & Robertson B.J. (eds.). *The Johns Hopkins Guide to Digital Media*. Maryland: Johns Hopkins University Press, pp. 497–500.

Wang, Y. 2020. Influence of camera view on TikTok users' presence, immersion and adoption intent. Available from: https://www.sciencedirect.com/science/article/pii/S0747563220301266?via%3Dihub. [14 April 2020].

We are social. 2020. Digital in 2020. Available from: https://wearesocial.com/digital-2020. [27 April 2020].

Weller, K., Bruns, A., Burgess, J., Mahrt, M. & Cornelius, P. (eds.). 2014. *Twitter and society*. Katrin Weller. Available from: https://katrinweller.files. wordpress.com/2012/08/twitter-and-society-introduction-2014.pdf. [7 September 2019].

West, T. & Turner, L.H. 2018. *Introducing communication theory: Analysis and application*. 5th edition. New York, NY: McGraw-Hill Education.

Woodworth, A. 2018. Amplify your impact: My body is ready. Best practices for using memes on library social media. *Reference & User Services Quarterly*, 58(2): 87–90.

World Wide Worx. 2019. SA social media landscape 2019: Executive summary. https://www.iabsa.net/assets/Usedebbieiabsanet/Social_Media_ Landscape_2019_report,_Executive_Summary.pdf. [19 April 2020].

Xu, L., Yan, X. & Zhang, Z. 2019. Research on the causes of the "Tik Tok" App becoming popular and the existing problems. *Journal of Advanced Management Science*, 7(2): 59–63.

Yang, S., Quan-Haase. A, Nevin A.D. & Chen, Y. 2017. The role of online reputation management, trolling, and personality traits in crafting of the virtual self on social media. In Sloan, L. & Quan-Haase, A. (eds.). *The Sage handbook of Social media research methods*. Los Angeles: SAGE Publications. pp. 74–89.

Zhang, D., Zhou, L., Briggs, R.O., & Nunamaker Jr, J.F. 2006. Instructional video in e-learning: Assessing the impact of interactive video on learning effectiveness. *Information & management*, 43(1): 15–27.

CHAPTER 2

Asiamah, N. Mensah, H.K & Oteng-Abayie, E.F. 2017. General, target, and accessible population: Demystifying the concepts for effective sampling. *The Qualitative Report*, 22(6): 1607–1622.

Allen, A. (Ed.). 2017. *The SAGE Encyclopedia of Communication Research Methods*. SAGE Publications.

Austin, Z. & Sutton, J. 2015. Qualitative research: Data collection, analysis and management. *The Canadian Journal of Hospital Pharmacy*, 68(3): 226–231.

Buffer. *State of Social*. 2019. Available from: https://buffer.com/state-of-social-2019 [12 June 2019].

Bruns, A. & Stieglitz, S. 2013. Towards more systematic Twitter analysis: metrics for tweeting activities. *International Journal of Social Research Methodology*, 16(2):91–108.

Buntain, C., McGrath, E., Golbeck & LaFree, G.J. 2016. *Comparing social media and traditional surveys around the Boston Marathon Bombing*. 6th Workshop on Making Sense of Microposts. Available from: http://microposts2016.seas.upenn.edu/ [26 August 2019].

Carrigan, M. 2016. *Social media for academics*. University of Cambridge: SAGE Publications.

Carson, B. 2016. Social media as a research methodology. Available from: https://blog.marketresearch.com/social-media-as-a-research-methodology [20 June 2019].

Chan, J. nd. *How to find consumer insights on social media: The expert guide*. Available from: https://www.linkfluence.com/blog/consumer-insights-social-media-guide [17 June 2019].

Creswell, J.W. 2018. *Qualitative inquiry and research design: Choosing among the five approaches*. 4th edition. Thousand Oaks, CA: SAGE Publications.

Creswell, J.W. 2014. *Research design: Qualitative, quantitative, and mixed methods approaches*. 4th edition. Thousand Oaks, California: SAGE Publications.

Devault, G. 2018. *Avoid these bias errors of samples in social media research*. Available from: https://www.thebalancesmb.com/avoid-bias-errors-in-social-media-research-2297091 [17 June 2019].

Dharmapalan, B. 2012. *Scientific research methodology*. Oxford: Alpha Science International Ltd.

Doody O. & Bailey M.E. 2016. Setting a research question, aim and objective. *Nurse Researcher*, 23(4): 19–23.

Efron, S.E. & Ravid, R. 2019. *Writing the literature review. A practical guide*. New York: The Guilford Press.

Feehan, B. 2019 *Social media industry benchmark report*. Available from: https://www.rivaliq.com/blog/2019-social-media-benchmark-report/ [17 June 2019].

FoodRisc Resource Centre. 2019. *Social media research*. http://resourcecentre.foodrisc.org/social-media-research_35.html [17 June 2019].

Given, L.M. 2008. *The SAGE encyclopedia of qualitative research methods*. UK: SAGE Publishing.

Guba, E.G. & Lincoln, Y.S. 1994. Competing paradigms in qualitative research. In Denzin, N.K. & Lincoln, Y.S. (eds.). *Handbook of qualitative research*. Thousand Oaks, CA: SAGE Publications, pp. 105–117.

Hynd, M. 2018. Will social research replace traditional market research? Available from: https://nealschaffer.com/will-social-research-replace-traditional-market-research/ [17 June 2019].

Kivunja, C. & Kuyini, A.B. 2017. Understanding and applying research paradigms in educational contexts. *International Journal of Higher Education*, 6(5): 26–41.

Kuhn, T.S. 1962. *The structure of scientific revolutions*. 1ˢᵗ edition. Chicago, IL: University of Chicago Press.

Lee, S. 2008. Population parameter. In Lavrakas, P.J. (ed.). *Encyclopedia of survey research methods*. Thousand Oaks, CA: SAGE Publications. Available from: http://dx.doi.org/10.4135/9781412963947.n386 [22 July 2019].

Leedy, P.D & Ormrod, J.E. 2013. *Practical research: Planning and design*. 10ᵗʰ edition. University of Northern Colorado: Pearson Education.

Marwick, A.E. & Boyd, D. 2011. I tweet honestly, I tweet passionately: Twitter users, context collapse, and the imagined audience. *New Media & Society*, 13(1): 114–133.

McLeod, S.A. 2019. Qualitative vs. quantitative research. *Simply Psychology*. Available from: https://www.simplypsychology.org/qualitative-quantitative.html [14 April 2020]

McCorkindale, T. & DiStaso M.W. 2014. The state of social media research: Where are we now, where we were and what it means for public relations. *Research Journal of the Institute for Public Relations*, 1(1): 1–17.

Mills, J. & Birks, M. 2014. *Qualitative methodology: A practical guide*. London: SAGE Publications Ltd.

Mollett, A., Brumley, C., Gilson, C. & Williams, S. 2017. *Communicating your research with social media. A practical guide to using blogs, podcasts, data visualisation and video*. London: SAGE Publications.

Morstatter, F., Dani H., Sampson, J. & Liu H. 2016. 'Can one tamper with the sample API?' Proceedings of the WWW'16 Companion, 81–82. Available from: ACM Portal: ACM Digital Library [25 June 2019].

Neuendorf, K.A. 2017. *The content analysis guidebook*. Thousand Oaks: SAGE Publications.

Nguyen, H. 2014. Should social media analysis replace traditional marketing research? Available from: https://www.netbase.com/blog/social-media-analysis-replace-traditional-marketing-research/ [22 July 2019].

Olteanu, A., Vieweg, S. & Castillo, C. 2015. 'What to expect when the unexpected happens: Social media communications across crises,' in Proceedings of 18th ACM Computer Supported Cooperative Work and Social Computing, 994–1009. Available from: ACM Portal: ACM Digital Library [25 June 2019].

Pather, S. & Remyenyi, D. 2019. 'Reflections on being a successful academic researcher' *Proceedings of 18th European Conference on Research Methodology for Business and Management Studies,* Stacey, A (ed.) UK; Academic Conferences and Publishing International Limited, Johannesburg, pp 3–14.

Petitt, A. 2011. *Using social media research to complement traditional methods.* Available from: https://www.quirks.com/articles/using-social-media-research-to-complement-traditional-methods [22 July 2019].

Phillips, M.L. 2011. *Using social media in your research.* Available from: https://www.apa.org/gradpsych/2011/11/social-media [20 June 2019].

Poynter, R. 2018. Researchers should be aware of the problems with observational data. Available from: https://greenbookblog.org/2018/05/31/researchers-should-be-aware-of-the-problems-with-observational-data/ [25 July 2019].

Randell K., Schmidt, MM., Smyth, V.K. & Kowalski, K. 2014. *Teaching the scientific literature review: Collaborative lessons for guided inquiry.* 2nd edition. Santa Barbara: Libraries Unlimited.

Ravitch, S.M. & Carl, N.M. 2016. *Qualitative research: Bridging the conceptual, theoretical, and methodological.* California: SAGE Publications.

Ruths, D. & Pfeffer, J. 2014. Social media for large studies of behaviour. *Science,* 346(6213): 1063–1064.

Sajuria, J. & Fábrega, J. 2016. Do we need polls? Why Twitter will not replace opinion surveys, but can complement them. In H. Snee, C. Hine, Y. Morey, S. Roberts & H. Wawtson, H. (eds). *Digital methods for social science. An interdisciplinary guide to research innovation.* London: Palgrave Macmillan, pp. 87–104.

Segal, S. nd. The what, why, and how of social media data. Available from: https://www.oktopost.com/blog/social-media-data/ [22 July 2019].

Shi, N-Z & Tao, J. 2008. *Statistical hypothesis testing: Theory and methods.* Singapore: World Scientific.

Sloan, L & Quan-Haase, A (eds). 2017. *The Sage handbook of social media Research Methods*. London: SAGE Publications.

Snaptrends 2019. Why social media data collection is a good idea. Available from: http://snaptrends.com/social-media-software/data-collection/ [22 July 2019].

Snelson, C.L. 2016. Qualitative and mixed methods social media research: A review of the literature. *International Journal of Qualitative Methods*, January to December: 1–5.

Smith, K. 2016. Conducting social media research: How to find real consumer insights. Available from: https://www.brandwatch.com/blog/social-media-research/ [22 July 2019].

Smith, K. 2019. *The best free and paid social media analytics tools*. Available from: https://www.brandwatch.com/blog/social-media-analytics-tools/ 23 July

Social Media Research Group. 2016. Using social media for research: An introduction. Available from: https://assets.publishing.service.gov.uk/government/uploads/system/uploads/attachment_data/file/524750/GSR_Social_Media_Research_Guidance_-_Using_social_media_for_social_research.pdf [22 July 2019].

Snelson, C.L. 2016. Qualitative and mixed methods social media research: A review of the literature. *International Journal of Qualitative Methods*, January-February: 1–15.

Sreejesh, S., Mohapatra, S. & Anusree, M.R. 2014. *Business research methods: An applied orientation*. Switzerland: Springer International Publishing.

Interpreting your results: The role of the literature review. Available from: https://www.statisticssolutions.com/interpreting-your-results/ [22 July 2019].

Tufekci, Z. 2014. 'Big questions for social media big data: Representativeness, validity and other methodological pitfalls,' in Proceedings of the 8th International AAAI Conference on Weblogs and Social Media, American Association for Artificial Intelligence (AAAI) ed. Available from: http://www.aaai.org/Library/ICWSM/icwsm14contents.php [26 August 2019].

Vis, F & Thelwall, M. 2013. *Researching social media*. UK: SAGE Publishing.

Wagner, C., Kawulich, B. & Garner, M. 2012. *Doing social research: A global context*. UK: McGraw-Hill Higher Education.

Will, T. 2016. Social media as a research method. *Communication Research and Practice*, 2(1): 7–19.

Zhang, H., Hill, S., & Rothschild, D. 2018. Addressing selection bias in event studies with general purpose social media panels. *Journal of Data and Information Quality*, 10(1): 24 pages, https://doi.org/10.1145/3185048.

Zheng, X., Zeng, Z., Chen, Z. & Rong, C. 2015. Detecting spammers on social networks. *Neurocomputing*, 159: 27–34.

CHAPTER 3

Adom, D., Hussein, E.K. & Agyem, J.A. 2018. Theoretical and conceptual framework: Mandatory ingredients of a quality research. *International Journal of Scientific Research*, 7(1): 2277–8179.

Ajzen, I. 1985. From intentions to actions: A theory of planned behaviour. In Khul, J. & Beckman, J. (eds.). *Action-control: From cognition to behaviour.* Heidelberg: Springer, pp. 11–39.

Ajzen, I. 2011. The theory of planned behaviour: Reactions and reflections. *Psychology and Health*, 26(9): 1113–1127.

Babbie, S. 2007. *The practice of social research.* 11th ed. Belmont, CA: Thomson Wadsworth.

Baker, R.K. & White, K.M. 2010. Predicting adolescents' use of social networking sites from an extended theory of planned behaviour perspective. *Computers in Human Behaviour*, 26(6): 1591–1597.

Barnes, J. 1954. Class and committees in a Norwegian island parish. *Human Relations*, 7(1): 39–58.

Bell, F. 2011. Connectivism: Its place in theory-informed research and innovation in technology-enabled learning. *International Review of Research in Open and Distance Learning*, 12(3): 98–118.

Blanchard, A.L. 2008. Testing a model of sense of virtual community. *Computers in Human Behaviour*, 24(5): 2107–2123.

Blau, P.M. 1964. *Exchange and power in social life.* New York: Wiley.

Bosch, T. 2017. What are social media? Introductory definitions. In Fourie, P.J. (ed.). *Media studies: Social (new) media and mediated communication today.* 4th ed. Cape Town: Juta, pp. 40–58.

Bott, E. 1957. *Family and social network.* London: Tavistock Publications.

Bourdieu, P. 1985. The forms of capital. In Richardson, J.G. (ed.). *Handbook of theory and research for the sociology education.* New York: Greenwood Press, pp. 241–258.

Bryman, A. 2012. *Social research methods*. 4th edition. New York: Oxford University Press.

Caldwell, M. 2017. Thinking about the public sphere and new (social) media. In P.J. Fourie (ed.). *Media studies: Social (new) media and mediated communication today*. 4th ed. Cape Town: Juta, pp. 112–165.

Chang, H.C. 2010. A new perspective on Twitter hashtag use: Diffusion of Innovation Theory, *Proceedings of the American Society of Information Science and Technology*, 47(1): 22–27.

Chang, Y.P. & Zhu, D.H. 2011. Understanding social networking sites adoption in China: a comparison of pre-adoption and post adoption. *Computers in Human Behaviour*, 27(5): 1840–1848.

Cheung, C.M.K. & Lee, M.K.O. 2010. A theoretical model of intentional social action in online social networks. *Decision Support Systems*, 49(1): 24–30.

Chiu, C. M., Hsu, M.H. & Wang, E.T.G. 2006. Understanding knowledge sharing in virtual communities: An integration of social capital and social cognitive theories. *Decision Support Systems*, 42(3): 1872–1888.

Chung, N., Han, H. & Koo, C. 2015. Adoption of travel information in user-generated content on social media: the moderating effect of social presence. *Behavior and Information Technology*, 34(9): 902–919.

Cline, B. J. 2016. Media ecology and the 21st century classroom. In Yildiz, M. & Keengwe, J. (eds.). *Handbook of research on media literacy in the digital age*. Hershey, PA: IGI Global, pp. 275–290.

Colliander, J. & Dahlén, M. 2011. Following fashionable friend: The power of social media. *Journal of Advertising Research*, 51(1): 313–320.

Collins, R.L., Martino, S. & Shaw, R. 2011. Influence of new media on adolescent sexual health: Evidence and opportunities: RAND corporation. Available from http://www.rand.org/pubs/working_papers/WR761.html.

Coombs, W.T. & Holladay, S.J. 2012. Internet contagion theory: How internet communication channels empower stakeholders. In Duhé, S. (ed.). *New media and public relations*. New York: Peter Lang, pp. 21–30.

Corley, K.G. & Gioia, D.A. 2011. Building theory about theory building: What constitutes a theoretical contribution? *Academy of Management Review*, 36(1): 12–32.

Coverdale, T.S. & Wilbon, A.D. 2013. The impact of in-group membership on e-loyalty of women online shoppers: An application of the social identity approach to website design. *International Journal of e-Adoption*, 5(1): 17–36.

Cropanzano, R. & Mitchell, M.S. 2005. Social exchange theory: An interdisciplinary review. *Journal of Management*, 31(6): 874–900.

Daft, R.L. & Lengel, R.H. 1983. Information richness: A new approach to managerial behavior and organization design. *Research in Organizational Behavior*, 6: 191–233.

Davis, F.D. 1989. Perceived usefulness, perceived ease of use and user acceptance of information technology. *MIS Quarterly*, 13(3): 319–340.

Dennis, A.R. & Valacich, J.S. 1999. 'Rethinking media richness: Towards a theory of media synchronicity', in *Proceedings of the 32nd Hawaii international conference on system sciences*, W.G. Chismar, W.G. & Mittman, R. (eds.). Maui, Hawaii.

DeSantis, G & Poole, M.S. 1994. Capturing the complexity in advanced technology use: adaptive structuration theory. *Organization Studies*, 5(2): 121–147.

Digman, J. M. (1990). Personality structure: Emergence of the five-factor model. *Annual Review of Psychology*, 41: 417–440.

Dore, M.M. 2012. Family systems theory. In Thyer, B.A., Dulmus, C.N. & Sowers, K.M. (eds.). *Human behaviour in the social environment: Theories for social work practice.* Hoboken, New Jersey: John Wiley & Sons, pp. 369–409.

Dwyer, C. 2007. Task technology fit, the social technical gap, and social networking sites, in *Proceedings of the Thirteenth Americas Conference on Information Systems*, Keystone, Colorado, 1–7.

El Said, G.R. 2015. Understanding knowledge management system antecedents of performance impact: Extending the Task-technology fit model with intention to share knowledge construct. *Future Business Journal*, 1(1/2): 75–87.

Emerson, R.M. 1962. Power-dependence relations. *American Sociological Review*, 27(1): 31–41.

Fischer, E. & Reuber, A.R. 2011. Social interaction via new social media: (How) can interactions on Twitter affect effectual thinking and behavior. *Journal of Business Venture*, 26(1): 1–18.

Fishbein, M. & Ajzen, I. 1975. *Belief, attitude, intention and behavior: An introduction to theory and research. Reading.* MA: Addison-Wesley.

Frank, K.A., Zhao, Y. & Borman, K. 2004. Social capital and the diffusion of innovations within organizations: The case of computer technology in schools. *Sociology of Education* 77(2): 148–171.

Freeman, L. 1979. Centrality in social networks: Conceptual clarification. *Social Network*, 1(3): 215–239.

Fulk, J., Steinfield, C.W., Schmitz, J. & Power, J.G. 1987. A social information processing model of media use in organizations. *Communication Research*, 14(5): 529–552.

Goodhue, D.L. & Thompson, R.L. 1995. Task-technology fit and individual performance. *MIT Quarterly*, 19(2): 213–236.

Grix, J. 2010. *The foundations of research*. 2ⁿᵈ edition. London: Palgrave Macmillan.

Hartmann, T. 2008. Parasocial interactions and paracommunication with new media characters. In Konijn, E.A., Utz, S. Tanis, M. & Barnes, S.B. (eds.). *Mediated Interpersonal Communication*. Routledge. pp.177–199.

Hau, Y.S. & Kim, Y.G. 2011. Why would online gamers share their innovation-conducive knowledge in the online game user community? Integrating individual motivations and social capital perspectives. *Computers in Human Behaviour*, 27(2): 956–970.

Hornsey, M.J. 2008. Social identity theory and self-categorization theory: A historical review. *Social and Personality Psychology Compass*, 2(1): 204–222.

Horton, D.R. & Wohl, R. 1956. Mass communication and para-social interaction: Observations on intimacy at a distance. *Psychiatry*, 19(3): 215–229.

Hsu, C.L. & Lin, J.C.C. 2008. Acceptance of blog usage: The roles of technology acceptance, social influence and knowledge sharing motivation. *Information and Management*, 45(1): 65–74.

Kapoor, K.K., Tamilmani, K., Rana, N.P., Patil, P., Dwivedi, Y.K. & Nerur, S. 2018. Advances in social media research: Past, present and future. *Information Systems Frontiers* 20: 531–558.

Katz, E. 1959. Mass communications research and the study of popular culture: An editorial note on a possible future for this journal. *Studies in Public Communication* 2: 1–6.

Katz, E., Blumler, J. & Gurevitch, M. 1974. Utilization of mass communication by the individual. In Blumler, J. & Katz, E. (eds.). *The uses of mass communication: Current perspectives on gratifications research*. Beverley Hills, CA: SAGE Publications, pp. 19–32

Kim, E., Lee, J., Sung, Y. & Choi, S.M. 2016. Predicting selfie-posting behavior on social networking sites: An extension of theory of planned behavior. *Computers in Human Behavior*. 62(1): 116–123.

Koo, C., Wati, Y. & Jung, J.J. 2011. Examination of how social aspects moderate the relationship between task characteristics and usage of social communication technologies (SCTs) in organizations. *International Journal of Information Management*, 31(5): 445–459.

Legris, P., Ingham, J. & Collerette, P. 2003. Why do people use information technology? A critical review of the technology acceptance model. *Information & Management*, 40(3): 191–204.

Lezin, N. 2007. Theories and approaches: Theory of reasoned action. Available from: http://recapp.etr.org/recapp/index.cfm?fuseaction=pages. TheoriesDetail&PageID=517. [4 August 2019].

Lin, N. 1999. Building a network theory of social capital. *Connections* 22(1): 28–51.

Littlejohn, S.W., Foss, K.A. & Oetzel, J.G. 2017. *Theories of human communication*. 11th ed. Long Grove, IL: Waveland Press.

Liu, W., Sidhu, A., Beacom, A.M., Valente, T.W. 2017. Social network theory. In, Rössler, P. Hoffner, C.A. & Van Zoonen, L. (eds.). *The international encyclopedia of media effects*. John Wiley and Sons, pp 2–12.

Lu, H. O. & Hsiao, K. L. 2010. The influence of extro/introversion on the intention to pay for social networking sites. *Information & Management*, 47(3): 150–157.

Lu, H-P. & Yang, Y-W. 2014. Toward an understanding of the behavioral intention to use a social networking site: An extension of task-technology fit to social-technology fit. *Computers in Human Behavior*, 34: 323–332.

McLuhan, M. 1964. *Understanding media; the extensions of man*. 1st ed. New York: McGraw Hill.

Meraz, S. 2009. Is there an elite hold? Traditional media to social media agenda setting influence in blog networks. *Journal of Computer-Mediated Communication*, 14(3): 682–707.

Mitchell, J.C. 1969. *Social networks in urban situations*. Manchester: Manchester University Press.

Moreno, M. & Koff, R. 2016. 11 Media theories and the Facebook influence model. *The Psychology of Social Networking*, 1: 130–142.

Ngai, E.W.T., Moon, K.K, Lam, S.S., Chin, E.S.K. & Tao, S.S.C. 2015. Social media models, technologies and applications. *Industrial Management and Data Systems*, 111(5): 769–802.

Olaniran, B.A., Rodriquez, N. & Williams, I.M. 2012. 'Social information processing theory (SIPT): A cultural perspective for international online communication environments.' In St. Amant, K. & Kelsey, S. (eds.). *Computer-mediated communication across cultures: International interactions in online environments*. Hershey, PA: IGI Global, pp. 45–65.

Pelling, E.L. & White, K.M. 2009. The theory of planned behaviour applied to young people's use of social networking web sites. *Cyber Psychology and Behavior* 12(6): 755–759.

Pettenati, M. C. & Cigognini, M. 2009. Social networking theories and tools to support connectivist learning activities. In Ang, C. & Zaphiris, P. (eds.), *Human Computer Interaction: Concepts, Methodologies, Tools, and Applications*. Hershey, PA: IGI Global, pp. 961–978.

Pinho, J.C.M.R. & Soares, A.M. 2011. Examining the technology acceptance model in the adoption of social networks. *Journal of Research and Interactive Marketing*, 5(2/3): 116–129.

Plugh, M. 2018. What is media ecology? *Explorations in Media Ecology*, 17(2): 181–186.

Porter, C.E., & Donthu, N. 2008. Cultivating trust and harvesting value in virtual communities. *Management Science*, 54(1): 113–128.

Putnam, R.D. 2000. *Bowling alone: The collapse and revival of American community*. New York: Simon and Schuster Paperbacks.

Qi, J., Monod, E., Fang, B. & Deng, S. 2018. Theories of social media: Philosophical foundations. *Engineering*, 4(1): 94–102.

Quan-Haase, A. & Young, A.L. 2010. Uses and gratifications of social media: A comparison of Facebook and Instant messaging. *Bulletin of science, technology and society*, 30(5): 350–361.

Reid, W.J. 1978. *The task centred system*. New York: Columbia University Press.

Rice, R.E. 1992. Task analyzability, use of new media, and effectiveness: A multi-site exploration of media richness. *Organization Science*, 3(4): 475–500.

Riva, G., Widerhold, B. & Cipresso, P. (2020) *The psychology of social networking Vol.1: Personal experience in online communities*. Berlin: De Gruyter Open, pp. 130–142.

Rogers, E.M. 1962. *Diffusion of innovations*. 1st ed. New York: Free Press.

Ruehl, C.H. & Igenhoff, D. 2015. Communication management on social networking sites: Stakeholder motives and usage types of corporate Facebook, Twitter and YouTube pages. *Journal of Communication Management*, 19(3): 288–302.

Saffer, A.J. 2019. Fostering social capital in an international multi-stakeholder issue network. *Public Relations Review*, 45(2): 282–296.

Scolari, C.A. 2012. Media ecology: Exploring the metaphor to expand the theory. *Communication Theory*, 22(2): 204–225.

Sheer, V.C. 2011. Teenagers' use of MSN features, discussion topics, and online friendship development: The impact of media richness and communication control. *Communication Quarterly*, 59(1): 82–103.

Shiue, Y.C., Chiu, C.M., & Chang, C.C. 2010. Exploring and mitigating social loafing in online communities. *Computers in Human Behavior*, 26(4): 768–777.

Siemens, G. 2004. Connectivism: A learning theory for the digital age. Available from: https://pdfs.semanticscholar.org/a25f/84bc55488d01bd5f5ac ac4eed0c7d8f4597c.pdf [Accessed 10 August 2019].

Silverman, D. 2013. *Doing qualitative research: A practical handbook.* 4th edition. Thousand Oaks, CA: SAGE Publications.

Sinclaire, J.K. & Vogus, C.E. 2011. Adoption of social networking sites: an exploratory adaptive structuration perspective for global organizations. *Information Technology and Management*, 12: 293–314.

Stefanone, M.A., Lackaff, D. & Devan Rosen, D. 2010. The relationship between traditional mass media and "Social Media": Reality television as a model for social network site behavior. *Journal of Broadcasting & Electronic Media*, 54(3): 508–525.

Taifel, H. 1974. Social identity and intergroup behaviour. *Social Science Information*, 13(2): 65–93.

Thibaut, J.W. & Kelley, H.H. 1996. Controlling supplier opportunism in industrial relationships. *Journal of Marketing Research*, 33(4): 431–441.

Thyer, B.A., Dulmus, C.N. & Sowers, K.M. 2012. *Human behaviour in the social environment: Theories for social work practice.* Hoboken, New Jersey: John Wiley & Sons.

Trafimow, D. 2009. The Theory of Reasoned Action: A case study of falsification in psychology. *Theory and Psychology*, 19(4): 501–518.

Urquhart, C. & Vaast, E. 2012. Building social media theory from case studies: A new frontier for IS research, in *Proceedings of the thirty-third international conference on information systems*, Orlando, pp. 1–20.

Veltri, G.A. & Atanasova, D. 2015. Climate change on Twitter: Content, media ecology and information sharing behaviour. *Public Understanding of Science*, 26(6): 721–737.

Walhter, J.B. 1992. Interpersonal effects in computer-mediated interaction: A relational perspective. *Communication Research*, 19(1): 52–90.

Wu, Q., Wu, J. & Ling, J. 2009. 'Applying social network theory to the effects of information technology implementation'. In Dwivedi, Y., Lal, B., Williams, M., Schneberger, S. & Wade, M. (eds.), *Handbook of research on contemporary theoretical models in information systems.* Hershey, PA: IGI Global, pp. 325–335.

You, L. & Hon, L. 2019. How social ties contribute to collective actions on social media: A social capital approach. *Public Relations Review*, 45(4). Available from: https://www.sciencedirect.com/science/article/abs/pii/S0363811118302650. [10 August 2019].

Yousafzai, S.Y., Foxall, G.R. & Pallister, J.G. 2010. Explaining internet banking behaviour: Theory of reasoned action, theory of planned behaviour, or technology acceptance model? *Journal of Applied Social Psychology*, 40(5): 1172–1202.

Zhang, S, Jiang, H., Carroll, J.M. 2010. Social identity in Facebook community life. *International Journal of Virtual Communities and Social Networking*, 2(4): 66–78.

CHAPTER 4

Agwuele, A. 2016. *The symbolism and communicative contents of dreadlocks in Yorubaland*. Switzerland: Palgrave MacMillan.

Altheide, D.L. 2008. Ethnographic content analysis. In Given, L.M. (ed.). *The SAGE encyclopedia of qualitative research methods*. Thousand Oaks, Los Angeles: SAGE Publications.

Alton, L. 2018. 7 Ways to segment your social media audience. Available from: https://socialmediaweek.org/blog/2018/03/7-ways-to-segment-your-social-media-audiences/ [2 August 2019].

Andreotta, M., Nugroho, R., Hurlstone, M.J. 2019. Analyzing social media data: A mixed-methods framework combining computational and qualitative text analysis. Available from: https://doi.org/10.3758/s13428-019-01202-8 [3 July 2020].

Ang, S.H. 2014. *Research design for business and management.* Available from: http://dx.doi.org/10.4135/9781473909694 [19 February 2019].

Atkinson, P. 2015. *For ethnography.* SAGE Publications.

Ballantine, J.H., Roberts, K.A. & Korgen, K.O. 2014. *Our social world: Introduction to sociology.* Thousand Oaks, Los Angeles: SAGE Publications.

Behar-Horenstein, L.S. 2018. Qualitative research methods. In Frey, B.B. (ed.). *The SAGE encyclopedia of educational research, measurement and evaluation.* Singapore: SAGE Publications.

Belgrave, L.L. 2014. Grounded theory. In Coghlan, D. & Brydon-Miller, M. (eds.). *The Sage encyclopedia of action research.* Thousand Oaks, Los Angeles: SAGE Publications.

Berg, B.L. 2008. Qualitative research in social sciences. In Given, L.M. (ed). *The SAGE encyclopedia of qualitative research methods.* Thousand Oaks, Los Angeles: SAGE Publications.

Biesenthal, C. 2014. Pragmatism. In Coghlan, D. & Brydon-Miller, M. (eds.). *The SAGE encyclopedia of action research.* Thousand Oaks, Los Angeles: SAGE Publications.

Bock, T. 2018. What is market segmentation research? Available from: https://www.displayr.com/what-is-market-segmentation-research/ [1 August 2019].

Boellstorff, T., Nardi, B., Pearce, C. & Taylor, TL. 2012. *Ethnography and virtual worlds: A handbook of method.* NJ: Princeton University Press.

Boje, D.M. 2008. *Storytelling organisations.* Thousand Oaks, Los Angeles: SAGE Publications.

Bosch, T. 2013. Conducting media ethnographies in Africa. In Darling-Wolf, F. (ed.). *Blackwell's international companion to media studies: Research methods in media studies.* Oboken, NJ: Wiley-Blackwell.

Braun, V. & Clarke, V. 2006. Using thematic analysis in psychology. *Qualitative Research in Psychology* 3(2):77–101.

Bryman, A. 2012. *Social research methods.* 4th ed. New York, NY: Oxford University Press.

Bryman, A., Bell, E., Hirschsohn, P., Dos Santos, A., Du Toit, J., Masenge, A., Van Aardt, I. & Wagner, C. 2014. *Research methodology.* Cape Town: Oxford University Press.

Burton, D. & Bartlett, S. 2009. *Key issues for education researchers.* London: SAGE Publications.

Byrne, D. 2017a. *Philosophy of research: Project planner*. Available from: https://
methods.sagepub.com/project-planner/philosophy-of-research [22 August
2019].

Byrne, D. 2017b. *Data analysis and interpretation: Project planner*. Available
from: https://dx.doi.org/10.4135/9781526408570 [5 August 2019].

Caliandro, A. 2017. Digital methods for ethnography: analytical concepts for
ethnographers exploring social media environments. *Journal of Contemporary
Ethnography*, 47(5): 551–578.

Chandler, D. 2017. *Semiotics: the basics*. 3rd ed. London: Routledge.

Charmaz, K. & Bryant, A. 2008. Grounded theory. In Given, L.M. (ed.). *The
SAGE encyclopedia of qualitative research* methods. Thousand Oaks, Los
Angeles: SAGE Publications.

Clandinin, D.J. & Caine, V. 2012. Narrative inquiry. In McGaw, B., Baker, E.
& Peterson, P.P. (eds.), *International encyclopedia of education*. 3rd ed. New
York: Elsevier.

Cobley, P. & Jansz, L. 2014. *Introducing semiotics: a graphic guide*. London: Icon
Books.

Cockerham, L. 2016. Marketer's guide to the corporate video production
process: how to plan your way to success. Available from: https://www.
skeletonproductions.com/insights/corporate-video-production-process
[13 August 2019].

Collins, T. 2015. Creating personas vs customer segments: What's the
difference? Available from: https://www.acquia.com/blog/creating-
personas-vs-customer-segments-whats-difference [14 April 2020].

Cook, J., Laidlaw, J. Mair, J. 2009. What if there is no elephant? Towards
a conception of an un-sited field. In Flazon, M.A. (ed.). *Multi-sited
ethnography: Theory, praxis and locality in contemporary research*. Farnham:
Ashgate.

Devault, G. 2019. Market segmentation for target market research: identifying
target markets for improved return on investment. Available from: https://
www.thebalancesmb.com/market-segmentation-for-target-market-
research-2296840 [01 August 2019].

Dudovskiy, J. 2018. *The ultimate guide to writing a dissertation in business studies:
A step-by-step assistance*. Available from: https://research-methodology.net/
about-us/ebook/ [19 June 2019].

Du Plessis, C. 2015. Brand storytelling: The case of the Coca Cola journey corporate website. *Communitas: Journal for Community Communication*, 20(1): 84–103.

Eco, U. 1976. *A theory of semiotics*. Bloomington, IN: Indiana University Press.

Friese, S. 2014. *Qualitative data analysis with ATLAS.Ti*. 2ⁿᵈ edition. London: SAGE Publications.

Gabriel, D. 2013. Inductive and deductive approaches to research. Available from: https://deborahgabriel.com/2013/03/17/inductive-and-deductive-approaches-to-research/ [13 September 2019].

Gephart Jr, R.P. 2018. Qualitative research as interpretive social science. In Cassell, C., Cunliffe, A.L. & Grandy, G. *The SAGE handbook of qualitative business and management research methods: History and traditions*. London: SAGE Publications.

Gergen, K.J. & Gergen, M.M. 2012. Social constructionism. In Given, L.M. (ed). *The Sage encyclopedia of qualitative research methods*. Thousand Oaks, Los Angeles: SAGE Publications.

Hand, M. 2017. Visuality in social media: researching images, circulation and practices. In Sloan, L. & Quan-Haase, A. (eds.). *The SAGE handbook of social media research methods*. Thousand Oaks, Los Angeles: SAGE Publications.

Harrison, A.K. 2018. *Ethnography*. Canada: Oxford University Press.

Hawkes, T. 2003. *Structuralism and Semiotics*. 2ⁿᵈ ed. New York: Routledge.

Highfield, T. & Leaver, T. 2016. Instagrammatics and digital methods: studying visual social media, from selfies and GIFs to memes and emoji. *Communication Research and Practice*, 2(1): 47–62.

Hiles, D., ermk, I. & Chrz, V. 2017. Narrative inquiry. 2ⁿᵈ edition. In Willig, C. *The SAGE handbook of qualitative research in psychology*. London: SAGE Publications.

Hine, C. 2015. *Ethnography for the internet*. London: Bloomsbury Publishing.

Hine, C. 2017. Digital ethnography. Available from: https://onlinelibrary.wiley.com/doi/10.1002/9781118430873.est0628 [29 February 2019].

Hine, C. 2000. *Virtual ethnography*. London: SAGE Publications.

Hines, T. & Quinn, L. 2005. Socially constructed realities and the hidden face of market segmentation. *Journal of Marketing Management*, 21(5-6): 529–543.

Holton, J.A. 2018. From grounded theory to grounded theorizing in qualitative research. In Cassell, C., Cunliffe, A.L. & Grandy, G. (eds.). *The SAGE handbook of qualitative business and management research methods*. London: SAGE Publications.

Hsieh, H. & Shannon, S. 2018. Content analysis. In Frey, B.B. (ed.). *The SAGE encyclopedia of educational research, measurement, and evaluation*. Singapore: SAGE Publications.

Jansen, B.J., Jung, S.G., Salminen, J., An, J. & Kwak, H. 2017. Viewed by too many or viewed too little: using information dissemination for audience segmentation, in *Proceedings of the Annual Meeting of the Association for Information Science & Technology*, Washington, DC. (Oct 27 – Nov 1).

Jewitt. C. & Oyama, R. 2001. Visual meaning: a social semiotic approach. In Van Leeuwen, T. & Jewitt, C. (eds). *A handbook of visual analysis*. London: SAGE Publications.

Kaplan-Weinger, J. & Ullman, C. 2014. Methods for the ethnography of communication: Language in use in schools and communities. New York: Routledge.

Kariko, A.A.T. 2013. Analysis on internet memes using semiotics. Available from: http://english.binus.ac.id/2013/06/24/analysis-on-internet-memes-using-semiotics/ [12 February 2019].

Kartch, F. 2018. Narrative interviewing. In Allen, M. (ed). *The SAGE encyclopedia of communication research methods*. Thousand Oaks, Los Angeles: SAGE Publications.

King, N. & Brooks, J. 2018. Thematic analysis in organisational research. In Cassell, C., Cunliffe, A.L. & Grandy, G. (eds.). *The SAGE handbook of qualitative business and management research methods: Methods and challenges*. London: SAGE Publications.

King, N. & Horrocks, C. 2010. *Interviews in qualitative research*. London: SAGE Publications.

Kowal, S. & O'Connell, D.C. 2014. Transcription as a crucial step of data analysis. In Flick, U. (ed.). *The SAGE handbook of qualitative data analysis*. London: SAGE Publications.

Lapadat, J.C. 2010. Thematic analysis. In Mills, A.J., Durepos, G. & Wiebe, E. (eds.). *Encyclopedia of case study research*. Thousand Oaks, Los Angeles: SAGE Publications.

Latzko-Toth, G., Bonneau, C. & Millette, M. 2017. Small data, thick data: thickening strategies for trace-based social media research. In Sloan, L. & Quan-Haase, A. (eds.). *The SAGE handbook of social media research methods*. Thousand Oaks, Los Angeles: SAGE Publications.

Markos-Kujbus, E. & Gáti, M. 2012. Social media's new role in marketing communication and its opportunities in online strategy building. Paper presented at ECREA 2012, 4th European Communication Conference, 24–27 October, Istanbul.

Marwick, AE. 2013. Ethnographic and Qualitative Research on Twitter. In Weller, K., Bruns, A., Puschmann, C., Burgess, J. & Mahrrt, M. (eds.). *Twitter and society*. New York: Peter Lang, pp. 109–122.

Matusitz, J. 2018. Semiotics. In Allen, M. (ed.). *The SAGE encyclopedia of communication research methods*. Thousand Oaks, Los Angeles: SAGE Publications.

Mazur, R. 2018. Narrative research. In Frey, B.B. (ed.). *The SAGE encyclopedia of educational research, measurement, and evaluation*. Singapore: SAGE Publications.

Mead, G.H. 1934. *Mind, self, and society: from the standpoint of a social behaviourist*. Chicago: University of Chicago Press.

Morgan, D.L. 2014. Pragmatic as a paradigm for social research. *Qualitative Inquiry* 20(8):1045–1053.

Nevius, F. 2018. New media analysis. In Allen, M. (ed.). *The SAGE encyclopedia of communication research methods*. Thousand Oaks, Los Angeles: SAGE Publications.

Nöth, W. 2012. Visual semiotics: Key features and an application to picture ads. In Margolis, E. & Pauwels, L. (eds.). *The SAGE handbook of visual research methods*. London: SAGE Publications.

Ollison, M. 2017. 5 Simple ways to segment your social media audience. 28 July 2017. Markiesha Ollison: Blog. Available from: https://blog.hubspot.com/marketing/segment-social-media-audience [2 August 2019].

O'Reilly, K. 2015. Ethnography: Telling practice stories. In Scott, R. & Kosslyn, S. (eds.). *Emerging trends in the social and behavioural sciences*. Available from: https://onlinelibrary.wiley.com/doi/pdf/10.1002/9781118900772.etrds0120 [24 July 2019].

Payne, G. & Payne, J. 2004. *Sage key concepts in social research*. London: SAGE Publications.

Rasmussen Pennington, D. 2017. Coding of non-text data. In Sloan, L. & Quan-Haase, A. (eds.). *The SAGE handbook of social media research methods.* LA: Sage.

Postill, J., & Pink, S. 2012. Social media ethnography: the digital research in a messy web. *Media International Australia*, 145(1):123–133.

Pritchard, K. & Whiting, R. 2018. Analysing web images. In Cassell, C., Cunliffe, A.L. & Grandy, G. (eds.). *The SAGE handbook of qualitative business and management research methods.* London: SAGE Publications.

Quan-Haase, A. & McCay-Peet, A. 2017. *Building interdisciplinary social media research teams: motivations, challenges, and policy frameworks.* Thousand Oaks, Los Angeles: SAGE Publications.

Quan-Haase, A. & Sloan, L. 2017. *Introduction to the handbook of social media research methods: Goals, challenges and innovations.* Thousand Oaks, Los Angeles: SAGE Publications.

Romenti, S., Murtarelli, G. & Valentini, C. 2014. Organisations' conversations in social media: Applying dialogue strategies in times of crises. *Corporate Communications: An International Journal* 19(1):10–33.

Rose, G. 2007. *Visual methodologies: An introduction to the interpretation of visual materials.* London: SAGE Publications.

Salmons, J. 2012. Qualitative methods in social media research. (Video file). Available from: https://www.youtube.com/watch?reload=9&v=BS70gVapaXs [8 August 2019].

Salmons, J. 2017. Using social media in data collection: designing studies with the qualitative e-research framework. In L. Sloan & A. Quan-Haase (eds.). *The SAGE handbook of social media research methods.* Thousand Oaks, Los Angeles: SAGE Publications.

Salmons, J. 2018. Multimodal qualitative research to study complex problems. Available from: https://www.methodspace.com/multimodal-qualitative-research-study-complex-problems/ [26 February 2019].

Schreier, M. 2013. Qualitative content analysis. In Flick, U. (ed.). *The SAGE handbook of qualitative data analysis.* London: SAGE Publications.

Schwandtr, T.A. 2007. *The SAGE dictionary of qualitative inquiry.* Available from: http://dx.doi.org/10.4135/9781412986281 [22 February 2019].

Shank, G. 2008. Semiotics. In L. Given (ed.). *The SAGE handbook of qualitative research methods.* Available from: http://dx.doi.org/10.4135/9781412963909.n419 [12 February 2019].

Shukairy, A. n.d. Personas vs. market segmentation. Available from: https://www. invespcro.com/blog/personas-vs-market-segmentation/ [14 April 2020].

Siegel, S. 2018. Discourse analysis. In Frey, B.B. (ed.). *The SAGE encyclopedia of educational research, measurement, and evaluation.* Singapore: SAGE Publications.

Smith, JK. 2008. Interpretive inquiry. In L. Given (ed.). *The SAGE handbook of qualitative research methods.* Available from: http://dx.doi. org/10.4135/9781412963909.n233 [19 June 2019].

Stan, L. 2010. Content analysis. In Mills, A.J., Durepos, G. & Wiebe, E. (eds.). *Encyclopedia of case study research.* Thousand Oaks, Los Angeles: SAGE Publications.

Swart, C. 2018. A conceptual framework for social media brand communication in non-profit organisations in South Africa: An integrated communication perspective (Doctoral dissertation). University of South Africa (Unisa), Pretoria.

Van Leeuwen, T. 2012. Multimodality and multimodal research. In Margolis, E. & Pauwels, L. (eds.). *The SAGE handbook of visual research methods.* London: SAGE Publications.

Venkatesh, A., Crockett, D., Cross, S. & Chen, S. 2017. *Ethnography in marketing and consumer research (Foundations and Trends(r) in Marketing).* Delft: Now Publishers Inc.

Williams, I. 2018. Personas vs. segments – what's the story? Available from: https://www.meltwater.com/sg/blog/personas-vs-segments-whats-the-story/ [14 April 2020].

Williams, M.L., Burnap, B. & Sloan, L. 2016. *Crime sensing with big data: the affordances and limitations of using open-source communications to estimate crime patterns.* Oxford University Press.

Yang, S., Quan-Haase, A., Nevin, A.D. & Chen, Y. 2017. The role of online reputation management, trolling, and personality traits in the crafting of the virtual self on social media. In Sloan, L. & Quan-Haase, A. (eds.). *The SAGE handbook of social media research methods.* Thousand Oaks, Los Angeles: SAGE Publications.

CHAPTER 5

Ampofo, L., Collister, S., O'Loughlin, B., Chadwick, A., Halfpenny, P.J. & Procter, P.J. 2015. Text mining and social media: When quantitative meets qualitative and software meets people. In Halfpenny, P.J., & Procter, P.J. (eds.). *Innovations in digital research methods*. Thousand Oaks, Los Angeles: SAGE Publications pp. 161–192.

Barbier, G. & Liu, H. 2011. Data mining in social media. In Aggarwal, C.C. (ed.). *Social network data analytics* pp. 327–352. Hawthorne, New York: Springer.

Bastian, M., Heymann, S. & Jacomy, M. 2009. Gephi: An open source software for exploring and manipulating networks. *Third international AAAI conference on weblogs and social media*. Available from: https://gephi. org/publications/gephi-bastian-feb09.pdf. [18 June 2020].

Bosch, T. 2016. Twitter and participatory citizenship: #FeesMustFall in South Africa. In Mutsvairo, B. (ed.). *Digital activism in the social media era: Critical reflections on emerging trend in Sub-Saharan Africa*. Cham: Palgrave Macmillan, pp. 159–173.

Bosch, T. 2019. Social media and protest movements in South Africa: #FeesMustFall and #ZumaMustFall. In Dwyer, M. & Molony, T. (eds.). *Social media and politics in Africa: Democracy, censorship and security*. London: Zed Books, pp. 66–83.

Boyd, D., & Crawford, K. 2012. Critical questions for Big Data: Provocations for a cultural, technological, and scholarly phenomenon. *Information, Communication & Society*, 15(5): 662–679.

Bruns, A. & Burgess, J. 2016. Methodological innovation in precarious spaces: The case of Twitter. In Snee, H., Roberts, S., Hine, C., Morey, Y. & Watson, H. (eds.). *Digital methods for social science: An interdisciplinary guide to research innovation*. United Kingdom: Palgrave Macmillan.

Bruns, A. (2019) After the 'APIcalypse': Social media platforms and their fight against critical scholarly research. *Information, Communication & Society* 22(11): 1544–1566.

Buchel, O. & Pennington, D. 2017. Geospatial analysis. In Sloan, L. & Quan-Haase, A. (eds.). *The SAGE Handbook of Social Media Research Methods*. Thousand Oaks, Los Angeles: SAGE Publications.

Conroy, N.J., Rubin, V.L., & Chen, Y. 2015. Automatic deception detection: Methods for finding fake news. *Proceedings of the Association for Information Science and Technology*, 52(1): 1–4.

Creswell, J.W. 2014. *Research design: Qualitative, quantitative, and mixed methods approaches.* 4th edition. Thousand Oaks, California: SAGE Publications.

Deacon, D., Pickering, M., Murdock, G. & Golding, P. 1999. *Researching communications: A practical guide to methods in media and cultural analysis.* New York: Oxford University Press.

Gaffney, D. & Puschmann, C. 2014. Data collection on Twitter. In Weller, K., Bruns, A., Burgess, J., Mahrt, M. & Puschmann, C. *Twitter and society (Digital Formations).* New York: Peter Lang, New York.

Gandomi, A & Haider, M. 2015. Beyond the hype: Big Data concepts, methods, and analytics. *International Journal of Information Management,* 35(2): 137–144.

Gerlitz, C., & Rieder, B. 2013. Mining one percent of Twitter: Collections, baselines, sampling. *M/C Journal,* 16(2): 1–16.

Giglietto, F., Rossi, L. & Bennato, D. 2012. The open laboratory: Limits and possibilities of using Facebook, Twitter, and YouTube as a research data source. *Journal of Technology in Human Services,* 30(3–4): 145–159.

Günther, W.A, Mehrizi, M.H.R, Huysman, M & Feldberg, F. 2017. Debating Big Data: A literature review on realizing value from Big Data. *Journal of Strategic Information Systems,* 26(3): 191–209.

Heer, J. & Boyd, D. 2005. Vizster: Visualizing online social networks. In *IEEE Symposium on Information Visualization, 2005. INFOVIS 2005.* pp. 32–39. IEEE.

Hollander, J. Graves, E., Renski, H., Foster-Karim, C., Wiley, A. & Das, D. 2016. *Urban social listening: potential and pitfalls for using microblogging data in studying cities.* London: Palgrave Macmillan.

Jensen, E. & Laurie, C. (2016). *Doing real research. A practical guide to social research.* Los Angeles and London: SAGE Publications.

Jünger, J & Keyling, T. 2018. Facepager 3. An application for generic data retrieval through APIs. Source code and releases. Available from: https://github.com/strohne/Facepager/ [18 June 2020].

Kitchin, R. 2014. Big Data, new epistemologies and paradigm shifts. *Big Data & Society,* 1(1): 1–12

Marres, N. 2016. Foreword. In Snee, H., Roberts, S., Hine, C., Morey, Y. & Watson, H. (eds.). *Digital methods for social science: An interdisciplinary guide to research innovation.* United Kingdom: Palgrave Macmillan.

Mostafa, M. 2013. More than words: Social networks' text mining for consumer brand sentiments. *Expert Systems with Applications* 40(10): 4241–4251.

Neuenhof, K.A. 2016. *The content analysis guidebook*. 2nd edition. Thousand Oaks, California: SAGE Publications.

Olshannikova, E. Olsson, T., Huhtamaki, J. & Karkkainen, H. 2017. Conceptualizing Big Social Data. *Journal of Big Data*. 4(3): 1–9.

Oussous, A., Benjelloun, F.Z., Lahcen, A.A. & Belfkih, S. 2018. Big Data technologies: A survey. *Journal of King Saud University – Computer and Information Sciences*, 30(4): 431–448.

Oweis, N.E., Owais, S.S., George, W., Suliman, M.G. & Snasel, V. 2015. A survey on Big Data, mining: Tools, techniques, applications and notable uses. Available from: https://www.researchgate.net/publication/282845795_A_Survey_on_Big_Data_Mining_Tools_Techniques_Applications_and_Notable_Uses [5 April 2019].

Putting Big Data to "good" use. 2017. Available from: https://www.youtube.com/watch?v=VuXEyFX0fSg&feature=youtu.be&utm_source=twitter&utm_medium=SAGE_social&utm_content=sageoceantweets&utm_term=586afadf-b104-429b-a663-0cb06a5af84a [25 June 2019].

Quan-Haase, A. & Sloan, L. 2017. Introduction to the handbook of social media research methods: Goals, challenges and innovations. London: SAGE Publications.

Rieder, B. 2013. Studying Facebook via data extraction: The Netvizz application. In *Proceedings of the 5th annual ACM web science conference*. Available from: https://dl.acm.org/doi/10.1145/2464464.2464475 pp. 346–355.

Rubin, V. 2017. Deception detection and rumour debunking for social media. In Sloan, L. & Quan-Haase, A. (eds.). *The Sage handbook of social media research methods*. Thousand Oaks, Los Angeles: SAGE Publications.

Shah, D.V., Cappella, J.N., & Neuman, W.R. 2015. Big Data, digital media, and computational social science: Possibilities and perils. *The ANNALS of the American Academy of Political and Social Science*, 659(1): 6–13.

Smith, M.A., Hansen, D.L. & Shneiderman, B. 2009. Analysing (social media) networks with NodeXL. *Proceedings of the fourth international conference on Communities and technologies*. Available from: https://dl.eusset.eu/bitstream/20.500.12015/2665/1/00374.pdf [1 October 2019].

Shu, K., Sliva, A., Wang, S., Tang, J. & Liu, H. 2017. Fake news detection on social media: A data mining perspective. *ACM SIGKDD Explorations Newsletter*, 19(1): 22–36.

Stieglitz, S, Mirbabaiea, M, Rossa, B & Neubergerb, C. 2018. Social media analytics – Challenges in topic discovery, data collection, and data preparation. *International Journal of Information Management*, 39: 156–168.

Tinati, R., Halford, S., Carr, L. & Pope, C. 2014. Big Data: Methodological challenges and approaches for sociological analysis. *Sociology*, 48(4): 663–681.

Williams, M.L., Burnap, P. & Sloan, L. 2016. Crime sensing with big data: The affordances and limitations of using open-source communications to estimate crime patterns. *The British Journal of Criminology* 57(2): 320–340.

CHAPTER 6

Adams, K.M. 2015. *Non-functional requirements in systems analysis and design.* Cham: Springer.

Campbell, D.T. & Fiske, D.W. 1959. Convergent and discriminant validation by the multi trait multimethod matrix. *Psychological Bulletin,* 56(2): 81–105.

Castro, F.G., Kellison, J.G., Boyd, S.J. & Kopak, A. 2010. A methodology for conducting integrative mixed methods research and data analyses. *Journal of Mixed Methods Research*, 4(4): 342–360.

Collins, K.M.T., Onwuegbuzie, A.J. & Sutton, I.L. 2006. A model incorporating the rationale and purpose for conducting mixed methods research in special education and beyond. *Learning Disabilities. A Contemporary Journal,* 4: 67–100.

Creswell, J.W. 2013. Steps in conducting a scholarly mixed methods study. DBER Speaker Series 48. Available from: https://digitalcommons.unl.edu/dberspeakers/48/ [14 April 2020].

Creswell, J.W. 2016. A concise introduction to mixed methods research. *Evaluation Journal of Australasia,* 16(2): 36–37.

Creswell, J.W. & Plano Clark, V.L. 2011. *Designing and conducting mixed methods research.* 2nd ed. London: SAGE Publications.

Creswell, J.W. & Plano Clark, V.L. 2007. *Designing and conducting mixed methods research.* London: SAGE Publications.

Creswell, J.W., Plano-Clark, V.L., Gutmann, M.L. & Hanson W.E. 2003. *Advanced mixed methods research designs.* In Tashakkori, A. & Teddlie, C. (eds.). *SAGE handbook of mixed methods in social and behavioural research.* Thousand Oaks, California: SAGE Publications pp. 159–196.

Davis, C.H.F., Deil-Amen, R., Rios-Aguilar, C. & Canche, M.S.G. 2012. *Social media in higher education: A literature review and research directions.* Arizona, USA: The Centre for the Study of Higher Education at The University of Arizona and Claremont Graduate University.

Fuchs, C. 2014. *Social media: A critical introduction.* Thousand Oaks, California: SAGE Publications.

Guetterman, T.C., Babchuk, W.A., Howell Smith, M.C. & Stevens, J. 2017. Contemporary approaches to mixed methods-grounded theory research: A field-based analysis. *Journal of Mixed Methods Research*, 13(2): 179–195.

Greene, J.C., Caracelli, V.J. & Graham, W.F. 1989. Toward a conceptual framework for mixed-method evaluation designs. *Educational Evaluation and Policy Analysis*, 11(3): 255–274.

Guest G. 2012. Describing mixed methods research: An alternative to typologies. *Journal of Mixed Methods Research*, 7(2): 141–151.

Jahoda, M., Lazarsfeld, P.F. & Zeisel, H. 1933. *Die Arbeitslosen von Marienthal. English translation published in 1971, as Marienthal: The sociography of an unemployed community.* Chicago, IL: Aldine Atherton.

Johnson, R.B. 2012. Dialectical pluralism and mixed research. *American Behavioural Scientist,* 56(6): 751–754.

Johnson R.B., Onwuegbuzie, A.J. & Turner L.A. 2017. Towards a definition of mixed methods research. *Journal of Mixed Methods Research*, 1(2): 112–133.

Johnson, R.B. & Onwuegbuzie, A.J. 2004. Mixed methods research: A research paradigm whose time has come by. *Educational Researcher,* 33(7): 14–26.

Kelly, M., Dowling M. & Miller M. 2018. The search for understanding: The role of paradigmatic worldviews. *Nurse Researcher*, 25(4): 9–13.

Leech, N.L. & Onwuegbuzie, A.J. 2009. A typology of mixed methods research designs. *Qual Quant*, 43(2):2 65–275.

Kivunja, C. & Kuyini, A. B. 2017. Understanding and Applying Research Paradigms in Educational Contexts. *International Journal of Higher Education*, 6(5):26-41.

Kong, S.Y., Yaacob, N.M. & Ariffin, A.R.M. 2018. Constructing a mixed methods research design: Exploration of an architectural intervention. *Journal of Mixed Methods Research*, 12(2): 148–165.

Malina, M, Nørreklit, H. & Selto, F. 2011. Lessons learned: Advantages and disadvantages of mixed method research. *Qualitative Research in Accounting & Management*, 8(1): 59–71.

Maxwell, J.A. 2011. Paradigms or toolkits? Philosophical and methodological positions as heuristics for mixed methods research. *Mid-Western Educational Researcher*, 24(2): 27–30.

Maxwell, J.A. & Loomis, D.M. 2003. *Mixed methods design: An alternative approach*. In Tashakkori, A. & Teddlie, C. (eds.). *SAGE handbook of mixed methods in social and behavioural research*. Thousand Oaks, California: SAGE Publications pp. 241–272.

Mertens, D.M., Bazeley, P., Bowleg, L., Fielding, N., Maxwell, J., Molina-Azorin & J.F., Niglas, K. 2016. The future of mixed methods: A five-year projection to 2020. Available from: https://mmira.wildapricot.org/resources/Documents/MMIRA%20task%20force%20report%20Jan2016%20final.pdf.

McCay-Peet, L. & Quan-Haase, A. 2017. In Sloan, L. & Quan-Haase, A. 2017. *The SAGE handbook of social media research methods*. Thousand Oaks California: SAGE Publications.

McKim, C.A. 2017. The value of mixed methods research: A mixed methods study. *Journal of Mixed Methods Research*, 11(2) 202–222.

Molina-Azorin, J.F. & Fetters, M.D. 2019. Building a Better World Through Mixed Methods Research. *Journal of Mixed Methods Research*, 13(3): 275-281.

Morgan, D. L. 2007. Paradigms Lost and Pragmatism Regained: Methodological Implications of Combining Qualitative and Quantitative Methods. *Journal of Mixed Methods Research*, 1(1): 48-76.

Ngai, E.W.T, Tao, S.S.C & Moon, K.K.L. Social media research: Theories, constructs, and conceptual frameworks. *International Journal of Information Management*, 35: 33–44.

Onwuegbuzie, A.J. & Combs, J.P. 2010. *Emergent data analysis techniques in mixed methods research: a synthesis*. In Tashakkori, A. & Teddlie, C. (eds.). *SAGE handbook of mixed methods in social and behavioural research*. 2nd ed. Thousand Oaks California: SAGE Publications.

Onwuegbuzie, A.J. & Combs, J.P. 2011. Data analysis in mixed research: A primer. *International Journal of Education*, 3(1): 1–25.

Onwuegbuzie, A.J. & Collins, K.M.T. 2007. A typology of mixed methods sampling designs in social science research. *The Qualitative Report*, 12(2): 281–316.

Onwuegbuzie, A.J. & Frels R.K. 2013. Introduction: Toward a new research philosophy for addressing social justice issues: Critical dialectical pluralism 1.0. *International Journal of Multiple Research Approaches*, 7(1): 9–26.

Plano Clark, V.L., Anderson, N., Wertz, J.A., Zhou, Y., Schumacher, K. & Miaskowski, C. 2015. Conceptualizing longitudinal mixed methods designs: A methodological review of health sciences research. *Journal of Mixed Methods Research*, 9(4): 297–319.

Plano-Clark, V.L. and Creswell, J.W. (eds.). 2008. *The mixed methods reader.* Thousand Oaks California: SAGE Publications.

Poynter, R. 2010. *The handbook of online and social media research: Tools and techniques for market researchers.* United Kingdom: John Wiley & Sons.

Rossman, G.B. & Wilson, B.L. 1985. Numbers and words: Combining quantitative and qualitative methods in a single large-scale evaluation study. *Evaluation Review*, 9(5): 627–643.

Schutt, R.K. 2015. *Investigating the social world: The process and practice of research.* Thousand Oaks, California: SAGE Publication.

Shannon-Baker, P. 2016. Making paradigms meaningful in mixed methods research. *Journal of Mixed Methods Research*, 10(4): 319–334.

Shirky, C. 2008. *Here comes everybody.* London: Penguin.

Snelson, C.L. 2016. Qualitative and mixed methods social media research: A review of the literature. *International Journal of Qualitative Methods*, 15(1): 1–15.

Tashakkori, A. & Teddlie, C. 1998. *Mixed methodology: Combining qualitative and quantitative approaches (Applied Social Research Methods, No. 46).* Thousand Oaks, Thousand Oaks California: SAGE Publications.

Teddlie, C & Tashakkori, A. 2009. *Foundations of mixed methods research: Integrating quantitative and qualitative approaches in the social and behavioural sciences.* Thousand Oaks, Thousand Oaks California: SAGE Publications.

Teddlie, C & Tashakkori, A. 2006. A general typology of research designs featuring mixed methods. *Research in Schools*, 13(1): 12–28.

Webb, E.J., Campbell, D.T., Schwarz, R.D. & Sechrest, L. 1966. *Unobstrusive measures: Nonreactive research in the social sciences.* Chicago, IL: Rand McNally.

Whitehead, D. & Schneider, Z. 2012. *Mixed-methods research.* In Schneider Z., Whitehead D., LoBiondo-Wood G. & Haber J. *Nursing & midwifery research: Methods and appraisal for evidence-based practice.* 4th edition. Mosby, Marrickville, Sydney: Elsevier pp. 263–284.

CHAPTER 7

Albers, C. 2019. The problem with unadjusted multiple and sequential statistical testing. *Nature Communications*, 10(1): 1–4.

Baesens, B. 2014. *Analytics in a Big Data world: The essential guide to data science and its applications.* New York: John Wiley & Sons.

Bamman, D., Eisenstein, J. & Schnoebelen, T. 2014. Gender identity and lexical variation in social media. *Journal of Sociolinguistics*, 18(2): 135–160.

Baruch, Y. & Holtom, B.C. 2008. Survey response rate levels and trends in organizational research. *Human Relations*, 61(8): 1139–1170.

Batterham, A.M. & Hopkins, G. 2006. Making meaningful inferences about magnitudes. *International Journal of Sports Physiology and Performance*, 1(1): 50–57.

Bica, M. 2019. Twitter in the eye of the storm: Assessing the public's risk perceptions. Available from: https://items.ssrc.org/chancing-the-storm/twitter-in-the-eye-of-the-storm-assessing-the-publics-risk-perceptions/ [6 August 2019].

Blackstone, A. 2012. *Principles of sociological inquiry – qualitative and quantitative methods.* Maine: Saylor Foundation.

Bornstein, M.H., Jager, J. & Putnick, D.L. 2013. Sampling in developmental science: Situations, shortcomings, solutions, and standards. *Developmental Review*, 33(4): 357–370.

Braun, V. & Clarke, V. 2013. *Successful qualitative research – A practical guide for beginners.* London: SAGE Publications.

Brooker, P., Barnett, J. & Cribben, T. 2016. Doing social media analytics. *Big Data and Society.* July–December: 1–12.

Coyne, I.T. 1997. Sampling in qualitative research. Purposeful and theoretical sampling: Merging or clear boundaries? *Journal of Advanced Nursing*, 26(3): 623–630.

Creswell, J.W. 2014. *Research Design. Qualitative, quantitative, and mixed approaches.* Thousand Oaks, Los Angeles: SAGE Publications.

Daniel, J. 2012. *Sampling Essentials. Practical Guidelines for Making sampling Choices.* Thousand Oaks, Los Angeles: SAGE Publications.

Davis, R. 2018. Listeriosis outbreak: The blame games begin. *Daily Maverick* 5 March 2018. Available from: https://www.dailymaverick.co.za/article/2018-03-05-listeriosis-outbreak-the-blame-games-begin/ [5 March 2018].

De Choudhury, M., Lin, Y.R., Sundaram, H., Candan, K., Xie, L. & Kelliher, A. 2010, How does the data sampling strategy impact the discovery of information diffusion in social media? in *ICWSM 2010 – Proceedings of the 4th International AAAI Conference on Weblogs and Social Media*, 34–41. Available from: https://asu.pure.elsevier.com/en/publications/how-does-the-data-sampling-strategy-impact-the-discovery-of-infor [6 August 2019].

De Leeuw, E.D. 2005. To mix or not to mix data collection modes in surveys. *Journal of Official Statistics*, 21(2): 233–255.

Driscoll, K. & Walker, S. 2014. Big Data, big questions—working within a black box: Transparency in the collection and production of big Twitter data. *International Journal of Communication* 8: 1745–1764.

Du Plessis, C. 2019. Prosumer engagement through story-making in trans-media branding. *International Journal of Cultural Studies*, 22(1): 175–192.

Duffy, J. 2013. LinkedIn. *PCMag*. Available from: http://www.pcmag.com/article2/0,2817,2120736,00.asp [1 February 2014].

Durrheim, K & Painter, D. 2006. Collecting quantitative data. Sampling and measuring. In Terre Blanche, M., Durrheim, K. & Painter, D. (eds.). *Research in practice. The applied methods for the social sciences.* 2nd edition. Cape Town: UCT. pp. 131–159.

Eisner, E.W. 1991. *The enlightened eye: Qualitative inquiry and the enhancement of educational practice.* New York: Macmillan.

Farrokhi, F. & Mahmoudi-Hamidabad, A. 2012. Rethinking convenience sampling: Defining quality criteria. *Theory and Practice in Language Studies*, 4(4): 784–792.

Frankenfield, J. 2019. Data analytics. Investopedia. Available from: https://www.investopedia.com/terms/d/data-analytics.asp [3 September 2019].

Golafshani, N. 2003. Understanding reliability and validity in qualitative research. *The Qualitative Report,* 8(4): 597–607.

Golder, S.A., Wilkinson, D.M. & Huberman, B.H. 2007. Rhythms of social interaction: Messaging within a massive online network. In Steinfield, C., Pentland, B.T., Ackerman, M. & Contractor, N. (eds.). *Communities and Technologies 2007: Proceedings of the Third Communities and Technologies Conference, Michigan State University 2007.* London: Springer pp. 41–66.

Goodman, L. 2011. Comment: On respondent-driven sampling and snowball sampling in hard-to-reach populations and snowball sampling not in hard-to-reach populations. *Sociological Methodology*, 41(1): 347–353.

Goodman, L.A. 1961. Snowball sampling. *Annals of Mathematical Statistics*, 32(1): 148–170.

Grodzinsky, F.S. & Tavani, H.T. 2011. Privacy in 'the cloud': Applying Nissenbaum's theory of contextual integrity. *ACM SIGCAS Computers and Society*, 41(1): 38–47.

Handcock, M.S. & Gile, K.J. 2011. Comment: On the concept of snowball sampling. *Sociological Methodology*, 41(1): 367–371.

Hayes, A. 2019. Systematic sampling. *Investopedia*. 29 April 2019. Available from https://www.investopedia.com/terms/s/systematic-sampling.asp [2 October 2019].

Hayes, A.F. 2005. *Statistical methods for communication science*. Mahwah, N.J.: Lawrence Erlbaum & Associates.

Heimann R. & Danneman, N. 2014. *Social media mining with R*. Birmingham: Packt Publishing.

Hill, C.A., Dean, E., & Murphy, J. 2013. *Social media, sociality, and survey research*. New York: John Wiley & Sons.

Hill, K. 2014. Facebook added 'research' to user agreement 4 months after emotion manipulation study. *Forbes*. Available from: http://onforb.es/15DKfGt. [7 August 2019].

Howison, J., Wiggins, A. & Crowston, K. 2011 Validity issues in the use of social network analysis with digital trace data. *Journal of the Association of Information Systems*, 12(12): 767–797.

Hutton, L. & Henderson, T. 2013. An architecture for ethical and privacy-sensitive social network experiments. *ACM SIGMETRICS Performance Evaluation Review*, 40(4): 90–95.

Iarossi, G. 2006. *The power of survey design. A user's guide for managing surveys, interpreting results, and influencing respondents*. Washington DC: The World Bank.

Jing, Y., Liu, D., Kislyuk, D., Zhai, A., Xu, J., Donahue, J. & Tavel, S. 2015. Visual search at Pinterest. In *Proceedings of the 21th ACM SIGKDD International Conference on Knowledge Discovery and Data Mining* (KDD '15). ACM, New York, NY, USA, 1889–1898. DOI:https://doi.org/10.1145/2783258.2788621 [16 August 2019].

Johnson, B.R. 1997. Examining the validity structure of qualitative research. *Education*, 118(2): 282–292.

Johnson, T., & Owens, L. 2003. Survey response rate reporting in the professional literature. In *58th Annual Meeting of the American Association for
Public Opinion Research, Nashville*. Available from http://www.amstat.org/
sections/srms/Proceedings/y2003/Files/JSM2003-000638.pdf [28 June
2019].

Joppe, M. (2000). The Research Process. Available from http://www.ryerson.
ca/~mjoppe/rp.htm [3 October 2019].

Jouhki, J., Lauk, E., Penttinen, M., Sormanen, N. & Uskali, T. 2016. Facebook's
emotional contagion experiment as a challenge to research ethics. *Media
and communication*, 4(4): 75–85.

Kim, J.K. & Wang, Z. 2018. Sampling techniques for big data analysis.
International Statistical Review, 87(1): 177–191.

Kelly, K. 2006. Calling it a day: Reaching conclusions in qualitative research.
In Terre Blanche, M., Durrheim, K. & Painter, D. (eds.). *Research in practice.
The applied methods for the social sciences*. Cape Town: UCT, pp. 370–387.

Kramer, A.D.I., Guillory, J.E. & Hancock, J.T. 2014. Experimental evidence
of massive-scale emotional contagion through social networks. *Proceedings
of the National Academy of Sciences*, 111(24): 8788–8790.

Krippendorf, K. 2018. *Content analysis. An introduction to its methodology*. 2nd
ed. London: SAGE Publications.

Lewis, K., Kaufman, J., Gonzalez, M., Wimmer, A. & Christakis, N. 2008.
Tastes, ties, and time: A new social network dataset using Facebook.com.
Social Networks, 30(4): 330–342.

Lincoln, Y.S. & Guba, E.G. 1985. *Naturalistic inquiry*. Beverly Hills, California: SAGE Publications.

Liujuan C.A., Rongrong J.B.N., Yue G.C., Wei L.B. & Qi T., 2013. Mining
spatiotemporal video patterns towards robust action retrieval. *Neurocomputing*,
105: 61–69.

Lohr, S.L. 2010. *Sampling design and analysis*. 2nd ed. Boston, MA: Cengage
Learning.

Lyon, T.P. & Montgomery, A.W. 2013. Tweetjacked: The impact of social
media on corporate greenwash. *Journal of Business Ethics*, 118(4): 747–757.

Mawson, N. 2014. #oscarpistorius hype causes Twitter fatigue. *IT Web*
4 March 2014. Available from https://www.itweb.co.za/content/
lP3gQ2MGOmDMnRD1 [8 October 2019].

Mecatti, F. & Singh. A.C. 2014. Estimation in multiple frame surveys: A simplified and unified review using the multiplicity approach. *Journal de la Société Française de Statistique*, 155(4): 51–69.

Minelli, M., Chambers, M., Dhiraj, A., Rajaram, D. & Chambers, M. 2012. *Big Data, big analytics: Emerging business intelligence and analytic trends for today's businesses*. New York: John Wiley & Sons.

Mokati, N. 2018. #Listeriosis gets South Africans talking on social media. *iol* 5 March 2018. Available from https://www.iol.co.za/news/politics/listeriosis-gets-south-africans-talking-on-social-media-13603887 [6 March 2018].

Murphy, J., Hill, C.A. & Dean, E. 2013. *Social media, sociality, and survey research in social media, sociality and survey research*. Hoboken, NJ: John Wiley & Sons.

National Center for Education Statistics. (NCES). n.d. Overcoverage. *Statistical Standards*. Available from: https://nces.ed.gov/statprog/2002/glossary.asp#overcoverage [19 July 2019].

Noble, H. & Smith, J. 2015. Issues of validity and reliability in qualitative research. *Evidence Based Nursing*, 18(2): 34–35.

Olteanu, A., Castillo, C. Diaz, F. & Kiciman, E. 2016. *Social data: Biases, methodological pitfalls, and ethical boundaries*. SSRN Scholarly Paper ID 2886526, Rochester, NY: Social Science Research Network. A1-A43.

Osborne, J.W. 2013. *Best practices in data cleaning. A complete guide to everything you need to do before and after collecting your data*. London: SAGE Publications.

Osman, M. 2019. Mind-Blowing LinkedIn statistics and facts. Available from: https://kinsta.com/blog/linkedin-statistics/ [30 September 2019].

Patel, H. 2018. *How web scraping is transforming the world with its applications*. Available from: https://towardsdatascicnce.com/https-medium-com-hiren 787-patel-web-scraping-applications-a6f370d316f4 [23 August 2019].

Patton, M.Q. 2002. *Qualitative evaluation and research methods*. 3rd ed. Thousand Oaks, Los Angeles: SAGE Publications.

Pew Internet & American Life. 2012. *Trend data (adults): What Internet users do online*. Available from: http://www.pewinternet.org/Trend-Data-(Adults)/ Online-Activites-Total.aspx. [9 April 2015].

Pfeffer, J., Mayer, K. & Morstatter, F. 2018. Open access tampering with Twitter's sample API. *EPJ Data Science* https://doi.org/10.1140/epjds/s13688-018-0178 [2 September 2019].

Phan, T.Q. & Airoldi, E.M. 2015. A natural experiment of social network formation and dynamics. *Proceedings of the National Academy of Sciences of the United States of America* 112(21): 6595–6600.

Saravan, D. 2016. Literature survey on multimedia data retrieval techniques using data mining. *i-manager's Journal on Software Engineering*, 10(3): 27–33.

Schofield, W. 2006. Survey sampling. In Sapsford, R. & Jupp, V. (eds.). *Data collection and analysis.* 2nd ed. London: SAGE Publications, pp. 26–54.

Schultz, J. 2019. *How much data is created on the Internet each day?* Available from: https://blog.microfocus.com/how-much-data-is-created-on-the-internet-each-day/#targetText=There%20are%201440%20minutes%20per,of%20Youtube%20videos%20each%20day [4 October 2019].

Staff reporter. 2019. Twitter hits back over ConCourt ruling on corporal punishment in the home. *iol.* Available from: https://www.iol.co.za/news/south-africa/western-cape/twitter-hits-back-over-concourt-ruling-on-corporal-punishment-in-the-home-33204862 [12 July 2019].

Statscounter. 2019. *Social media stats in South Africa. August 2019.* Available from: https://gs.statcounter.com/social-media-stats/all/south-africa [19 September 2019].

Stenbacka, C. 2001. Qualitative research requires quality concepts of its own. *Management Decision*, 39(7): 551–556.

Suresh, K.P. 2011. An overview of randomization techniques: An unbiased assessment of outcome in clinical research. *Journal of Human Reproductive Sciences*, 4(1): 8–11.

The American Association for Public Opinion Research. 2015. *Standard definitions: Final dispositions of case codes and outcome rates for surveys.* 8th ed. Oakbrook Terrace, Il: AAPOR.

Thompson. S.K. 2012. *Sampling.* New York: John Wiley and Sons.

Trip Advisor SA. 2017. Can we trust Agoda.com Review? Available from: https://www.tripadvisor.co.za/ShowTopic-g1-i12334-k10319402-Can_We_Trust_Agoda_com_Review-Holiday_Travel.html [17 September 2019].

Trochim, W. 2006. *Random selection & assignment.* Web Center for Social Research Methods. Available from: https://socialresearchmethods.net/kb/random.htm [20 October 2006].

Van der Vyver, A.G. 2017. The State versus Oscar Pistorius: A critical analysis of media coverage and the court of public opinion. *The International Journal of Technology, Policy and Law*, 3(1): 16–27.

Yang, K. 2010. *Making sense of statistical methods in social research.* London: SAGE Publications.

CHAPTER 8

Adithya, S.R. & Ambika, M., Prabhu, R. & Krishnakumar, R. 2017. Real time data collection and analytics of social media sites using Netlytic. *Middle-East Journal of Scientific Research*, 25(1): 174–180.

Ahmed, W. 2019. Using Twitter as a data source: an overview of social media research tools. Available from: https://blogs.lse.ac.uk/impactofsocialsciences/2019/06/18/using-twitter-as-a-data-source-an-overview-of-social-media-research-tools-2019/ [18 June 2019].

Barnhart, B. 2018. How to mine your social media data for a better ROI. Available from: https://sproutsocial.com/insights/social-media-data/ [13 September 2019].

Baruffa, O. 2018. How data gets cleaned – An example. Available from: https://oscarbaruffa.com/how-data-gets-cleaned-an-example/ [20 April 2018].

Bickman, L. & Rog, D.J. 2008. *Handbook of applied social research methods*. 2nd edition. Thousand Oaks, Los Angeles: SAGE Publications.

Biroscak, B.J., Scott, J.E., Lindenberger, J.H. & Bryant, C.A. 2017. Leximancer software as a research tool for social marketers: application to a content analysis. *Social Marketing Quarterly* 23(3): 223–231.

Boxiner, A, Vaknin, E, Volodin, A, Barda, D & Zaikin, R. 2019. *Tik or Tok? Is TikTok secure enough?*. [O]. Available: https://research.checkpoint.com/2020/tik-or-tok-is-tiktok-secure-enough/ [25 April 2020].

Brown, S.C., Stevens, R.A., Troiano, P.F. & Schneider, M.K. 2002. Exploring complex phenomenon: grounded theory in student affairs research. *Journal of College Student Development*, 43(2): 1–11.

Cheliotis, G., Lu, X. & Song, Y. 2015. Reliability of data collection methods in social media research, in *Proceedings of the Ninth International AAAI Conference on Web and Social Media*: 586–589.

Creps, J. 2019. *InstaLoader – an OSINT tool for scraping Instagram metadata*. Available from: https://jakecreps.com/2019/07/12/instaloader/ [13 September 2019].

Creswell, J.W. 2007. *Qualitative inquiry and research design: choosing among five approaches*. 2nd edition. Thousand Oaks, Los Angeles: SAGE Publications.

Davies, L. 2019. Social media data in research: a review of the current landscape. Available from: https://ocean.sagepub.com/blog/social-media-data-in-research-a-review-of-the-current-landscape?utm_source=twitter&utm_medium=SAGE_social&utm_content=sageoceantweets&utm_term=c6a8b96a-8b46-4efa-bf14-2bf6862e8b0e [7 June 2019].

DeGennarro, T. 2019. Is TikTok the next big thing in social media marketing? [O]. Available: https://nealschaffer.com/is-tiktok-the-next-big-thing-in-social-media-marketing/ [25 April 2020].

Desjardins, J. 2019a. What happens in an Internet minute in 2019? Available from: https://www.visualcapitalist.com/what-happens-in-an-internet-minute-in-2019/ [14 August 2019].

Desjardins, J. 2019b. How much data is generated each day? Available from: https://www.weforum.org/agenda/2019/04/how-much-data-is-generated-each-day-cf4bddf29f [14 August 2019].

Dhawraj, R. 2013. *An investigation of the Democratic Alliance's political public relations campaign in the 2009 South African general elections including how social networking site Facebook was leveraged to help increase the party's vote-share.* Master's dissertation, University of South Africa.

Dhawraj, R. 2019. *A conceptual framework for digital political communication to promote party-political issue ownership via an urban electioneering platform.* PhD thesis, University of South Africa.

Dobre, C. & Xhafa, F. 2014. Intelligent services for big data science. *Future Generation Computer Systems,* 37: 267–281.

Expert Panel, Forbes Agency Council. 11 reasons TikTok is a sleeping social media giant. 2019. [O]. Available: https://www.forbes.com/sites/forbesagencycouncil/2019/09/03/11-reasons-tiktok-is-a-sleeping-social-media-giant/#27ce591d5062 [25 April 2020].

Fiesler, C., Young, A., Peyton, T., Bruckman, A.S., Gray, M., Hancock, J. & Lutters, W. 2015. Ethics for studying online socio-technical systems in a big data world, in *Proceedings of the 18th ACM Conference Companion on Computer Supported Cooperative Work & Social Computing,* New York, NY, 289–292.

Gantz, J. & Reinsel, D. 2012. The digital universe in 2020: Big data, bigger digital shadows, and biggest growth in the Far East IDC – EMC Corporation. Available from: https://www.emc.com/leadership/digital-universe/2012iview/big-data-2020.htm [5 June 2019].

Haimson, O., Andalibi, N. & Pater. J. 2016. Ethical use of visual social media content in research publications. Available from: https://ahrecs.com/uncategorized/ethical-use-visual-social-media-content-research-publications [20 September 2019].

Haynes, E., Garside, R., Green, J., Kelly, M.P., Thomas, J. & Guell, C. 2019. Semiautomated text analytics for qualitative data synthesis. *Research Synthesis Methods* 10(3): 452–464.

Historical Twitter data and hashtag Twitter archive search – TrackMyHashtag. 2019. Available from: https://www.trackmyhashtag.com/historical-twitter-data [13 September 2019].

Holsti, O.R. 1969. *Content analysis for the social sciences and humanities.* Reading, Mass: Addison-Wesley.

How to use Twitter analytics: 2019. Analyze your tweets and understand your followers. Available from: https://business.twitter.com/en/analytics.html [27 March 2019].

Hu, J.C. 2019. *The tricky ethics of using YouTube videos for academic research.* Available from: https://psmag.com/social-justice/the-tricky-ethics-of-digital-academic-research [13 September 2019].

Hu, Y., Manikonda, L. & Kambhampati, S. 2014. *What we Instagram: A first analysis of Instagram photo content and user types.* Available from: https://www.public.asu.edu/~lmanikon/icwsm2014.pdf [3 April 2019].

Hutchinson, A.J, Johnston, L.H. & Breckon, J.D. 2010. Using QSR-NVivo to facilitate the development of a grounded theory project: An account of a worked example. *International Journal of Social Research Methodology,* 13(4): 283–302.

Instaloader. 2019. Available from: https://instaloader.github.io/ [13 September 2019].

Katapally, T. 2019. Citizen science can help solve our data crisis. Available from: https://www.weforum.org/agenda/2019/03/citizen-science-can-help-solve-our-data-crisis [14 August 2019].

Kemp, S. 2019. Digital 2019: Global Internet use accelerates. Available from https://wearesocial.com/blog/2019/01/digital-2019-global internet-use-accelerates [14 August 2019].

Liang, H. & Zhu, J.J.H. 2017. Big data, collection of (social media, harvesting). In Matthes, J. (ed). *The International Encyclopedia of Communication Research Methods.* Hong Kong: John Wiley, pp. 1–18.

Ma, Ding. 2020. Visualisation of social media data: mapping changing social networks. [O]. Available: https://webapps.itc.utwente.nl/librarywww/papers_2012/msc/gfm/dingma.pdf [25 April 2020].

Markham, A. 2012. Fabrication as ethical practice: Qualitative inquiry in ambiguous Internet contexts. *Information, Communication & Society*, 15(3): 334–353.

McCourt, A. 2018. Social media mining: The effects of big data in the age of social media. Available from: https://law.yale.edu/mfia/case-disclosed/social-media-mining-effects-big-data-age-social-media [6 May 2019].

Moakes, J., CEO, Democratic Alliance. 2011. Interview by author. [Transcript]. 29 February. Cape Town.

Montgomery, E. 2020. What is TikTok & how does it affect your social media strategy? [O]. Available: https://www.threegirlsmedia.com/2020/01/06/what-is-tiktok-how-does-it-affect-your-social-media-strategy/ [25 April 2020].

Olshannikova, E., Olsson, T., Huhtamäki, J. & Kärkkäinen, H. 2017. Conceptualizing big social data. *Journal of Big Data* 4(3): 1–19.

Patnaik, S. & Barik, S.S. 2018. Social media analytics using visualization. *International Journal of Scientific Research Engineering & Technology (IJSRET)*, 7(4): 260–267.

Pearce, W., Özkula, S.M., Greene, A.K., Teeling, L., Bansard, J.S., Omena, J.J. & Rabello, E.T. 2018. Visual cross-platform analysis: Digital methods to research social media images. *Information, Communication & Society*, 1–21.

Pila, E., Mond, J.M., Griffiths, S., Mitchison, D. & Murray, S.B. 2017. A thematic content analysis of #cheatmeal images on social media: Characterizing an emerging dietary trend. *International Journal of Eating Disorders*, 50(6): 698–706.

Priya, D. 2017. Introduction to data mining and its process (Video file). Available from: https://www.youtube.com/watch?v=A682An06Vq4 [28 August 2019].

Radford, J. 2019. Collecting social media data for research. Available from: https://ocean.sagepub.com/blog/collecting-social-media-data-for-research [7 June 2019].

Rolfe, G. 2004. Validity, trustworthiness and rigour: Quality and the idea of qualitative research. *Methodological Issues in Nursing Research* 53(3): 304–310.

Ryklief, L. 2018. Learn how to source & clean data. Available from: https://openup.org.za/articles/openintake-2018-feb.html [20 April 2018].

Saad, M., Mohammad, A., Hamri, R. & Fahad, G. 2018. Data mining: Analysis of a social data visualization web site (Instagram). *International Journal of Computer Networks and Communications Security*, 6(4): 76–78.

Saylor, L. 2012. Synchronous and asynchronous communication (Video file). Available from: https://www.youtube.com/watch?v=ONGtUTGc9sE [16 August 2019].

Schulz-Herzenberg, C. 2009. Trends in party support and voter behaviour, 1994-2009. In Southall, R. & Danile, J. (eds) *Zunami*. Johannesburg: Jonathan Ball: pp. 23–46.

Shleyner, E. 2018. 19 Social media metrics that really matter—and how to track them. Available from: https://blog.hootsuite.com/social-media-metrics/ [25 August 2019].

Sikolia, D., Biros, D., Mason, M. & Weiser, M. 2013. Trustworthiness of grounded theory methodology research in information systems. Available from: https://aisel.aisnet.org/cgi/viewcontent.cgi?referer=https://www.google.com/&httpsredir=1&article=1006&context=mwais2013 [5 April 2017].

Singh, S. 2017. *Mining data from social media with Python*. Available from: https://www.youtube.com/watch?v=pVmCI9zIMbc&list=PLmcBskOCOOFW1SNrz6_yzCEKGvh65wYb9 [25 June 2019].

Sivarajah, U., Kamal, M.M., Irani, Z. & Weerakkody, V. 2016. Critical analysis of big data challenges and analytical methods. *Journal of Business Research*, 70: 263–286.

Sloan, L., Jessop, C., Al Baghal, T. & Williams, M. 2019. Linking survey and Twitter data: Informed consent, disclosure, security, and archiving. *Journal of Empirical Research on Human Research Ethics*, 1 (14): 1–14.

Smith, K. 2019. 126 Amazing social media statistics and facts. Available from: https://www.brandwatch.com/blog/amazing-social-media-statistics-and-facts/ [31 May 2019].

Social media fires up election season. 2014. Available from: https://www.sabcnews.com/sabcnews/social-media-fires-up-election-season/ [18 May 2016].

Social media stats worldwide. 2019. Available from: http://gs.statcounter.com/social-media-stats [21 January 2019].

Southall, R. & Daniel, J. 2009. The South African election of 2009. *Africa Spectrum*, 44(2): 111–124.

Spaountzi, A & Psannis, K.E. 2016. Social networking data analysis & challenges. *Future Generation Computer Systems*, 1–39.

Statt, N. 2019. *TikTok's global social media takeover is starting to slow down.* [O]. Available: https://www.theverge.com/2019/11/4/20948731/tiktok-bytedance-china-social-media-growth-users-decline-first-time Accessed on 2020/04/25

Stieglitz, S, Mirbabaiea, M, Rossa, B & Neubergerb, C. 2018. Social media analytics – Challenges in topic discovery, data collection, and data preparation. *International Journal of Information Management*, 39: 156–168.

Using social media for social research: an introduction. 2016. [O]. Available: https://assets.publishing.service.gov.uk/government/uploads/system/uploads/attachment_data/file/524750/GSR_Social_Media_Research_Guidance_-_Using_social_media_for_social_research.pdf [25 April 2020].

Vela, G. 2020. TikTok: The next frontier of social media is here. [O]. Available: https://www.forbes.com/sites/forbesagencycouncil/2020/03/19/tiktok-the-next-frontier-of-social-media-is-here/#70fc88792426 [25 April 2020].

Watkins, E. & Sutton, J. 2018. Cambridge Analytica files for bankruptcy. Available from: https://edition.cnn.com/2018/05/18/politics/cambridge-analyticabankruptcy/index.html?sr=twCNNp051818cambridge-analyticabankruptcy0627AMStory& CNNPolitics=Tw [18 May 2019].

Wronski, M. 2015. The SA social media landscape in 2015. Available from: http://www.mikewronski.co.za/2015/09/07/the-sa-social-media-landscape-in-2015/ [4 October 2016]

Yu, J.X. 2019. Research on TikTok app based on user-centric theory. *Applied Science and Innovative Research* 3(1): 28–36.

CHAPTER 9

Ahmed, W., Bath, P. A., & Demartini, G. 2017. Using Twitter as a data source: An overview of ethical, legal, and methodological challenges. In Woodfield, K. (ed). *The Ethics of Online Research.* Bingley, United Kingdom: Emerald Publishing Limited, pp. 79–107.

Ahmed, W. 2017. Using Twitter as a data source: An overview of social media research tools (updated for 2017). *Impact of Social Sciences Blog.* Available from: https://blogs.lse.ac.uk/impactofsocialsciences/2017/05/08/using-twitter-as-a-data-source-an-overview-of-social-media-research-tools-updated-for-2017/ [22 August 2019].

Ahmed, W. 2018. *Using Twitter data to provide qualitative insights into pandemics and epidemics* (Doctoral dissertation, University of Sheffield).

Ahmed, W. & Lugovic, S. 2019. Social media analytics: Analysis and visualisation of news diffusion using NodeXL. *Online Information Review*, 43(1):149–160.

Al-Saqaf, W. 2016. *Mecodify: A tool for Big Data analysis & visualisation with Twitter as a case study*. Working Paper in the MeCoDEM series. United Kingdom: University of Leeds.

Anderson, S. & Clarke, V. 2017. Disgust, shame and the psychosocial impact of skin picking: Evidence from an online support forum. *Journal of Health Psychology*, 24(13): 1773–1784.

Andreotta, M., Nugroho, R., Hurlstone, M.J., Boschetti, F., Farrell, S., Walker, I., Paris, C. 2019. Analyzing social media data: A mixed-methods framework combining computational and qualitative text analysis. *Behavior Research Methods*, 51(4): 1766–1781.

Archer, E., Janse van Vuuren, H & Van der Walt, H. 2017. *Introduction to Atlas Ti*. 6th edition. Pretoria: Research Rescue.

Bengtsson, M. 2016. How to plan and perform a qualitative study using content analysis. *NursingPlus Open*, 2: 8–14.

Boyd, D. & Crawford, K. 2011. Six Provocations for Big Data (September 21, 2011). A Decade in Internet Time: Symposium on the Dynamics of the Internet and Society, September 2011. Available at SSRN: https://ssrn.com/abstract=1926431 or http://dx.doi.org/10.2139/ssrn.1926431.

Braun, V. & Clarke, V. 2006. Using thematic analysis in psychology. *Qualitative Research in Psychology*, 3(2):77–101.

Braun, V, & Clarke, V. 2012. Thematic analysis. In H. Cooper (ed). *Handbook of research methods in psychology: Research designs*. Washington DC, US: American Psychological Association, pp. 57–71.

Braun, V. 2008. 'She'll be right"? National identity explanations for poor sexual health statistics in Aotearoa/New Zealand. *Social Science & Medicine*, 67(11): 1817–1825.

Brooks, J., McCluskey, S., Turley, E. & King, N. 2015. The utility of template analysis in qualitative psychology research. *Qualitative Research in Psychology*, 12(2): 202–222.

Clarke, V., Braun, V., Terry, G & Hayfield N. 2019). Thematic analysis. In Liamputtong, P. (ed.). *Handbook of research methods in health and social sciences*. Singapore: Springer, pp. 843–860.

Clarke, V. & Kitzinger, C. 2004. Lesbian and gay parents on talk shows: Resistance or collusion in heterosexism. *Qualitative Research in Psychology*, 1(3): 195–217.

Creswell, J.W. 2013. *Qualitative inquiry & research design: choosing among the five approaches*. Thousand Oaks, Los Angeles: SAGE Publications.

Creswell, J.W. 2014. *Research design: Qualitative, quantitative, and mixed methods approaches*. 4th edition. Thousand Oaks, California: SAGE Publications.

De Bruin, A. & McAuliffe, E. 2018. Social network analysis as a methodological approach to explore health systems: A case study exploring support among senior managers/executives in a hospital network. *International Journal of Environmental Research and Public Health*, 15(3): 511.

Everson-Hock, E.S., Taylor, A.H., Ussher, M. & Faulkner, G. 2010. A qualitative perspective on multiple health behaviour change: Views of smoking cessation advisors who promote physical activity. *The Journal of Smoking Cessation*, 5(1): 7–14.

Fang, E. 2019. ML Study Jam – Vision API (June 11, 2019). Available from: https://towardsdatascience.com/ml-study-jam-detect-labels-faces-and-landmarks-in-images-with-the-cloud-vision-api-a80e89feb66f [3 October 2019].

Fereday, J. & Muir-Cochrane, E. 2006. Demonstrating rigor using thematic analysis: A hybrid approach of inductive and deductive coding and theme development. *International Journal of Qualitative Methods* 5(1): 80–92.

Flick, U. 2014. Mapping the field. In Flick, U. (ed). *The SAGE handbook of qualitative data analysis*. London: SAGE Publications, pp. 3–18.

Followthehashtag. (n.d.). Available from: http://www.followthehashtag.com/. [22 August 2019].

Fusch, P.I., & Ness, L.R. 2015 Are we there yet? Data saturation in qualitative research. *The Qualitative Report*, 20(9): 1408–1416. Available from: http://nsuworks.nova.edu/tqr/vol20/iss9/3 [19 June 2020].

Guest, G., MacQueen, K.M. & Namey, E.E. 2012. *Applied thematic analysis*. Thousand Oaks, Los Angeles: SAGE Publications.

Hand, R. 2018. Social media: The ever-changing landscape. Available from: https://www.business2community.com/social-media/social-media-the-ever-changing-landscape-02125597 [15 August 2019].

Hawkins, J.M. 2018. Thematic analysis. In M. Allen (ed). *The Sage Encyclopedia of Communication Research Methods*. Thousand Oaks: SAGE Publications, pp. 01–07.

Hawksey, M. (n.d.). TAGS. [Online]. Available from: https://tags.hawksey. info/. [22 August 2019].

Hu, X. & Liu, H. 2012. Text analytics in social media. In Aggarwal, C.C. & Zhai, C.X. (eds.). *Mining Text Data*. Boston: Springer, pp 385–414.

4 Major ways in which big data is impacting social media marketing. 2018. Available from: https://insidebigdata.com/2018/10/06/4-major-ways-big-data-impacting-social-media-marketing/ [16 August 2019].

Ivanov, I. 2018. What is big data analytics on social media? Available from: https://locowise.com/blog/what-is-big-data-analytics-on-social-media [16 August 2019].

Krystyanczuk, M. & Chatterjee, S. 2017. *Python social media analytics*. Birmingham, United Kingdom: Packt Publishing.

Pearce, W., Özkula, S.M., Greene, A.K., Teeling, L., Bansard, J.S., Omena, J.J. & Teixeira Rabello, E. 2018. Visual cross-platform analysis: Digital methods to research social media images. *Information, Communication & Society*, 23(2): 161–180.

Poulsen, S.V., Kvåle, G. & Van Leeuwen, T. 2018. Special issue: Social media as semiotic technology. *Social Semiotics*, 28(5): 593–600.

Pila, E., Mond, J.M., Griffiths, S., Mitchison, D. & Murray, S.B. 2017. A thematic content analysis of# cheatmeal images on social media: Characterizing an emerging dietary trend. *International Journal of Eating Disorders*, 50(6): 698–706.

Provalis Research. 2020. Products. Available from https://provalisresearch. com/products/qualitative-data-analysis-software/ [6 April 2020].

Pulsar [Online] (n.d.). *Pulsar Social Data Intelligence*. Available from http:// www.pulsarplatform.com/. [22 August 2019].

Openrefine.org, computer software. 2019. Available from: https://github.com/ OpenRefine [17 August 2019].

QSR International, computer software. (n.d.). Available from: http://www. qsrinternational.com/product [22 August 2019].

Smith, M.A., Shneiderman, B., Milic-Frayling, N., Mendes Rodrigues, E., Barash, V., Dunne, C. & Gleave, E. 2009. Analyzing (social media) networks with NodeXL. In *Proceedings of the fourth international conference on Communities and technologies* (pp. 255–264). ACM.

Sloan, L. & Quan-Haase, A. (eds). 2017. *The Sage handbook of social media research methods*. London: SAGE Publications.

Smith, M. A., Rainie, L., Shneiderman, B. & Himelboim, I. 2014. Mapping Twitter topic networks: From polarized crowds to community clusters. *Pew Research Center*, 20: 1–56.

SocioViz. (n.d.) [Online]. Retrieved from http://socioviz.net/SNA/eu/sna/login.jsp. [22 August 2019].

Statistical Cybermetrics Research Group. (n.d.). *Mozdeh Twitter time series analysis*. Available from http://mozdeh.wlv.ac.uk/. [22 August 2019].

Tabassam, S. 2017. Security and privacy issues in cloud computing environment. *Journal of Information Technology and Software Engineering*, 7(5): 1–6.

Tjora, S. 2019. *Qualitative research as stepwise-deductive induction*. New York: Routledge.

Track My Hashtag. (n.d.). [Online]. Available from https://www.trackmyhashtag.com/ [22 August 2019].

Twitonomy. (n.d.). [Online]. Available from https://www.twitonomy.com/. [22 August 2019].

Veek, A. 2013. Analyzing the content of social media data. Quirks. Available from: https://www.quirks.com/articles/analyzing-the-content-of-social-media-data [22 August 2019].

Visibrain. (n.d.). Available from http://www.visibrain.com/en/ [22 August 2019].

Webometric Analyst. (n.d.). Available from http://lexiurl.wlv.ac.uk [22 August 2019].

Wang, Y. 2014. *Data preparation for social network mining and analysis*. Dissertation. Singapore Management University, Singapore.

Zamawe, F.C. 2015. The implication of using NVivo software in qualitative data analysis: Evidence-based reflections. *Malawi Medical Journal*, 27(1): 13–15.

Zheng, X., Zeng, Z., Chen, Z. & Rong, C. 2015. Detecting spammers on social networks. *Neurocomputing*, 159: 27–34.

CHAPTER 10

Alm, J.G. 2014. Sharing copyrights: The copyright implications of user content in social media. *Hamline Journal of Public Law and Policy*, 35:103.

Anthonysamy, P., Greenwood, P. & Rashid, A. 2013. Social networking privacy: Understanding the disconnect from policy to controls. *Computer*, 46(6): 60–67.

Association of Internet Researchers. 2012. Ethical decision-making and internet research. Recommendations from the AoIR ethics working committee (Version 2.0). Available from: http://aoir.org/reports/ethics2.pdf. [5 August 2019].

Ayalon, O. & Toch, E. 2013. Retrospective privacy: Managing longitudinal privacy in online social networks. *Proceedings of the Ninth Symposium on Usable Privacy and Security*, 4. Available from: https://dl.acm.org/doi/10.1145/2501604.2501608. [10 July 2019].

Bahri, L., Carminati, B. & Ferrari, E. 2018. Decentralized privacy-preserving services for online social networks. *Online Social Networks and Media*, 6: 18–25.

Beigi, G., Shu, K., Zhang, Y. & Liu, H. 2018. Securing social media user data: An adversarial approach. *Proceedings of the 29th on Hypertext and Social Media*, 165–173. Available from: https://dl.acm.org/doi/10.1145/3209542.3209552 [6 July 2019].

Bender, J.L., Cyr, A.B., Arbuckle, L. & Ferris, L.E. 2017. Ethics and privacy implications of using the internet and social media to recruit participants for health research: A privacy-by-design framework for online recruitment. *Journal of Medical Internet Research*, 19(4): 104–122.

Beninger, K., Fry, A., Jago, N., Lepps, H., Nass, L. & Silvester, H. 2014. Research using social media: Users' views. *NatCen Social Research*, 1–40.

Benton, A., Coppersmith, G. & Dredze, M. 2017. Ethical research protocols for social media health research. *Proceedings of the First ACL Workshop on Ethics in Natural Language Processing*, 94–102. Available from: https://www.aclweb.org/anthology/W17-1612/ [19 June 2020].

Boyd, D.M. 2014. *It's complicated: The social lives of networked teens*. New York: Yale University Press.

Boyd, D.M. 2011. Social network sites as networked publics: affordances, dynamics, and implications. In Papacharissi, Z. (ed.). *A networked self: Identity, community, and culture on social network sites*. New York: Routledge, pp. 39–58.

Boyd, E.B. 2010. A third of Facebook users customized their privacy settings after the policy changes (and why Facebook thinks that's a good thing). *Bay Newser*. Available from: http://www.mediabistro.com/baynewser/privacy/a_third_of_facebook_users_customized_their_privacy_settings_after_the_policy_changes_and_why_facebook_thinks_thats_a_good_thing_150409.asp. [17 June 2019].

Bull, S.S., Breslin, L.T., Wright, E.E., Black, S.R., Levine, D. & Santelli, J.S. 2011. Case study: An ethics case study of HIV prevention research on Facebook: The Just/Us study. *Journal of Pediatric Psychology*, 36(10): 1082–1092.

Burns, A. 2015. In full view: Involuntary porn and the postfeminist rhetoric of choice. In Nally, C. & Smith, A. (eds.). *Twenty-first century feminism*. Basingstoke, UK: Palgrave Macmillan, pp. 93–118.

Cheng, Y., Park, J. & Sandhu, R. 2013, May. Preserving user privacy from third-party applications in online social networks. *Proceedings of the 22nd International Conference on World Wide Web*, 723–728. Available from: https://dl.acm.org/doi/10.1145/2487788.2488032 [24 March 2019].

Choi, T.R. & Sung, Y. 2018. Instagram versus Snapchat: Self-expression and privacy concerns on social media. *Telematics and Informatics*, 35(8): 2289–2298.

Clark, K., Duckham, M. & Guillemin, M. 2015 *Guidelines for the ethical use of digital data in human research*. Melbourne: Carlton Connect Initiative, University of Melbourne.

Consumers International. 2018. The state of data protection rules around the world: A briefing for consumer organisations. *Consumer International*. Available from: https://www.consumersinternational.org/media/155133/gdpr-briefing.pdf [31 July 2019].

Correa, D., Silva, L.A., Mondal, M., Benevenuto, F. & Gummadi, K.P. 2015. The many shades of anonymity: Characterizing anonymous social media content. *Ninth International AAAI Conference on Web and Social Media*, 71–80. Available from: https://www.aaai.org/ocs/index.php/ICWSM/ICWSM15/paper/view/10596 [19 June 2020].

Crow, G. & Wiles, R. 2008. Managing anonymity and confidentiality in social research: The case of visual data in community research. *International Journal of Social Research Methodology*, 11(5): 417–428.

Custers, B. 2016. Click here to consent forever: Expiry dates for informed consent. *Big Data & Society*, 3(1): 1–6.

Custers, B., Van der Hof, S., Schermer, B., Appleby-Arnold, S. & Brockdorff, N. 2013. Informed consent in social media use-the gap between user expectations and EU personal data protection law. *SCRIPTed*, 10(4): 435–457.

Cutillo, L.A, Molva, R. & Önen, M. 2011. Safebook: A distributed privacy-preserving online social network. In *2011 IEEE International Symposium on a World of Wireless, Mobile and Multimedia Networks*, 1–3. Available from: https://ieeexplore.ieee.org/document/5986118 [19 June 2020].

Davies, R. & Rushe, D. 2019. Facebook to pay $5bn fine as regulator settles Cambridge Analytica complaint. *The Guardian* 24 July. Available from: https://www.theguardian.com/technology/2019/jul/24/facebook-to-pay-5bn-fine-as-regulator-files-cambridge-analytica-complaint [26 July 2019].

Donath, J. 2007. Signals in social supernets. *Journal of Computer-Mediated Communication*, 13(1): 231–251.

Dubinko, M., Kumar, R., Magnani, J., Novak, J., Raghavan, P. & Tomkins, A. 2007. Visualizing tags over time. *ACM Transactions on the Web (TWEB)*, 1(2): 1–22.

Dutton, W.H., Blank, G. & Groselj, D. 2013. *Cultures of the Internet: The Internet in Britain: Oxford Internet Survey 2013 Report.* Oxford Internet Survey 2013 Report. Oxford Internet Institute.

Ellison, N.B., Steinfield, C. & Lampe, C. 2007. The benefits of Facebook 'friends:' Social capital and college students' use of online social network sites. *Journal of computer-mediated communication*, 12(4): 1143–1168.

Freelon, D. 2014. On the interpretation of digital trace data in communication and social computing research. *Journal of Broadcasting & Electronic Media*, 58(1): 59–75.

Fuster, G.G. & Gellert, R. 2012. The fundamental right of data protection in the European Union: in search of an uncharted right. *International Review of Law, Computers & Technology*, 26(1): 73–82.

Gao, H., Hu, J., Huang, T., Wang, J. & Chen, Y. 2011. Security issues in online social networks. *IEEE Internet Computing*, 15(4): 56–63.

Goga, O., Loiseau, P., Sommer, R., Teixeira, R. & Gummadi, K.P. 2015. On the reliability of profile matching across large online social networks. *Proceedings of the 21st ACM SIGKDD International Conference on Knowledge Discovery and Data Mining*, 1799–1808. Available from: https://dl.acm.org/doi/10.1145/2783258.2788601 [2 May 2019].

Gelinas, L., Pierce, R., Winkler, S., Cohen, I.G., Lynch, H.F. & Bierer, B.E. 2017. Using social media as a research recruitment tool: Ethical issues and recommendations. *The American Journal of Bioethics*, 17(3): 3–14.

Gibson, S., Benson, O. & Brand, S.L. 2013. Talking about suicide: Confidentiality and anonymity in qualitative research. *Nursing Ethics*, 20(1): 18–29.

Hargittai, E. 2010. Facebook privacy settings: Who cares? *First Monday*, 15(8): Available from: https://journals.uic.edu/ojs/index.php/fm/article/view/3086 [19 June 2020].

Henderson, M., Johnson, N.F. & Auld, G. 2013. Silences of ethical practice: dilemmas for researchers using social media. *Educational research and evaluation*, 19(6): 546–560.

Henderson, M., de Zwart, M., Lindsay, D. & Phillips, M. 2010. *Legal risks for students using social networking sites*. Doctoral dissertation, Australian Council for Computers in Education.

Highfield, T. & Leaver, T. 2016. Instagrammatics and digital methods: Studying visual social media, from selfies and GIFs to memes and emoji. *Communication Research and Practice*, 2(1): 47–62.

Holloway, D., Green, L. & Livingstone, S. 2013. *Zero to eight: Young children and their internet use*. LSE, London: EU Kids

Holmes, S. 2009. Methodological and ethical considerations in designing an Internet study of quality of life: A discussion paper. *International Journal of Nursing Studies*, 46: 394–405.

Humphry, J. 2014. *Homeless and Connected: Mobile phones and the Internet in the lives of homeless Australians*. Australian Communications Consumer Action Network, Sydney.

Hutton, L. & Henderson, T. 2015. 'I didn't sign up for this!': Informed consent in social network research, *Proceedings of the Ninth International AAAI Conference on Weblogs and Social Media (ICWSM)*, 178–187. Available from: https://www.aaai.org/ocs/index.php/ICWSM/ICWSM15/paper/viewFile/10493/10501 [19 June 2020].

International Council on Human Rights Policy. 2011. *Navigating the database: Privacy, technology, human rights*. Geneva, Switzerland.

Jamieson, T., & Güez, S. 2018. Protecting human subjects in the digital age: Issues and best practices of data protection. *Survey Practice* 11(2): 1–9.

Jerome, S. & Kollipara, P. 2010. *Good Morning Tech, Hillicon Valley*. Available from: http://thehill.com/ blogs/silicon-valley/technology/110519-good-morning-tech (reporting that a bill introduced in the House 'would require companies to get consent from individuals before collecting their personal information') [10 May 2019].

Jing, F., Zhang, L. & Ma, W.Y. 2006. Virtual Tour: an online travel assistant based on high-quality images. *Proceedings of the 14th ACM international conference on multimedia*, 599–602. Available from: https://dl.acm.org/doi/abs/10.1145/1180639.1180762 [6 April 2019].

Jouhki, J., Lauk, E., Penttinen, M., Sormanen, N. & Uskali, T. 2016. Facebook's emotional contagion experiment as a challenge to research ethics. *Media and Communication*, 4(4):75–85.

Jungherr A. 2015. *Analyzing Political communication with digital trace data: The role of Twitter messages in social science research*. Cham, Switzerland: Springer.

Kang, R., Brown, S. & Kiesler, S. 2013. Why do people seek anonymity on the internet? Informing policy and design. *Proceedings of the SIGCHI Conference on Human Factors in Computing Systems*, 2657–2666). Available from: https://dl.acm.org/doi/10.1145/2470654.2481368 [10 March 2019].

Kaiser, K. 2009. Protecting respondent confidentiality in qualitative research. *Qualitative Health Research*, 19(11): 1632–1641.

Kayes, I. & Iamnitchi, A. 2017. Privacy and security in online social networks: A survey. *Online Social Networks and Media*, 3(4): 1–21.

Keep, T., Oksanen, A. & Räsänen, P. 2015. Who prefers anonymous self-expression online? A survey-based study of Finns aged 15–30 years. *Information, Communication & Society*, 18(6): 717–732.

Kietzmann, J.H., Silvestre, B.S., McCarthy, I.P. & Pitt, L.F. 2012. Unpacking the social media phenomenon: Towards a research agenda. *Journal of Public Affairs*, 12(2): 109–119.

Kitchin, H.A. 2007. *Research ethics and the internet: Negotiating Canada's Tri-Council policy statement*. Halifax & Winnipeg, Canada: Fernwood.

Kleinig, J. 2010. The nature of consent. In: Miller Wertheim (ed.) *The ethics of consent: Theory and practice*. New York, NY: Oxford University Press.

Krasnova, H., Kolesnikova, E. & Guenther, O. 2010. Leveraging trust and privacy concerns in online social networks: An empirical study, *Proceedings of the 18th European Conference on Information Systems*, June 6–9, South Africa, University of Pretoria.

Kumar, S., Saravanakumar, K. & Deepa, K. 2016. On privacy and security in social media–A comprehensive study. *Procedia Computer Science*, 78: 114–119.

Leiker, M. 2011. When to 'friend' a patient: social media tips for health care professionals. *WMJ: Official Publication of the State Medical Society of Wisconsin*, 110(1): 42–43.

Leon, P.G., Ur, B., Wang, Y., Sleeper, M., Balebako, R., Shay, R., Bauer, L., Christodorescu, M. & Cranor, L.F. 2013. What matters to users?: factors that affect users' willingness to share information with online advertisers. *Proceedings of the ninth symposium on usable privacy and security*, 7. Available from: https://dl.acm.org/doi/10.1145/2501604.2501611 [5 March 2019].

Lewis, K. 2015. Studying online behaviour: Comment on Anderson et al. 2014. *Sociological Science*, 2: 20–31.

Li, J. 2013. Privacy policies for health social networking sites. *Journal of the American Medical Informatics Association*, 20(4): 704–707.

Livingston, J.S. 2011. Invasion contracts: The privacy implications of terms of use agreements in the online social media setting. *Albany Law Journal of Science and Technology*, 21: 591–637.

Livingstone, S. & Brake, D.R. 2010. On the rapid rise of social networking sites: New findings and policy implications. *Children & Society*, 24(1): 75–83.

Lunnay, B., Borland, J., McNaughton, D. & Ward, P. 2015. Ethical use of social media to facilitate qualitative research. *Qualitative Health Research*, 25(1): 99–109.

Ma, X., Hancock, J. & Naaman, M. 2016, May. Anonymity, intimacy, and self-disclosure in social media, *Proceedings of the 2016 CHI conference on human factors in computing systems*, 3857–3869. Available from: https://dl.acm.org/doi/10.1145/2858036.2858414 [25 May 2019].

Madden, M., Lenhart, A., Cortesi, S., Gasser, U., Duggan, M., Smith, A. & Beaton, M. 2013. Teens, social media, and privacy. *Pew Research Center*, 21: 2–86.

Mantello, A. 2013. The EU Proposal for a General Data Protection Regulation and the roots of the 'right to be forgotten'. *Computer Law & Security Review*, 29(3): 229–235.

Markham, A. & Buchanan, E. 2012. *Ethical decision-making and internet research: Version 2.0.* Recommendations from the AOIR Ethics Working Committee. Available from: http://www.aoir.org/reports/ethics2.pdf [3 July 2019].

Marwick, A.E. & Boyd, D. 2014. Networked privacy: How teenagers negotiate context in social media. *New media & society*, 16(7): 1051–1067.

McFerran, B., Aquino, K. & Duffy, M. 2010. How personality and moral identity relate to individuals' ethical ideology. *Business Ethics Quarterly*, 20(1): 35–56.

Mehmood, A., Natgunnathan, I., Xiang, Y., Hua, G., & Guo, S. 2017. Protection of Big Data privacy. *IEEE Access*, 4, 1821–1834.

Moreno, M.A., Goniu, N., Moreno, P.S. & Diekema, D. 2013. Ethics of social media research: common concerns and practical considerations. *Cyberpsychology, Behavior, and Social Networking*, 16(9): 708–713.

Negoescu, R.A., Adams, B., Phung, D., Venkatesh, S. & Gatica-Perez, D. 2009. Flickr hypergroups, *Proceedings of the 17th ACM international conference on Multimedia*, 813–816. Available from: https://dl.acm.org/doi/10.1145/1631272.1631421 [24 April 2019].

Nunan, D. & Yenicioglu, B. 2013. Informed, uninformed and participative consent in social media research. *International Journal of Market Research*, 55(6): 791–808.

Oswald, M., James, H. & Nottingham, E. 2016. The not-so-secret life of five-year-olds: legal and ethical issues relating to disclosure of information and the depiction of children on broadcast and social media. *Journal of Media Law*, 8(2): 198–228.

Parsons, S., Sherwood, G. & Abbott, C., 2016. Informed consent with children and young people in social research: is there scope for innovation? *Children & Society*, 30(2): 132–145.

Penneck, S. 2018. Confidentiality in an era of Big Data: An official statistics perspective. *Statistical Journal of the IAOS*, 1–6.

Petrova, E., Dewing, J. & Camilleri, M. 2016. Confidentiality in participatory research: Challenges from one study. *Nursing Ethics*, 23(4): 442–454.

Radin, M.J. 2004. Regime change in intellectual property: superseding the law of the state with the law of the firm. *University of Ottawa Law & Technology Journal*, 1:173.

Rainie, L., Kiesler, S., Kang, R., Madden, M., Duggan, M., Brown, S. & Dabbish, L. 2013. Anonymity, privacy, and security online. *Pew Research Internet Project*. Available from: http://www.pewinternet.org/2013/09/05/anonymity-privacy-and-security-online/ [5 May 2019].

Regan, PM. 2002. Privacy and commercial use of personal data: Policy developments in the US. Paper presented at the *Rathenau Institute Privacy Conference*, 17 January, Amsterdam

Rivers, C.M. & Lewis, B.L. 2014. Ethical research standards in a world of Big Data. *F1000Research*, *3*. Available from: https://doi.org/10.12688/f1000research.3-38.v1 [10 February 2019].

Robinson J., Rodrigues M., Fisher S., Bailey E. & Herrman, H. 2015. Social media and suicide prevention: Findings from a stakeholder survey. *Shanghai Archives of Psychiatry*, 27(1): 27–35.

Rosser, B.S., Oakes, J.M., Horvath, K.J., Konstan, J.A., Danilenko, G.P. & Peterson, J.L. 2009. HIV sexual risk behavior by men who use the Internet to seek sex with men: results of the Men's INTernet Sex Study-II (MINTS-II). *AIDS and Behavior*, 13(3): 488–498.

Saunders, B., Kitzinger, J. & Kitzinger, C. 2015. Participant anonymity in the internet age: From theory to practice. *Qualitative research in psychology*, 12(2): 125–137.

Saunders, B., Kitzinger, J. & Kitzinger, C. 2015. Anonymising interview data: challenges and compromise in practice. *Qualitative Research*, 15(5): 616–632.

Schroeder, R., 2014. Big Data and the brave new world of social media research. *Big Data & Society*, 1(2) 1–14

Shamoo, A.E., & Resnik, D.B. 2009. *Responsible conduct of research*. Oxford, UK: Oxford University Press. Available from: DOI: 10.1093/acprof:oso/9780195368246.001.0001 (30 June 2019)

Sharkey, S., Jones, R., Smithson, J., Lewis, E., Emmens, T., Ford, T. & Owens, C. 2011. Ethical practice in internet research involving vulnerable people: lessons from a self-harm discussion forum study (SharpTalk). *Journal of Medical Ethics*, 37(12): 752–758.

Shim, K., & Oh, S.K.K. 2018. Who creates the bandwagon? The dynamics of fear of isolation, opinion congruency and anonymity-preference on social media in the 2017 South Korean presidential election. *Computers in Human Behavior*, 86: 181–189.

Sleeper, M., Balebako, R., Das, S., McConahy, A.L., Wiese, J., & Cranor, L.F. 2013. 'The post that wasn't: Exploring self-censorship on Facebook', Proceedings of the ACM Conference on Computer Supported Cooperative Work, 793–802. Available from: https://dl.acm.org/doi/10.1145/2441776.2441865 [24 June 2019].

Social Research Association. 2003. *Ethical Guidelines*. Social Research Association. Available from: http://www.the-sra.org.uk/ethics03.pdf [2 May 2019.

Starr FM. 2019. 'New 'gagging' social media policy sparks uproar at Daily Graphic'. *Starr FM* Available from https://starrfm.com.gh/2019/08/new-gagging-social-media-policy-sparks-uproar-at-daily-graphic/ [9 August 2019].

Staksrud, E., Ólafsson, K. & Livingstone, S. 2013. Does the use of social networking sites increase children's risk of harm? *Computers in Human Behavior*, 29(1): 40–50.

Stefanidis, A., Crooks, A. & Radzikowski, J. 2013. Harvesting ambient geo-spatial information from social media feeds. *GeoJournal*, 78(2): 319–338.

Tiidenberg, K. 2015. Boundaries and conflict in an NSFW community on Tumblr: The meanings and uses of selfies. *New Media & Society*, 18(8): 1563–1578.

Topcu, Ç., Yıldırım, A. & Erdur-Baker, Ö. 2013. Cyber bullying@ schools: What do Turkish adolescents think? *International Journal for the Advancement of Counselling*, 35(2): 139–151.

Townsend, L. & Wallace, C. 2016. *Social media research: A guide to ethics*. Aberdeen: University of Aberdeen.

Tufekci, Z. 2008. Can you see me now? Audience and disclosure regulation in online social network sites. *Bulletin of Science, Technology and Society*. 28(1): 20–36.

Ur, B. & Wang, Y. 2013. A cross-cultural framework for protecting user privacy in online social media. In *Proceedings of the 22nd International Conference on World Wide Web*, 755–762. Available from: https://dl.acm.org/doi/10.1145/2487788.2488037 [4 May 2019].

Van Slyke, C., Shim, J.T., Johnson, R. & Jiang, J.J. 2006. Concern for information privacy and online consumer purchasing. *Journal of the Association for Information Systems*. 7(6): 415–444.

Varnhagen, C.K., Gushta, M., Daniels, J., Peters, T.C., Parmar, N., Law, D., Hirsch, R., Sadler Takach, B. & Johnson, T. 2005. How informed is online informed consent? *Ethics & Behavior*, 15(1): 37–48.

Warin, J. 2011. Ethical mindfulness and reflexivity: Managing a research relationship with children and young people in a 14-year qualitative longitudinal research (QLR) study. *Qualitative Inquiry*, 17(9): 805–814.

Weller, K. & Kinder-Kurlanda, K.E. 2016. A manifesto for data sharing in social media research. In *Proceedings of the 8th ACM Conference on Web Science*, 166–172. Available from: https://dl.acm.org/doi/10.1145/2908131.2908172 [24 July 2019].

Whiteman N. 2012. *Undoing ethics*. New York: Springer

Williams, M.L., Burnap, P., Sloan, L., Jessop, C. & Lepps, H. 2017. Users' views of ethics in social media research: Informed consent, anonymity, and harm. In Woodfield, K. (ed.). *Advances in research ethics and integrity: The ethics of online research Vol 2*. London: Emerald Publishing Limited, pp. 27–52.

Wisniewski, P.J., Knijnenburg, B.P. & Lipford, H.R. 2017. Making privacy personal: Profiling social network users to information privacy education and nudging. *International Journal of Human-Computer Studies*, 98: 95–108.

Zheleva, E. & Getoor, L. 2011. Privacy in social networks: A survey. In Aggarwal, C.C. (ed.). *Social network data analytics*. Boston: Springer, pp. 277–306

Zimmer, M. 2010. 'But the data is already public': on the ethics of research on Facebook. *Ethics and Information Technology*, 12(4): 313–325.

CHAPTER 11

Adami, E. & Jewitt, C. 2016. Special Issue: Social media and visual communication. *Visual Communication*, 15(3): 263–270.

Agratchev, A. 2012. Big data in the offline world: How data from brick-and-mortar stores trumps online analytics. *VentureBeat*. Available from: https://venturebeat.com/2012/06/29/big-data-in-the-offline-world/. [30 January 2019]

Airike, P.E. 2013a. Armchair advocates and social media. 14 October 2013. *Peppi-Emilia Airike*. Available from: http://wpmu.mah.se/nmict132group10/2013/10/14/armchair-advocates-   and-social-media/. [21 February 2019].

Airike, P.E. 2013b. Please like and share, and save the world! Slacktivism – what is it? 18 October 2013. *Peppi-Emilia Airike*. Available from: http://wpmu.mah.se/nmict132group10/2013/10/14/please-like-and-share-and-save-the- world-slacktivism-what-is-it/. [21 February 2019].

Alampi, A. 2012. Social media is more than simply a marketing tool for academic research. *The Guardian*. Available from: https://www.theguardian.com/higher-education-network/blog/2012/jul/24/social-media-academic-research-tool. [22 July 2019].

Anderson, M., Toor, S., Rainie, L. & Smith, A. 2018. An analysis of #BlackLivesMatter and other Twitter hashtags related to political or social issues. 11 July 2018. *Pew research Centre: Internet & Technology*. Available from: https://www.pewinternet.org/2018/07/11/public-attitudes-toward-political-engagement-on-social-media/. [30 August 2019].

Andrews, L. 2019. #FairnessFirst: stepping up to keep SA's females safe. 9 September 2019. *BizCommuinty*. Available from: https://www.bizcommunity.com/Article/196/813/195314.html. [21 September 2019].

Aral, S., Dellarocas, C. & Godes, D. 2013. Introduction to the special issue social media and business transformation: a framework for research. *Information Systems Research*, 24(1): 3–13.

Armchair politician or advocate for change? n.d. *Fresh Brew Marketing*. Available from: http://www.freshbrewmarketing.com/armchair-politician-or-advocate-for-change/. [23 February 2019].

Auman-Bauer, K. 2019. Researchers analyze use of social media to influence politics during uprising. 23 August 2019. *Phys.org*. Available from: https://phys.org/news/2019-08-social-media-politics-uprising.html. [30 August 2019].

Barboni, E., Brooks, N., Wheatley, B. & Schlebusch, N. 2018. *(Anti)social media: the benefits and pitfalls of digital for female politicians*. Atalanta and Brandseye: UK.

BBC. 2018. Joseph Kony – child kidnapper, warlord, 'prophet'. 27 July 2018. *BBC: Africa*. Available from: https://www.bbc.com/news/world-africa-17299084. [30 August 2019].

Benfield, M.D. 2009. 'Net-Geo-Politics', in *Decolonizing the Digital/Digital Decolonization, Volume 3, Dossier 1*. 18 September 2009. The Worlds & Knowledges Otherwise Projects (WKO). Duke University, Trinity College of Arts and Sciences, Durham, NC: Center For Global Studies and the Humanities. Available from: https://globalstudies.trinity.duke.edu/projects/wko-digital-1. [20 October 2018].

Baer, J. 2018. 6 unexpected trends in 2018 social media research. Available from: http://www.convinceandconvert.com/social-media-measurement/6-unexpected-trends-in-2018-social-media-research/. [5 January 2019].

Benetoli, A., Chen, T. F. & Aslani, P. 2018. Consumer perceptions of using social media for health purposes: benefits and drawbacks. *Health Informatics Journal*, 25 (4): 1661–1674.

Bentley, C. A. 2013. Are you an armchair advocate? *Huffpost*. Available from: https://www.huffingtonpost.com/charles-a-bentley/are-you-an-armchair-advocate_b_2890670.html. [20 July 2019].

Berry, D. M. 2011. The computational turn: thinking about the digital humanities. *Culture Machine*, 12: 1–22. ISSN 1465–4121.

Boellstorff, T. 2016. For whom the ontology turns: theorizing the digital real. *Current Anthropology Volume*, 57 (4): 387– 407.

Brooker, P., Dutton, W. & Greiffenhagen, C. 2017. What would Wittgenstein say about social media? *Qualitative Research*, 17 (6): 610–626.

Bruns, A. & Burgess, J. 2015. Twitter hashtags from ad hoc to calculated publics. In Rambukkana, N. (ed.). *Hashtag publics: The power and politics of discursive networks*. Peter Lang, New York, pp. 13–28.

Bruns, A., Moon, B., Paul, A. & Münch, F. 2016. Towards a typology of hashtag publics: a large-scale comparative study of user engagement across trending topics. *Communication Research & Practice*, 2(1): 20–46.

Bruns, A. & Moon, B. 2019. Twitter isn't just for political hashtag warriors. Many still use the social network to just hang out. 25 July 2019. *The Conversation: Africa*. Available from: https://theconversation.com/twitter-isnt-just-for-political-hashtag-warriors-many-still-use-the-social-network-to-just-hang-out-120505. [10 September 2019].

Burgess, J. 2014. From 'broadcast yourself!' to 'follow your interests': making over social media. *International Journal of Cultural Studies,* 18 (3): 281–285.

Burma Campaign UK. 2007. For human rights, democracy & development in Burma. *Burma Campaign UK.* Available from: http://burmacampaign.org.uk/2007/. [21 October 2019].

BusinessTech. 2016. 8 critical elements to the #FeesMustFall debate. 9 October 2016. *BusinessTech.* Available from: https://businesstech.co.za/news/general/139369/8-critical-elements-to-the-feesmustfall-debate/. [24 October 2019].

Campbell, A. 2013. What is hashtag hijacking? 19 August 2013. *Small Business Trends.* Available from: https://smallbiztrends.com/2013/08/what-is-hashtag-hijacking-2.html. [24 October 2019].

Carpi, D. 2020. Introduction: Digital Ontology and Epistemology. Between Law, Literature and the Visual Arts, *Pólemos,* 14(1): 1-4.

Cele, N. 2018. Icasa regulation a 'data must fall' win for the consumer. 19 Novemebr 2018. *Kayafm.co.za.* Available from: https://www.kayafm.co.za/icasa-regulation-data-must-fall/. [30 July 2019].

Chadwick, A. & Dennis. D. 2016. Social media, professional media and mobilisation in contemporary Britain: Explaining the strengths and weaknesses of the citizens' movement 38 Degrees, *Political Studies,* 65(1): 42–60.

Chae, B. K. 2015. Insights from hashtag #supplychain and Twitter Analytics: Considering Twitter and Twitter data for supply chain practice and research. *International Journal of Production Economics,* 165 (July 2015): 247–259.

Chaffey, D. 2020, April 17. Global social media research summary 2020. *Smart Insights.* Available from: https://www.smartinsights.com/social-media-marketing/social-media-strategy/new-global-social-media-research/ [19 April 2020].

Change.org. 2019. *The world's platform for change.* Available from: https://www.change.org/. [24 October 2019].

Cheliotis, G., Lu, X. & Song, Y. 2015. Reliability of data collection methods in social media research, in Association for the Advancement of Artificial Intelligence: *Proceedings of the Ninth International AAAI Conference on Web and Social Media,* California, 586-589.

Clement, J. 2020, April 1. Number of global social network users 2010-2023. *Statista.com.* Available from: https://www.statista.com/statistics/278414/number-of-worldwide-social-network-users/ [19 April 2020].

Chiluwa, I & Ifukor, P. 2015. 'War against our Children': Stance and evaluation in #BringBackOurGirls campaign discourse on Twitter and Facebook. *Discourse & Society*, 26 (3):267–296.

Cooper, A. & Mann, R. 2016. Using social media for social research: An introduction. *Social media research group*. UK: Government Social Research. Available from: https://assets.publishing.service.gov.uk/government/uploads/system/uploads/attachment_data/file/524750/GSR_Social_Media_Research_Guidance_-_Using_social_media_for_social_research.pdf. [20 February 2019].

Cooper, P. 2020, February 20. 140+ Social media statistics that matter to marketers in 2020. *Hootsuite*. Available from: https://blog.hootsuite.com/social-media-statistics-for-social-media-managers/ [19 April 2020].

Crano, R.D. 2019. The real terror of Instagram: Death and disindividuation in the social media scopic field. *Convergence: The International Journal of Research into New Media Technologies*, 25(5-6): 1123–1139.

Crawford, K & Finn, M. 2015. The limits of crisis data: analytical and ethical challenges of using social and mobile data to understand disasters. *GeoJournal*, 80: 491–502.

Dailey, K. 2012. Kony2012: The rise of online campaigning. 9 March 2012. *BBC: News Magazine*. Available from: https://www.bbc.com/news/magazine-17306118. [20 February 2019].

DaSilva, C. 2018. Has occupy Wall street changed America? 9 September 2018. *NewsWeek: U.S.* https://www.newsweek.com/has-occupy-wall-street-changed-america-seven-years-birth-political-movement-1126364. [15 July 2019].

Delgado, R. 2018. The impact of big data on social media. *Dataflog*. Available from: https://datafloq.com/read/impact-big-data-social-media/3548. [15 July 2019].

Dennis, J. 2018a. It's better to light a candle than to fantasise about a sun. In Dennis, J. (ed.). *Beyond Slacktivism*. Cham: Palgrave MacMillan, pp. 1–23.

Dennis, J. 2018b. #stopslacktivism: why clicks, likes, and shares matter. In Dennis, J. (ed.). *Beyond Slacktivism*. Cham: Palgrave MacMillan, pp. 25–69.

Dermody, A. 2016. What will advocacy organizations do after change. org's big announcement? 25 July 2016. *Connectivity*. Available from: https://info.cq.com/resources/advocacy-organizations-change-orgs-big-announcement/. [20 October 2019]. Digital Evolution. n.d. Digital evolution: past, present and future outlook of digital technology. Available from: https://flatworldbusiness.wordpress.com/digital-evolution/. [24 October 2019].

DOMO. 2019. *Data Never Sleeps 6.0*. Available from: https://www.domo. com/learn/data- never-sleeps-6. [22 February 2019].

Drahošováa, M. & Balcob, P. 2017. The analysis of advantages and disadvantages of use of social media in European Union. *Procedia Computer Science*, 109C: 1005–1009.

Dwyer, R. & Fraser, S. 2019. Celebrity enactments of addiction on Twitter. *Convergence: The International Journal of Research into New Media Technologies*, 25(5-6): 1044–1062.

Eland, 2016. Beyond hashtags: how a new wave of digital activists is changing society. 11 April 2016. *The Conversation*. Available from: https:// theconversation.com/beyond-hashtags-how-a-new-wave-of-digital-activists-is-changing-society-57502 [20 September 2019].

Eluère, P. 2018. UNHCR Innovation Service: 'Three times the world actually cared about refugees and what we can learn'. 12 June 2019. *Medium*. Available from: https://medium.com/unhcr-innovation-service/three-times-the-world-actually-cared-about-refugees-and-what-we-can-learn-b69df80e05c6. [22 October 2019].

Elwell, S.J. 2014. The transmediated self: Life between the digital and the analog. *Convergence: The International Journal of Research into New Media Technologies*, 20(2): 233–249.

Farman, J. 2012. *Mobile interface theory: Embodiment and the mobile interface*. London: Routledge.

Filo, K., Lock, D. J. & Karg, A. 2015. Sport and social media research: A review. *Sport Management Review*, 18(2): 166–181.

Gaitho, M. 2018. What Is the Real Impact of Social Media? *Simplilearn*. Available from: https://www.simplilearn.com/real-impact-social-media-article. [28 July 2019].

Fuentes, M. 2014. Digital activism. 25 June 2014. *Encyclopedia Britannica: encyclopedia of activism and social justice*. Available from: https://www. britannica.com/topic/digital-activism. [3 October 2019]

Garber, M. 2015. #PrayForParis: When Empathy Becomes a Meme. 16 November 2015. *The Atlantic: Culture*. Available from: https://www. theatlantic.com/entertainment/archive/2015/11/pray-for-paris-empathy-facebook/416196/. [24 October 2019].

Gardner, A.S. 2019. YouTube, ageing and PJ Harvey: an 'everyday' story of the erasure of age. *Convergence: The International Journal of Research into New Media Technologies*, 25(5-6): 1155–1167.

George, J.J. & Leidner, D.E. 2019. From clicktivism to hacktivism: understanding digital activism. *Information & Organization (in print)*. Available from: https://www.researchgate.net/publication/332738189_From_Clicktivism_to_Hacktivism_Understanding_Digital_Activism. [24 October 2019].

Grandoni, 2012. On the unlikely viral success of 'Kony 2012'. 9 March 2012. *The Atlantic: Technology*. Available from: https://www.theatlantic.com/technology/archive/2012/03/unlikely-viral-success-kony-2012/330723/. [24 October 2019].

Harper, S. 2018. APIs: what they are and why they matter for your data. 28 April 2018. Safe Software. Available from: https://www.safe.com/blog/2016/04/apis-what-are-they-and-why-they-matter-for-your-data/. [30 September 2019].

Hodes, R. 2017. Questioning 'Fees Must Fall'. *African Affairs*, 116(462): 140–150.

Holmes, L. 2015. The 'Post It Forward' blog is working to change the way we talk about mental health. 5 April 2015. HuffPost. Available from: https://www.huffpost.com/entry/post-it-forward-tumblr_n_7274444. [21 October 2019].

Hong Kong: from the Umbrella Movement to the Anti-Extradition Protests. 2015. Wordpress. 20 March 2015. Available from: https://victoriatbhui.wordpress.com/2014/11/23/unity-is-the-key-to-success-vs-failure/. [20 February 2019].

Huss, M. 2019. Web 1.0, 2.0, 3.0, and the print v. web debate. 24 September 2019. *Meghan Huss*. Available from: https://blog.meganhuss.com/?p=5. [24 October 2019].

Hutchinson, J. 2016. An introduction to digital media research methods: how to research and the implications of new media data. *Communication Research and Practice*, 2(1): 1–6.

InfluenceWatch. 2019. MoveOn Civic Action (MoveOn.org). Available from: https://www.influencewatch.org/non-profit/moveon-civic-actionmoveon-org/. [26 September 2019].

Intellipaat. 2019. Algorithms: the backbone of big data analytics! 17 October 2019. *Intellipaat*. Available from: https://intellipaat.com/blog/algorithms-backbone-of-data-analytics/. [26 September 2019].

Invisible Children. 2019. Five years after Kony 2012. How have things changed? *Invisible Children*. Available from: https://invisiblechildren.com/blog/2017/03/16/five-years-kony-2012/. [26 September 2019].

Joyce, M. (ed.). 2010. *Digital activism decoded: the new mechanics of change*. NY: International Debate Education Association.

Karombo, T. 2019. #Datamustfall: SA data more expensive than in rival and neighboring economies. 6 March 2019. *Business Report*. Available from: https://www.iol.co.za/business-report/economy/datamustfall-sa-data-more-expensive-than-in-rival-and-neighboring-economies-19660907. [30 August 2019].

Kahla, C. 2019. Am I Next: Gender-based violence protesters take to the streets [photos]. 4 September 2019. *The South African*. Available from: https://www.thesouthafrican.com/news/am-i-next-gender-based-protest-photos/. [30 September 2019].

Kgabane, E. 2019. What will it take to end gender-based violence? 4 October 2019. *LeadSA*. Available from: http://www.leadsa.co.za/articles/362844/what-will-it-take-to-end-gender-based-violence. [15 October 2019].

Khanzode, K.C.A. & Sarode, R.D. 2016. Evolution of the World Wide Web: from Web 1.0 to 6.0. *International Journal of Digital Library Services*, 6(2): 1–11.

Koopman, C. 2018. Campaign victory for Data Must Fall – Press Release. *Amandla.mobi*. Available from: https://www.amandla.mobi/data_must_fall_icasa_victory. [21 July 2019].

Liao, S, 2019. Facebook, Instagram, and WhatsApp are still down for some users around the world: while you can open the apps, they're missing major functions. 13 March 2019. *The Verge*. Available from: https://www.theverge.com/2019/3/13/18264092/facebook-instagram-down-partially-post-messages-profile-loading. [30 September 2019].

Leetaru, K. 2019, February 11. How big is social media and does it really count as 'Big Data'? Forbes: AI & Big Data. Available from https://www.forbes.com/sites/kalevleetaru/2019/02/11/how-big-is-social-media-and-does-it-really-count-as-big-data/#16000b04f2c1 . [26 April 2020].

Leung, H. 2019. Five years on, Hong Kong activist Joshua Wong speaks to TIME about the Umbrella Revolution. 27 September 2019. *Time: World*. Available from: https://time.com/5685733/joshua-wong-hong-kong-umbrella-movement-revolution-anniversary/. [30 September 2019].

Levitin, M. 2015. The triumph of Occupy Wall Street. 10 June 2015. *The Atlantic: Politics*. Available from: https://www.theatlantic.com/politics/archive/2015/06/the-triumph-of-occupy-wall-street/395408/. [12 September 2019].

Lotame Solutions. 2018. *How to combine online and offline data*. Available from: https://www.lotame.com/combining-online-and-offline-data-to-drive-success/. [12 September 2019].

Mahrt, M. & Scharkow, M. 2013. The value of big data in digital media research. *Journal of Broadcasting & Electronic Media*, 57(1): 20–33.

McAuley, V. & Rivera, D. 2019. Digital activism. 28 February 2019. *The University of British Columbia: Vancouver Campus*. Available from: https://digitaltattoo.ubc.ca/2019/02/28/digital-activism/. [20 October 2019].

McKeon, R.T. & Gitomer, D. H. 2019. Social media, political mobilization, and high-stakes testing. *Frontiers in Education*, 4 (11 June 2019).

McNair, C. 2018. *Worldwide Social network users update: eMarketer's estimates and forecast for 2016–2021, with a focus on Instagram*. London: eMarketer. Available from: https://www.emarketer.com/Report/Worldwide-Social-Network-Users-Update-eMarketers-Estimates-Forecast-20162021-with-Focus-on-Instagram/2002170. [4 November 2018].

Mole, J. 2017. Understand your online and offline data to build defined data strategy. 7 September 2017. *ACXIOM*. Available from: https://www.acxiom.co.uk/blog/understand-your-online-and-offline-data-to-build-defined-data-strategy/. [12 February 2019].

MoveOn.org. 2019. *MoveOn: people-powered progress*. Available from: https://front.moveon.org/. [15 July 2019].

Mui, Y.Q. 2012. Change.org emerges as influential advocate on issues from bullying to bank fees. 23 January 2012. *The Washington Post: Business*. Available from: https://www.washingtonpost.com/business/economy/changeorg-emerges-as-influential-advocate/2012/01/09/gIQAoCJHLQ_story.html. [22 February 2019].

Nayyar, S. 2016. *Digital media and society implications in a hyperconnected era: World Economic Forum shaping the future implications of digital media for society*. Project report prepared in collaboration with Willis Towers Watson. World Economic Forum: USA.

Netivist. n.d. Does online activism work? Does it have a positive impact on society? *Netivist.com*. Available from: https://netivist.org/debate/online-activism-pros-and-cons?fbclid=IwAR3boCtfuLeTIfI36bDzJZXK43u4it mHbowKQ9upqChZHzlQSZEI-LeMTXA#. [24 October 2019].

Olsen, A. E. 2018. What is algorithm analysis? 29 August 2018. *DZone:Blog.* Available from: https://dzone.com/articles/what-is-algorithm-analysis. [25 August 2019]

Olshannikova, E., Olsson, T., Huhtamäki, J. & Kärkkäinen, H. (2017). Conceptualizing Big Social Data. *Journal of Big Data*, 4(3): 1–19.

Perez-Rivera, D.T., Torres-Lugo, C. & Santos-Lozada, A. 2019. Engaging for Puerto Rico: #RickyRenuncia (and #RickySeQueda) during El Verano del 19 and digital identities. *SocArXiv.* Available from: https://osf.io/preprints/socarxiv/wdk9u/ [13 August 2019].

Price-Mitchell, M. 2019. Disadvantages of social networking: surprising insights from teens. 6 September 2019. *Roots of Action.* Available from: https://www.rootsofaction.com/disadvantages-of-social-networking/. [18 September 2019].

Rein, J. & Lee, S. 2019. Using LinkedIn for professional development and networking: how to build your network and engage with other professionals. *Learn how to become.* Available from: https://www.learnhowtobecome.org/career-resource-center/linkedin-professional-development-and-networking/. [22 September 2019].

Rees, A. 2015. Digital and online activism. March 2015. *Reset.org: Digital for Good.* Available from: https://en.reset.org/knowledge/digital-and-online-activism. [21 September 2019].

Reines, R. 2015. I Instagram, therefore I Am. 17 November 2015. *The Daily Telegraph: RendezView.* Available from: https://www.dailytelegraph.com.au/rendezview/put-your-money-where-your-mouth-is/news-story/e87a450bac8051ede6e1fc6fdf7ec374. [24 October 2019].

Richterich, A. 2019. Hacking events: project development practices and technology use at Hackathons. *Convergence: The International Journal of Research into New Media Technologies*, 25(5-6): 1000–1026.

Riley, A. 2013. Slacktivism: 'liking' on Facebook may mean less giving. 8 November 2013. *UBC News.* Available from: https://news.ubc.ca/2013/11/08/slacktivism-liking-on-facebook-may-mean-less-giving/. [21 February 2019].

Rishika, R., Kumar, A., Janakiraman, R., Bezawada, R. 2013. The effect of customers? Social media participation on customer visit frequency and profitability: an empirical investigation. *Information Systems Research*, 24(1): 108–127.

Ruths, D. & Pfeffer, J. 2014. Social media for large studies of behavior: Large-scale studies of human behavior in social media need to be held to higher methodological standards. *Science*, 346(6213): 1063–1064.

Schradie, J. 2019. The revolution that wasn't: How inequalities in digital activism spaces challenge the democratic promise of the Internet. 3 June 2019. *The ForumNetwork: Digitalisation.* Available from: https://www.oecd-forum.org/users/262949-jen-schradie/posts/49498-the-revolution-that-wasn-t-how-inequalities-in-digital-activism-spaces-challenge-the-democratic-promise-of-the-internet. [24 October 2019].

Sebei, H., Hadj Taieb, M.A. & Ben Aouicha, M. (2018). Review of social media analytics process and Big Data pipeline. *Social Network Analysis and Mining*, 8(1): 1–28.

Shapshak, T. 2019. #DataMustFall says South Africa's President ahead of new spectrum policy. 21 June 2019. *Forbes.com.* Available from: https://www.forbes.com/sites/tobyshapshak/2019/06/21/datamustfall-says-south-africas-president-ahead-of-new-spectrum-policy/#1141d43a3cec. [18 September 2019].

Siapera, E., Boudourides, M., Lenis, S. & Suiter, J. 2018. Refugees and network publics on Twitter: Networked framing, affect, and capture. *Social Media + Society*, 4(1): 1–21.

Smith, C. 2018. Evolution of the World Wide Web From Web 1.0 to Web 5.0. 9 April 2018. *Geeks with Blogs.* Available from: http://geekswithblogs.net/Xicomtech/archive/2018/04/09/244669.aspx. [24 October 2019].

Smith, S. 2016. Pervasive theatre: New writing for new environments. *Convergence: The International Journal of Research into New Media Technologies*, 24(3): 321–336.

Statista. 2018. Number of social network users worldwide from 2010 to 2021 (in billions). Available from: https://www.statista.com/statistics/278414/number-of-worldwide-social-network-users/. [27 July 2019].

Statista. 2019. Global mobile social network penetration rate as of January 2019, by region. Available from: https://www.statista.com/statistics/412257/mobile-social-penetration-rate-region/. [27 July 2019].

Steinberg, S.B. 2016. #Advocacy: social media activism's power to transform law. *Kentucky Law Journal*, 105(3): 413–452.

Subrahmanyam, K., Reich, S.M., Waechter, N. & Espinoza, G. 2008. Online and offline social networks: Use of social networking sites by emerging adults. *Journal of Applied Developmental Psychology*, 29(6): 420–433.

Taylor, A. 2014. Is #BringBackOurGirls helping? 6 May 2014. *Washington Post: Worldviews.* Available from: https://www.washingtonpost.com/news/worldviews/wp/2014/05/06/is-bringbackourgirls-helping/. [24 October 2019].

Tsung-gan, K. 2017. The Umbrella Movement after three years: So much accomplished, and much still to do. 24 September 2017. *Hong Kong Free Press: Opinion Politics & Protest.* Available from: https://www.hongkongfp.com/2017/09/24/umbrella-movement-three-years-much-accomplished-much-still/. [24 October 2019].

Van Rijmenam, M. 2013. The advantages of big social data for your organisation. 15 January 2013. *Datafloq.* Available from: https://datafloq.com/read/big-social-data/236 . [26 April 2020]

Vines, S. 2017. Those who think the Umbrella Movement failed need to learn a little history. 1 October 2017. *Hong Kong Free Press: Opinion Politics & Protest.* Available from: https://www.hongkongfp.com/2017/10/01/think-umbrella-movement-failed-need-learn-little-history/. [24 October 2019].

Walker, A. 2019. #AmINext is not a hashtag, it's the reality of life as a woman in South Africa. 3 September 2019. *BizCommunity.* Available from: https://www.bizcommunity.com/Article/196/669/195154.html. [21 September 2019].

Walton, A.G. 2017. 6 ways social media affects our mental health. *Pharma & Healthcar*e. Available from: https://www.forbes.com/sites/alicegwalton/2017/06/30/a-run-down-of-social-medias-effects-on-our-mental-health/#2de975932e5a. [30 August 2019].

Yuen, S. 2017. Hong Kong after the UmbrellaMovement: An uncertain future for 'One Country Two Systems'. *Current Affairs: China Perspectives,* 25(1): 49–53.

Index

This is a subject index arranged alphabetically in word-by-word order, so that 'Big Data' is filed before 'Big Social Data'. *See* and *see also* references guide the reader to the preferred or alternative access terms used. Illustrations are expressed in **bold *italic* font**. Case studies are expressed in *italics*.

www.ingramcontent.com/pod-product-compliance
Lightning Source LLC
Chambersburg PA
CBHW061126210326
41518CB00034B/2506